Mark Twain

MAN IN WHITE

Mark Twain

MAN IN WHITE

The Grand Adventure of His Final Years

MICHAEL SHELDEN

Random House   New York

Published in the United States by
Random House, an imprint of
The Random House Publishing Group,
a division of Random House, Inc., New York.

RANDOM HOUSE and colophon are registered trademarks
of Random House, Inc.

Library of Congress Cataloging-in-Publication Data
Shelden, Michael.
Mark Twain : man in white : the grand adventure of his final years / Michael Shelden.
p. cm.
Includes bibliographical references.
ISBN 978-0-679-44800-6
eBook ISBN 978-1-58836-928-4
1. Twain, Mark, 1835–1910. 2. Authors, American—19th century—Biography.
3. Humorists, American—19th century—Biography. I. Title.
PS1331.S45 2010
818'.409—dc22
[B]   2009019719

Printed in the United States of America on acid-free paper

www.atrandom.com

2 4 6 8 9 7 5 3 1

First Edition

Book design by Liz Cosgrove

To Sue, Sarah, Vanessa, and June

Don't part with your illusions.
When they are gone you may still exist,
but you have ceased to live.

MARK TWAIN

CONTENTS

PART FOUR: TEMPEST

ILLUSTRATIONS

Clothes make the man.
Naked people have little or no influence in society.

MARK TWAIN[1]

. . .

How the Man in Black
Became the Man in White

CITIZEN TWAIN

ON A BLUSTERY Friday afternoon in December 1906, Mark Twain arrived for a special appearance at the Library of Congress, trailing smoke from his usual brand of cheap cigar. The temperature hovered at freezing and the skies were gloomy, but he was dressed warmly in a long dark overcoat and a derby from which thick curls of white hair protruded on either side. At the main doors, facing the Capitol, he entered the Great Hall of the Library and made his way down a long marble corridor to the Senate Reading Room, where a hearing was in progress on copyright legislation. The Librarian of Congress—a dapper middle-aged man named Herbert Putnam—was expecting him and emerged from the hearing to escort Twain inside.

All heads turned as the famous guest strode to the front of the chamber, which was full of lobbyists, lawyers, authors, and publishers. Normally used as a private study for senators, the high-ceilinged room had the look and feel of an elegant club, with oak paneling, mahogany desks, black leather chairs, and a big marble fireplace. At a long conference table facing the gathering were the dozen or so members of the Joint Congressional Committee on Patents, chaired by a jowly Republican lawyer from South Dakota, Senator Alfred Beard Kittredge.

A representative of the player piano industry, a Mr. Low, was droning on about copyright protection for perforated music rolls—"May I suggest an addition to clause (b) of section 1"—when Twain reached his seat and paused to remove his overcoat. By this simple gesture he caused—as one observer later put it—"a perceptible stir." That was an understatement. Against the fading light of the afternoon Twain emerged as a figure clothed all in white. His outfit perfectly matched his hair, from his white collar and cravat—held in place by a "creamy moonstone"—to his white shoes. Among so many soberly dressed fellows in black and gray, he stood out as a gleaming apparition, impossible to ignore.[2]

"Mark Twain Bids Winter Defiance," said the headline in the *New York Herald* the next day. "Resplendent in a White Flannel Suit, Author Creates a Sensation." The *New York World* called his costume "the most remarkable suit" of the season, and another paper said he was a "vision from the equator" who warmed the hearts of his audience while "the wintry wind whistled around the dome of the Capitol." The best comment came from the *Boston Herald:* "Oh, that all lobbyists could enter the congressional corridors in raiment as spotless as Mark Twain's."[3]

All day long, Senator Kittredge and his colleagues had been listening to various experts explain the fine points of the nation's copyright laws, and much of the discussion had been dry and tedious. The committee members had grown restless and bored as they listened to yet another lobbyist argue his case with statistics and legal precedents. But the moment Twain removed his overcoat, the room came to life, and the legislators stared wide-eyed at the man in white as he waited his turn to speak.

Twain's good friend and fellow novelist William Dean Howells, who was sitting nearby, was so taken aback by this unconventional outfit that the first words from his mouth were "What in the world did he wear that white suit for?" Appearing in such clothing at a formal gathering was a shocking breach of etiquette. In summer months, Washington was full of people in white suits, but in December nobody dared to dress that way.[4]

Twain's suit is now so famous that modern depictions of the author rarely show him in any other garb. The common assumption is that it was his signature look for much of his career. In fact, Senator Kittredge's otherwise dull committee hearing marked not only the public debut of Twain's uniform, but the beginning of an extraordinary period in which the author—who had just turned seventy-one—fashioned much of the image by which he is still known a century afterward.

He planned this debut carefully, and knew how the world would react. As a man who had spent years bedazzling audiences at lectures and banquets, he had a keen appreciation for the power of theatrical effects, and was sure that no one would forget the way he looked in white. Only two months earlier he had confessed privately, "I hope to get together courage enough to wear white clothes all through the winter. . . . It will be a great satisfaction to me to show off in this way." He wasn't ashamed to seek attention, explaining, "The desire for fame is only the desire to be continuously conspicuous and attract attention and be talked about." Indeed, his debut in white provoked comment on front pages everywhere. For several days it was all anyone could talk about.[5]

It wasn't by chance that he chose to reveal his new look in one of the most conspicuous places in America—the nation's greatest library. Though the building was only ten years old, it was already regarded as a monument for the ages. Built in the style of the Paris Opera House, it had the kind of splendor usually associated with great landmarks of the Old World—with soaring columns, grand arches, and a massive dome. Admirers boasted that it was "the largest, the costliest, and the safest" library in the world. For a literary man wanting to stage a sensational event, there wasn't a better backdrop.[6]

Though the extensive press coverage pleased him, Twain wasn't merely showing off. He had serious business to conduct at the hearing, where he wanted to urge legislators to change the system of copyright law, which he considered archaic and unjust. It was a subject close to his heart. For years he had been fighting to improve the system, but now he regarded the problem with a greater sense of urgency. His long career was nearing its end, and the future of his life's work was at stake.

When he stood up to speak, he knew that he would command complete attention. Like a good showman, he understood that his words

...ll the more impressive coming after so many lackluster ...ordinary men in conventional attire. For almost half an hour, ...floor, addressing the room directly instead of speaking only to ...ators. Though he had composed a few rough notes earlier in the ...n, he didn't bother to refer to them. He preferred to speak from the ...rt, and did so without hesitation, employing sound reasoning and amusing anecdotes, and making an occasional sardonic swipe at the glacial pace of reform. His real audience was not the men in the room, but the larger American public who would read of his appearance in their newspapers the next day.

Many writers, unaccustomed to addressing such a gathering, would have felt intimidated. But not Twain, whose confidence in his own rhetorical powers was as high as his opinion of most congressmen was low. He once said that America had "no native criminal class except Congress." Two weeks before coming to the hearing he had remarked privately, "All Congresses and Parliaments have a kindly feeling for idiots, and a compassion for them, on account of personal experience and heredity." For the benefit of his case, however, he treated the committee as though they were a group of thoroughly upright and thoughtful men and spoke to them as politely as possible.[7]

At the time, copyrighted works enjoyed protection for a period of forty-two years following the date of publication. Senator Kittredge was sponsoring a bill with a new limit—one that began with the death of the author and continued for fifty years. He considered this provision more than generous, and Twain was willing to accept it. But what America's most famous writer really wanted was something that most authors were too modest to suggest—copyright in perpetuity for all literary works.

Why should the rights of someone possessing literary property, he asked, be any different from those of a landowner? "I am quite unable to guess why there should be a limit at all to the possession of the product of a man's labor. There is no limit to real estate. . . . You might just as well, after you had discovered a coal mine and worked it for forty-two years, have the government step in and take it away."

What was worse, he went on, the current system didn't benefit anyone except publishers. "It merely takes the author's property, merely takes from his children the bread and profit of that book, and gives the publisher *double* profit. . . . And they continue the enjoyment of these ill-gotten gains generation after generation, for they never die. They live forever, publishers do."[8]

He was the last speaker of the day, and there was a general feeling among the audience "that they were being rewarded for the long waiting." Their faces softened, and they leaned forward to catch every word. As one reporter noted, "He made a speech the serious parts of which created a strong impression, and the humorous parts set the Senators and Representatives in roars of laughter."[9]

Though he was one of the oldest men in the room, he didn't act it. His mind was as sharp as ever, his eyes full of life, his figure straight and trim. His long speech was—in the words of the *New York Times*—"a star performance," and the response couldn't have been better. "When the last sentence was spoken," an eyewitness wrote, "the applause came like an explosion."[10]

As much as his audience enjoyed the speech, it was what he wore that made the strongest impression. There were a few dissenting voices. The *Washington Post* made fun of him for "wearing a linen duster in the middle of winter," and a Chicago paper joked that he was parading through the capital in "last summer's yachting clothes." But the author was oblivious to such criticism, and—as he expected—his new look as the Man in White quickly became fixed in the popular imagination. William Dean Howells revised his initial opinion that the outfit was inappropriate and admitted that his friend's appearance at the hearing was "a magnificent coup." (He would later joke that he always felt underdressed when Twain wore white, "as if I had come in my nighty.")[11]

As soon as the news of his appearance at the Library of Congress became widely known, everyone wanted to see the new costume, and he obliged by wearing it often, and by posing in it for photographers again and again. He asked his tailor to produce a set of six identical suits in both serge and flannel with matching shirts, ties, and waistcoats. More were added later, while a few gray suits were reserved for travel and ordinary wear.

In the twilight of his career Twain was making visual what his friends had long accepted as factual—that he was one of a kind, an American original who would be talked about long after he was gone, and whose works would surely last as long as the Library of Congress itself. He could dress in white and get away with it because he was Mark Twain, and that was the only excuse he needed. As he had explained to a New York audience earlier in the year, "I was born modest, but it didn't last."[12]

A GREAT EXAGGERATION

I have achieved my seventy years in the usual way:
by sticking strictly to a scheme of life which would
kill anybody else.[13]

· · ·

It is easy to understand why Mark Twain's new look made such a powerful and enduring impression on the world.* There isn't much agreement, however, on why he suddenly wanted to wear white for the rest of his life. Some have said that he was obsessed in old age with cleanliness. It's true that he once told an audience he could wear one of his suits "for three days without a blemish." But as an old man who tended to scatter cigar ash wherever he went, he didn't mean for this boast of immaculate grooming to be taken any more seriously than his occasional claim that he didn't like "to attract too much attention" when he wore white.[14]

He was having fun with reporters when he informed them that his suit was "the uniform of the American Association of Purity and Perfection, of which I am president, secretary, and treasurer, and the only man in the United States eligible to membership." In his bright new clothes there was a mock suggestion of the virginal, which appealed to his sense of the absurd while at the same time suggesting a real spirit of innocence and freshness that reinforced his reputation for boyish high jinks and recalled his youth in the Mississippi Valley, where—in Huck

---

* Some writers go to great lengths to keep the life of Samuel L. Clemens separate from his career as Mark Twain, using the pen name only when referring to the literary figure. But neatly sorting out the many differences between his public and private characters is impossible, and the problem is unnecessarily complicated by constantly switching between two names for the same person. For convenience, I tend to stick with the name by which most readers know him.

Finn's words—successful men often appeared in "linen so white it hurt your eyes to look at it."[15]

There was also a hint of rebellion against adult conformity by one who had never wanted to grow old. As Howells once said of him, "He was a youth to the end of his days, the heart of a boy with the head of a sage; the heart of a good boy, or a bad boy, but always a willful boy." Sounding like an overgrown Huck Finn among fancy Easterners, Twain once referred to his white outfit as "my dontcareadam suit." To a reporter for the *New York Tribune,* he declared, "When you are seventy-one years old you may at least be pardoned for dressing as you please. . . . When I look around at the men in their black evening clothes I am disagreeably impressed with the fact that they are no more cheerful and no more pleasant to look at than a lot of crows."[16]

Though he was inclined to say amusing things about his new look whenever he spoke of it to the press, the uniform signaled more than a simple defiance of winter's gloom and the tyranny of fashion. There was something more significant behind his choice of such an unconventional outfit. Wearing white at his age was a kind of joke on death—a playful way of pretending that it had little power over him, and that he wouldn't submit to it until he was good and ready. Determined not to waste his last years in a dreary shuffle toward extinction, he wanted to go out in the grand fashion of a man who had made a deep impression on the world, and who was convinced that nothing about him—including the manner of his passing—would be forgotten.

In a candid discussion with his friend and authorized biographer, Albert Bigelow Paine—who later published the details of their talk— Twain confessed that in his old age he wanted to set himself free from gloomy reminders of past sorrows, final partings, and—inevitably—from his own approaching end.

"I can't bear to put on black clothes again," he told Paine. "If we are going to be gay in spirit, why be clad in funeral garments? . . . When I put on black it reminds me of my funerals. I could be satisfied with white all the year round."

A little while later he came back to his biographer and announced, "I have made up my mind not to wear black any more, but white, and let the critics say what they will."[17]

After returning from his first outing in "snow-white"—to use his description—he made much of the fact that everyone else had looked "funereal" as they stood around in ordinary dark suits. "Like delegates to an undertaker's convention," he scoffed. "As for black clothes," he said, "my aversion for them is incurable."[18]

Black clothing brought to mind some of the most painful moments from his intimate life as a father and husband. Three deaths haunted him: first, the sudden passing of his infant son, Langdon, more than thirty years earlier; then, in the 1890s, the death of his favorite daughter— Susy—after a brief illness ended her life at twenty-four; and, finally, the loss of his beloved wife, Olivia—or "Livy," as he called her—who slowly succumbed to heart disease. Her death took place only two and a half years before he made his grand debut in white. The timing—as always with Twain—was crucial.

In the aftermath of his wife's death, he and his two surviving children— Clara and her younger sister, Jean, both adults—dressed in black for an extended period, as was the custom. But Clara took her mourning to an extreme, retiring from the world for several months and wearing not only black dresses, but also heavy black veils. A striking photograph from the period captures her grief-stricken figure swathed in black, looking as lifeless as a statue positioned beside her solemn father. The picture was taken during the return voyage from Italy, where Livy's effort to regain her health had failed after a stay of eight months. She died on June 5, 1904.

For a time, this grim atmosphere was all-pervasive, and Twain came to feel that it was suffocating him. Shortly after losing his wife, he lamented, "The world is black today, & I think it will never lighten again." A few days later he wrote, "In my life there have been 68 Junes— but how vague and colorless 67 of them are contrasted with the deep blackness of this one."[19]

As the weeks of mourning turned to months, the dark cloud slowly lifted, and he tried to shun any oppressive thoughts of death. He began to take an active part in society again, seeing old friends, going to small parties, and giving talks in New York. By the end of 1906, he was ready to make a dramatic break from the past. Going to the opposite extreme of Clara's behavior, he decided to wear only white from head to toe as often

Mark Twain's older surviving daughter, Clara, was so
fond of wearing black that her piano teacher in Vienna,
Theodor Leschetizky, nicknamed her "Night."

as possible. It was a sign of affirmation, a show of faith in what remained
of his life.

As it happened, he didn't have much time left—only three and a half
years. But he would turn this period into one of the most eventful of his
life. He would make new friends, create a few enemies, pursue some old
dreams, develop fresh ambitions, and stir up trouble by testing the limits
of what he could say and do.

And there would be no lack of drama. In this short period he built a
mansion in Redding, Connecticut, survived a burglary by a couple of gun-
toting thieves, enjoyed flirtatious friendships with some of the prettiest
actresses on Broadway, debated female sexuality with the woman who
coined the phrase "the It girl," helped a group of slum children start a the-

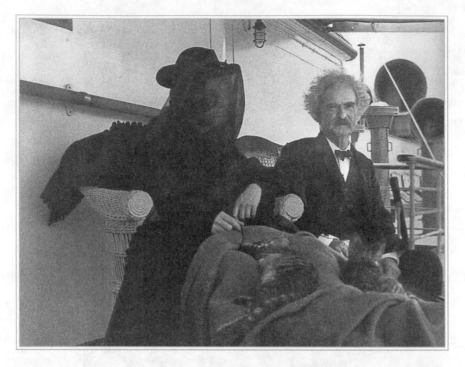

On the return voyage from Italy after her mother's death, Clara was inconsolable and covered herself from head to toe in black. She remained in mourning for many months. Two years later Twain remarked, "When I put on black it reminds me of my funerals. I could be satisfied with white all the year round."

ater, entertained a Texas Ranger, stayed out until four in the morning partying with showgirls and dancing dogs, explored Bermuda, pretended that he had been lost at sea, joked with the king and queen of England on the grounds of Windsor Castle, recited Romantic poetry to society ladies at the Waldorf-Astoria, used his influence to avoid being called for jury duty in the ragtime era's "Trial of the Century," taught little girls how to play billiards and cards, published books on heaven and Shakespeare, and almost allowed himself to be swindled out of everything he had.

And while all these things were happening, he held fast to his stated policy and took every opportunity to make himself conspicuous in white.[20]

Among the rich and powerful, he regarded himself as the equal of anyone and often made that clear in this last stage of his life. He picked fights with King Leopold of Belgium and Mary Baker Eddy of the

Christian Science church, upstaged Theodore Roosevelt at an international exhibition, talked politics with Winston Churchill at the House of Commons, drank whiskey with Andrew Carnegie, played golf with Woodrow Wilson, and appeared in a film made by Thomas Edison's company. In the literary world, he gave encouragement to a wide range of writers, sharing ghost stories with the author of *Dracula*, finding promise in the talents of the young Willa Cather, and forming a bond of mutual admiration with George Bernard Shaw.

Just before turning seventy-one, he looked ahead and acknowledged the usual worries about what he once called "troubled and foreboding Age." But he also found reasons to be optimistic, agreeing with a friend's claim that "the best of life begins at seventy." He wanted to enjoy his money and fame before it was too late, and he relished the idea of doing exactly as he pleased for the rest of his life. "You have earned your holiday," he told himself. Instead of fretting over how much time he had left, he decided that he wouldn't be ruled by the calendar and would concentrate on having fun.[21]

He had a long history of dismissing the question of his death with artful, and memorably comic, statements. He was a relatively robust sixty-one when a journalist—Frank Marshall White—asked for his response to a rumor that he was dying. White sent a cable to his New York editor with Twain's famous comment "The report of my death was an exaggeration." Other press accounts altered this to read, "The reports of my death are grossly exaggerated," and "grossly" was soon replaced by "greatly" in the more popular version. "Of course I'm dying," Twain told White, "but I'm not dying any faster than anybody else." He was amused at how often his initial comment was reprinted and embellished, wryly observing, "It keeps turning up . . . in the newspapers when people have occasion to discount exaggeration."[22]

He liked to joke about the possibility of preparing his own obituary. It was an idea that he may have taken from the greatest showman of the age, P. T. Barnum, whose dying wish was to see his own obituary printed. To oblige Barnum, the *New York Evening Sun* famously arranged to publish a "premature" report. "Great and Only Barnum," the headline said two weeks before he died in 1891. "He Wanted to Read His Obituary; Here It Is."

Several years later, Mark Twain went to the trouble of writing a mock letter to the press, politely asking for "access to my standing obituaries, with the privilege—if this is not asking too much—of editing, not their Facts, but their Verdicts." As an incentive for compliance to his request, he suggested a reward of no small value: "For the best Obituary—one suitable for me to read in public, and calculated to inspire regret—I desire to offer a Prize, consisting of a Portrait of me done entirely in pen and ink without previous instruction." A few papers responded by printing tongue-in-cheek tributes to the "dead" author. The *New York World* trumpeted its eulogy with a nice pun on the false assertion in the headline, "Here Lies Mark Twain."[23]

A subversive at heart, Twain loved undercutting easy assumptions—even his own. Which is one reason why he was so fond of exaggeration. It undercuts itself. He jested so often about death that many of his contemporaries stopped taking him seriously on the subject and wondered whether he might outlive most of his generation and die in his late eighties—as his mother had done—or even survive into his nineties and beyond. His admirers couldn't imagine a world without him. And sometimes he felt that way himself, toying with the notion that his ghostly appearance in white clothes created the impression that he was already beyond death's reach. "Time is pushing me inexorably along," he said at the turn of the twentieth century. "I am approaching the threshold of age; in 1977 I shall be 142."[24]

As long as he planned on being around for a while, it made sense in an odd way to choose a hearing on copyright legislation as the place to reveal his new look. There was an extra incentive for extending his life if he could also extend the life of his books by keeping them under copyright. If Congress agreed to pass a new law guaranteeing protection for at least fifty years after the author's death, then the longer Twain lived, the longer his work would survive for the benefit of his heirs.

For years he had been piling up manuscripts to be published only after he was gone. He wanted to entertain posterity by leaving to his heirs the job of issuing new works every decade or so. These were meant to go off like time bombs, each intended to cause a periodic ruckus, keeping his name in the news and his fame alive. Such would prove to be the case when some of the more sensational autobiographical pieces began appearing in the 1930s and 1940s—especially those collected in a volume called, appropriately, *Mark Twain in Eruption*. These works were enthusiastically received in just the manner the author intended—as defiant protests from the grave. "He said things after his death," a surprised Theodore Dreiser declared of Twain in 1935, "that he never dared say in his life."[25]

While diligently dictating his autobiography in old age, Twain often paused to consider the amazement with which his manuscripts would be greeted by posterity. Never one to think small, he had no doubt that his vast literary output would continue attracting readers into the next century, and that the demand would always exist for fresh revelations from his manuscript hoard. Speculating in 1906 on what future audiences would say of his unpublished comments on religious bigotry and social hypocrisy, he took a long view. "The edition of A.D. 2006 will make a stir when it comes out," he wrote confidently. "I shall be hovering around taking notice, along with other dead pals." (If he managed to continue hovering through the summer of 2008, he would have seen his face adorning the cover of *Time,* which called him "Our Original Superstar.")[26]

As an author who was used to seeing his works lavishly illustrated, and who appreciated the importance of images, he was aware that his new look made an unforgettable illustration of his own star appeal. The Man in White was not only an entertaining sight, but one that seemed to require comment. He was a cigar-store angel come to life, with a mischievous eye on this world, and a curious one on the next. Such a figure furnished a spectacle that was both comic and tragic, a spirited celebration of life's rewards and a clown's lament of his own mortality.

The full effect may have been lost on contemporaries who thought he was simply trying to amuse them, but he made it clear from the beginning that his decision to adopt a new image was inextricably linked to his unavoidable encounter with death. "I have reached the age where dark clothes have a depressing effect on me," he told the press in 1906. "Light-colored clothing is more pleasing to the eye and enlivens the spirit. Now, of course, I cannot compel everyone to wear such clothing just for my especial benefit, so I do the next best thing and wear it myself."[27]

Though his literary career was largely at an end, he wanted to use all the creative force remaining in him to put the finishing touches on a life

as complex and dazzling as anything in his fiction. As Howells remarked
of the final years, "His literature grew less and less and his life more
and more." In many ways Twain was never more alive—and never more
perceptive—than in this eventful period that lasted a mere forty months.
He turned it into an epic progress, beginning with his appearance in
Washington at the end of 1906 and concluding with the world's parting
glimpse of him in April 1910, when the many mourners at his funeral in
New York looked down at his open casket and saw Mark Twain still
splendidly arrayed in white.[28]

STRAINED RELATIONS

> All of us contain Music & Truth,
> but most of us can't get it out.[29]

· · ·

Though Twain's old age was much sadder than many of his contemporaries would have guessed—especially at the very end—it was also funnier and a lot happier than later generations of critics and biographers
have been willing to admit. But the temptation to see the writer's old age
as blighted in one way or another is considerable.

It is true that much of his writing in his last years is full of rage
against the frailties of human nature, the cruelties of life, and the chaos
of the universe. Surely, the reasoning goes, the bitter, scathing antagonist
of the "damned human race" felt overwhelmed by the darkness of the
world, and suffered accordingly. The septuagenarian Twain who is so
often portrayed as nothing but an acerbic old cynic is supposed to sound
like this: "*Is*n't human nature the most consummate sham & lie that was
ever invented? Isn't man a creature to be ashamed of in pretty much all
his aspects? Is he really fit for anything but to be stood up on the street
corner as a convenience for dogs? Man, 'Know thyself'—& then thou wilt
despise thyself, to a dead moral certainty."

These would seem to be the words of an American Lear, gnashing his
teeth and pulling out his white hair in an old man's rant. But, no, these
are Mark Twain's words in a letter written to a friend in 1884, when he

was still in his forties—at the peak of his powers, in the bloom of health, and surrounded by adoring friends and a loving family in one of the finest houses in the fair city of Hartford, Connecticut.[30]

In fact, he was always fond of savagely attacking the moral failings of his fellow humans and of exposing their distorted views of themselves and their world. He didn't need to wait until old age to discover that humanity wasn't all it pretended to be. The main thing that changed between middle age and old age was that he became less guarded about sharing his unvarnished opinions, putting them in formal literary pieces intended for eventual publication rather than merely venting his feelings to sympathetic friends in letters or conversations.

With close companions such as Howells and Joseph Twichell—his Hartford neighbor and family minister—he was accustomed to launching vitriolic outbursts against all kinds of injustice, knowing they would understand that his fierce tirades didn't represent the sum of his views nor the full measure of his character. At the end of an especially angry letter to Reverend Twichell on the subject of political hypocrisy, he declared, "I have written you to-day, not to do you a service, but to do myself one. There was bile in me. I had to empty it. . . . I have used you as an equilibrium-restorer more than once in my time, & shall continue, I guess."[31]

Twain's moods changed frequently, and it is unrealistic to saddle him with one dominant emotion during his final years, when he was as likely to assume the part of the joker as that of the angry prophet. As Clara once observed of her father, he was always a man of many emotions, a "cyclonic warrior one moment—lily-of-the-valley the next." He could easily shift from merry to morose in the blink of an eye, attacking human folly one minute and penning Valentine's Day verses to little girls the next. Writing in 1906 to the wife of a close friend, he was in typical form when he shrugged off the fact that he was feeling low and worn out emotionally after a hard night. He explained that it was only a short bout of "a disease I am not much subject to—depression of spirits," and added, "I am all right, this morning, in *all* ways."[32]

He was fearless in his ability to delve deep into the shadows of life and to confront the painful truths lurking there. But what sets him apart from so many other writers with a talent for staring into the abyss is his ability to face the worst and still find reason to laugh. Sometimes his laughter was derisive, mocking, or weary, but often it was simply an expression of his inexhaustible love of the comic and the absurd. He was never so glum that he couldn't find some reason to lighten his anger with a joke.

In our modern eagerness to highlight his darker side, we do him a disservice by pretending that his matchless sense of humor suddenly failed him in his last years. At his best, he was never merely funny. Or merely serious. Rather, he delighted in slyly mixing the two, and loved nothing better than creating confusion between them. When a pious lady approached him and gushed, "How God must love you!" he solemnly replied, "I hope so," but out of her hearing added in a perfect deadpan, "I guess she hasn't heard of our strained relations."[33]

If he had been an ordinary man, he might have been crushed by the various disappointments he suffered in a tumultuous life that began in the steam age and ended almost seventy-five years later at the dawn of the aviation age. But modern critics who so easily imagine him crippled by misfortune and blind anger forget how difficult his life had been from the beginning. He survived into his seventies for a reason. He was made of strong stuff, having learned early to cope with adversity in a frontier environment that was demanding and unforgiving.[34]

He grew up with two thousand miles of wilderness at his back and the continent's mightiest river at his feet. As a young steamboat pilot he learned to follow the twists and turns of that river for hundreds of miles, in daylight and in darkness, upstream and down. And he also learned how to take the measure of the many men and women who flocked to the river from all parts of the world. Some came to revel in the freedom of frontier life, some to undermine and corrupt it.

He saw the worst and best in humanity, from the generous residents of Memphis who cared for the brother he lost in an explosion on the river, to the slavers who plied their awful trade in human beings from Missouri to Louisiana. Though he spent half his life in comfort among genteel Easterners, his character was forged in the West among people of exceptional toughness and resourcefulness. They provided him with a view of the world that mixed hard realism with a boisterous love of life.

He lived at a time when everyone took it for granted that existence was short, and that a good run of luck could end at any moment, wiping out fortunes and destroying whole families. No private empire was safe, no happy family secure. Stupendous success was often merely a prelude to stupendous failure. Swindlers and speculators ruined innocent lives, banks failed, and financial panics put old established firms out of business overnight. Young brides and their infants were swept into early graves by the perils of childbirth. Even in the best towns, epidemics of cholera and typhus and deadly influenza were constant threats.

In 1876, when his own happiness seemed unthreatened, Twain was well aware that his world could collapse at any moment: "What a curious thing life is. We delve away, through years of hardship, wasting toil, despondency; then comes a little butterfly season of wealth, ease, & clustering honors.—Presto! the wife dies, a daughter marries a spendthrift villain, the heir & hope of the house commits suicide, the laurels fade & fall away. Grand result of a hard-fought, successful career & a blameless life. Piles of money, tottering age, & a broken heart."[35]

He would come to know the pain of such misfortunes, and would complain bitterly of them. Some of his worst fears did, in fact, come true—a fortune lost, a wife and a beloved daughter in their graves, and another child plagued by chronic disease. But to think that these tragedies—hard as they were to bear—were enough to break Mark Twain's spirit is to misjudge his character completely. Resilient and restless in the best tradition of the West, he did not merely endure old age, but repeatedly demonstrated an ability to rise above its limitations and tragedies, and to seek out pleasures to offset its pains.

One of his admirers during his last decade—Willa Cather—was flabbergasted when she later encountered Van Wyck Brooks's argument in *The Ordeal of Mark Twain* (1920) that the old humorist was a "storm-beaten human drift, a derelict, washing about on a forlorn sea." Having known the famous man well enough to be granted an audience while he spent a lazy morning in bed, she believed that if Van Wyck Brooks "had ever seen that old lion in bed telling stories, he never could have written his book." Cather was right. Twain had the spirit of a lion as well as the roar.[36]

THE UNIVERSE OF MARK

It "gravels" me, to this day, to put my will
in the weak shape of a request, instead of
launching it in the crisp language of an order.[37]

· · ·

At the height of his glory Mark Twain was a literary giant in a gilded age filled with legendary movers and shakers of all kinds—Carnegie, Edison, Rockefeller, Theodore Roosevelt. But none of these titans enjoyed the kind of affection that greeted Twain wherever he went. It isn't an exaggeration to say that, in the first decade of the twentieth century, he was the most famous, and the most beloved, person in America. His image was so familiar that it was regularly featured in advertising for everything from cigars to kitchen stoves. The press eagerly reported even the slightest events in his life. Dockhands cheered him at foreign ports; policemen stopped traffic to let him cross the road; customs agents allowed him to travel without inspection; and postal authorities tracked him down to deliver letters addressed to him by name only. When he entered a restaurant or theater, people would stand up to applaud.

Long before he left this world, his status as an immortal figure in popular culture seemed assured. His books were classics, and occupied a place of honor in many American homes. His spectacular rise from humble beginnings to national hero was almost as familiar as Abraham Lincoln's similar story. In fact, after his death, he was praised as the "Lincoln of our literature."[38]

Throughout his last decade he received the deferential treatment worthy of a legend. When he visited the Capitol on his mission to lobby for copyright legislation, he took over the Speaker's private chamber as his temporary office. The next day he ambled over to the White House, and was promptly taken to see Theodore Roosevelt after casually telling the doorkeeper, "I want the usual thing—I want to see the President." When he came out a few minutes later, he announced confidently, "The President is one with us on the copyright matter."[39]

In New York, where he kept a leased house on Fifth Avenue, he liked to go out on Sundays when the sidewalks were full of crowds leaving church and stroll along in a cloud of cigar smoke, pausing occasionally to nod regally when someone said hello. If the press accused him of being too proud, he was always ready with a mock response of contrite humility. Told that he had been too familiar in a conversation with King Edward VII, he replied that he had done nothing of the kind: "I was reared in the most exclusive circles of Missouri and I know how to behave."[40]

He enjoyed a pampered existence, lounging in bed for a good part of the day, "propped against snowy pillows" and looking like an emperor in "a handsome silk dressing gown of rich Persian pattern." It was a family joke that he spent so much time in bed his hair had "assumed the color of his pillow." His unruly mane prompted one irreverent critic to speculate that Twain's "principal recreation is not parting his hair." At whatever hour he chose to get up, he would be disappointed if he found the house empty and would seek out companions. Depending on his mood, he liked the company of cats, impressionable young men, innocent girls, well-bred ladies of various ages, or a few elderly gentlemen whose renown was great, but not nearly as great as his own. If he could find anyone willing to join him in a game of billiards, he was happy to continue playing until midnight and beyond.[41]

In an age when many people lived on less than two dollars a day, his income rose to as much as a hundred thousand dollars a year. He was the highest paid writer in America, and it was widely reported that his magazine contributions could earn a dollar a word. In fact, his last contract with Harper & Brothers guaranteed him only a third of that, but it was still a better deal than anyone else could have expected, and he always insisted on a strict word count from his editors, even going so far as to demand that hyphenated words be counted as two. Legend has it that when an admirer enclosed a dollar with a request for his autograph, he replied not with his signature but with the single word "Thanks," in accordance with his rumored rate.[42]

After he was described in the *Atlantic Monthly* as "Mark Twain, originally of Missouri, but then of Hartford, and now ultimately of the solar system, not to say the universe," he took pleasure in thinking of his name floating somewhere among distant planets. "If we can prove that my fame has reached to Neptune and Uranus, and possibly to some systems a little beyond there, why, that would satisfy me." When an English journalist asked his opinion of a Russian plan for disarmament, he saw no reason why his powers should not extend to the establishment of world peace. "The Tsar is ready to disarm. I am ready to disarm. Collect the others; it should not be much of a task now."[43]

Until his final months, he looked hearty enough to most observers. (Just shy of five foot nine, he weighed a trim 158 pounds.) "You couldn't never think of him as old," said a family servant. "Why he used to run upstairs three steps at a time." As Clara recalled, "He was fundamentally young to the day of his death.... His movements were quick and decided. His laugh was spontaneous and hearty." Twain himself frequently declared that he always felt young inside. "I am only able to perceive I am old by a mental process," he said at seventy. "I am altogether unable to feel old in spirit."[44]

He liked to boast that, after having survived a sickly period in his youth, his health improved so much that it had remained exceptionally good ever since. In his forties he wrote, "During the first seven years of my life I had no health—I may almost say that I lived on allopathic medicine, but since that period I have hardly known what sickness is." The improvement was so remarkable that even an early addiction to tobacco didn't cause a relapse. "I began to smoke immoderately when I was eight years old," he claimed. Smoking cigars, he believed, had proven "to be the best of all inspirations for the pen, and, in my particular case, no sort of detriment to the health." When his pen was moving at top speed, he could go through twenty or more cigars a day. At such times, he added, "I smoke with all my might, and allow no intervals."[45]

A FIRST-CLASS LIFE

I know if I was going to be hanged I could get up and
make a good showing, and I intend to.[46]

···

The thick haze of his favorite cigar may have left Twain confused about the exact age at which his love affair with tobacco began. But he was right about the sudden break from his early years of sickness. In a matter of months, young Samuel Langhorne Clemens of Hannibal, Missouri, had gone from being "a pale, sickly boy who did a great deal more thinking than was good for him" to a constant companion of the most adventurous boys in his little hometown on the Mississippi. No one was more shocked by this change than his mother, Jane Clemens, who doubted from the start that he would survive childhood. Recalling the day of his birth—November 30, 1835—she said, "When I first saw him, I could see no promise in him. . . . He was a poor looking object to raise."[47]

She knew from hard experience how quickly death could strike in frontier villages where disease spread easily. She lost her husband—John Clemens, a dignified but impecunious country lawyer and storekeeper—to an attack of pneumonia when he was only forty-eight. Three of her seven children fell victim to illness early in life. She never forgot the morning when Margaret, the younger of her two daughters, left for school reciting lines from the day's lesson—"God is a spirit & they that worship him must worship him in spirit & in truth"—for these were the last words she remembered her daughter saying before sickness overcame the girl. When Margaret arrived home at the end of the day, she was in the grip of a high fever and was put to bed. She lingered for nearly a week, becoming increasingly incoherent and lapsing into a coma from which she never awoke.[48]

Such a painful loss might have been a devastating blow to a weaker woman, but Jane was remarkably strong and held the family together through many hardships and tragedies. As young Sam—the sixth of her seven children—observed of her, she was not one to dwell on misfortune, but kept "a sunshiny disposition" until the end of her days. Quick-witted and playful, she was able to banter with her famous son even in old age. When she used to spin tales about his childhood illnesses, he would tease her by raising an eyebrow and inquiring earnestly, "Afraid I wouldn't live?" And she would tease him back: "No—afraid you would."[49]

Though her memory often failed her in later years, she remained a spirited, engaging character until her death at eighty-seven. Her son admired the way she never let her troubles—not even the pains of age—diminish her love of life. And, no doubt, the pride he felt in her frontier resiliency was also partly a reflection of the pride he felt in his own. "To the very day of her death," he wrote a month after the event, "she felt a strong interest in the whole world and everything and everybody in it. In all her life she never knew such a thing as a half-hearted interest in affairs and people. . . . I am certain it was this feature of my mother's make-up that carried her so far toward ninety."[50]

Only a few years before Twain's own death, a reporter was sufficiently impressed by his lively manner to declare confidently, "One must see this big, boisterous man, with the red-veined cheeks of health and the little gray-blue eyes sparkling with the light of laughter, half hidden under the drooping bristles of his eyebrows, to appreciate why he can afford to joke even with death. He is 72, and any insurance company, one would hazard, would take him to-day as a 'first-class life,' and be glad of the opportunity."[51]

But the rosy surface was deceptive, and Twain couldn't ignore it. The ill effects of having lived so self-indulgently for so long were unavoidable, though it wasn't until very late in life that he was forced to face them. His smoking habit left him with a chronic cough, occasional bouts of bronchitis, and a "tobacco heart," as he called his angina after it began to trouble him. Giving up his cigars—which were so strong most of his friends wouldn't touch them—was out of the question. "I stopped smoking, about a fortnight," he wrote in the last year of his life, "because the doctor said smoking would kill me. But I thought it over & resumed. I don't care for death, & I do care for smoking." He cared for it so much that he knew he wouldn't last long if he gave it up. "When I get smoked out—well, it will be a sign!" He was remarkably successful at not allowing his ailments to slow him down. Up until the last few weeks of his life, he remained active.[52]

Clara worried that he was living so freely in old age that he might do something dangerous or disgraceful. She feared that after her mother's death he wouldn't feel obliged to follow anyone's opinion but his own. "He frightens me almost to death sometimes," she confessed. But he wasn't concerned. As he explained to a fellow septuagenarian, "Before seventy we are merely respected . . . and have to behave all the time. . . . After seventy we are respected, esteemed, admired, revered, and don't have to behave unless we want to."[53]

What follows is the story of Mark Twain's last great adventure—his bold effort to make "a good showing" in his long farewell to a public that adored him, and to a world whose charms he treasured, but whose failings he never could forgive. With great imagination and verve, he crafted an image that would endure for many decades, and burnished a reputation that would survive the ups and downs of fashion. Rather than a time of bitterness and retreat, as many writers have suggested, his slow exit from a "first-class life" was full of energy and hope, and deserves a close look because it allows us to see Twain in all his unvarnished splendor, living larger than anyone else, and proud of it. "Everybody lives," he wrote in 1907, "but only Genius lives richly, sumptuously, imperially."[54]

I have chosen to focus on this final period of three and a half years because it seems to capture the essence of the man, giving us a deeper understanding of his extraordinarily complex character and a better appreciation of his genius. His flame burned brightly at the end, and he was intensely conscious of the spectacle, relishing the pleasures of the moment while also eagerly speculating on the afterglow of his legacy. My book is the story of how this consummate showman staged his parting scenes, what he did to perpetuate his fame, and how he made it pay long after he was gone.

I haven't a particle of confidence in a man
who has no redeeming petty vices whatever.

MARK TWAIN

. . .

PART ONE

BLITHE SPIRIT

Seated at Clara's piano, Twain plays a tune for his daughter and her friend, violinist Marie Nichols. The author loved music of many kinds, from Beethoven sonatas to popular songs.

ONE

Ragtime on Tap

Many a small thing has been made large
by the right kind of advertising.
Mark Twain[1]

. . .

ON THE FINAL NIGHT of 1906 the fog was so heavy in Manhattan that even the powerful new searchlight shining over Times Square could barely penetrate it. Rain had been falling all day, and the sidewalks were full of frustrated revelers huddled under umbrellas. But as midnight approached, the air cleared a little, the moon came out, and the searchlight broke through the clouds, projecting a glowing "1907" against the black sky. In the distance, factory whistles blared as thousands of partygoers broke into cheers and the restaurants on Broadway dimmed their lights. Crowds poured into Times Square throwing confetti, shaking cowbells, and blowing toy horns.

A few blocks away—inside the cavernous hall of the New York Electric Music Company—the street celebrations were drowned out by the sound of "Auld Lang Syne" being played on an enormous new device called a Telharmonium. Weighing two hundred tons, and requiring more than two thousand electrical switches to amplify its notes, the organlike instrument was undergoing the first major test of its capability to transmit music through telephone lines to listening stations around town. Though it was a crude effort to do what radio broadcasts would later do much better, the invention was greeted as a great technological breakthrough, and there was talk that it would soon be available to anyone with ordinary telephone service. For its New Year's Eve demonstration, lines were connected to large megaphones at several cafés and hotels. The only private residence to receive the transmission was Mark Twain's tall corner house at 21 Fifth Avenue—near Washington Square—where twenty guests were invited to listen to the Telharmonium's music fill his parlor a few minutes before the stroke of twelve.

Just before the special equipment began to reverberate with sound, Twain gathered his audience around him, paused dramatically, and then commanded, "Listen." As if by magic, the music began to pour from the megaphone. The author's face lit up, and he stepped aside to allow his guests to appreciate this modern wonder. In a letter written the next day, he proudly described the moment: "At 11:55 there was a prepared surprise; lovely music—played on a silent piano of 300 keys at the corner of Broadway a mile and a half away, and sent over the telephone wire to our parlor—the first time this marvelous invention ever uttered its voice in a private house."

It seemed a dream come true to a man who counted among his most cherished possessions a massive player organ encased in an eight-foot-high mahogany frame. He was so fond of his "Aeolian Orchestrelle" that he used it almost every night—playing a simple melody on the keyboard himself or listening to something from his collection of sixty music rolls. His favorites were Beethoven sonatas and Chopin nocturnes, but he also liked popular songs and Scottish airs. Now he could look forward to having the wizards of the New York Electric Music Company supply him with tunes of all kinds on demand, making available—in the words of the Telharmonium's supporters—"opera, symphony and ragtime on tap."[2]

He had first heard of the Telharmonium only two weeks earlier when he came across a newspaper article about it. He was so thrilled by the report that he had gone straight to the company's headquarters at Thirty-ninth and Broadway—across the street from the Metropolitan Opera House—to see the device for himself.

A reporter had tagged along and watched as Twain sat near the keyboard dais of the massive instrument, swinging his legs while he listened contentedly to a private demonstration. The quality of the sound pleased him, but what really fascinated him was the sheer mechanical complexity of the device, whose workings seemed almost beyond comprehension. Eagerly, he agreed on the spot to take out the first individual subscription to the new service. Later, he proudly declared that this put him once again at the forefront of modern technological progress, noting that he had been among the first to use a fountain pen, a typewriter, and a home telephone.

The one regret he expressed was that the device had not been invented sooner. "The trouble about these beautiful, novel things," he remarked, "is that they interfere so with one's arrangements. Every time I see or hear a new wonder like this I have to postpone my death right off. I couldn't possibly leave the world until I have heard this again and again."[3]

For his New Year's Eve celebration, he allowed half a dozen reporters into his home to observe the festivities. In the front hall they gathered with notebooks in hand and listened politely as he explained the wonders of his new musical device. But everyone seemed to understand that the main attraction of the evening wasn't the workings of the new machine but the antics of the old man in white. He didn't disappoint the men of the press. Striking a pose, he declared, "This is the famous suit I wore when I went to interview the copyright committee of Congress in Washington. Yes, I insist that white is the best color for men's clothes. If men were not so near insane they would appreciate the fact."

One reporter teased him about his fame, suggesting that he run for governor. He pretended to take the idea seriously. "I am the real man," he shot back. "I am sure I would make a great Governor." While he was talking, a small wagon was wheeled into the parlor behind his back. It was carrying "a bewhiskered old gentleman" who was supposed to represent 1906. "There he comes butting in," Twain joked, looking behind him. "He doesn't know when to quit."[4]

The party had a circuslike atmosphere, with the host presiding over various games and comic skits throughout the evening. Twain wanted his guests to be in high spirits when they were treated to the first magical notes from the Telharmonium. At one point he wandered off for a short time, and then suddenly reappeared at the top of the stairs with a young man whose arm was tied to his by a pink ribbon. In identical white suits, they descended the stairs slowly, each trying to match the steps of the other but not quite succeeding. As they entered the parlor, Twain announced that they were Siamese twins and were going to enlighten the guests by presenting a lecture on the evils of strong drink. While the older "brother" explained the dangers of liquor, the younger stood silently and took furtive drinks from a flask of rum.

As some of the guests may have known, P. T. Barnum's famous conjoined twins—Chang and Eng—used to have violent arguments with each other over religion and alcohol. So Mark and his twin pretended that the drinking habits of one affected the sobriety of the other. The more Mark denounced rum, the more intoxicated he became, staggering and hiccupping and slurring his words as his other half finished off the contents of the flask.

Twain was in rare form, playing his part effortlessly and behaving like a much younger man. "We are so much to each other, my brother and I," he explained, as he pretended to succumb slowly to the effects of alcohol, "that what nourishes him and what he drinks—ahem!—nourishes me. . . . It has often been a source of considerable annoyance to me, when going about the country lecturing on temperance, to find myself at the head of a procession . . . so drunk I couldn't see."

His guests laughed so hard that he was forced to end his mock lecture because he couldn't be heard above the noise. In a front-page story the next day, the *New York Times* began its report of the party by going along with Twain's joke, declaring, "The last thing that Mark Twain did in 1906 was to get drunk and deliver a lecture on temperance. . . . [He] took all the glory for the lecture to himself while he blamed his Siamese brother for the jag. Those who have never heard that Mr. Clemens has a Siamese brother, must be told that he only had such a relative for one night."[5]

This "partially impromptu performance" was inspired by an idea that had been at the back of Twain's mind for years. In the 1890s he had written "Those Extraordinary Twins," which features conjoined brothers who are at odds over everything—one is a hard-drinking Democrat, the other a Whig champion of the Teetotalers' League. But his first treatment of such a farcical pairing goes all the way back to a short piece called "Personal Habits of the Siamese Twins," which was written in the late 1860s, when Chang and Eng were at the height of their fame.

Pretending to be an intimate friend of the famous pair, Twain claimed to know all their secrets. It was true that one brother was a temperance man and the other was not, but Twain added the outrageous charge that the two had been bitter enemies in the Civil War. "During the War they were strong partisans," he wrote, "and both fought gallantly all through the great struggle—Eng on the Union side and Chang on the Confederate. They took each other prisoners at Seven Oaks."[6]

This was the sort of comedy that played particularly well in the boom-and-bust culture of the frontier, and though Twain was now a New York gentleman with a house on Fifth Avenue, nothing made him happier than indulging in some of the old inspired nonsense that had fueled his rise as a Western humorist. By deciding to dress the "twins" at his party in white, and by inventing dialogue for the skit as he went along, he seemed eager to prove that he could still breathe fresh life into an old concept.

His partner in the skit was a young friend named Witter Bynner— a wealthy, Harvard-educated poet and editor. Blessed with neither acting ability nor a great sense of humor, Bynner nevertheless made a good sidekick. All that he needed to do was drink and look serious, for the funniest thing about him was the sharp contrast his age and size made to his twin's. According to one observer, Mark looked much shorter and older beside his "brother," who was "very tall, very slight and had black hair."

Bynner was delighted to help out and never forgot his starring moment opposite the great author. He had nothing but good memories of Twain, who acted as his mentor for a time, and who enjoyed exposing the young man's tender ears to coarse language that included—the poet fondly recalled—some moments of "sublime profanity."[7]

By the time Twain stepped forward to begin the Telharmonium's brief midnight demonstration, his guests were suitably primed to greet the new marvel with gasps of joy and admiration. One of the amazed reporters thought the sound from the device had "all the richness of a great orchestra." Many of the guests lingered long after the music ended, continuing to celebrate the occasion, but the newspapermen had to race off to file their stories for the morning papers. Twain was good copy, and everyone agreed that the author had given 1906 "a merry funeral." The proud host declared that he was pleased with the whole affair.*

"Next to the day I was put in trousers," he said with no small degree of hyperbole, "this is the happiest occasion of my life."[8]

· · ·

LIKE HIS DEBUT in white at the Library of Congress, Twain's party was a sign of his determination not only to liven up his old age, but to give his fame a good boost. One reason he wanted the publicity was to draw attention to his most important project of this period—his autobiography. Since September, the *North American Review* had been running excerpts from the work. Though much of his ever-expanding manuscript was not meant to be seen by his contemporaries, he had been allowing selected parts to appear in print under a lucrative agreement with the magazine's editor and owner—Colonel George Harvey, who was also president of Harper's. The work was being featured in twenty-five installments as "Chapters from My Autobiography," and was scheduled to continue appearing until the end of the year. The deal called for Twain to be paid $30,000. For that much money, white suits and funny parties were easy ways for the author to advertise himself and his autobiography-in-progress.

It was also a great pleasure for him to pretend that he could be an old reprobate and stay up late and get drunk if he wanted to. During the long years of his marriage to the very proper Olivia Langdon, he wouldn't have dared to throw a big New Year's Eve party in which he played an alcoholic. She would have been scandalized by the subheading in the *New York Times,* "Twin Gets Drunk and the Joy of It Penetrates to Twain While

---

* Unfortunately, the Telharmonium's transmissions proved so powerful that they affected ordinary telephone calls, interrupting conversations with blasts of music or deafening static. There were even reports that the navy's communications with its ships at sea were disrupted by interference from the device. Complaints poured in, the service was cut back, and subscriptions were canceled. By the end of the year, the Broadway headquarters was closed, and the gargantuan instrument was dismantled, its parts sold for scrap.

Lecturing on Temperance." But, much as he adored his wife's memory, he clearly relished the freedom to take new liberties with his public image. He was entering into his second bachelorhood, and was ready to return to some of the mischievous ways of his youth.

He was quick to share his new look and his new attitude with the rest of New York. For the next three months he brightened the winter by making frequent appearances in white at matinees, fund-raising events, and testimonial luncheons. He even wore his famous suit when he visited Police Headquarters one day to pay a social call on an old admirer, Commissioner Theodore Bingham. The press dutifully recorded such comings and goings, and Twain usually paused long enough to exchange a few pleasantries with the reporters and have his picture taken.

Reminiscing that winter about a public appearance he had made long ago in Boston, he explained to one journalist the first rule of entertaining an audience at a lecture or reading. Keep it short, he advised. According to his calculations, after twelve minutes every audience knows that the speaker "ought to be gagged." After fifteen minutes "they know that he ought to be shot."[9]

But nobody was in any danger of being bored by Twain. He was constantly in demand, and was overwhelmed with invitations. He particularly enjoyed being seen in the company of some of the rising young stars in the entertainment world. The Broadway actresses Ethel Barrymore and Billie Burke—both of whom were then in their twenties—were two of his favorites. He was especially close to Burke, whose warm manner and trilling voice he adored. (She would later use both to great advantage as the Good Witch in the 1939 film of *The Wizard of Oz*). He called her "Billie Burke, the young, the gifted, the beautiful, the charming," and liked to rave about the beauty of her red hair.

"It was always exciting and enjoyable to see him," she was to recall. "He would shake that beautiful shock of snowy white hair and lean his wonderful head against mine to say, 'Billie, we redheads have to stick together.' "[10]

He had met young Ethel Barrymore the previous summer at a garden party, where he watched in amazement as she frolicked in a fountain for the amusement of the guests. Whenever he saw her afterward, he liked to address her fondly as "the water sprite!" ("He was always very nice to

(*Left*): At a midnight ball in 1908, Ethel Barrymore and Twain spent much of the party together. Afterward, Twain said that he "enjoyed it thoroughly till 4:05 a.m., when I came away with the last of the rioters." (*Right*): Billie Burke, the young Broadway star, visited Twain often in the final years of his life.

me," she would later say.) One day in March he and Ethel joined forces to raise money for women college students at a performance of one-act plays. He served as master of ceremonies, and she played a boy of fifteen in a dramatic piece called *Carrots*.[11]

He sometimes sat next to her at dinner parties given by their mutual friend Robert J. Collier, the young publisher of *Collier's Weekly*. Naturally, Twain was always the center of attention at these gatherings, and he loved every minute of them, especially when the ladies treated him to a few innocent gestures of affection. He once described an evening at Collier's large home in Gramercy Park as "a kissing bee."[12]

After basking in the limelight at one of his friend's Sunday night parties, he said he was reminded of a favorite saying by Mary Ann Cord, the former slave who used to cook for his family at their summer cottage in Livy's hometown of Elmira, New York. "Auntie Cord"—whose "vigorous eloquence" had often enchanted him—coined a phrase for social luminaries: "de queen o' de magazines." He thought her phrase fit him perfectly because his "full evening dress of white broadcloth" seemed to charm both men and women. "I dined with a dozen other guests," he boasted, "and was 'de queen o' de magazines.' "[13]

· · ·

THE OUTPOURING OF AFFECTION and admiration that greeted his new look encouraged Twain to believe that he could appear in white at almost any kind of event. He seemed eager to test the reactions of widely different audiences. During that winter he was surely the only celebrity in town who was applauded at both a billiards tournament and a poetry reading. The warm reception he received at the first event is hardly surprising, given his well-known love of the game. An accomplished player, he claimed that billiards "exercises all your body and half of your soul." When he discovered in the first week of March that the National Amateur Billiard Championship was taking place at a concert hall in midtown Manhattan, he decided to show up unannounced and arrived during the middle of a big match.[14]

As he entered the smoke-filled hall—wearing what one observer fancifully described as a "pearl-colored sack suit"—the defending national champion was getting ready to take an important shot. Suddenly, the spectators turned their attention away from the game and began to applaud Twain. Soon they were standing and cheering.

According to one account, the loud cheers "so disconcerted" the champ—Edward Gardner—that he missed his shot. Twain didn't seem to notice. He was too busy waving and smiling as he walked to his seat. But after the commotion died down and play resumed, there was no more attentive spectator in the crowd than the famous author, who stayed for almost two hours and kept his eyes riveted on the action.

"At the good shots," a reporter noted, the author "puffed furiously at a big black cigar."

The reigning champ put on a thrilling show. After dropping behind in the score, he made a roaring comeback and pulled out a victory, winning by a single point.

Twain was at ease in the rough and rowdy crowd, and didn't seem to mind sitting the whole time beside a shady character named Calvin

Demarest, a champion player known for his volatile temper. (Several years later Demarest would be charged with attempted murder and spend time in an insane asylum.)[15]

Twain was less comfortable at the poetry reading, but he was much more than a mere spectator at that event. He had an important part to perform, reading two poems to a packed house. His appearance was in support of the new Keats-Shelley Memorial in Italy. An Anglo-American organization had purchased the house in Rome where John Keats died in 1821 and wanted to raise money to establish a museum. After President Theodore Roosevelt gave the idea his blessing in a public letter of support, high society turned its attention to the cause and organized a large charity event on Valentine's Day, 1907, in the ballroom of the Waldorf-Astoria.

The Vanderbilt family purchased a box seat, as did the wife of former president Grover Cleveland. The room was decorated with Italian, British, and American flags, and at the door attractive ladies sold Valentine's cards with verses from Keats and Shelley. Twain was one of several celebrities invited to take the stage and read from the works of the Romantic poets.

The crowd at the billiards tournament probably would have been surprised to know that their hero Mark Twain was a longtime admirer of Percy Bysshe Shelley. In those days an American male who unashamedly admitted to a fondness for Romantic poetry was regarded as something of a freak. In its account of the festivities at the Waldorf, the *Washington Post* couldn't help taking a dismissive tone, describing the crowd as a lot of "highbrows" and joking that "a number of long-haired poets" attended the affair. The paper seemed surprised not only that Twain recited a poem by Shelley, but that he didn't drawl the words or turn them into an occasion for comedy.[16]

In fact, he spoke the lines of "To a Skylark" with great care and intelligence. It was one of his favorites. As the more respectful account in the *New York Times* explained, Twain associated the poem "with the happiest period of his life, when he read it more than any other to his wife." It is easy to imagine Livy listening with delight while her husband read to her Shelley's tribute to the "blithe Spirit," the bird that sings "hymns" with "unpremeditated art." Though she may have had conventional tastes, and have tried too hard to push Twain into writing more sentimental works—telling him *The Prince and the Pauper* and his book about Joan of Arc were his best—Livy recognized in him what many of his contemporaries did not: a talent for lyricism.[17]

His style may not have much in common with Shelley's, but there are several passages in *Life on the Mississippi* and *Huckleberry Finn* that are stirring examples of lyric prose at its best. Huck reveals a touch of the poet when he says, "It's lovely to live on a raft. We had the sky, up there, all speckled with stars, and we used to lay on our backs and look up at them, and discuss about whether they was made, or only just happened."[18]

As a bonus, Twain followed "To a Skylark" with a reading of Robert Browning's "Memorabilia," which famously begins, "Ah, did you once see Shelley plain." Among the British writers he admired, Browning ranked near the top. He studied his works with almost scholarly zeal, and considered himself an expert at reading them aloud. He liked entertaining both family and friends with his passionate interpretations of Browning's verse. One observer described these readings as "rich, sympathetic, and luminous." And Reverend Joseph Twichell said of his friend, "Whoever may have had the good fortune to hear his rendering of anything from Browning . . . will not be likely to forget the pleasure of it." Twain was so fond of the poet's works that he once tested even Livy's patience when he suggested reading Browning during dinner. She said no.[19]

Despite all his experience on the platform, he was struck by a case of nerves just before he appeared at the Waldorf. He knew that he would seem out of place at such an event where high culture—not humor—was dominant. "I have never done anything of quite so serious a nature before," he said. But when he stood up to read, he suddenly felt at ease. Though he seems to have been bored by the other performers, he remarked afterward that he was "quite entirely satisfied" with his own readings. And, to everyone's relief, the event turned out to be a great success, raising almost $3,000 for the Keats-Shelley Memorial.[20]

· · ·

FULL OF RESTLESS ENERGY, Twain wasn't content to limit his early appearances in white to Washington and New York. Impatient to try out his new look in a warmer climate, he turned up at the docks one day to announce he was going to make a brief getaway to a place where he would have "an opportunity to appear logical in March in a suit of white flannels."[21]

His destination was Bermuda. He had visited the island in his thirties, and again in his forties, but on those early trips the voyage from New York had taken three and a half days. Now a new ship had reduced the time to a mere forty-five hours each way. The steamer *Bermudian* proudly advertised its speedy service with the slogan "A short ocean voyage to a foreign land."[22]

Separated from the American mainland by six hundred miles of ocean, the British colony of Bermuda was an ideal backdrop for a man dressed in white. If he had searched the world over for a place more in harmony with his suit, he wouldn't have found it. A coral island, Bermuda was a place where for centuries people had built their houses from the thick layer of the shiny rocklike material that lay only six inches under the soil. For good measure, the houses were also covered in a heavy coat of whitewash that Twain once described as "the whitest white you can conceive of. . . . The white of marble is modest and retiring compared with it." Like the writer's new uniform, the painted blocks of coral created a stunning effect. As Twain said of a cluster of bright houses, "The sun comes out and shines on this spectacle, and it is time for you to shut your unaccustomed eyes, lest they be put out." Moreover, even the roads crisscrossing the island were white, having been scraped clean of dirt to allow the underlying layer of coral to shine through. Over time, the substance underfoot turned to powder and looked—as Twain noted—like "coarse white sugar."[23]

The island was so much to his liking that he would visit it repeatedly over the next three years, making sure that on his way there and back he always spoke to reporters at the pier in New York to remind them that his appearance was even more impressive in Bermuda than in America. "I wore that all the time I was in Bermuda," he said of his uniform after one of his quick trips, "and all said it exactly suited my complexion and style of beauty."

He was also happy to promote the notion that each trip to the island's balmy climate did wonders for his health and kept him young. He liked to say that the island—which he always pronounced "Bermooda"—was "better than four or five or six million doctors." No tourism bureau could have done more to enhance the little colony's appeal, and the grateful residents gave Twain an enthusiastic welcome each time he came back.[24]

He liked to stay at the Princess Hotel in Hamilton. It was a four-story wooden structure by the water's edge with long verandas and room enough for four hundred guests. He enjoyed the view from the main veranda, where he could sit in one of the many wicker rocking chairs and watch the boats leaving the harbor to maneuver their way across Bermuda's large western inlet, the Great Sound. The tight-knit community of Hamilton—with its busy waterfront, sleepy back streets, and row after row of white houses—bore some resemblance to his nostalgic image of Hannibal, Missouri, as "the white town drowsing in the sunshine of a summer's morning."[25]

The shallow waters of Bermuda's bays and the dark mysteries of its grottoes offered as much pleasure and adventure as any swimming hole or cave in his old home state. One important difference, however, was that the relationship between the island's blacks—who made up almost 60 percent of the population—and its white community—who controlled the government—was far better than in old Hannibal. The two races tended to treat each other with respect, though segregation was the rule in many public places.

But the colony's political and social concerns didn't interest Twain as much as its natural beauty and its peaceful atmosphere. For the most part, he went there to relax and dream, and to congratulate himself on finding a place that seemed to have been made for him.

· · ·

NOT ALL TWAIN'S OUTINGS that winter turned out well. In January he was a reluctant guest at a disastrous weekend dinner honoring one of the richest and most powerful politicians of the time—United States senator William Andrews Clark.

When he was invited to attend the dinner, he was led to believe that it was going to be a routine affair to celebrate an art exhibition at the Union League Club on Fifth Avenue, a few miles uptown from his own house. He was wary of accepting invitations to such formal events if he suspected they might drag on until late at night and leave him feeling trapped. With luncheons and matinees—or private dinners with friends—he always assumed that he could get away quickly if he grew tired or bored. His first instinct in this case was to make an excuse and stay home, but on second thought he agreed to go and soon regretted it.

After he arrived at the exhibition, he discovered that all the paintings belonged to Senator Clark, and that the dinner was to thank the wealthy politician from Montana for generously loaning works from his large personal collection of European masters. Though his personal knowledge of the sixty-eight-year-old senator was slight, Twain was familiar with his record of greed and corruption, and considered him "as rotten a human being as can be found anywhere under the flag," and "the most disgusting creature that the republic has produced since [Boss] Tweed's time."

Twain was escorted to an exclusive dining room of the club, where—to his dismay—he was seated at a long table with the senator and other important guests. In one corner sat a piano player and a few "fiddlers" ready to entertain the gathering with patriotic tunes. As the festivities began, the author realized that he was stuck. The only thing he could do was sit and wait it out.

Everyone except Twain seemed pleased to be there and content to listen for hours while praise was heaped on Clark. But the author was appalled by the humorless vanity of the senator and the self-abasement of his admirers.

"I am a person of elevated tone and of morals that can bear scrutiny," Twain reassured himself afterward, "and am much above associating with animals of Mr. Clark's breed. . . . While I am willing to waive moral rank and associate with the moderately criminal of the Senators . . . I have to draw the line at Clark of Montana."[26]

In this case, Twain wasn't exaggerating. William Clark—the "Copper King"—was a brazen scoundrel who built up a mining fortune partly by underpaying his miners and then overcharging them for food and other supplies. He silenced his enemies in the Montana press by buying up their newspapers and throwing them out of work; he then used bribery on a massive scale to win election to the Senate, later defending his actions by declaring shamelessly, "I never bought a man who wasn't for sale." In financial matters, he was so heartless that when one of his new motor cars ran over an eleven-year-old boy, he refused to appear in a civil trial brought by the injured child's parents until they posted a bond of $250 to cover *his* legal costs.[27]

After his first wife died when he was in his fifties, he began chasing very young girls—including his teenage ward, the daughter of a former employee. After the girl became pregnant, he had no choice but to marry her, but the grown children from his first marriage were stunned when he returned from a European vacation to announce that his young ward, Anna, was now their new stepmother. As one Western newspaper remarked in a tactful understatement, "The rich old senator has been as active in the lists of love as he has been in the arena of politics."[28]

A lanky man with a fierce squint and a wiry beard, he made money in shady ventures throughout the West, even convincing scores of buyers to pay inflated sums for apparently worthless desert real estate at a tiny watering hole in Nevada called Las Vegas. He took their cash and ran, but they named the county after him anyway. Back East, he tried to buy respectability by lavishing money on his collection of paintings and rare books, and by building a home in Manhattan that was grander than anyone else's. His 121-room mansion on Fifth Avenue and East Seventy-seventh Street was still under construction when Twain dined with him, but it was already the talk of the town. Some people were impressed, but others ridiculed it as a crude monstrosity.

The roguish aspects of Clark's career might have won him a little admiration from Twain if the senator had not taken himself so seriously and had not behaved so boorishly. He fit to perfection the character type that tended to arouse Twain's greatest anger—the pompous vulgarian. "Assfulness and complacency" were the hallmarks of his personality, according to Twain. As his admirers stood up and paid fulsome tributes to him in the smoke-filled room, Clark sat silently at the head of the table, savoring each word of praise. It is doubtful that he noticed the occasional wince or roll of the eye from Twain, who could barely contain his disgust. By the time the speeches had ended and the little band "frantically sawed and thumped" its way through a few tunes, Clark's reluctant guest was ready to burst.

"If a stranger had come in at that time," Twain was to recall, "he might have supposed that this was a divine service and that the Divinity was present. . . . I wish I may never die if the worshippers present at this religious service did not break out in grateful applause . . . and I wish I may never permanently die, if the jailbird didn't smile all over his face and look as radiantly happy as he will look some day when Satan gives him a Sunday vacation in the cold storage vault."[29]

Much as the experience of that night pained him, he took his revenge a little later when he called in his stenographer and rained insults on Clark in an autobiographical dictation, inventing elaborate condemnations for the entertainment of posterity. It was enjoyable to let loose and say what he really thought of an event that courtesy had prevented him from assailing on the spot. To imagine the old senator in the clutches of the devil was at least some compensation for having been forced to endure his presence on that long winter evening. And though there was a serious point to be made about society's worship of men like Clark, there was also for Twain the sheer delight of cutting one of the high and mighty down to size, and doing it in a style meant to shock and amuse.

Because it was too risky to expose him while he was alive, all the pleasure of abusing the senator had to be enjoyed in private. It was a sly pleasure for Twain, like hiding something and pretending to be unaware of it. He was satisfied that sooner or later the world would read his remarks on Clark, and that the only thing sure to survive from the event was his condemnation of it.

All of which helps to explain why he placed so much importance on his autobiographical dictations. They allowed him to speak his mind without regard to the consequences. His anger spent, he could then save the stenographer's written record for posthumous publication in his extended autobiography, relishing the thought of setting off another time bomb at some far distant period. In his estimation this was serious work and gave a purpose to his social activities beyond the immediate amusement or annoyance they caused him. And since he was such a fluent public speaker, he found that dictating was "pleasanter work" than laboring with a pen.

What he wanted to achieve in his autobiography wasn't a straightforward narrative of his life, but a series of impromptu sketches depicting the author in the act of being himself. As he confided to William Dean

Howells, his ambition was to capture "the subtle something which makes good talk so much better than the best imitation of it that can be done with a pen." In other words, he wanted to give readers the sensation of meeting Mark Twain in the flesh and listening to him as an audience of one, "with the result being that the reader knows the author."[30]

The goal was to preserve the most perishable part of his appeal—the charm of his conversational style in free flow. In a great burst of hyperbole, he claimed that his dictations would emerge as "one of the most memorable literary inventions of the ages." Because of his combination of artistic talent and commercial ambition, he was convinced that he was creating something that "ranks with the steam engine, the printing press and the electric telegraph." Before even a word had been published, he was imagining himself as the Edison of literature, boldly declaring, "I'm the only person who has ever found out the right way to build an autobiography."[31]

Despite the fact that it would take a hundred years before a full edition would be published, his autobiography has indeed served its purpose well. The straight-talking, cigar-smoking septuagenarian who stands impressively at the center of it is exactly the persona that has survived with such effectiveness into the twenty-first century. As he might have said himself, he was aiming at that result all along.

"I have not known, and shall never know, anyone who could fill the place of the wife I have lost," Twain said of his beloved Livy, who died in 1904.

Domestic Circle

He did nothing by halves; nothing without
unquestioning confidence and prodigality.
Albert Bigelow Paine on Mark Twain.[1]

. . .

ALTHOUGH HE ENTERTAINED FREQUENTLY at 21 Fifth Avenue,
Mark Twain wasn't satisfied with the look and feel of his house. When he
first saw it in August 1904—shortly after his return from the Italian villa
where Livy had died in June—he was sufficiently pleased with its possibilities to sign a three-year lease. The house itself was almost as old as he
was, but had not aged nearly as well and required three months of renovation before he could move in. He described it as "an old-time house . . .
badly out of repair." Though it had its flaws, the basic structure was
sound. It was a three-story townhouse from the 1840s, with large rooms
and elegant fixtures on every floor.[2]

The interior was too dark, he complained, and he blamed both its design and its location. He didn't notice the problem on his first inspection
of the house, primarily because he was still distracted by grief in the aftermath of his wife's death. When he finally realized he had made a mis-

take, it was too late to go elsewhere. "We put the furniture in," he recalled, "then moved in ourselves, and made a discovery straightway. There was not a window in the whole house, either on the Fifth Avenue front or on the long Ninth Street side that had ever known what a ray of sunshine was like. It was a bad business, and too late to correct it. The entire house is in shadow at all seasons of the year except dead summertime."

Filled with regret at having taken the long lease, he thought the gloomy atmosphere affected everything. "Nobody thrives in this house," he complained. "Nobody profits by our sojourn in it except the doctors. They seem to be here all the time. We must move out and find a house with some sunshine in it."[3]

It really wasn't as bad as that. For one thing, there was a big bay window at the side of the house that not only allowed light to fill the parlor, but also gave Twain a comfortable place where he could sit and watch passersby at the busy corner. And the house was so large that he didn't suffer from a lack of space. There was room enough not only for himself and his daughters, but also for the housekeeper, Katy Leary, the French butler, Claude Beuchotte, and at least three or four other servants.

The neighborhood was peaceful and bright. Two major hotels were a few doors away—the Grosvenor and the Brevoort. Twain knew the Grosvenor well, having stayed there many times and finding it "the nicest, quietest, genteelest little hotel in all New York." In fact, it was the last place in America where he and Livy had been together before going to Italy, which may be one reason why he chose to return to the neighborhood. The Grosvenor advertised itself as an establishment serving guests "of the highest class . . . in the old aristocratic Knickerbocker section." By contrast, the Brevoort was a much more informal place. It was a favorite of the literary and artistic crowd, who liked its intimate atmosphere and the good food at its French café, where Twain sometimes dined.[4]

The area seemed anything but gloomy to one of Twain's neighbors at the time—Willa Cather. She was so entranced by the play of light and shadow on the long, tree-lined street that she liked to pause in Washington Square by the fountain and admire the scene framed by the great white Arch. In a short story set around 1906, she describes the view on a sunny afternoon: "Looking up the Avenue through the Arch, one could see the young poplars with their bright, sticky leaves, and the Brevoort glistening in its spring coat of paint, and shining horses and carriages,—occasionally an automobile, mis-shapen and sullen, like an ugly threat in a stream of things that were bright and beautiful and alive."[5]

However pleasant the scene may have looked from the outside, the tall brownstone simply had too many dark corners for Twain. Sunlight and white suits were what he wanted, and 21 Fifth Avenue couldn't supply enough of the former to satisfy him. What it lacked for Twain was "that elusive trick, that intangible something, whatever it is . . . that gives the home look and the home feeling to an American house."

He tried to find some structural way to brighten the place, but there was no easy solution. He had to make the best of things until the lease was up and a better home could be found. As one compensation, he began amusing himself by making jokes about the dismal look of the old property, calling it "the House of Mirth."[6]

The problem with the townhouse could have been avoided, he often told himself, if only his wife had been alive to advise him. He was certain she would never have overlooked something as basic as the lack of natural light in a new home.

"Livy would have thought of that," he lamented. "Livy always thought of everything."[7]

· · ·

THOUGH HE ENJOYED his independence and surprised himself with how well he was able to function on his own, Twain was often reminded of how Livy had helped to smooth his way through life. During their thirty-four years of marriage, she had done everything in her power to give him and their children a perfect home. In Hartford—where they had lived for twenty years—she had helped to oversee the design and construction of the house that was supposed to be their ideal home for a lifetime. It was everything the Fifth Avenue brownstone was not.

Bright and fanciful, with tall gables and "bricks of various hue" in intricate patterns, the Hartford mansion—which was built in 1874—stood on high ground in the parklike neighborhood of Nook Farm. The interior was lavishly furnished and included a library, a large upstairs room for billiards and smoking, comfortable guest rooms, a playroom for the children, and separate quarters for the servants. Several balconies offered wide views over the town and the surrounding countryside. In all seasons sunlight streamed through the long glass panels of its ground-floor conservatory.[8]

From the start, Olivia Langdon Clemens envisioned their home as a haven from worldly cares, where her husband could relax after tending to his work, and where they could raise their daughters in peace and comfort. Twain was right when he said that his wife would never have overlooked the lack of light in a new house. For her, home life was everything, and she always wanted every detail to be just right.

Heiress to a large fortune accumulated by her coal merchant father in Elmira, New York, Livy was a delicate woman with black hair, kind eyes, and a small but perfectly formed mouth. She grew up in a sheltered world where her parents indulged her every wish and patiently nursed her through a long period of poor health in her late teens and early twenties. The spirit of domestic harmony fostered by her parents in their prosperous home was a crucial influence on her upbringing, and she worked to maintain a similar atmosphere for her own children and husband.

When their mansion was built, Livy was in her late twenties, and her husband was in his late thirties. Married for only four years, they had already endured the loss of their nineteen-month-old son, Langdon, to diphtheria. Moving into the new house had been one way of making a fresh start for their family. By then, Susy was a toddler, and Clara was only a few months old. (Jean came along six years later.) Though the house was meant to be a showplace, it was always a home first. The whole family came to feel that "it had a heart, & a soul, & eyes to see us with." In a poignant tribute written a few years after moving away from Hartford, Twain said of the house, "We never came home from an absence that its face did not light up & speak out its eloquent welcome—& we could not enter it unmoved."[9]

Life in Hartford was so good for so long that Twain often thought he was dreaming, and was fond of musing in those happy times on "the story of his life, the inexhaustible, the fairy, the Arabian Nights story." It was hard to imagine a more satisfying existence. He had a devoted wife and three loving daughters, servants to wait on him, a prosperous career, a wide circle of friends, and an enthusiastic literary following. It took almost twenty years for this happy arrangement to turn tragic, but the same spendthrift ways that fueled the family's rise triggered its decline.[10]

In the 1890s he was nearly ruined by his bad investment in the Paige typesetter, which was supposed to revolutionize the printing industry. By some estimates, he lost almost a quarter of a million dollars on the unsuccessful machine. When this loss was added to the rising costs of running his own publishing firm—which launched its first title, *Adventures of Huckleberry Finn,* in 1885—he quickly found himself short of cash and surrounded by creditors. His money troubles forced him out of his mansion—which he could no longer afford to maintain—and led to a long exile abroad. He and his family lived in various hotels and rented houses until his debts were finally cleared.

His finances gradually recovered, but the magic of his previous life in Hartford proved impossible to recapture. He knew he couldn't live there again after his heart was broken by Susy's death from spinal meningitis in 1896. Several years later—following Livy's death at fifty-eight—the mansion was sold at a considerable loss, and the widower and his two surviving daughters—each painfully aware of the family's misfortunes—carried on as best they could in New York. It wasn't easy, not least because the shortcomings of 21 Fifth Avenue only served to remind them of the things that had made their old place so inviting. Many men Twain's age wouldn't have wanted to bother with another move, but he seemed to feel instinctively that his new life as the Man in White required him to find a more appropriate domestic setting.

· · ·

ONE REASON TWAIN LEASED No. 21 was that he thought Clara would like it. But she often found excuses to stay elsewhere. Troubled with insomnia and sensitive to noise, she complained of her father's late hours, and of the loud noises coming from his billiards room at the back of the house. She even went to the trouble of putting up a sign in the room: "NO BILLIARDS AFTER 10 P.M." But she was fighting a losing battle. She had a habit of making rules for her father's conduct that he had a habit of breaking.

Though they were close and often affectionate, the outspoken father and his high-strung daughter had an uneasy relationship. Their wills often clashed, and it didn't take much to upset the delicate balance of Clara's emotions. Her father said she suffered from "nervous affections." Whatever name can be given to them, her nerves were certainly quick to fray and slow to mend. She would sometimes lose control when she was upset, screaming and knocking over furniture. After one of her outbursts of temper, she wrote that it had come from "controlling, controlling, controlling oneself, till one just bursts at last in despair."[11]

Part of the trouble was that her nerves had never fully recovered from the trauma of losing her mother. She was so distraught at the funeral that she had needed to be restrained, at one point letting out a heartrending cry and almost collapsing over her mother's grave. For many months afterward, she found it necessary to put herself under the care of various doctors. They prescribed long rest cures at private nursing homes in New York and Connecticut. Her father paid the bills and waited patiently for her to get better, explaining to friends, "The shock of her mother's death was crushing."[12]

She seemed content to prolong her recovery. On the eve of going into a long period of seclusion in the fall of 1904, she was almost cheerful about the prospect of seeing no one but doctors and nurses until at least the spring. Calling her father "dearest little Marcus," she wrote him a sentimental farewell note full of childlike comments about herself and her cat, Bambino: "I feel like sending you one more fluttering goodbye before the bars are bolted. . . . Au revoir Marcus dear. My deep love to you with a warm hug. Bambino lightly touches a lock of your hair with a forepaw and wishes you plenty of milk all winter—there goes his back up again; he's most capricious. Again goodbye— Your loving Saphead."[13]

These words may sound like those of a girl of eighteen who is trying to confront her troubles with a brave face, but Clara was actually thirty at the time. In many ways her emotional development had been stifled for years, especially since the death of her sister Susy, which had caused such deep distress to her and the rest of the family. Her mother never came to terms with that loss and had turned increasingly to Clara for comfort and support. Livy was so insistent on having her second daughter near her that it was difficult for the young woman to break away long enough to develop a life of her own. When heart disease caused Livy to suffer almost daily pain in the last two years of her life, it was Clara who acted as her nurse and constant companion.

The daughter's devotion to her mother was intense, but she had a strong will of her own and was frustrated by her inability to establish a separate life. There were times in her youth when a different sort of future had seemed possible—one in which her best qualities would have been free to shine on their own. She had many charms and no small degree of musical talent. Of the three Clemens girls, she was the most attractive. Her best features were her large eyes and her dark wavy hair, which was rich and full. She had a pleasing figure and dressed fashionably, and she never found it difficult to attract men. A newspaper columnist of the time called her "as dainty and pretty as a cameo." Though she was inclined to take herself too seriously, she had a sharp wit and could hold her own in conversations with her father.[14]

A good pianist, she had hopes of becoming an exceptional one and talked her parents into taking her to Vienna in 1897, where she became a pupil of one of the great piano teachers of the period, Theodor Leschetizky. She was twenty-three at the time, Vienna was dazzling in all its fin-de-siècle glamour, and her father's reputation in Austria was so high that everyone treated her family like royalty. But in her struggles to prove herself as a musician, she was easily discouraged. In less than a year she lost patience and gave up the piano. She suddenly announced one day that she wanted to become a singer instead. Her parents were shocked by her decision, but rationalized it as best they could and started paying for voice lessons. She would spend the next eight years preparing for a career as a concert singer, "leapfrogging from one voice method to another" as she moved with her family to London, and then to New York.[15]

It was not until 1906 that Clara made her professional debut as a singer. The event took place only a few months before her father's Telharmonium party. After an intense period of preparation interrupted by periodic rest cures, she gave her performance on the stage of a small gymnasium in the little town of Norfolk, Connecticut, with her most recent voice coach, Isidore Luckstone, providing the accompaniment.

Her father was in the third row, pretending to look inconspicuous but not doing a very good job of it. All eyes in the room were on him. At the conclusion of the recital he was asked to say a few words. He spoke for at least ten minutes, expressing gratitude for the audience's warm response to Clara's singing ("which is, by the way, hereditary"), recalling his own debut as a lecturer, and making jokes about stage fright, which he claimed to have conquered so thoroughly that he was ready now to face any audience. "I know if I was going to be hanged I could get up and make a good showing, and I intend to."[16]

Of course, he stole the show, much to Clara's distress. Inevitably, the newspaper reports of her performance made much of the fact that she was Mark Twain's daughter.

"This was vinegar for Clara," her father later commented, "but saccharin for me, for I had been pretending for two years that for her there could be no glory comparable to the glory of being my daughter, and that therefore she ought to suppress herself and sail altogether under my name. Naturally, she wouldn't listen to this most reasonable suggestion, but perversely wanted to succeed upon her own merit or not at all."[17]

In fact, he was immensely proud of her performance and boasted of her success for many days afterward, calling it "a beautiful, and blood-stirring, and spirit-satisfying triumph." Yet he couldn't resist "pretending" to be envious and provoking what he called "skirmishings" with Clara. His tone of mock combat was an intrinsic part of his humor, but was easy to confuse with the real thing, especially for an oversensitive daughter who had been exposed to it too often, and who needed as much straightforward support as she could get.

Twain could always sense that these games with Clara created "a vexation for her which was not wholly fictitious," yet he persisted in them because it was part of his nature to do so. Tact wasn't one of his strong points. He enjoyed the ability to relieve tension by making light of it. Clara didn't. She always wanted him to be more serious, especially in regard to her needs.

Though the world loved his irrepressible wit, she was often exasperated by it. She came to see it as part of the price she had to pay for being Mark Twain's daughter. In later life she tried to view their "skirmishings" in a more tolerant light and to act as though she had shared in the fun. "Father and I," she recalled, "used to play the little game of pretending to be jealous of each other." During his lifetime, however, she was not always so understanding of such games. Even the white suits annoyed her. She was embarassed by his new look and tried to talk him out of wearing the suits in public.[18]

Twain was so pleased by Clara's debut that he encouraged her to give more performances and agreed to pay her expenses. But instead of taking the plunge and trying to establish her career in the big city, she preferred to limit her appearances to small towns. As the follow-up to her professional debut in Connecticut, she went on a concert tour in February and March of 1907, singing in such places as Utica, New York; Fitchburg, Massachusetts; and Portsmouth, New Hampshire. In these small towns she hoped that her singing would have a better chance of being judged on its own merits.

"Warbling around the country" was the way Twain cheerfully referred to her winter tour. But the results were not encouraging. As Clara soon discovered, it wasn't easy attracting paying customers. She often found herself staring at rows of empty seats. When she took the stage at the Cummings Theater in Fitchburg—a new vaudeville palace with a thousand seats—she sang her heart out, but few people came to listen, despite tickets selling for as little as twenty-five cents each. "The attraction deserved a better attendance," the local paper lamented the next day. "The few that had the pleasure of hearing the concert found nothing to criticize in the singing of Miss Clemens, who possesses a beautiful contralto voice."[19]

In the four weeks she spent on the road Clara not only didn't make money, but ran up big losses. The cost of her wardrobe seems to have been especially high. When she returned home, her debts amounted to $2,500. It was the kind of disastrous outcome that would have ended most singers' hopes of touring again. But Clara was full of enthusiasm and insisted she wanted to go back on the road for another four weeks. As far as the debts were concerned, she assumed her father would take care of them, and she was right.

· · ·

GIVEN CLARA'S IMMATURE WAYS and uncertain prospects, Twain had good reason to worry that if anything happened to him, she would find it hard to support herself. He feared that she might end up penniless if he couldn't secure his copyrights for many years to come and leave her other works for posthumous publication. The problem was all the more urgent because of the difficulties facing his other daughter, Jean, whose troubles were much worse than Clara's, and who was sure to need considerable assistance for the rest of her life.

Twenty-six years old and—like her sister—unmarried, Jean had recently left home to live in the little village of Katonah, New York, where she was staying at a place known locally as the Hillbourne Club. Set on a private estate of forty-two acres, the Club included a large three-story house, a few modern cottages, and a spacious lodge. Surrounding it were steep hills and some of the reservoirs that formed the water supply of New York City, forty-five miles away. Though a passing traveler might easily have mistaken the Club for a country retreat catering to wealthy city dwellers, all its guests were there under doctor's orders. A few had suffered nervous breakdowns, but most were being treated for epilepsy—the disease that had afflicted Jean for a decade. She had experienced her first serious attack in 1896, when she was approaching sixteen, but this was her first extended stay at a sanitarium specializing in the treatment of the disease.

Except for the deaths of Susy and Livy, nothing caused Twain more distress than his youngest child's long ordeal with a chronic disease that defeated all attempts to remedy it. Yet he never gave up trying to help her. Over the years he had made countless attempts to seek treatment for her in America and abroad. Since 1896 he had been frustrated repeatedly by doctors who knew little of the disease, and who had no idea of how to help. "I have worn my soul out," he lamented in 1900, "trying to get hold of some body who had enough sense to ask straight questions & send me informing answers, but I have struck nothing but fools & incapables."[20]

For a decade Jean tried to deal with her illness without having to live away from her family. Sometimes she could go for months without suffering a major seizure, but then a bad week would come along, and she might have three or four attacks in a single day. The unpredictability of her illness, the trauma of her convulsions, and the complete absence of any effective medication took a heavy toll on her and her family. Monitoring the erratic course of her disease, Twain said, "was like watching a house that was forever catching fire, & promised to burn down if you ever closed an eye."[21]

JEAN CLEMENS, 1884   JEAN CLEMENS, 1898

JEAN CLEMENS, 1909

In her carefree girlhood, before she began suffering the first symptoms of epilepsy, Jean was described by a family friend as being "in face and mind the replica of her father, who adored her and was fond of repeating good stories about her."

Twain believed he had finally found some reason for hope when she agreed to enter the sanitarium at Katonah. It was one of the best facilities of its kind in America. Opened in 1904, it was equipped with a medical office, a modern clinical laboratory, and a room for the latest therapeutic treatments, including hydrotherapy. The number of patients was limited to just fifteen, with most living in separate rooms in the main house, while the rest had accommodations in the adjacent cottages. Unlike the little nursing homes where Clara preferred to take her rest cures, the sanitarium was a serious medical establishment offering first-rate care for an illness that the society of the time tended to regard as embarrassing or even shameful.

The owner and "medical superintendent"—a local physician named Edward A. Sharp—didn't like to refer to the Club as a sanitarium, preferring to identify it as a "private health resort." Dr. Sharp and his staff saw their main mission as providing a humane environment that was as free and natural as possible in a quiet setting of rural beauty "where the hum and roar, the wear and tear and strain put upon the strong in the outside world do not penetrate." Instead of being confined like inmates in an asylum, patients were treated almost like guests in a hotel and encouraged to socialize and to enjoy the outdoors. In good weather, they could play lawn tennis, go boating or canoeing, and take walks in the neighborhood. The winter activities included skating and sledding. The lodge at the entrance to the grounds served as a "club house," with a music room, a solarium, a bowling alley, and a squash court. Patients had access to a greenhouse for year-round gardening, as well as to a large "arts and crafts shop" with a resident teacher. The system couldn't promise a cure, and Dr. Sharp's administration didn't always live up to its own ideals, but in many ways the establishment was far ahead of its time.[22]

One of its sponsors was America's leading authority on epilepsy—Dr. Frederick Peterson, a talented physician who was clinical professor of psychiatry at the medical college of Columbia University. Jean was his patient, and it was on his recommendation that she decided to give the sanitarium a try. She listened carefully to Peterson's plan for her treatment and gave her approval. As she noted in her diary before she left home, "Dr. Peterson said . . . that a strictly regular regime was imperative, that in order to have any hope at all of wearing this disease out, an absolutely regular and quiet, unexcited life must be led. Well, then, if that is true, then the one and only thing for me to do is to go into a sanitarium next winter and lead as monotonous and healthy a life as is physically possible—out in the country."[23]

In general, the effects of Jean's disease were not obvious to outsiders. She usually gave the appearance of being perfectly well, as is often the case with epileptics. The tallest of the Clemens daughters, she was the most physically active in the family. She had a trim, almost athletic build, with strong arms and long legs. At twelve, she was described by her father as a robust "colt" full of energy and high spirits. After the first symptoms of her epilepsy appeared, she refused any suggestion that she embrace the quiet life of an invalid. She loved being outdoors with her dog, or going for long walks with a friend or servant. Fond of horses, she loved to ride and resisted efforts to persuade her to give it up for a safer activity. When the weather was pleasant, she kept so busy that her father was both amazed and alarmed by her "continuous carnival of riding, driving, walking, climbing, romping—I don't know how she has survived it."[24]

Though Susy was Twain's favorite daughter, he recognized that Jean was a kindred soul in many ways. Writing of Jean's girlhood, a family friend described her as being "in face and mind the replica of her father, who adored her and was fond of repeating good stories about her." William Dean Howells was struck by the close understanding between Twain and his youngest daughter, "whom he alone knew in the singular force of her mind."[25]

Like her father, Jean was an avid reader. She loved language and enjoyed discussing the fine points of English usage. She once wrote to the editors of the *New York Times* offering her views on a question of modern spelling, and her letter was considered good enough to be published, appearing under the name "Jean L. Clemens" with no hint that she was Mark Twain's daughter. She was so good with words that her father was of the opinion that "if it were not for her affliction, she would have been a writer."[26]

Foreign languages also fascinated her, and she became fluent in at least three—German, French, and Italian. Her friend Nancy Brush said that Jean not only "spoke beautiful Italian" but also "knew yards of

Italian poetry by heart." She was equally proficient in the other two languages. "When she talks German," her father proudly observed, "it is a German talking—manner & all; when she talks French, she is French—gestures, shrugs & all." While the family was staying in Vienna, he was even more impressed when her "fine gift for language" helped her to learn some basic Polish from a teacher who gave instruction in French.[27]

Though the problem of Jean's disease weighed heavily on Clara's mind, the older sister had enough trouble simply trying to steer her own course in life, and the two weren't as close as they had been in childhood. "I am afraid we have grown apart," Jean wrote of her sister after their mother's death. "I know she cannot understand or sympathize with, my curious nature, and while my love for her has not diminished, I cannot help feeling that lack of sympathy in her."[28]

The family secretary, Isabel Lyon, was someone who might have befriended Jean. A former governess in her early forties, "Miss Lyon"—as she was known in the family—had been hired in 1902 to help with household duties and general correspondence. After Livy's death, she gradually took charge of every aspect of Twain's domestic life and seemed content to give herself entirely to serving the family. Living under the same roof, she was always near at hand when Twain or his daughters needed her. Sometimes her boss treated her like a member of the family, and sometimes like an ordinary servant. He certainly paid her an ordinary wage—only fifty dollars a month, with room and board.

Almost by default, she was put in the position of being a frequent companion and helpmate to Jean. But she didn't like it. The epileptic attacks alarmed her, and she overreacted, convincing herself that the young woman was dangerous. Doing her best to hide her fears, Lyon always tried to give Twain the impression that she was keen to help his daughter, but she was greatly relieved when the move to the sanitarium took place. Barely five feet tall, she was much smaller than Jean and was easily frightened when a seizure overcame the young woman. She seems to have been the only one, however, who ever recorded any fear of violence from her. In truth, the attacks never harmed anyone but Jean, usually because she blacked out and fell or hit herself inadvertently.[29]

It was a tearful scene when the young woman—accompanied by a personal maid—boarded a train in Manhattan on October 25, 1906, for the short journey to Katonah. She had no idea how long her treatment would last, but she was prepared for a long stay.

She and her father wanted to believe that this painful separation would eventually bring her some relief from what he once referred to as her "unearned, undeserved and hellish disease." Her seizures had been growing more frequent of late, and he was increasingly anxious about her future. He wanted to try every possible measure before it was too late to help at all. A few days after they parted, he wrote her and tried to sound optimistic, declaring, "You will be sure to improve there."[30]

· · ·

IN HIS EFFORT to keep his books alive and to provide for his family, Twain wanted an oversized biography to supplement the oversized auto-biography already in the works. In Albert Bigelow Paine he found a part-ner who could produce the necessary product. Totaling half a million words, the four volumes of the book that would eventually be published as *Mark Twain: A Biography* are roughly equal in length to the complete typescript of Twain's dictated memoirs. When both works are taken to-gether, their million words represent the kind of massive commemoration a dying emperor might have planned for himself in another time and place. Like white suits, they were meant to inspire awe and admiration.

Twenty-five years younger than his subject, Paine knew that he had been given the chance of a lifetime, and he was tireless in his devotion to the task. A slender, dapper man with a long nose and short dark hair parted in the middle, he was an amazing workhorse, and was willing to travel far and wide to do biographical research while also doing other editorial work and freelance writing to support himself and his young family.

Having spent a hard youth on the prairies of Illinois and Kansas, he was now entering middle age as a familiar—but minor—figure on the New York literary scene. In the eleven years since his arrival in New York from the Midwest, he had produced more than a dozen works of adult fic-tion, children's literature, and biography—including one book of almost six hundred pages. His novel about Antarctic explorers—*The Great*

White Way (1901)—was better known for its title than its content, having inspired a few New York journalists to apply the phrase to Broadway after heavy snows left the street under a blanket of white in December 1901. (The term caught on when it later became associated with the growing use of electric lights in the theater district.)

He also wrote sentimental verse and worked as an editor at *St. Nicholas*—the most popular children's magazine of the time, where he created a special department, "The St. Nicholas League," which featured contributions by talented young readers. (His most recent discovery was a fourteen-year-old poet named Edna St. Vincent Millay, whose first poem—"The Land of Romance"—appeared in his magazine in early 1907.)[31]

With a wife and four young daughters at home, he needed all the work he could get to pay the bills. After trying for years to find a large enough place for his family in an affordable New York neighborhood, he had given up on the city as too expensive for his needs and had moved the family to rural Connecticut, where he acquired an old farmhouse and became a commuter.

As a writer of poetry and fiction, he had shown only modest talent. But as a biographer, he had achieved significant success, producing in 1904 a critically acclaimed work on the life and art of the legendary political cartoonist Thomas Nast, who had died two years earlier. With a subject of Twain's stature, he had the chance to flex all his literary muscles and to make a major contribution to biography. It was his moment to shine, and he was determined to make the most of it.

He became Twain's official biographer just as the older man was adjusting to life as a widower and thinking hard about the future. Twain had been vaguely considering the possibility of choosing an official biographer, but had not yet made up his mind on the subject when Paine offered himself for the job in January 1906.

After hearing from a mutual friend that Twain thought his book on Nast was "damn good," the biographer moved quickly to seize his opportunity. Near the end of a dinner party honoring Twain at the Player's Club, Paine approached him and asked whether he could call on him at home. They agreed to meet a few days later, and though nothing was said in advance about a biography, Twain must have known what was coming. He didn't need much convincing when Paine stood nervously before him on Saturday, January 6, and explained why the time was right to undertake an official Life, and why he was the man to do it.

As was often the case in his old age, Twain was enjoying a late morning in bed, idly reading and smoking. So his visitor began on a light note by telling him how much he admired his work. This bit of flattery was unnecessary and seemed not to interest Twain. "He had heard it so often," Paine reflected afterward. But when the question of writing his biography was finally brought up, he was ready with a quick response.

"When would you like to begin?" he asked bluntly, fixing Paine with a sharp gaze.

The biographer couldn't believe his luck, but answered promptly that he was ready to start immediately. Twain gave his approval just as quickly, and the deal was soon fixed. Paine suddenly went from being a new acquaintance to a trusted confidant. Right away, he was given a tour of the author's study and shown where the private papers were stored. He was also invited to take his own notes from Twain's autobiographical dictations and to use whatever he liked. Then he was handed a key to the house and informed that he could come and go as he pleased. (By the end of the year, he even had a room of his own, with Twain inviting him to stay as long as he wanted.)

"That was always his way," the grateful biographer recalled in his account of that momentous interview. "He did nothing by halves; nothing without unquestioning confidence and prodigality." From that moment until Twain's death, they worked closely together and were rarely out of touch for more than a few weeks at a time. Paine would be a ready and eager witness to the closing scenes of his subject's life, a fact never lost on Twain, who made sure that his new biographer was at his side when he went to Washington and staged his first appearance in white.

Two years before his biographer came along, Twain had made his first serious effort at dictating his autobiography. He thought that he had found the right person to help him get started—Isabel Lyon, who was immensely fond of him and was willing to sit for hours taking dictation. As it turned out, however, it wasn't the best arrangement. She wrote in longhand, and Twain found that she simply couldn't keep up with the flow of words. But Lyon performed well enough in the beginning to prove that the method could work.

After Paine appeared on the scene, Twain began dictating again, and the autobiography proceeded almost in tandem with the biography, each giving momentum to the other. It was Paine who brought on board a professional stenographer to take Twain's dictation, a woman named Josephine Hobby—who had worked for Richard Watson Gilder's *Century Magazine*. She prepared accurate copies of the autobiographical dictations for the use of both Twain and his biographer, who was expected to suggest topics and to serve as an appreciative audience. For much of 1906, Twain made a point of meeting regularly with his biographer, using their time together for dictations and chats, and—by the end of year—game after game of billiards.

It was an arrangement that both men found stimulating. Twain liked having the full attention of an intelligent admirer, and Paine was grateful for the chance to watch his subject in action: "It was absorbingly interesting; his quaint, unhurried fashion of speech, the unconscious movement of his hands, the play of his features as his fancies and phrases passed in mental review and were accepted or waved aside." Paine soon came to feel that he and Josephine Hobby had been given an extraordinary opportunity: "We were watching one of the great literary creators of his time in the very process of his architecture. We constituted about the most select audience in the world enjoying what was, likely enough, its most remarkable entertainment."

As one way of showing his gratitude, Paine took up billiards and did his best to master the game. Before he met Twain, he had played only a few times and was a mediocre shot. "No matter," the older man had told him, relishing the prospect of endless victories. "The poorer you play, the better I shall like it."

His game improved, but only because Twain made a point of playing him day and night. In early 1907 they spent a good part of every week competing vigorously against each other, and sometimes the owner of the table would find himself the loser at the end of a long evening. "He was willing to be beaten," Paine observed dryly, "but not too often."[32]

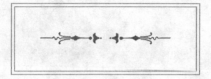

At a New York pier, Twain jokes with Standard Oil millionaire Henry Rogers, opening his friend's overcoat to "borrow" some money.

THREE

Pirates of Broadway

We lectured and robbed and raided
for thirteen months. . . . I sent the book-money
and lecture-money to Mr. Rogers
as fast as we captured it.

Mark Twain[1]

. . .

ON A VISIT to Mark Twain's house in the winter of 1907, his publisher, George Harvey, overheard the author conducting an unusual telephone conversation. Instead of speaking into the mouthpiece himself, Twain was sitting in bed and using one of his servants to relay comments to Henry Rogers—his old friend and financial adviser—at the other end of the line.

"You tell Henry Rogers that I am not feeling very well this evening," he said to the servant, "and that I should like to take dinner with him at his home."

The servant did as instructed and came back with the response that Mr. Rogers "would be glad to have Mr. Clemens as his guest at dinner."

"Well, you ring up Henry Rogers again and tell him that I have a cold and can't go unless he sends his automobile for me."[2]

The message was conveyed, and Rogers happily agreed to send his new Oldsmobile touring car to Twain's house and bring him to the family mansion on East Seventy-eighth Street, where he and his second wife lived in modern splendor. "I do not own a motor-car," Twain had told an automobile journal a little while back, "but I recommend them to all my friends and advise them to buy a car—so that they will come around and take me out in it."

If Twain had requested a whole fleet of cars on this cold night at the end of January, his friend would have obliged him. Henry Huttleston Rogers had the money for it, and his affection for the author knew no bounds. When they were together, they tended to behave like old school chums skipping class. But for many others—including the president of the United States—Rogers was a villain who represented the very worst excesses of the age. A New England paper said he was nothing less than "a peril and a menace to the republic."[3]

Twain had good reason to think otherwise. A decade earlier this Standard Oil millionaire and Wall Street speculator had saved the day when Twain was in danger of losing everything. At that time, their acquaintance was slight, but Rogers had generously agreed to help the beleaguered writer arrange new credit and avoid financial disaster. Rogers asked nothing in return, believing that he was repaying a debt of his own—one that he owed to the author for all the pleasure he had taken from his books over the years. The task required a great deal of time and effort—with some setbacks along the way—but after five years the debts were paid and Twain's finances were once again on a sound footing.

A friendship developed between the two that grew deeper with the years. "I am his principal intimate," Twain said of their relationship. "We were strangers when we met, and friends when we parted, half an hour afterward." If Rogers had been able to escape more often from the demands of his wide network of business enterprises, the two friends might easily have spent months at a time in each other's company without complaint. Each helped to raise the spirits of the other, and to keep them high as long as they were together.[4]

It helped that Rogers found enjoyment in indulging Mark Twain's wishes, for the writer's idea of fun was to test this goodwill from time to time. To Twain's amazement, his friend always proved equal to the test. "I do things which ought to try any man's patience," he wrote of Rogers in a private essay, "but they never seem to try his." When he felt restless or low, his mood always seemed to brighten in the presence of this powerful friend, whose imposing figure was several inches taller than his own. With deep-set eyes, a square jaw, and broad shoulders, Rogers had the look of a man whose confidence in his own abilities was supreme. "The sight of him is peace," Twain once said. Proudly, he informed the tireless Rogers, "You and I are a team: you are the most useful man I know, and I am the most ornamental."[5]

Rogers usually spent the better part of the day at his office, rising before dawn to work a few hours at home before going downtown to Standard Oil's sixteen-story headquarters at 26 Broadway, where he was a director and vice president. He occupied a spacious suite on the eleventh floor of the gray stone building, with a majestic view of the harbor. The view was important, for his favorite weekend pastime was racing his yacht in Long Island Sound. He was often heard to boast that the only vacation he needed was "a shave and a trip up the Sound."[6]

He was quite serious about the shave. An especially handsome man in his youth, he was always particular about his appearance, and was usually so well groomed that not a hair was out of place. He liked tight-fitting dark suits with high buttons and a black derby, and often sported a diamond stick pin in his cravat. His silver hair was styled rather grandly in two sleek waves that matched the long curve of his mustache, and he carried himself with such an air of authority that almost everyone from elevator boys to his fellow executives tended to show him deference.

Only four years Twain's junior, he had given some thought to retirement, but was too intent on expanding his business empire to slow his pace. He was the fourth-largest individual shareholder in the Standard Oil Trust, and it was this solid base of wealth—with its steady flow of fat dividends—that allowed him to amass a second fortune on Wall Street.

He made large investments in dozens of companies, big and small—including Union Pacific and U.S. Steel. Among the enterprises he controlled personally were mining companies in Montana, a railroad in Virginia, the local gas monopoly in Brooklyn, the streetcar lines on Staten Island, and a factory in New England that was the world's largest producer of brass tacks. The total value of his assets was enormous. By some estimates, it was as high as $100 million, which put him in the top rank of America's biggest tycoons—just below Andrew Carnegie, J. P. Morgan, and Standard Oil's biggest stockholder, John D. Rockefeller.[7]

He enjoyed so much independence at 26 Broadway that he was able to spend more time managing his own interests than those of Standard Oil. Some people considered him a brilliant and audacious speculator and financier, while others charged that he was a ruthless manipulator of the stock market who made his money through backroom deals. His critics bitterly joked that H. H. Rogers didn't want the public to know that his initials really stood for "Hell Hound."

Twain wasn't influenced by any of the name-calling. He always felt compelled to stand up for his friend no matter what. In fact, it was partly his devotion to Rogers that had fueled his anger toward Montana's Senator William Clark. The two millionaires had battled each other for years over their competing interests in copper mines, and each had employed smear tactics against the other. In his home state, Clark had turned his rivalry with Rogers into a political campaign issue, portraying himself as a defender of Montana's resources against "rapacious" villains from Standard Oil. Rogers and his associates fought back by acquiring local newspapers and using them to spread stories of Clark's moral and financial misdeeds.[8]

As far as Twain was concerned, any enemy of Rogers was an enemy of his. Showing passionate disdain for his friend's critics, he declared with an ironic verbal twist, "The only man I would give a *damn* for . . . is a Standard Oil fiend." He enthusiastically celebrated him as "the best friend I ever had," and refused to accept that he was compromising his reputation by associating with a robber baron. The general public didn't know quite what to make of such a relationship, but he was rarely criticized for it. "Mark Twain is so popular," one newspaper observed, "he can withstand the friendship of even H. H. Rogers and the Standard Oil."[9]

It is typical of their relationship that—for the sheer amusement of it—Twain had decided on this cold winter evening to engage Rogers in a game of relaying telephone messages. He was confident that his friend would take each interruption in stride and let the joke play out. In fact, before the car could be dispatched to 21 Fifth Avenue, there were more interruptions.

"You ring up Henry Rogers again," Twain commanded his servant, "and tell him that I can't go unless there is a bed convenient; it's too cold for me to return in the night air."

More calls went back and forth until it was agreed that Twain would not only spend the night, but would "waive etiquette" — as he put it — and bring only a nightshirt instead of more formal robes. The whole conversation left George Harvey bewildered but amused. It was obvious that the two friends were enjoying an obscure private game, toying with each other over the phone like two youths who had just discovered the device.

But as Harvey would have appreciated, the author loved nothing better than developing an elaborate joke with a friend who understood it, and who was eager to play along. Indeed, Rogers was the best straight man Mark Twain ever had. They made an unusual comic pair, though this was lost on some people who found their high jinks confusing or simply unseemly for two elderly gentlemen.

It didn't matter to them if no one else understood their banter. In this case what an outsider wouldn't have known was that the two friends shared a long-standing joke that Twain in a nightshirt on the loose after dark could be a frightening spectacle to the uninitiated.

As Rogers had told him years ago, "If you ever are startled by housebreakers . . . I am sure your appearance, as I have once or twice seen you in the night, would be quite enough to drive them away, if they did not drop dead on the spot. I might suggest that you put your spectacles on the tip of your nose to add to the effect."[10]

. . .

FROM TIME TO TIME, Twain liked to go down to the Standard Oil Building in his white outfit and surprise the clerks and secretaries as he wandered idly among the offices before visiting his friend. Normally, the employees were expected to maintain a dignified and sober air befitting a place where so much wealth and power were concentrated. Plainclothes detectives discreetly guarded the main entrance, which was marked only by the address number. "There is an absence of bustle and noise," a contemporary observer said of the headquarters. "While transactions involving millions may be involved, the negotiations are conducted in a quiet, methodical manner, apparently free from excitement." But there was no way to suppress the stir of excitement Twain caused whenever he entered the building. Around him, even the most subdued employees would suddenly show signs of life.[11]

There was one person in the building, however, who might have been expected to disapprove of Twain's intrusions. Few people at Standard Oil put up a more forbidding front than Rogers's own secretary, Katharine Harrison, who was known in Wall Street circles as "the Sphinx." She maintained such a strict attitude of secrecy about her boss's activities that she rarely gave straight answers to anyone except in response to the most basic questions. "She keeps thousands of secrets," one newspaper said of her, "secrets that would be worth hundreds of thousands of dollars to men in the market place of finance. . . . Are the Rockefellers buying or selling steel? . . . The Sphinx knows, but never tells." Behind a pair of glinting spectacles, she kept a close watch over the dozens of callers who wanted a few minutes of Rogers's time. Most of them were turned away with a hard glance.[12]

Wearing high collars and thin ties, the forty-year-old private secretary seemed all business and—at six feet—was almost as imposing as her boss. She was paid well for her work—$10,000 a year, which was said to be the highest salary earned by any woman in America at the time. Thanks to investment tips from Rogers, she had also accumulated a stock portfolio worth half a million dollars. Little was known about her private life, except that she shared a house with her mother on a quiet street in Brooklyn. One female visitor to the office described her as a model of "business competency," but noted that she seemed "as impersonal as the chairs in the room."[13]

Yet whenever Twain appeared, she was no more immune to his charms than anyone else. In his presence, she was all sympathy and deference, responding to his every wish and serving him tirelessly as if she were his private banker. She helped her boss oversee Twain's accounts, withdrawing money when the author needed it, and arranging investments at his direction or that of Rogers. She even allowed him glimpses into her carefully guarded private life, sharing with him her secret passion for art. In fact, she spent much of her money building up a large collection of valuable paintings.

Whenever Twain came calling at 26 Broadway and found Rogers busy with someone else, Miss Harrison would gently steer him to a nearby sofa where he could stretch out and relax with one of his cigars. He found something soothing about the low hum of activity around him and often fell asleep on the sofa. No one dared disturb him. One visitor remembered passing a conference room and hearing the "rhythmic measures" of a man snoring loudly. Of course, it was Twain fast asleep, while in the adjacent rooms Miss Harrison and other employees of Standard Oil were quietly going about their work.

"It's only Mark," Henry Rogers would say if anyone mentioned the snoring. "He's taking a well-earned rest—he was born tired, you know."[14]

Some of the most important business at the office was conducted over lunch in a private dining room at the top of the building. "There was no surer proof of favor in the Standard Oil empyrean," one historian of the company has written, "than to receive an invitation to dine at the long table." Twain was one of the few men unaffiliated with the company who not only received such invitations but was allowed to show up unannounced. A junior lawyer at the firm recalled being in the middle of a serious discussion over lunch with the directors about a pending lawsuit "when Rogers suddenly looked up and called to the waiter, 'Hide the pie. Here comes Mark Twain.' "[15]

The author often liked to boast that he was the one with too much work and too much money, and that Rogers was the impractical spendthrift. "You see, it's like this," he would explain in his best drawl. "Rogers furnishes the plans and I foot the bills." He even suggested they start a new firm with himself as the senior partner and Rogers as the junior. "Spread it around quietly that Clemens, Rogers & Co. are solvent," he joked; "it may have a good effect on the market."[16]

But when it came time for bills to be paid, he always kept in mind whose pockets were deeper. Asked by a fellow humorist why he wanted to invite Rogers to a literary luncheon, Twain was incredulous. "Why ask Rogers? . . . Why ask Rogers? To pay for the lunch, you idiot."[17]

As a favorite prank, he liked to involve his friend in writing outrageous letters under false names to strangers. When a letter arrived one day from the head of a literary society in New Zealand asking "Samuel Clemence Esq" to comment on his career as Mark Twain, the author handed the letter to Rogers and said, "*You* send him a line." The tycoon put aside more pressing business and took up the challenge, writing to the man as "P. Huttleston," the ninety-three-year-old father-in-law of "Mr. Clemence." With a deadpan wit worthy of Twain himself, Rogers explained that the famous author couldn't reply because he was ill and had "lost his sense of humor entirely," and was now writing only on religious subjects and on such metaphysical questions as "Do calves need water?"[18]

One day in 1907, Twain sent Rogers an incendiary letter addressed to the editor of the *New York Times* and dared him to mail it. It was supposedly written by William Dean Howells, but it was all Twain's work and was not meant to be taken seriously. The joke was that no one as reserved in language and manner as Howells would pen such an illiterate and intemperate letter, and that he would be horrified if the newspaper ever printed it:

Sir to you, I would like to know what kind of a goddam govment this is that discriminates between two common carriers & makes a goddam railroad charge everybody equal & lets a goddam man charge any goddam price he wants to for his goddam opera box

W D Howells

Tuxedo Park   Oct 4

(goddam it)[19]

Unlike Howells—who, as one friend noted, "never swore, never used vulgar phrases"—Rogers used profanity openly and often, and probably roared with laughter at the idea of anyone agreeing to print such a magnificent verbal explosion under the name of the distinguished, well-mannered novelist. Of course, he didn't send it, but the mere thought of doing so would have amused Rogers, whose own use of salty language had occasionally caused him trouble at Standard Oil.[20]

In fact, he might have made millions more out of the company if he hadn't been so fond of swearing, drinking, and card playing. Though these activities never interfered with his business abilities, they did affect his standing in the eyes of straitlaced John D. Rockefeller, who strongly disapproved of such conduct. A Baptist who claimed that "the power to make money is a gift of God," Rockefeller thought that Standard Oil's monopoly in the petroleum industry (it was twenty times the size of its nearest rival) was good for America and wanted to believe that the moral character of his fellow directors was—like his own—above reproach. He had no objection to pocketing the profits Rogers helped to generate for the directors, but he was adamantly opposed to letting him assume the title of company president. His opposition was based solely on moral grounds. As one of his biographers put it, "Rockefeller was irked by Rogers's gambling and profanity, his strutting in public and mingling with high society."[21]

To the end of his days, Rogers was unapologetic about his reputation within the company. "I was never a favorite," he said. "I suppose I was a born gambler." He also didn't pretend there was anything sacred about the Standard Oil Trust. It was a financial enterprise, not an arm of the Baptist Church. "We are not in business for our health," he declared bluntly, "but are out for the dollars."[22]

Like many others, Twain believed that even if Rogers didn't have the title to prove it, he was the true head of Standard Oil. The author was convinced that no one knew the refinery business better than his friend, and he was happy to swear about it. "Jessus! but I had a narrow escape," he told Rogers one day. "Suppose you had gone into humor instead of oil—where would I be?"[23]

The answer to this question is, of course, broke. It was only because Rogers continued to keep a close eye on his finances that Twain didn't return to his old ways and lose more money on one bad investment after another. As the author was well aware, his friend had intervened many times to keep him from drifting toward insolvency again. "He has continued to break up my bad schemes," he gratefully acknowledged, "and put better ones in their place, to my great advantage."

Rogers negotiated Twain's publishing contracts and played a crucial part in protecting the future life of his books. In 1894, when Twain's unpaid debts soared to $160,000, and his creditors were threatening to seize all his assets—including his copyrights—it was an especially clever maneuver by Rogers that rescued him.[24]

"They were bent on devouring every pound of flesh in sight and picking the bones," Rogers later said of the creditors. He met with them one afternoon and heard their demands. They confidently insisted "that Mark Twain should turn over his copyrights," and wouldn't entertain any compromise or further delay. But their "high-handed manner" offended Rogers, who wasn't used to accepting other people's terms.

Rising to his full height, he looked down at the bankers and other creditors and told them flatly, "Gentlemen, you are not going to have this thing all your way." Then he surprised them with an argument they had not expected. Noting that Twain had borrowed more money from his wife's personal fortune than from any other source, he announced that she qualified as the "chief creditor," and that therefore she had first claim on the copyrights. He made the point with such conviction and force that nobody in the room was willing or able to rebut him. In due course all the copyrights were assigned to Livy. Single-handedly, Rogers saved his friend's most valuable assets. As far as Twain was concerned, there was no higher service anyone could have provided him.[25]

Because the author placed absolute trust in Rogers, he turned over thousands of dollars to him for investment, beginning with the proceeds from lectures given during his world tour of 1895–96. He was handsomely rewarded. Almost without fail the price of his stocks went up and brought him large gains. He was happy to take the money and not look too closely into how Rogers performed these feats of financial wizardry. It was easier to assume that his powerful friend simply possessed a talent for turning whatever he touched into gold. "Why, it is just splendid!" Twain wrote to him after receiving a nice windfall. "I have nothing to do but sit around and watch you set the hen and hatch those big broods and make my living for me. Don't you wish you had somebody to do the same for you?—a magician who can turn steel and copper and Brooklyn gas into gold."[26]

According to Rogers's critics on Wall Street, there was nothing magical about some of his more spectacular gains from the stock market. He rigged the system, they charged, guaranteeing profits for himself and his friends, and losses for everyone else who was blind to his tactics. His most infamous case involved his rivalry with Senator William Clark over control of Montana's copper reserves. Through a series of complex financial tricks, he acquired mines with borrowed funds, and then offered stock in a new company called Amalgamated Copper, whose value was advertised at a wildly inflated rate. He made millions when speculators caught "copper fever" and bought up every share. When Wall Street insiders began selling their stock to make a quick profit, the price fell and many ordinary investors were left with huge losses. Howls of protest erupted against Henry Rogers—the Pirate of 26 Broadway.

"He's a pirate all right," Twain admitted, "but he owns up to it and enjoys being a pirate. That's the reason I like him."[27]

In any other case involving such shady financial dealings, Twain would have happily poured scorn on the culprit. It was easy for him to denounce the corruption of Senator Clark or—to use other names he gave in an interview from this period— "the Goulds and Vanderbilts and other professional grafters." More than thirty years earlier, he had mercilessly satirized such men in *The Gilded Age*. Lately, he had given a sharp public rebuke to Rockefeller, telling a Boston paper that John D.'s success had played a part in lowering the ethical standards of American business. "We gave to the world the spirit of liberty more than one hundred years ago," he told the *Boston Transcript* in 1905, "and now we are giving the world the spirit of graft."

But he was never going to associate Rogers with such corruption. In his eyes, his friend occupied a plane far above that of the other tycoons. He was more generous, more amiable, and more interesting. Twain knew that Rogers often made a point of hiding his more generous side for fear that it would be taken as a sign of weakness by Wall Street rivals. It was only after his death that the public learned how freely Rogers had supported a number of worthy causes. At Twain's urging, he had become one of Helen Keller's benefactors, paying her way through college and giving her a lifetime annuity. Deeply appreciative, Keller called Rogers "one of the noblest men that ever lived." He was also a supporter of over sixty schools for the children of black farmworkers in the South, donating money every year to construct new buildings and hire teachers. The man who quietly disbursed these educational funds on Rogers's behalf was Booker T. Washington, who came to know him well and considered him "one of the best and greatest men I have ever met."[28]

Nothing could make Twain denounce a loyal confidant. As his closest friends knew, if you had his trust, you had all of it. If you lost it, it was almost impossible to get it back. Major J. B. Pond—Twain's lecture manager in the 1880s and 1890s—once remarked of his star performer, "He possesses some of the frontier traits—a fierce spirit of retaliation, and the absolute confidence that life-long 'partners,' in the Western sense, develop."[29]

It didn't hurt that Twain had a soft spot in his heart for uncommon buccaneers like Rogers. He thought a few pirates must have been among his own Clemens ancestors in the Elizabethan era, when playing that part in the queen's service was "a respectable trade." As he confessed in an autobiographical dictation from 1906, "In my time I have had desires to be a pirate myself."[30]

For Rogers, playing the fearless buccaneer in the business world was a serious game. For Twain, it was just a game—the stuff of fantasy, like the daydreams of Tom Sawyer, whose favorite pastime is pretending to be a pirate on the river. Under an oak tree on Cardiff Hill, Tom sits back and imagines the joy of becoming famous one day as "the Black Avenger of the Spanish Main." He sees himself arrayed in glory with a plumed hat, red sash, "crime-rusted cutlass," and high boots. "How his name would fill the world," he muses in a moment of youthful ecstasy, "and make people shudder." As Twain jokes in *Life on the Mississippi,* the boys of his hometown "had a hope that if we lived and were good, God would permit us to be pirates."[31]

There is more than a touch of Tom in Mark Twain's lively description of his own moneymaking abilities as an internationally famous author giving talks during his world tour, and then sending the profits home to his trusted partner at 26 Broadway: "On the 15th of July, 1895, [I started] on our lecturing raid around the world. We lectured and robbed and raided for thirteen months. . . . I sent the book-money and lecture-money to Mr. Rogers as fast as we captured it." It pleased Twain to think of himself as a mildly disreputable but lovable figure in league with similar fellows. Part of his satisfaction in wearing the white suit was knowing that it was a joke against himself, a "whited sepulchre" that concealed a heart with darker moods and a character that was far from spotless.[32]

When a new installment of Ida Tarbell's muckraking history of Standard Oil appeared in 1904 with an account of Rogers that cast him in a better light than Rockefeller, Twain pretended to be greatly disappointed. He teased Rogers that the journalist had whitewashed his character, and he accused him of buying her off. "She gives you no rank as a conspirator—does not even let you say any dark things; does not even let you sit mute and awful in a Buffalo Court like John D., and lower the temperature of justice. Henry H., the woman has been *bought!*"

As both men were well aware, it was in fact Twain who had made the arrangements for Tarbell to meet Rogers at the beginning of her research, which in turn had helped the millionaire launch the charm offensive that resulted in a more favorable portrait from the journalist. Indeed, as she later admitted, she couldn't help liking Rogers, whose appearance and manner reminded her of Twain. Her final judgment on the tycoon—which she included in an autobiography published long after his death—was one that would have delighted both men. She called him "as fine a pirate as ever flew his flag in Wall Street."[33]

. . .

A PIRATE NEEDS A SHIP, and Rogers had a superior one. With all his millions, there was no luxury he couldn't afford, including a big yacht. His was a stunner—a 227-foot steam-powered vessel called the *Kanawha*. Built to serve as a racing yacht, the vessel could reach speeds in excess of twenty-two knots and was said to be faster even than J. P. Morgan's renowned *Corsair*. It was the star attraction of the New York Yacht Club's annual cruise at Newport, winning its racing prize—the Lysistrata Cup— two years in a row. Rogers entered the ship in many races and lost only once.[34]

The name of Rogers's yacht was an inside joke. For several years he had been secretly involved in a business venture of such magnitude that it represented the biggest gamble of his life. If it failed, he stood to lose half his fortune. Around the time that he acquired the *Kanawha*—in 1901—he was quietly buying up thousands of acres of cheap land around a little village in West Virginia called Deepwater, which bordered the Kanawha River. The land was located among some of the richest coal-fields in America, but there was no easy way to haul the coal to ports on the Atlantic coast, where it could be shipped to factories, generating plants, and homes up and down the Eastern Seaboard. Rogers's ambitious plan—which he estimated would require at least six years to complete— was to build his own railroad from the Kanawha River to the seaport at

Norfolk, Virginia. It was a distance of more than four hundred miles, and he was intending to pay for every mile of it out of his own pocket. The cost was estimated at between $30 and $40 million.

The trick was to keep his plan secret during as much of the construction period as possible. He couldn't afford to have competitors inflating prices for land or putting legal obstacles in his way. Rogers's ingenious solution was to build not one railroad, but two—neither of which would appear to have any connection with the other nor pose any great threat to his existing rivals. Using a few carefully chosen front men, Rogers stayed in the background and pulled all the strings from the safe distance of his office on Broadway. In West Virginia he secretly backed construction of the Deepwater Railroad, which stopped at the border with Virginia. On the other side of the state line, he poured money into the Tidewater Railroad, which started in Norfolk and stopped at the border with West Virginia. At the last minute he planned to connect the two, reveal his ownership of both, and merge them into what he hoped would become the most profitable freight operation in the world.

The whole scheme sounds like a practical version of the railway Colonel Sellers hopes will make him rich in *The Gilded Age*. His road is supposed to run from Slouchburg to Corruptionville. "Ain't it a ripping road, though?" Sellers asks after he has traced the imaginary route on his kitchen table. "I tell you, it'll make a stir when it gets along. Just see what a country it goes through. There's your onions at Slouchburg—noblest onion country that graces God's footstool; and there's your turnip country all around Doodleville—bless my life, what fortunes are going to be made there when they get that contrivance perfected for extracting olive oil out of turnips."[35]

It is unlikely that Twain knew much about Rogers's scheme until fairly late in the game. His friend liked keeping his business affairs shrouded in mystery, and Twain usually preferred talking about his own get-rich schemes rather than other people's. But when the secret finally leaked out at the end of January 1907, and Twain became fully aware of the monumental risk Rogers had taken, he had nothing but praise for the gamble. As he told his friend at a later time, he considered the project not merely a great achievement, but "the triumph of your life." There was still a lot of work to be done before the line was ready to send its first coal trains to the coast. But, unlike Colonel Sellers, Rogers knew how to turn bold visions into realities, and to make them pay.[36]

As for the *Kanawha*, Twain was almost as fond of the yacht as Rogers was. Whether the name was a clue to anything or not was of little concern to him. He simply enjoyed sailing on such a fine ship, and sharing that experience with "Admiral" Rogers, as he liked to call him. They had some of their best times together on the vessel, which was not only fast but luxurious.

When the time was right and the weather was fair, they liked to sail away from New York with several friends and stay out at least a few days. Frequently, the destination was Rogers's hometown of Fairhaven, Massachusetts, where he had built an eighty-five-room mansion for weekend escapes and family holidays. At night Twain and other pals liked to join the "Admiral" on the deck and spend hours playing cards, drinking strong whiskey, and swapping tall tales. So many hands of poker were played in the forward deckhouse that Twain called it the "poker chapel."

The smoke-filled atmosphere on the *Kanawha* often turned raucous, especially when Twain started telling ribald jokes with an innocent face. They always sounded funnier, and less juvenile, coming from him. He recorded one of his favorites in a notebook from this period: A drunk on the telephone asks, "Zis 'e S'iety for Saving Fallen Women?" The answer is yes. Well, the drunk responds, "Save two for me tonight."[37]

Both Rogers and Twain were inclined to exaggerate the extent of their dissipation on these cruises. Before leaving on a long ocean voyage with his goodhearted and patient wife, Emilie, Rogers invited Twain to come along and added in jest, "The only essentials this time will be drunkenness, profanity and sodomy."[38]

Unfortunately, Twain was unable to make that trip.

The one thing he didn't enjoy about the yacht was its performance in rough weather. Rogers liked to tell the story of seeing Twain clinging to the rail in a heavy storm.

"Mr. Clemens," a steward had asked, "can I get you something?"

"Yes," the seasick Twain replied. "Get me a little island."[39]

But in calm seas he was never happier than when he was sailing on the *Kanawha* with his friends. At night the vessel would chug gently

After returning from a cruise on Henry Rogers's steam yacht, the *Kanawha*, Twain looked "like a boy fresh from his wild oats."

along like a big steamboat in a smooth channel, rekindling in his heart some of the joy of his younger days. He could almost close his eyes and imagine himself back on the river, listening to the talk of the crew and the drone of the steam engine. On his return from one of the yacht's bracing voyages, he seemed so full of life that Isabel Lyon said he looked "like a boy fresh from his wild oats."[40]

It must have been a great disappointment to Rogers that no one in the press or on Wall Street seemed curious about the origin of the yacht's name. In any case, when the secret was finally revealed on January 28, 1907, it was the *Wall Street Journal* that had the scoop. The paper declared that H. H. Rogers was the mastermind behind "one of the remarkable railroad enterprises of recent years." The report also included a detailed description of how the rival lines had been fooled into assuming the Deepwater and the Tidewater railroads were separate entities, and of how Rogers had created a superior road that would be difficult for anyone to compete against.[41]

To celebrate his triumph, he planned a big yachting adventure for the end of April 1907, and asked Twain to come along. They were going to sail from New York to Virginia and attend the opening of the Jamestown Exposition, a "world's fair" commemorating the three hundredth anniversary of the first English settlement. The location of the original

Jamestown was considered unsuitable for the fair, so Norfolk was chosen instead. President Theodore Roosevelt and many other dignitaries planned to be there.

It wasn't, however, the fair or the president that Rogers wanted to see. He wanted to admire the new piers he had built in Norfolk to receive the contents of all the coal cars he would soon be sending to the coast on the Virginian Railway, which was his new name for the combined Deepwater and Tidewater lines. And his white-clad partner in crime was eager to make an appearance at his side. Twain saw it as a golden opportunity to expand his own fame when the world's attention would be focused on the great fair.

"Yes, I'm going to be a buccaneer," he boasted to the press shortly before leaving New York. "The bucks and buccaneers on this cruise to the Spanish Main will be the guests of Henry H. Rogers, aboard his yacht *Kanawha*. We expect to have a bully time, and our first port of entry will be Jamestown."[42]

· · ·

TWAIN'S USE OF THE WORD "bully" was probably meant as a little joke at the expense of the other famous visitor to the fair. As everyone knew, President Roosevelt and Henry Rogers were on the worst possible terms. Indeed, as a trustbuster, the president regarded Rogers and the rest of the Standard Oil millionaires as among the worst of what he memorably called "malefactors of great wealth." He saw himself locked in battle with "a few ruthless and determined men whose wealth makes them particularly formidable, because they hide behind the breastworks of corporate organization." His Justice Department was doing everything in its power in the federal courts to break up the oil trust and to reduce the influence of Rogers and his partners. (By the end of the year, Standard Oil would be facing legal suits in no fewer than seven federal and six state courts.) A famous cartoon of the period shows a defiant Roosevelt as the "infant Hercules" trying to wrestle a two-headed serpent into submission. One head belongs to John D. Rockefeller, the other to Henry Rogers.[43]

Rather than antagonize the president any further, one of the heads of that serpent—Rockefeller—had decided to play it safe and was keeping a

low profile. But Rogers was less cautious, and wasn't going to allow anyone to stop him from celebrating his great success with the Virginian
Railway—not even the president of the United States.

"He would go to Halifax for half a chance to show off," Mark Twain
complained of Roosevelt in 1907, "and he would go to hell for a whole
one."[44]

At the new Exposition both the leader of America and the nation's
greatest living writer would be given a "whole" chance to demonstrate
their star power without straying beyond Hampton Roads. Quite an expert himself at showing off, Twain felt that he knew his man. Whereas he
considered himself a harmless self-promoter, he thought the president
was a dangerous egotist whose policies—both foreign and domestic—
were undermining America.

Whenever they had met, however, he was civil to the president, and
didn't hesitate to use his wit to win Roosevelt's approval for causes near
to his heart, such as copyright reform. Face-to-face, he always found the
president's personal charm difficult to resist. After a lunch at the White
House in 1905, he told Isabel Lyon, "You can't help liking [Roosevelt] for
he is a magnetic creature, and he shows his teeth in his forceful smile, just
as much as ever, and he unconsciously says that he is 'De-lighted' to see
you, just as the caricaturists have it on the record." For his part, the president always said that he thought highly of the author, calling him "not
only a great humorist, but a great philosopher."

But the politician in Roosevelt made Twain cringe. As he remarked in
private, "Whenever (as a rule) I meet Roosevelt the statesman & politician, I find him destitute of morals & not respectworthy."[45]

Arriving in Norfolk a day before the president, Twain was quick to get
ashore and draw a crowd. After chatting with the local press, he paraded
around the docks in a yachting cap and his white clothes, then took an
automobile ride to the Exposition, where he made an early tour of the
grounds before the official opening. A crowd of 25,000 was expected the
next day. As for Rogers, he had his own business to attend to and went off
immediately to inspect the new railroad. Accompanying him was his son,
Harry, who was in his late twenties, and who was being groomed to take
over his father's empire.

Besides the typical exhibits of historical interest, the fair featured

amusement rides, a Wild West show, animal acts, military displays, souvenir shops, and—as a modern novelty—a building full of premature ba-
bies in incubators. The electric sign outside announced in big letters,
"Baby Incubators with Living Infants." For those who missed the original
event, there was also a theatrical reenactment of the San Francisco
earthquake of the previous year, with crashing scenery, explosions, and
fires. As for the original Jamestown settlers, they were represented in a
life-size diorama featuring Captain John Smith trading goods with the
Powhatan tribe.[46]

On opening day—Friday, April 26, 1907—President Roosevelt arrived
right on time for his part in the official ceremonies. An armada of sixteen
American battleships and dozens of foreign warships had been assembled to welcome him with twenty-one-gun salutes. The spring weather
was ideal, with a sunny sky and a light breeze. After cruising down the
Chesapeake Bay on the presidential yacht, USS *Mayflower,* Roosevelt
woke at dawn and was dressed and ready at half past eight, standing on
the deck and watching the horizon through the shiny ovals of his pince-
nez. Wearing a top hat and frock coat, he was attended by members of his
administration and various naval officers.

When his ship entered Hampton Roads, the naval guns roared their
welcome. For a solid hour the battleships boomed away, sending out
white clouds of smoke as the *Mayflower* slowly sailed down the line.
From the shore, an artillery battery gave a three-hundred-gun salute.
Most of the American warships were relatively new—ten had been built
in the last three years—and each was painted a dazzling white. At the
end of the year, the president would send this "Great White Fleet" on a
cruise around the world to show potential adversaries that America's
naval might was second to none.

Asked about the fleet, Twain told the press that he didn't think it was
necessarily a bad thing for America to have "a whacking big navy." The
problem, he explained, was that the country had too many politicians
who seemed eager to unleash "the martial canines." For Twain—who had
been named in 1901 an honorary vice president of the Anti-Imperialist
League of New York—America's brutal conquest of the Philippines in the
early years of the century had been a sobering example of the enormous
damage a modern military could create in the service of jingoistic lead-

ers. As he would say later in the year, he considered the Philippines campaign "a stain upon our flag that can never be effaced." In the rapid buildup of the navy he feared that the president and others were preparing to engage in more misadventures abroad. Privately, he complained that Roosevelt had to be watched because he was tempted "to do insanely spectacular things."

Asked if he considered himself a man of peace, Twain answered honestly, saying that sometimes he was, and sometimes he wasn't. "I could get up and shout for peace, whatever that means, just as well as any of the rest of us. Then I might get mad afterward and do just what I had been declaring with the utmost positiveness, that I wouldn't and oughtn't to do."[47]

As he had tried to make clear in "The War Prayer"—which was written in 1905 but rejected for publication in March of that year by *Harper's Bazaar* as "not quite suited to a woman's magazine"—Twain loathed men of war who pretended to be men of peace. No author has ever satirized sanctimonious warmongers better than Mark Twain. If such people spoke truthfully, he pointed out, any prayer for divine assistance in war would reveal its hypocrisy instantly, exposing the real horrors of a victorious campaign against a supposedly unrighteous enemy: "Lord, blast their hopes, blight their lives, protract their bitter pilgrimage, make heavy their steps, water their way with their tears, stain the white snow with the blood of their wounded feet! We ask it in the spirit of love, of Him Who Is the Source of Love, and Who is the ever-faithful refuge and friend of all that are sore beset . . . Amen."[48]

At the Jamestown celebration, Twain didn't engage in any public dispute about the patriotic glorification of the Great White Fleet, but some members of the Exposition's advisory board did complain that its participation in the festivities was an example of an "extravagant militarism" imposed on an event whose purposes were peaceful. But as an old Rough Rider and a former assistant secretary of the navy, Roosevelt wanted an extravagant display of firepower, and he got it. The performance of the fleet filled him with joy. "It was an inspiring sight," he wrote a few days later, "and one I would not have missed for a great deal."[49]

While the warships were busy impressing the dignitaries on the presidential yacht, the *Kanawha* was steaming among the many sailboats and other pleasure craft that had gathered at a distance to observe the festivities. The news quickly spread that Mark Twain was aboard Henry Rogers's yacht, and soon the vessel was being shadowed by the large excursion steamer *John Sylvester*, which was taking more than five hundred eager tourists to the fair. The passengers began calling out the author's name, and at one point the steamer came close enough to the yacht to graze its bow. To satisfy their curiosity, Twain appeared on deck, waving and bowing. To those who asked if the contact between the two vessels had caused any damage, he stepped forward and shouted proudly, "Never touched me."

But playing to the crowd only made things worse. When hundreds of passengers on the steamer raced to one side for a closer view of Twain, they almost caused their vessel to capsize. In fact, there was so much activity on the water that, before the day was over, the *Sylvester* nearly collided with another ship. Realizing the danger in the overcrowded waters, the captain of the *Kanawha* found a safe spot where he could anchor, and then Twain and the rest of the Rogers party were transferred to a launch, which safely transported them to the fair.[50]

The Exposition opened with a long military parade down the newly paved street along the waterfront, where the various state exhibitions were housed in large colonial-style buildings. Roosevelt watched from a reviewing stand surrounded by so much security that neither Twain nor Rogers would have been able to get near him if they had wanted to. There were rumors that an anarchist like the one who had killed President William McKinley six years earlier at the Pan-American Exposition had come from Chicago with the sole purpose of shooting Roosevelt at the Jamestown Exposition. As the *Washington Post* reported, "A strong force of troops lined the space in front of the grand stand, half a hundred Secret Service men mixed with the crowd, and everybody who attempted . . . to get to the grand stand was stopped."[51]

Despite the fact that Rogers and Roosevelt remained at a safe distance from each other at the fair, the president knew from press reports that the tycoon was in Norfolk. Though he was supposed to be celebrating America's past, Roosevelt couldn't pass up an opportunity to bash his current foes—"the predatory classes," as he called them—and to issue a warning that may have been meant for Rogers personally. "This country,"

Roosevelt declared in his speech at the fair, "should move to the reform of abuses of corporate wealth. The wrong-doer, the man who swindles and cheats, whether on a big scale or a little one, shall receive at our hands mercy as scant as if he committed crimes of violence or brutality."

As dire as these words may have sounded to most people, they wouldn't have made much of an impression on Rogers, who knew how to play the legal system to his advantage. In several high-profile suits against Standard Oil and other companies in which he held a large stake, he had proven himself to be such a slippery defendant that the *Wall Street Journal* had started calling him "the Artful Dodger."[52]

But regardless of what the president said or did, Rogers and Twain were determined to enjoy the day. After the main events were done, Rogers mingled with some of the employees of the Virginian Railway, all of whom had been given the day off, while Twain wandered over the grounds and admired the elegant row of state exhibition halls. Finally, he "blundered into the Virginia building"—as he put it—where he found himself interrupting a reception for the young Democratic governor, Claude Swanson. Seeing Twain, everyone soon forgot the politician and began to gather around the author. Swanson didn't seem to mind.

"I took it off his hands," Twain said of the reception afterward. "It gave him a rest & he was thankful."[53]

When the long day came to an end, Twain, Rogers, and the rest of their party returned to the yacht and spent the night at anchor near the battleships, all of which were illuminated with strings of electric lights that were visible for miles. Gazing at the long row of naval vessels from the dark shore, one reporter turned poetic and described the scene as a "line of fire which shimmered across the water."[54]

In good spirits, Twain retired to his cabin. His first day at the fair, he wrote later, "was very gay, & really paid for the excursion." He had every reason to be satisfied. In the view of the *New York Times*, the crowds had shown "more interest in him than they had in the big naval review at the opening of the Jamestown Exposition."[55]

· · ·

THE NEXT DAY—a Saturday—brought a change in the weather that kept Twain from going ashore for a few days. The sky turned overcast and a cold drizzle began to fall. Much of the Exposition was still under construction, and the rain left the grounds muddy. So while they waited for the sky to clear, Twain and his friends contented themselves with the entertainments available on the yacht.

It remained gloomy throughout the weekend, with a heavy fog descending over much of the Virginia coast. On Monday morning Rogers felt that pressing business in New York required him to return home immediately. To save time, he and his son, Harry, disembarked and took a fast train to New York. Rogers's son-in-law Urban Broughton, an English-born engineer, stayed behind to keep Twain company on the *Kanawha* while the yacht's captain waited for the weather to improve.

Twain grew restless as the fog persisted into Tuesday, and he finally went ashore to the Chamberlin Hotel, a large resort at Old Point Comfort. Holding court in the lobby with admirers—including a few reporters—he enjoyed portraying himself as an ancient mariner who had been marooned and was beginning to worry he would never see home again. Conveniently forgetting that Broughton was with him, he spun a sad tale for his audience.

"Here I am," he said, "all alone on Mr. H. H. Rogers's yacht *Kanawha*, anchored out there, and not a saint to look down in pity. . . . For two days we have been held up by the fog out by the Cape, and the navigation officer says that he won't risk the passage. . . . So here I remain, pacing the boards of the *Kanawha* or the carpets of the Chamberlin, utterly, unforgivably alone. I think of that Fifth Avenue and of the dear omnibus trundling up and down from the monument, and I feel that I am without a country."[56]

When some of his innocent listeners suggested that he simply take a train home, he answered that he detested rail travel and said he had no alternative but to "remain a marooned mariner until the fog lifts."[57]

He was so good at delivering such words with a straight face that some people concluded from his remarks that he was actually in distress, especially when the headlines the next day read, "Mark Twain in Gloom. Marooned at Old Point by Fog. Tells a Tale of Desertion," and "Humorist Only Unhappy Man at Hampton Roads. Refuses to Desert the Ship." But by the time these stories appeared in print, the weather had improved and the captain was ready to sail. With Broughton and the crew of forty attending to his every need, Twain was able to relax and enjoy himself on the return voyage. By Thursday, May 2, the old mariner was safely back at 21 Fifth Avenue, listening once again to the comforting rattle of the Washington Square omnibus as it passed his door.

But the joke that he had been "marooned" was not yet played out. It was taken up by Rogers himself, who saw the newspaper headlines about "desertion" and decided to match Twain's false story with one of his own. And his tall tale was much more outrageous. Though he was well aware that his beloved yacht had returned to New York the day before, he sent an urgent message on Friday to newspapermen in Norfolk saying that the *Kanawha* had not yet arrived at her home port, and that he feared his friend Mark Twain might be lost at sea. ("The only way [I] was lost at sea," Twain joked afterward, "was for something to do.") The reporters took Rogers at his word, forgetting that he was the same man who had fooled everyone by building one railroad disguised as two seemingly unconnected ones. "The Standard Oil wizard showed a remarkable willingness to let the newspapers into the workings of his mind," the *Washington Post* later remarked, "and the narrative of the missing humorist was born."[58]

It was said that the editor of the *Norfolk Ledger-Dispatch* was so worried by the possibility of Twain going down with the yacht that he "sat up all night with an 'extra' ready and with his heart in his mouth." Messengers were put on the alert at the telegraph office to convey to the paper any news of ships in distress. When the concerns expressed in Virginia were relayed to New York, the national press jumped on the story.

On Saturday morning readers found Mark Twain's name splashed across the front page of the *New York Times*. The news appeared very bad indeed. "Twain and Yacht Disappear at Sea," the headline read. "Humorist and the *Kanawha* Missing from Hampton Roads." The report on the front page of the *New York Tribune* was equally alarming, with an urgent message by telegraph from Norfolk appealing for help in locating "H. H. Rogers's yacht *Kanawha,* having on board Mark Twain. The yacht has been missing since Wednesday." To most readers, it must have seemed that the humorist was a goner.[59]

Twain was as surprised as anyone to learn that he was in peril on the open ocean. "I see you are lost in the fog," a neighbor teased after finding the author at home, and in good shape.

Bewildered, Twain asked, "Lost in a fog? What do you mean?" When the news report was shown to him, he quickly guessed that Rogers was behind the story and rose magnificently to the occasion.

"You can assure my Virginia friends," he solemnly informed the reporters who soon gathered at his door, "that I will make an exhaustive investigation of this report that I have been lost at sea. If there is any foundation for the report, I will at once apprise the anxious public."

The next day the papers had great fun playing with variations on Twain's old joke about exaggerated stories of his death. The *New York American* came up with the best headline: "Twain Hesitates to Admit He's Dead." [60]

Mark Twain enjoying a day of sailing during a visit to Bermuda.

Body and Soul

What God lacks is convictions—stability of character.
He ought to be a Presbyterian or a Catholic
or *something*—not try to be everything.

Mark Twain[1]

. . .

IN ONE OF HIS COMMENTS to the press about his supposed disappearance at sea, Twain denied that he was trying to hide from anyone. In particular, he joked, he didn't want people spreading rumors that he was "dodging Mrs. Eddy." He offered no further explanation, but contemporary readers of New York papers would have understood his joke right away. Over the past several years he had received considerable attention in the press for articles he had written that were critical of Mary Baker Eddy and the Christian Science movement she had founded. At the beginning of 1907, Harper's brought out a collection of his writings on the subject under the title *Christian Science, with Notes Containing Corrections to Date*. An earlier version of the book was supposed to have appeared in 1903, but at the last minute Harper's had decided not to publish it. Church members had already raised a fuss over Twain's articles, and—according to the author himself—Harper's asked him "not to insist upon

its publication, they being afraid it could hurt their house by antagoniz-
ing the Scientists."[2]

His publisher had good reason to be concerned. Reclusive and secre-
tive, Eddy—now in her eighties and not in good health—still exercised
absolute control over the affairs of her sect, and her teachings were
revered by thousands of members who attended services at more than
seven hundred churches. Her followers zealously defended their faith
from the frequent attacks launched against it in the popular press, insisting that Eddy was a benevolent mother figure who exercised her authority with a soft touch.

Twain's quarrel was not so much with the religion as with the character of its leader, whom he enjoyed criticizing in personal terms that were
bound to offend many of her admirers. In his view, Eddy ruled over her
church like an American pope, communing with God behind the lace cur-
tains of her Victorian parlor and giving orders with the certainty of one
who thought "her authority was from heaven, and had no limits." Though
Twain was Harper's most important author, the publishing house was understandably reluctant to issue a work that called the seemingly mild-
mannered Eddy a "remorseless tyrant"; "a brass god with clay legs"; "a
Christian for revenue only"; and a despot who was "grasping, sordid,
penurious, famishing for everything she sees—money, power, glory." For
good measure, Twain also accused Eddy of plagiarism, claiming that her
Science and Health—the textbook for believers—was entirely the work
of others.[3]

At the end of 1906 the Harper's office finally decided to risk publication after the *New York World* and *McClure's Magazine* launched investigations into Eddy's life that made Twain's portrait seem less extreme. The
author of the long series of articles that ran in *McClure's* came to a conclusion about Eddy's character that was every bit as harsh as Twain's, declaring, "Probably no other woman so handicapped—so limited in
intellect, so uncertain in conduct, so tortured by hatred and hampered by
petty animosities—has ever risen from a state of helplessness and de-
pendence to a position of such power and authority."[4]

It is sometimes suggested that Twain's criticisms of Eddy were the
product of a curmudgeon's bitterness or a misogynist's rage. But such

reasoning wouldn't explain the similar thoughts of the *McClure's* contributor, who was a promising young female writer with no predisposition to attack Christian Science or its leader. For more than a year Twain's neighbor in Manhattan, Willa Cather, had been investigating Eddy's career for *McClure's,* conducting much of her work in Boston, the church's home base. As a result of her own independent research, she had come to share Twain's conviction that the founder had misled her flock and had never, in Cather's words, "produced an original idea on her own account." In her opinion Eddy's principal ambitions were to enjoy a life of ease and "to exact homage from the multitude."[5]

A modern literary scholar has accused Twain of indulging in "paranoid fantasies" about Christian Science. It is true that both Cather and Twain overestimated Eddy's influence and the size of her following, but mistrust of Eddy and her inner circle was so widespread during the early years of the twentieth century that even the normally reserved editors of the *New York Times* became zealous foes of the church and led a relentless campaign to discredit it in ways that Twain never dared to employ. Again and again, the paper's editorial pages lambasted the church, calling it a "crude and squalid cult" and referring to a group of Eddy's faith healers as "wretched sorcerers" and "vampires." It warned the public against Christian Science "harpies," argued that Eddy was an outright fraud, and said her followers were "dupes." The campaign reached a fever pitch in 1904, when the *New York Times* said of Eddy, "To reverence, therefore, she has no faintest title, and it was through reverence that she and her associates in the miracle business were able to accomplish the little they have magnified into much."[6]

Rarely seen beyond the gates of her large home in Concord, New Hampshire—where she enjoyed a quiet, comfortable life, thanks to her various attendants and the resources made possible by a personal fortune of $3 million—Eddy provided an easy target for her foes. But, unlike the *New York Times* and many other critics of Christian Science, Twain sympathized with the basic concept of the religion and spoke admiringly of the potential for treating illness through mental and spiritual powers. Without any trace of irony, he used the words "gracious and beautiful" to describe "the power, through loving mercifulness and compassion, to heal fleshy ills and pains and griefs—all—with a word, with a touch of the hand!" To a correspondent who questioned his views, he explained that it was easy for him to separate the good in Christian Science from its leader, who, in his opinion, had distorted its purpose for personal gain. Though the "healing principle" was a real force, he explained, Eddy had "hitched it to the shirt-tail of a religion" and was like "a tramp stealing a ride on the lightning express." In private, his comic nickname for her was Eddypus.[7]

At various times in his life, Twain had wanted desperately to believe in mental healing. Livy's delicate health was often affected by her state of mind, and it was said that she had benefited in her youth from a faith healer who had supposedly helped her overcome a long bout of illness. Struggling to understand the slow decline of his wife's health in her last years, Twain searched for explanations that went beyond what the doctors could tell him. Miracle cures appealed to his imagination and offered the only alternative to the inadequate treatments available from the limited medical science of the day.

Similarly, in Jean's case, even her own doctors believed that her best hope of controlling her epilepsy was to adjust her way of thinking and to exert more control over her moods. At the time, no reliable drugs existed for her condition, so the next best thing was to help her establish a sense of calm in her mind and in her surroundings. Her treatment in Katonah was a kind of mental healing, a touch of Christian Science without the religion. It is little wonder that Twain was reluctant to discount its potential.

But part of his anger toward Eddy seems to have been driven by his own frustrated expectations for mental healing. It had failed to save Livy, and it had yet to produce much of a change in Jean. Moreover, in darker moments, he sometimes blamed Susy's death on her interest in various forms of mental science and spiritualism, believing that she had relied too much on these things to alleviate the pains of the spinal meningitis that killed her. If nothing else, attacking Eddy was one way of venting his frustration over all these private sorrows, especially since he considered her such a deserving target. For him, laughing at her personal failings was better than crying over the more serious problems created by incurable illnesses. "I am not combating Xn Science," he told a campaigner against the movement. "I haven't a thing in the world against it. Making fun of that shameless old swindler, Mother Eddy, is the only thing about it I take any interest in."[8]

Her writing style gave him endless amusement. Recalling his conversations with Twain about Christian Science, Howells said, "It would not be easy to say whether in his talk of it his disgust for the illiterate twaddle of Mrs. Eddy's book, or his admiration of her genius for organization, was the greater." Twain was convinced that she couldn't write a coherent paragraph and gleefully seized on examples of bad prose in her published work. Of her cryptic remark that a "spiritual noumenon" had "silenced portraiture," he dryly observed: "You cannot silence portraiture with a noumenon; if portraiture should make a noise, a way could be found to silence it, but even then it could not be done with a noumenon." His doubts about her authorship of *Science and Health* were based largely on his reading of her autobiography, which he considered a stylistic mess full of basic grammatical mistakes and misprints. Having spent much of his youth setting type by hand as a printer's apprentice, he offered the church some professional advice: "I think her proof-reader should have been shot."[9]

In case anyone thought he was being too hard on an old woman whose calling was religious rather than literary, he made a point of saying that his expectations for her prose weren't unreasonable. "I wish to say that of Mrs. Eddy I am not requiring perfect English, but only good English. No one can write perfect English and keep it up through a stretch of ten chapters. It has never been done. . . . It has been approached in several English grammars; I have even approached it myself; but none of us made port."[10]

Eddy's top officials responded to Twain's critique of their leader by undertaking a low-key effort to make peace with him. The Christian Science member responsible for press relations in New York—William McCrackan—contacted Twain after his early articles on the sect appeared and asked to speak with him in private. The author agreed, and a series of meetings and telephone conversations followed in which McCrackan did his best to soften Twain's views on Eddy. It didn't work,

Twain found little to admire in Mary Baker Eddy's *Science and Health*, the textbook for her Christian Science followers, saying of it, "I think her proof-reader should have been shot."

but the two men were polite to each other, and agreed to disagree. In one of their meetings Twain revealed his exasperation with a power greater than Eddy's.

"They tell me," he said to McCrackan, "that God is all powerful. He can do everything. Then I think of the miners down there in Pennsylvania working for a pittance in the dark. I think of the cruelties, oppressions, injustices everywhere and according to this, God is responsible for all of them. Why, I'd rather have Satan any day than that kind of a God."[11]

McCrackan was worried that Twain's mind had been poisoned against Eddy by false stories from an excommunicated member named Josephine Woodbury. A woman of considerable physical charm, Woodbury had been one of the church's prominent teachers until she had become pregnant by one of her students and had then claimed that mental science was the real cause of her pregnancy. She was a great believer in hypnosis and the power of suggestion, so she thought it perfectly natural to announce that

her child—christened "The Prince of Peace"—was the result of an immaculate conception. Eddy refused to go along with this ruse, and
Woodbury was banished from the church. For several years, however, she
waged a rearguard action against her former sect, and Twain was one of
the people she approached with disparaging tales of Eddy's private life.
After McCrackan found out that Twain had met with the disgraced former member, he concluded that she must have cast a spell over the old
man and turned him into her latest "victim of vulgar hypnotic trickery."
To the faithful, this may have seemed as good an explanation as any for
Twain's sharp criticisms of their leader.[12]

Accordingly, the church hierarchy decided that the best response
to Twain's new book from Harper's was simply to downplay its importance and to carry on with their own work, which would soon include establishing a daily newspaper designed to uphold Eddy's expressed ideal
of fair play in a country where the press was often her enemy. On
November 25, 1908, the *Christian Science Monitor* would make its first
appearance.

···

THERE WAS ONE wealthy member of the New York church, however,
who was convinced that Twain deserved a public rebuke for his new
book. Without any encouragement from other Christian Scientists, Genie
Holtzmeyer Rosenfeld decided to wage a one-woman battle against him.
A native of England, and a novelist in her youth, Rosenfeld was a middle-
aged society figure and patron of the arts who had abandoned her Jewish
roots and had become a fervent believer in Christian Science. As the wife
of Broadway producer Sidney Rosenfeld, she was well known in theatrical circles and was president of the Century Theatre Club, which boasted
a membership of four hundred women dedicated to promoting what they
called "intelligent" drama on the New York stage.

When one of her committees at the Theatre Club made the mistake of
not consulting the proud president before inviting Mark Twain to participate in a charity benefit, Genie Rosenfeld exploded with anger and
threatened to resign if the committee did not promptly withdraw the invitation. Her stand attracted the interest of the press, which reported on
her "stormy" confrontation with the offending committee. After remind-

ing her members that she was devoted to Christian Science, she rejected any suggestion that the club could raise money for charity by asking Twain to autograph copies of his books. She had no use for the author or his books and wanted everyone to know it. With a flair for overstatement common to the melodramas of the time, President Rosenfeld informed the committee that "Christ is dearer to me than anything else in this world, and so is Mrs. Mary Baker Eddy. I will not tolerate the reception of anybody who has attacked us as Mark Twain has done. I'll resign from the Century sooner than be forced into this position of seeming approval of his work."[13]

If Rosenfeld expected her members to support her, she was mistaken. Almost as one, they turned against her. Some said they would be happy to accept her resignation, and others threatened to resign if she prevailed. "I didn't know I had joined a Christian Science club," declared one angry member, "and I am going to get out."

At a hastily called meeting of the entire membership on May 1, 1907, the club voted not only to stand by the invitation to Twain, but to send him a formal message apologizing for the statements of their president. The apology took a light tone, but it represented a stunning defeat for Rosenfeld and—indirectly—the cause of Christian Science. The message to Twain affirmed the group's respect for him and specifically disavowed the president's remarks with the explanation that "Mrs. Rosenfeld is an Englishwoman and does not understand that, after the Constitution and the Emancipation Proclamation, you are our biggest native document and our best beloved institution."[14]

Twain might have enjoyed dealing with this controversy if it had arisen two weeks earlier. As it was, he was preoccupied with another matter at the end of the first week of May. This was the period when he was kept busy explaining why he had not perished at the bottom of the Atlantic. The Theatre Club's meeting took place on the day the *Kanawha* left Virginia, and by the time reporters found Twain safe at home three days later, his "disappearance" at sea was the only subject anyone wanted him to discuss. But he had seen enough in the newspapers of the past week to make a sly point of denying that he was trying to hide from Mrs. Eddy or her supporters.

Indeed, as though to prove his fearlessness, he put on his white uniform two days later and made a grand entrance at the charity event that had sparked all the controversy—the Actors' Fund Fair. It was held at the Metropolitan Opera House, and its purpose was to raise money for actors impoverished by illness or old age. Large crowds turned out to buy raffle tickets and various novelties sold by celebrities and chorus girls.

To avoid any conflicts, the management of the fair steered Twain away from Rosenfeld's club and arranged for him to autograph his books at another group's booth. He agreed to this plan, and took up his post at a table where he sold "autographs while you wait." Meanwhile, as the *New York Tribune* reported, "There was a gloom around the booth of the Century Theatre Club, across the way, that could have been cut with a knife. 'It's too bad, isn't it?' one of the members of the club said to a *Tribune* reporter, under her breath. 'I'm a Christian Scientist myself, but I don't believe in bringing religion into a thing of this kind. Mark Twain feels very bad about the fuss; I heard him say so. No, Mrs. Rosenfeld hasn't been here at all.' "[15]

When the fair opened, Mark Twain was asked to speak and was introduced to loud applause as "that American institution and apostle of wide humanity." He thanked the crowd for their good wishes, but urged them to "transmute" those feelings into hard cash for the benefit of the fund. Then, usurping the authority of President Roosevelt—who had officially opened the Actors' Fund Fair by pressing a button in Washington that switched on lights in the Opera House—Twain said, "By virtue of the authority in me vested I declare the fair open. I call the ball game. Let the transmuting begin!"[16]

He emerged as one of the best fund-raisers of the event, lending his star power to a couple of auctions, including one hosted by the society hostess Mrs. Stuyvesant (Mamie) Fish, whose floral booth was a big attraction. "Mrs. Fish was making sales yesterday," reported the *Tribune,* "and early in the afternoon Mark Twain assisted her by officiating at a floral auction in front of the booth." The fair also featured appearances by his friend Ethel Barrymore and another rising star of the stage, Douglas Fairbanks.[17]

As for Rosenfeld, she did indeed stay home, not wanting to risk any chance of meeting Twain. After her club had rejected her demands, she had no choice but to step down from the leadership. Humbled, she offered apologies and hoped she would be forgiven, but a new president was promptly elected, and she never recovered her place of importance in the group. In his brief remarks at the opening of the fair Twain made only one reference to the controversy. He chose not to joke about it, but spoke in terms that were broad and generous.

"There is to be no creed here," he said, "no religion except charity."[18]

· · ·

THOUGH MANY OF HIS CONTEMPORARIES were delighted by his campaign against Eddy, Twain always understood that his unvarnished views of mainstream Christianity were better saved for the edification of posterity. When he was dictating some of his angriest comments on the God of the Bible in the summer of 1906, he told Howells, "To-morrow I mean to dictate a chapter which will get my heirs & assigns burnt alive if they venture to print it this side of 2006 A.D." His abuse of Eddy pales beside that which he heaped on the "Lord of Creation" during this period, calling the Bible "the most damnatory biography that exists in print anywhere. It makes Nero an angel of light and leading, by contrast." The adjectives he applies to God include "repulsive," "malignant," "vindictive," and "pitiless." He was certainly right to think that his contemporaries weren't ready for such strong stuff, especially his scornful verdict on the concept of God the Father: "We know quite well that we should hang His style of father wherever we might catch him."[19]

Twain was a vociferous critic of Christian missionaries—especially those working in Asia, where the new American empire was making inroads. In 1901 he had expressed his views in the powerful essay "To the Person Sitting in Darkness," urging American missionaries and other ambassadors of "the Blessings-of-Civilization Trust" to quit meddling in the affairs of China or any other place where the natives were presumed to be living in darkness. "Give those poor things a rest," he said. They had already suffered enough from exposure to "Maxim Guns and Hymn Books, and Trade-Gin and Torches of Progress and Enlightenment (patent adjustable ones, good to fire villages with, upon occasion)."

As he argued privately, if the missionaries really wanted to do good work, they could return home and help stop lynchings and similar atrocities committed by supposedly God-fearing Americans. "O kind missionary," he joked bitterly, "O compassionate missionary, leave China! come home and convert these Christians!"[20]

In light of these views, it might seem hard to believe that Twain wrapped up his busy week at the beginning of May 1907 by making a four-hundred-mile round-trip train journey to raise money for the First Presbyterian Church of Annapolis, Maryland. He had never been to Annapolis before and knew only two people in the congregation, yet he was willing to go on the long trip merely for the sake of making a prosperous church a little more prosperous. It wasn't that he had suddenly experienced a change of heart about religion. The failings of Christianity always made his blood boil, but he still felt a sentimental attachment to the church of his youth and was inclined to help it. He could view such generosity as a public duty, whereas his feud with God was mostly a private affair. At any rate, even his fiercest tirades against Christianity couldn't manage to loosen some bonds that went back to his earliest days. His mother had been an active member of the First Presbyterian Church of Hannibal, and he had attended its Sunday school, whose traditions are gently mocked in *Tom Sawyer*.

As his closest friends understood, he never entirely escaped the influence of his Presbyterian upbringing, no matter how hard he tried to play the opposite of the much loathed figure of his boyhood—the congregation's Model Boy, who never missed a worship service and "was the pride of all the matrons." As Howells once told him, "If I had been your maker, I could have improved you I suppose, but for the creature of the Presbyterian deity who did make you, you are very well; and I am willing to take you as you are." On occasion Twain could even show a grudging sense of pride in Presbyterianism, praising it for its moderation: "You never see any of us Presbyterians getting in a sweat about religion and trying to massacre the neighbors."[21]

In any case, the particular Presbyterian who invited him to Annapolis was not an easy person to refuse. She was the first lady of Maryland, the wife of Governor Edwin Warfield, a Democrat who was then widely considered a strong choice for his party's presidential nomination in the next election. The governor belonged to one of the oldest families in Maryland and had patrician features suitable for the leader of a Border State, with a white mustache and long goatee. (One of his poor relations was then a young girl in Baltimore who would one day be known to the world as the woman for whom King Edward VIII surrendered the British throne— Wallis Warfield Simpson.)

When Governor Warfield's wife, Emma, wrote Twain asking him to participate in an "entertainment" to benefit her church, she caught him in an unusually good mood, and he promptly made up his mind to tell her yes. Discussing the invitation with Isabel Lyon—who would accompany him on the trip—he was not being entirely facetious when he explained that the offer was "right in my line for I'm nothing if I'm not a Presbyterian." Besides, he added, he had always wanted to see the Naval Academy at Annapolis and welcomed the chance to tour it as the governor's guest.[22]

The Warfields were in awe of the author and went out of their way to make sure his visit was a success. The governor himself met Twain and Lyon when they arrived in Baltimore on Thursday, May 9, and escorted them the rest of the way to Annapolis, where Twain was the guest of honor at a large dinner held in the Executive Mansion. So many tickets were sold for Twain's talk on behalf of the Presbyterians that Warfield had to move the event from the mansion to the marble chamber of the House of Delegates in the capitol. (In those days, nobody seemed to doubt the legality of a bunch of Presbyterians taking over the statehouse for the night.)

While preparations for the great event were underway, the governor and his wife took Twain to see the Naval Academy. For many years, the school had enforced a strict no-smoking policy on its grounds. Of course, the visiting author ignored the rule, and no one in the official party accompanying him was willing to point out his mistake. But the sentries knew their duty and told him twice to extinguish his cigar.

"Arrested again," Twain complained when he was caught the second time. "Constituted constabulary will run this country yet." Everyone laughed, but having to give up his cigar—even for a short time—was not a laughing matter to Twain. "I will fill the world with crime if I don't smoke," he said in a voice that seemed only partly joking. Fortunately, the governor intervened and quickly won special permission from the superintendent's wife to let Twain sit on her porch and smoke to his heart's content while he watched a special parade of midshipmen.

"I have smoked practically all my life," he explained to the Warfields, "and it has never done me any harm."[23]

Many of the state's newspapers sent correspondents to cover Twain's visit, and one overly excited journalist even went to the trouble of writing an original poem of thirty-six lines to celebrate the occasion. "Throw wide the sweet doors of the State," the newspaper poet rhapsodized about Twain's arrival in Annapolis. "And gather, ye bevies of beauty, with cheeks of the rose, at the gate!"[24]

On the evening of his talk there were no "bevies of beauty" waiting for Twain, but at least five hundred people bought tickets, and the author gave them a good show. He told a few anecdotes about his wayward youth and ended with his favorite ghost story, "The Golden Arm," which had been a staple of his act during his years on the lecture circuit. He still had the power to transfix an audience with his artful drawl and dramatic climaxes. Thirty years later, one of the spectators at the House of Delegates that night vividly recalled the powerful moment when the white-clad humorist ended his ghost story about the corpse with the golden arm. "He made everyone's flesh creep. 'Who's got my golden arm?' he demanded . . . and at the climax, when he shouted 'YOU!' everyone popped up out of his seat."[25]

During the evening Twain also discussed his earlier "arrest" at the Naval Academy and decided to embellish the details a bit. He claimed that he had been "caught red-handed" breaking a federal law and had escaped punishment only because someone had whispered to the sentries that they couldn't lock up a gentleman whom the governor considered "one of the greatest men in the world." He pleaded rhetorically, "Who am I to contradict the Governor of Maryland? Worm that I am, by what right should I traverse the declared opinion of that man of wisdom and judgment whom I have learned to admire and trust?"[26]

With his usual genius for such things, he managed to do a good deed for the Warfields and their church while at the same time casting himself as an endearing old rake who could barely stay one step ahead of the law. And the more he played the incorrigible sinner, the more the crowd loved him. He was proud to be a walking contradiction and was only too happy to point it out.

During a lull in the festivities he talked politics with the governor and told him that he usually tried to avoid siding with one party against another. He said he was a "mugwump," which he defined as someone unafraid to change his mind on any issue at any time.

"I want to change my mind every day if I feel like it," Twain said. "I vote for the men, not for their principles—sometimes I doubt if he has any principles."[27]

Warfield didn't take the comment personally. In fact, he seems to have been delighted by his guest's refreshing willingness to speak his mind. As for Mrs. Warfield, she considered Twain's visit one of the highlights of her time as first lady, posing proudly at his side for the official photographs in a heavy dress that covered her ample figure from neck to foot and made her look the very model of Presbyterian rectitude.

Though Twain was in Maryland for only forty-eight hours, the Warfield itinerary kept him busy nearly every waking minute. By the end of Friday night, he was exhausted. The original plan was for him to stay the weekend and return home on Monday, but living for two days on someone else's schedule was about all he could stand—especially if it included a lot of formal socializing. So when Saturday came along, he decided it was time to leave. Isabel Lyon offered a polite excuse to the Warfields, saying that Twain was suddenly needed in New York on urgent business. Adding apologies of his own, he was able to make an early exit without causing any offense.

It also helped that on the return trip to Baltimore he allowed the governor to accompany him and to have one more chance to show him off. During his short layover in the city, he went with Warfield to see the new headquarters of the *Sun* newspaper. While he toured the offices, Twain brought smiles to the faces of the editors when he paused near one of their rooms to admire its tidy appearance, exclaiming, "I could even write something good in here myself!"[28]

· · ·

THOUGH IT WASN'T EXACTLY URGENT, Twain did have business to attend to back home. He had an appointment coming up in June that he considered one of the most important in his life. He had learned about it only a week earlier when a message from England reached him as the *Kanawha* was leaving Virginia. It came from the American ambassador in

London, who was forwarding a request from Lord Curzon, formerly viceroy of India and now chancellor of the oldest institution of higher learning in the English-speaking world.

"Oxford University would confer degree of Doctor of Letters on you on June 26," the ambassador cabled. "But personal presence necessary."

The invitation didn't allow much time for making the necessary arrangements—especially given that the voyage alone would take at least nine days from New York to London—but Twain promptly sent a wire with the simple response: "I will come with greatest pleasure."

He was overjoyed by the news and wouldn't have missed the chance to accept the degree in person. "I never expected to cross the water again," he acknowledged, "but I would be willing to journey to Mars for that Oxford degree." Clara later remarked that this was "one of the great moments in Father's career," and recalled that the prospect of making such a long voyage didn't deter him because "the goal at the other end shone with magnetic brilliance." She remembered him exclaiming with a mixture of pride and regret, "If only Livy could have known of this triumph!"[29]

He sent off his response so quickly that it arrived in London just before the barrage of press cables went out announcing that the *Kanawha* was missing. For a while it amused him to imagine that the ambassador might think his reply had come from the next world. Chuckling over the possible confusion, he joked, "Those at the American Embassy must have figured that while on my way down to Davy Jones I had stopped long enough to tap the cable and send them the message."[30]

At any rate, he delayed publicizing the Oxford degree until after he had traveled to Maryland. With Governor Warfield at his side, he told the press the good news, which gave the announcement an official air, as though he meant to emphasize that the award was a rare honor for America as well as for himself. And that was, in fact, the way it came to be seen on both sides of the Atlantic. As the good women of the Century Theatre Club had already told him, he was now such a national icon that it was impossible for his admirers not to see his achievements as a reflection of the American spirit at its best.

But why did an academic honor—especially one from the Old World—mean so much to a self-made man such as Twain? He offered a facetious explanation in which he cast himself as a wily backwoods renegade taking an easy prize from the innocent university authorities, then skipping out before anyone was the wiser. "I take the same childlike delight in a new degree that an Indian takes in a scalp," he boasted, "and I take no more pains to conceal my joy than the Indian does."[31]

It was fun to pretend that he had not strayed far from his humble frontier roots. In truth, the education he had given himself over the years was better than anything Oxford or any other distinguished university could have provided him. Behind his folksy exterior was, of course, a sophisticated intelligence with a knowledge of literature and languages that was wide and deep. He was a voracious reader. Fiction didn't interest him as much as history, which he studied as though preparing for an examination—taking notes, making lists, writing comments in the margins of books, and repeatedly returning to certain texts for close analysis. An annotated scholarly catalogue of his large personal library runs to two hefty volumes of closely spaced print.

Some contemporaries who regarded Twain as simply a popular entertainer were shocked when he chose to show them his serious intellectual side in all its intensity. During a conversation with him in New York at the turn of the century, the Harvard-educated lawyer and novelist Owen Wister couldn't believe his eyes or ears when Twain suddenly launched into an impassioned, and very detailed, defense of French literary realism: "Mark Twain was striding up and down again, whirling on me once in a while, scowling fiercely at me, his blue eyes burning beneath the scowl, and the mound of hair all of a piece with the electric total of the man. . . . Zola was the subject, he was wholly serious, very concentrated."[32]

It always annoyed Twain when people failed to appreciate the full range of his intelligence. In his heart he knew he was as well read as anyone, but he was also keenly self-conscious that he lacked a traditional diploma. Honorary degrees helped to make up for it. The more the better. But until Oxford came along with its offer, he had received only three— two from Yale, and one from the University of Missouri.

He exaggerated this apparent slight, laughing it off even as he complained that he deserved better. "In these past thirty-five or forty years," he said after receiving the invitation from Oxford, "I have seen our universities distribute nine or ten thousand honorary degrees and overlook me every time. . . . This neglect would have killed a less robust person than I am, but it has not killed me; it has only shortened my life and weakened my constitution; but I shall get my strength back now."

Oxford, he now could argue, had come to the rescue in the nick of time. Just when he was brooding over the possibility that he might take his last breath before Harvard or Princeton had seen the error of their ways, the most famous university in the world stepped in to do the right thing, proving once and for all to "the rest of Christendom" that Mark Twain could hold his head high among even the most serious intellectuals.

Summarizing this pleasing turn of events in his autobiography, he declared that "an Oxford decoration is a loftier distinction than is conferrable by any other university on either side of the ocean, and is worth twenty-five of any other, whether foreign or domestic. Now then, having purged myself of this thirty-five years' accumulation of bile and injured pride, I will drop the matter and smooth my feathers down and talk about something else."[33]

Behind all the joking was his deeply felt conviction that his brand of humor had its serious purpose and deserved respect from academics. When Yale gave him his first honorary degree—an MA in 1888—he was so grateful that he wrote a public letter of appreciation to President Timothy Dwight. Noting that British poet and critic Matthew Arnold had recently been sharply critical of American culture for its "addiction to the 'funny man,' " Twain thanked Yale for giving its show of support to the "worthy calling" of a humorist who took his art seriously. No one has ever explained that art better than the author himself, who declared in his letter to President Dwight: "With all its lightness and frivolity it has one serious purpose . . . and it is constant to it—the deriding of shams, the exposure of pretentious falsities, the laughing of stupid superstitions out of existence."[34]

Twain's biographer Albert Bigelow Paine lived in Redding, Connecticut, at the foot of the hill where Twain decided to build his new mansion. It was Paine who recommend the spot, praising its rural charm, which an illustrator later captured in this view of the biographer's farm, with three of Paine's daughters frolicking in the foreground. The fence borders the lane leading up to Twain's property.

FIVE

Autobiography House

*The most satisfying refuge yet invented
by men—and women, mainly women.*
Mark Twain on the American home[1]

. . .

THE SPRING HAD BEEN so eventful that Twain was happy to cut down
on his activities during the few weeks before he was scheduled to sail for
England. Leaving behind the stuffy confines of his New York townhouse
and the small army of reporters eager to write about him, he settled temporarily in a rented house at the rural oasis of Tuxedo Park, about forty
miles northwest of Manhattan. Covering six thousand acres, the gated
enclave had its own lake, golf course, and tennis courts. It was a peaceful
place with large homes—many quite grand—set among woods and mead-
ows. "A place of manorial elegance and rustic charm," one of its histori-
ans has called it. Full of interesting neighbors and lively social activities,
the park hosted an annual ball for its residents, and at one of these in the
1890s the first tuxedo appeared when a local grandee showed up in a
dress jacket without the tails. "Tuxedo is a charming place," Twain told

Henry Rogers, whose family owned property there. "I think it hasn't its equal anywhere."[2]

Albert Bigelow Paine visited him at the new retreat to report on the progress of the biography. In a relatively short period the indefatigable biographer had managed to do a lot of fieldwork, traveling in March and April to the West Coast, with stops along the way in Hannibal and New Orleans. He was able to track down and interview some of Twain's old pals from the *Roughing It* period in California and Nevada, as well as a few steamboat pilots in New Orleans and some childhood friends in Missouri. In quick order, the biographer was gathering up the scattered pieces of an epic life.

Not all of Paine's informants were impressed to hear that a biography was in preparation. An old schoolmate in Hannibal still couldn't understand why people were making such a fuss over Sam Clemens. "I've studied and studied and studied," eighty-year-old Buck Brown told Paine, "but I can't think of a thing remarkable in the Clemens boy." Once the oldest and biggest boy in Sam's one-room schoolhouse, Brown had stayed in Hannibal almost all his life, operating the town's main drugstore and serving four terms as its mayor. He remembered the creator of Tom and Huck as a relatively well-behaved, harmless youth.

"Why, he wasn't even bad," he recalled, "not bad enough to remember. In his talk he tries to make out like he stole watermelons, played hookey from school and was a regular cut-up. Well, now, he wasn't that kind of a chap at all. Of course, I'm a little older than he and was not with him all the time, but the place was small then, and if he'd been the village terror I most certainly would have known it."[3]

Paine's interviews quickly taught him a vital lesson. Although Twain was scrupulously honest about many things, it was a mistake to underestimate his fondness for adjusting facts to make a good story. When Paine came to write the biography, he developed some polite ways to explain this tendency, saying on one occasion that it arose from "curious confusions of memory and imagination that more than once resulted in a complete reversal of the facts." For the time being, however, he kept such overwrought explanations to himself and continued his speedy collection of hard facts throughout the rest of the summer.[4]

He suffered one major setback. On a visit to Elmira he took with him the only copy of an important source of information—the unpublished manuscript of an autobiography by Twain's oldest brother, Orion Clemens. A failure at nearly everything he attempted, Orion died in 1897, leaving behind his worn manuscript, which gave little evidence of literary merit. At an information booth in Grand Central Station, Paine stopped to ask a question about the train to Elmira and set down his suitcase—which contained the bulk of Orion's work. "When he turned to pick it up," Isabel Lyon later wrote of the incident, "it was gone & no advertising found it again."[5]

· · ·

WHILE TWAIN CONFERRED with his biographer and prepared for his trip overseas, Isabel Lyon was overloaded with work. It wasn't an easy job supervising the move to Tuxedo Park while also tending to the usual household business. She performed her tasks well, however, and Twain was appreciative, calling her "extraordinarily competent." She provided a buffer between him and the demands of ordinary life, and was always on guard against any outsider who might try to disturb him. A young artist who had painted Twain's portrait a year earlier recalled that Lyon was always hovering nearby. He described her as "fiercely efficient" and "haughty to strangers."[6]

The boundaries of her relationship with her employer were never clear and were always subtly shifting, depending on Twain's mood. A woman with passionate feelings, an affectionate manner, and an attractive, sensitive face, she worshipped Twain in ways that suggested some kind of romantic impulse. She usually treated him with great tenderness and warmth, managing his needs with all the care that a wife might show a husband. She would play cards with him, pour his drinks, look after his clothes, and towel his hair dry after a bath. She even liked to sit at his side and smoke with him, puffing on a "little meerschaum."

Some people were convinced that she was in love with him, and assumed she wanted to be the next Mrs. Clemens. But she denied it. "There was positively no question of romance," she insisted in an interview many years later, saying that she looked on him as "an old man" and couldn't fall in love with him despite "their great congeniality."[7]

Her admiration was so deep that she often thought of him as a man who deserved as much devotion as she could give. In her surviving journals, it is not uncommon for her to burst forth with praise for even his minor accomplishments. "Oh, the king is so great" is a typical expression of her exuberance for the man she served.[8]

Flattered by her devotion, and impressed by her hard work, Twain had recently entrusted her with the biggest job she would undertake in her life. He wanted her to build a new home for him.

He had reached the point where he couldn't stand another year at his dark house in Manhattan. What he wanted Lyon to do was the same thing Livy had done long ago—build a bright, fanciful home where he could relax and entertain. He had already acquired the land for it on a wooded hillside in Redding, Connecticut.

Although only an hour and a half away from New York by train, Redding then had so few inhabitants that it seemed more remote than it was. Paine had recommended this little town in the southwestern corner of the state to Twain as a suitable spot for a rural mansion. The biographer was well acquainted with Redding's charms, having bought an abandoned farm there himself in 1905. He had recently finished renovating his two-hundred-year-old farmhouse, which was a typical New England saltbox. He turned it into a cozy home for his wife, Dora, and their four daughters, who fell in love with both the farm and the town.

During a pause in one of their many billiard games at 21 Fifth Avenue, the biographer had entertained Twain with stories about Redding, explaining that it offered a good way of enjoying a life close to nature without having to stray too far from the attractions of the city. He had acquired his little farm of thirty acres—along with the house, a large barn, and a clear-running brook with red-speckled trout—for the astonishingly low price of $900. Though it was ancient, the house was comfortable, with an enormous fireplace ten feet wide, solid oak floors, and plaster made from oyster shells hauled up from Long Island Sound. The neighbors were kind and helpful, wildlife was plentiful, the summer gardens teemed with produce, and the fall scenery was "not surpassed . . . this side of heaven."[9]

Building costs were as reasonable as the price of land. For $30,000, Paine estimated, Twain could build the house of his dreams. There was ample space available on the ridge just above Paine's property, with wide views over the Saugatuck River valley. Twain briefly thought it over and embraced the idea without even bothering to go out and see the land with his own eyes. Paine's exuberant descriptions were enough for him.

Over a period of several months in 1906 and 1907, the necessary land was acquired, an architect was recruited, the design of the house was completed, and a reputable builder from Danbury was hired. Construction was set to begin at the end of May. To cover all the costs, and to provide for contingencies, Twain put aside $50,000 in the Knickerbocker Trust Company. Most of the money came from the sale of his autobiographical dictations to the *North American Review*. Accordingly, Lyon suggested that they call the new place "Autobiography House," and Twain agreed, saying, "It's a good name, I think."[10]

· · ·

DURING THE MANY MONTHS of planning, he was content to leave the details to Lyon, not wanting to burden his "retirement" with the inevitable complications and delays that would try his patience and absorb too much of his energy. Whenever he told people that he was going to build a new house, few believed that he was willing to surrender so much control over its construction to just two individuals—his secretary and the architect. "I don't want to see it," he liked to say of the house, "until the cat is purring on the hearth." It pleased him to think that, like some potentate of old, he could make his wishes known with a few waves of his hand and wake up one day to find his palace ready and waiting. As Paine put it, "He wanted the dramatic surprise of walking into a home that had been conjured into existence as with a word."[11]

The architect John Mead Howells was a fortunate choice. For good reason, Twain trusted him to do the right thing. He was the thirty-eight-year-old son of William Dean Howells, and had always been on good terms with his father's friend. But apart from the personal connection, Twain also was aware of John's professional standing as a talented architect on the verge of launching a national career. In later years he would enjoy phenomenal success, designing such major buildings as the Beekman Tower and the *Daily News* headquarters in Manhattan, and the Tribune Tower in Chicago.

When the initial drawings of the house were finished, the *New York*

Times obtained copies and printed one showing the front elevation. Headlined "Mark Twain's Wanderings at an End," the Sunday feature revealed that the house would be built in the style of an Italian villa, with a tiled roof and a spacious loggia at one end. It was the kind of architecture that Twain and his daughters knew well from their past visits to Italy, especially during the eight months they had spent at the large villa near Florence where Livy died.

In large measure, Twain's reason for building the house was to provide a country place where Jean would be able to live with him in comfort and safety. He made this clear not only to her, but to many others, including his friends and even to the *New York Times*. After interviewing him for their Sunday feature, the paper referred specifically to Jean's illness, which the family rarely mentioned publicly.

"Mr. Clemens's younger daughter is an invalid much of the time, and the site of the house . . . was chosen so that the author might give his family a permanent home for both Summer and Winter that would be accessible from New York. Added to this motive was Mark Twain's ambition to have his family about him in what may be the closing scenes of his life."[12]

Twain put the matter more succinctly in a letter to Emilie Rogers, finishing a description of Jean's difficult separation from the family with the unambiguous declaration, "I must have a country home for her."[13]

In terms of rural comfort and healthy living, Katonah was no more beneficial for Jean than Redding—provided she had proper medical attention when necessary. The two places were only twenty miles apart, so moving from one to the other or back again wouldn't be difficult. But Twain wanted to give his daughter something to look forward to, and the beautiful villa offered her that.

Early in the planning stages for the house, this prospect of a better life in a large home of her own was put before Jean as an incentive to cooperate with her doctors at the sanitarium and to make the most of her treatment. As she recorded in her diary after one of her sister's visits to Katonah, she had learned "that we were going to build in Redding and that I might perhaps manage to stay there, if I were better, instead of here."[14]

As the time neared for construction to begin, Jean's attitude did indeed brighten. "Jean is improving," Lyon noted in early spring, "and is full of plans for the future home in Redding." It was taken for granted that she much preferred going to the new place than returning to the old house on Fifth Avenue. "She does not like the city," Lyon wrote. "No, she hates the city." Of course, what this meant for the secretary was that she would eventually have to share the house with a young woman she feared. Preoccupied with her work, Lyon preferred not to think about Jean's return until she had to.[15]

· · ·

TWAIN ORIGINALLY WANTED Clara to work with John Howells and to supervise construction of the house, but she had no more patience for such work than her father and was happy to see Lyon take the responsibility. Besides, she was too preoccupied with her singing career and was busy in the spring touring again. Playing it safe, she continued to limit her engagements to small towns. "We have heard that you carried your Utica house by storm," Twain wrote her in May, making it seem as though storming Utica was as good as storming bigger places. Then he added a little dig in accordance with their usual game of one-upmanship: "I suppose it is because you are Mark Twain's daughter."[16]

Playful or not, the rivalry between father and daughter was another reason Clara didn't show more interest in the construction of the new home. She would turn thirty-three in June and needed her own place. If she could make a career for herself in music, there was a chance she could finally become independent. And she seems to have decided that her independence wouldn't be compromised by a husband or children. Marriage, she insisted, was not in her plans. Even if she did allow herself to form some kind of romantic bond, she wanted to have a career above all else.

Her relationships with men tended to be more emotional than physical. In the last few months she had grown close to her new accompanist, twenty-nine-year-old Charles E. Wark, a native of Ontario, Canada, who had become a good companion and confidant during their tours of the Northeast. He took care of the practical details of their travels and kept a general watch over her, helping to steady her volatile artistic temperament when necessary. Twain gave his approval to a relationship that seemed to him entirely proper. "I like Mr. Wark & his honest blue eyes ever so much," he told Clara. "I think you are fortunate to be in his guardian-ship."[17]

In her circumstances, Jean couldn't help envying Clara's ability to attract men. Though her sister had never lacked admirers, Jean had always been self-conscious about her own looks and her illness. Now she was even beginning to worry that she was getting too old to interest men. In her diary she acknowledged that men were often kind and friendly to her, but she lamented the fact that most men showed no romantic interest. She desperately wanted someone to love her and to marry her. "This hunger," she wrote, "this passionate desire is so constant, that every time I see a young man that I like I begin to hope that he may before long do more than like me. . . . I cannot help wishing, wishing, wishing that some day they may overlook my age, my stupidities and especially my disease— if Dr. Peterson finds that he can do nothing real with it."[18]

There was only one time in her life when a man's passion for her had been aroused, and it had turned out badly. She was ashamed of the experience and kept it a secret. It happened a few weeks after her mother's death, when her family had come back to America, and she was temporarily staying in the Berkshires at Four Brooks Farm, the home of editor Richard Watson Gilder, her father's friend. She was twenty-four, it was summer, and her father was lost in his grief. A much older married man from a nearby farm in Tyringham began to show an interest in her and tried to seduce her. Desperate for affection, she encouraged him up to a point, and soon came to regret it. He wouldn't leave her alone and continued writing her letters for months afterward. Worried that he would "tell tales" about her, she forced herself to send him polite replies. It was only when she went to the sanitarium that she was able to stop the correspondence, telling him she couldn't write "on account of my health."

"I have had but one person care for me," she wrote in her diary at Katonah, recalling the experience at Tyringham, "& that was wholly improper—that old married farmer whom I shouldn't have allowed to say a word. . . . I would give anything if I could entirely forget the whole occurrence. . . . I don't believe I shall ever be that much of a fool again. I was a child in my behavior, at that time, & an ill one, too, which made me even weaker than I should really have been."[19]

What made this unhappy experience even more difficult to bear was the thought that her sister had all the opportunities in the world to find a husband and start a family, yet had chosen to turn her back on the very things Jean would have died for. In fact, as Jean was well aware, Clara had long ago rejected a serious proposal of marriage from a very eligible young bachelor—a romantic fellow whose early promise as a musician had recently blossomed into a brilliant career. He was everything that someone like Jean might have dreamed of, but Clara had spent years falling in and out of love with him, and had finally put an end to their relationship—apparently with no hope of reviving it. His name was Ossip Gabrilowitsch; he was a celebrated young Russian pianist whom the New York press idolized as the "Poet of the Piano."

Clara parted ways with Gabrilowitsch largely because they had become more like rivals than lovers. She feared that he would dominate her, and during their long, stormy relationship she had fought constantly to establish her independence. They had met in 1898, when both were studying music in Vienna. He was four years Clara's junior, but was clearly superior to her in talent and had already established himself as Theodor Leschetizky's prize protégé. He was thin with a pale face, high forehead, dark hair, and the kind of long supple fingers that Clara always envied. His American contemporary, the composer Charles Ives, once remarked that the young Gabrilowitsch "looked the way musicians are supposed to look in novels, from his long hair to his habit of screwing up one eye while he was talking." Even when he was still in his teens, everyone took it for granted that he had a great career ahead of him. He had made his debut at eighteen in Berlin and was in demand as a soloist in other major European cities. Devoted to his music since childhood, he didn't have much experience with the opposite sex, but he had a passionate nature and was known for his "tender and romantic" style of playing. When Clara's beauty caught his eye, a potent spell was cast over him.[20]

He was not the only one in their circle who was drawn to her. Noting the effect that the pretty American was having on his young male pupils, Leschetizky remarked to a group of them, "Boys, it seems to me that you are all suffering from the same trouble—'Delirium Clemens.' "[21]

Wanting to stand out in this crowd, Gabrilowitsch drew on his talent and wrote a song to impress Clara. It was the beginning of a very long courtship that was complicated not only by their competing wills but by

Clara met the Russian pianist Ossip Gabrilowitsch when
they were both young music students in Vienna during the
late 1890s. Their courtship was stormy and full of long
separations.

extended separations that followed her family's move from Vienna.
Whenever they were reunited, the buildup of tensions between them
made fights inevitable. She called him "that Cossack." He dashed off
angry notes with melodramatic one-liners, scribbling such things as "I
renounce our friendship." Emotionally, they behaved more like children
than adults. On occasion, their conflicts made Clara lose complete control
over her emotions. As she later confessed, she had an urge "to break
plates and hit people."

At the end of 1902, when she was twenty-eight and he was twenty-
four, they finally became engaged. But this proved to be only a short truce
in their ongoing battles. Unsure of herself and full of turbulent emotions,
she asked in one letter, "Why am I writing to you I wonder? Doubtless because it is evening and because I hate, *hate* everybody—not you; on the
contrary, I seem to like you the more I hate others." She used Livy's de-

clining health as one excuse for breaking off the engagement, but she was also reluctant to become intimate physically, signing some of her letters to Ossip, "Your Nun."

Her father liked the young Russian and enjoyed debating political questions with him. Clara was pleased by the verbal fireworks that broke out whenever the two men disagreed over some controversial issue of the day. "The Slav temperament against the West-Southern," she later wrote, "provided a thrilling duel of intellects." They were in complete accord, however, on the evil effects of racial prejudice. When Ossip—who was Jewish—brought up the issue of the "persecutions and brutal injustice" that his people had suffered, Twain responded that anti-Semitism arose from "the swollen envy of pigmy minds."

In 1903, Gabrilowitsch concluded a highly successful series of American concerts and returned to Europe in triumph. But Clara didn't follow him. Though they corresponded, they kept their distance from each other and remained out of touch for long periods, and "knew nothing of each other's lives," as Clara later put it. While Clara was developing a new relationship with Charles Wark, Ossip was involved in a brief but passionate affair with Alma Mahler, the wife of the great composer.[22]

Thoroughly mystified by these developments, Twain seems to have assumed that Clara would never marry. In Redding, he hoped, his daughters would always have a home like the one in that other part of Connecticut where they had grown up under their mother's close supervision. Before debts and illness had forced its surrender, hastening the end of her own life, Livy had expected that the Hartford house would always remain in the family. Selling it had seemed unthinkable. And though it had fallen into other hands, Twain now had the chance to begin a new life in a house almost as lovely and grand as the old one. Given the history of his long search for such a place, the name Autobiography House was especially appropriate for the Redding home. His work would finance its construction, and the finished structure would also provide the setting of his life's last chapter.

You ought never to have any part of the audience behind you;
you can never tell what they are going to do.

MARK TWAIN

. . .

The American press exulted in the daily reports of Twain's successful visit to England and gave it enormous coverage, portraying it as a national triumph.

SIX

College of One

*If everybody was satisfied with himself,
there would be no heroes.*

Mark Twain[1]

. . .

WHEN TWAIN FIRST RECEIVED NEWS of the Oxford degree, his impulse was to make quick work of the trip and to return home as soon as possible. He was worried about overtaxing his health and didn't want to risk falling ill overseas—always a possibility at his age, and something he particularly dreaded. His plan was to stay in England for about ten days, with seven of those reserved for London. That would allow just enough time, he reasoned, for a little "private dissipation" and a round of "last good-byeing with old friends whom I shan't meet again without their haloes." (On second thought, he added, "there's one or two whom I shan't ever meet *with* them. I am sorry for that, for they are among the best of the flock.")[2]

Twain had a soft spot in his heart for Britain. During eight previous visits he had lived in the country for months at a time, and had come to know it well. His irreverent but low-key humor always found a warm response among the British, who enjoyed the often subtle way that he teased them, and his witty criticisms encouraged them to laugh at their own prejudices and insecurities. When a very proper English gentleman once questioned his American habit of carrying a cheap cotton umbrella, he solemnly explained that it "was the only kind of an umbrella that an Englishman wouldn't steal." Far from causing offense, this remark was widely repeated in London and chuckled over for days.[3]

Though his view of British institutions and policies had suffered its ups and down, he was always fond of the people and the land. On his first visit—in 1872—he was so impressed by the warm welcome that he had told Livy in an outburst of enthusiasm, "I would rather live in England than America—which is treason." His early visits to such major landmarks as the Tower of London and Warwick Castle helped to make English history come alive for him, and continued to fire his imagination in later years as he worked on *The Prince and the Pauper* and *A Connecticut Yankee in King Arthur's Court*.[4]

Much of the romance that he found in the nation's history was connected to his infatuation with the beauty of the countryside. He loved exploring it, especially when the season was right. "The summer in England!" he once exclaimed after learning that William Dean Howells was planning a tour of Britain. "You can't ask better luck than that," he told Howells. Of the rural landscape, he wrote, "England is too absolutely beautiful to be left out doors—ought to be under a glass case."[5]

As soon as the news of his impending return to England had been widely circulated, dozens of cables and letters arrived pleading with him to attend events of all kinds—private luncheons and teas, charity and club dinners, public receptions and garden parties. Most people seemed to understand that this would likely be his final trip to Europe, and nobody wanted to miss the last chance to see the great Mark Twain.

Wisely, Paine advised him that "England was not going to confer its greatest collegiate honor without first being permitted to pay its wider and more popular tribute." Twain thought it over and decided to use the Oxford occasion as an excuse for turning his trip into a more elaborate public farewell. Instead of staying for a week or so, he agreed to extend his visit to almost a month. The effect of this decision was to transform his stay into something of a national celebration, allowing the press and his loyal readers to reflect at length on his accomplishments and his charms. He couldn't have asked for anything better.[6]

He discussed his plans with Jean, going out to see her in Katonah near the end of May. They had a good time together, partly because it was just the two of them. On a previous visit he had been accompanied by Isabel Lyon. Afterward, Jean wrote, "Father came & we had a real visit this time, without Miss Lyon & over an hour in length." Though Lyon tried to disguise it, Jean knew that the secretary wasn't comfortable visiting Katonah and was often quick to find fault with her. "When Miss Lyon is about," she wrote, "I am always more painfully conscious of my ignorance and stupidities."[7]

She was so proud of her father's Oxford degree that she wanted to go along on the voyage, but knew it was impossible. Saying goodbye to him over the telephone on the day of his departure was heart-wrenching. "It was fearfully painful to hear his voice," she wrote in her diary, "& not be able to see or squeeze him. To think of his going abroad without one is horrible."[8]

Clara expressed no desire to accompany her father. She was too absorbed in her own affairs. But she did worry about him being away for so long. Her biggest concern was that he might do something to make himself and the family look foolish. She urged him to act with decorum and wrote out a list of things he shouldn't do while in England. As she said her goodbyes to him at the pier, she slipped the list into his hand and said, "Read it when you get aboard the ship."

High on the list was the admonition "Don't . . . wear white clothes on ship or shore until you get back." Twain would make an effort to follow her instructions, but with mixed results.[9]

Isabel Lyon wanted to accompany her boss overseas, but Clara seems to have advised her not to go. Rumors about the secretary's relationship with Twain were beginning to circulate in America, especially after press reports of his Annapolis trip mentioned her as his sole companion. No doubt Clara didn't consider it a good idea for Lyon to be seen at Twain's side when so much attention would be focused on him in England. But the secretary didn't like being left behind. She was disconsolate for days and had difficulty sleeping at night. Because she shared Clara's fears that Twain would embarrass himself in some way, she regretted not being able to keep him under her watchful eye.

"When the King is on the ocean there is anxiety," she noted solemnly in her journal; "but there is more anxiety of another kind when he is on land. . . . He 'scares us to death,' with his inclination for the unconventional."[10]

As his companion and assistant for the trip, Twain chose a young man of thirty-two who was a relative newcomer to his circle. Ralph Ashcroft had known the author for only a few years, and their dealings with each other had been limited to financial matters. As secretary-treasurer of the Plasmon Company—the manufacturer of a nutritional powder— Ashcroft had become a business ally of Twain, who was a major investor in the company and who had great hopes for the powder's future as a high-protein food. Like most of the investments he made on his own, this was a bad one, and he would lose around $50,000 in the end. But Ashcroft was able to convince him that he had his interests at heart and was doing his best to protect them from the greedy intrigues of other shareholders.

Twain's faith in Plasmon encouraged him to think the best of the young businessman. He raved about the company's product to all his friends and advised them to invest heavily in its stock. "I'm afraid you think Plasmon is a speculative thing," he told Henry Rogers, "but really it isn't." In all seriousness Twain advised Rogers that Standard Oil should "buy control of the company." Of course, his friend laughed off the idea. Likewise, William Dean Howells found entertainment in Twain's blind devotion to the new super-food. "I was not surprised to learn," Howells recalled, "that the damned human race was to be saved by Plasmon, if anything, and that my first duty was to visit the Plasmon agency with him, and procure enough to secure my family against the ills it was heir to for evermore."[11]

Twain would come to regret putting his trust in Ashcroft, but at this stage the young man appeared to be a good choice as a companion for the trip overseas. He was English by birth and knew his way around London. A dapper fellow with a Vandyke beard, he had a smooth, amiable manner and seemed hardworking and efficient. More important, he gave the impression that he would be happy to stay in the background and selflessly attend to the writer's every need. It also helped that Lyon approved of him, though she worried that he would be too "timid" with Twain and fail to stop him "doing thoughtless things."

But he was in no doubt about his principal duty. As he later told an English journalist, he was supposed "to see that Mark behaves himself."[12]

With Ashcroft at his side, Twain left for England on June 8, sailing from New York on the big modern liner *Minneapolis*. It was forty years to the day that the *Quaker City* had set sail for the Mediterranean, taking the young Mark Twain on the voyage that would result in his first great literary triumph—*The Innocents Abroad*. On that trip—with his whole career ahead of him—he had been full of high hopes. It was his first crossing of the Atlantic, and he had been eager to make his name as a world traveler. "I feel good—I feel d——d good," the thirty-one-year-old writer had scribbled at two A.M. on June 8, 1867. He had stayed up all night drinking with friends, unable to sleep because he couldn't wait to get started. The journey lasted almost six months and altered the course of his life.[13]

Now, as an old man whose auburn curls of youth had long since turned white, he was preparing to receive one last burst of international acclaim. It isn't surprising that as he stood at the rail and gazed out at the skyline, he felt a wave of nostalgia come over him. So much had changed since he had observed the harbor from the deck of the old *Quaker City*—a paddlewheel steamship built before the Civil War. The new age of skyscrapers was in full bloom now, with some buildings rising as high as three hundred feet and overshadowing the church spires that had dominated the scene in his young manhood.

The new view didn't impress him. "By daylight these skyscrapers make the city look ugly," he had observed on an earlier occasion. To his eyes, the rising skyline was no more pleasing to look at than "a cemetery with all monuments and no gravestones."[14]

While the ship was preparing to sail, reporters went aboard and found Twain bundled up in an overcoat. Although it was a sunny Saturday afternoon, he was apparently anticipating a stormy voyage. His mood was solemn. Even his cigar had temporarily failed to brighten his outlook. He threw it overboard and rashly declared that he would never smoke again, then changed his mind a moment later and began searching for another cigar. One newspaperman noted that "there was a faint suspicion of moisture in his eyes as he declared that this might be his last visit to London."

Trying to shift to a less emotional subject, reporters asked what he was working on. Twain explained that he was trying to pile up as many pages of his autobiography as possible before he died. It was a demanding job and kept him busy "twenty-six hours a day." The result would shock many people, he said. "I have made it as caustic, fiendish, and devilish as I possibly could. I have spared no one. It will make people's hair curl. Even Mrs. Eddy's friends are there, all right."

But he confessed that it was such a devastatingly honest and unsparing masterpiece that he would have to postpone its publication. "I don't want it published until after I am dead," he explained, then thought for a moment and added, "I want to be thoroughly dead when it is published. No rumors, but really dead. . . . It will occupy many volumes, and I will go right on writing until I am called to the angels and receive a harp."[15]

Teasing journalists was always good sport, and brought a twinkle to his eye. By the time the ship was at sea, his mood was upbeat, and he began to mingle with the other passengers in a free and easy way. Besides the crew, there were only 150 people sharing the voyage with him. Though the ship was big, it doubled as a cargo vessel, and therefore its number of passengers was relatively small. The result was that a casual, almost family-like atmosphere prevailed aboard the *Minneapolis*. Twain seemed to prefer it that way, though he joked beforehand that he had booked his passage on "a cattle boat."[16]

· · ·

AMONG HIS FELLOW PASSENGERS on this luxurious "cattle boat" was Archibald Henderson, a multitalented professor of mathematics at the University of North Carolina. Only twenty-nine years old, Henderson had already earned his doctorate and was branching out into other fields far removed from mathematics. After making a study of George Bernard Shaw's plays, he had corresponded with the dramatist and had obtained permission to write his biography. This project was his reason for being aboard the *Minneapolis*—he was going to London to meet his subject and to begin the research for the book. In effect, he would become for Shaw what Paine was for Mark Twain. Before the voyage was over, however, his fascination with Twain would grow to the point where he would want to write his biography, too. (Henderson's later requests to do a full-scale Life were politely refused by Isabel Lyon, writing on her employer's behalf.)

On the morning of June 18, when the *Minneapolis* reached its berth at Tilbury Docks outside London, Twain was pleasantly surprised to find that large numbers of people were eagerly awaiting his arrival. The moment he arrived, the stevedores stopped what they were doing and gave him a loud welcome, tossing their caps and shouting a lusty "hurrah!" Then a crowd of photographers and reporters descended on him and followed along as his luggage was loaded onto the train. They stayed with him on the ride to St. Pancras station in central London, where the tall figure of George Bernard Shaw was waiting to meet Professor Henderson. The two literary titans were introduced and exchanged warm greetings. "I had the pleasure," Henderson would recall, "of presenting to each other . . . the greatest living humorist and the greatest living wit." Shaw said that he had just been telling a reporter how much he admired Twain. In fact, he had been explaining why he thought their works had important elements in common.

"He is in very much the same position as myself," Shaw had said of Twain. "He has to put matters in such a way as to make people who would otherwise hang him believe he is joking."[17]

It was an astute observation, and though the two were able to spend only a short time together at the railway station, they would meet again before the end of Twain's visit and enjoy a more leisurely conversation over lunch at Shaw's home.

The newspapers were soon full of stories about Twain's triumphant appearance on English soil. The London *Daily Express* explained why his arrival was worth celebrating: "He is just as much a national institution on this side of the Atlantic as he is in his native country. The fact that he was born in America merely constitutes him a citizen of the United States for voting purposes. Otherwise he is a citizen of the English-speaking world." There was so much coverage of his visit that an amazed correspondent from a New York paper cabled home the observation that Twain was "receiving as much attention as would a European potentate."

One of the few complaints from the British press was that the conquering hero had chosen to come in a "pale-grey lounge suit" and black bowler. Where, the reporters wondered, was "the famous suit of white, the costume that set two continents talking"?[18]

· · ·

DURING HIS VISIT to England, Twain spent most of his time in London, where he established a convenient headquarters in fashionable Mayfair. Tucked away on a quiet street just off Piccadilly, his hotel, Brown's, was not as new as the Ritz nor as grand as Claridge's, but its high ceilings and oak-paneled interiors were comfortable, and its white Georgian facade was elegant without being ostentatious. Of medium size, Brown's Hotel was a favorite with well-to-do Americans, such as Andrew Carnegie and the Roosevelt family. In 1886, when Theodore Roosevelt stayed there during preparations for his wedding to Edith Carow, he was unknown in England and identified himself as a "ranchman." Twenty years later, when his young relations Franklin and Eleanor spent a week of their honeymoon at the hotel, they were given the best rooms—the Royal Suite—because they were, in the words of the bride, "identified with Uncle Ted."[19]

Twain was so pleased with Brown's that he didn't seem to mind its association with the Roosevelts. Normally, that would have been enough to disqualify it. After all, he had taken a dislike to William Howard Taft simply because he was Roosevelt's vice president, ridiculing him as "Roosevelt's miscarriage preserved in alcohol." Fortunately, Brown's remained unspoiled for him. Its appeal wasn't based on its popularity, but on its simple dignity and quiet charm. He had savored both during an earlier visit, and was looking forward to enjoying them again. He scorned the larger hotels that were packed with tourists, and was grateful to have an old-fashioned but spacious suite with a snug parlor and two bedrooms. "A blessed retreat of a sort now rare in England," he said of the hotel, "and becoming rarer every year."[20]

Spirits in high gear, Twain threw himself into a whirlwind of social activity during his free week before the ceremony in Oxford. He was kept busy seeing old friends, making several new ones, and paying his respects to the families of a few dead ones. He dined out at the Ritz, spoke to a luncheon attended by 250 people at the Hotel Savoy, and drew admiring crowds when he strolled down Piccadilly or wandered into Green Park. So great was the demand to entertain him that at least a dozen London clubs offered honorary memberships for the length of his stay. Ralph Ashcroft spent much of each day trying to answer all the letters and calls that poured into the hotel. On at least one occasion he stayed up until three in the morning writing replies on Twain's behalf.

Invited to tour Parliament shortly after his arrival, Twain was allowed the privilege of listening to the debates in the House of Lords from the gallery reserved for ambassadors and visiting heads of state. A little later, visiting the Commons, he was welcomed by Prime Minister Henry Campbell-Bannerman and introduced to many of the leading politicians of the day, who gathered at an informal reception to shake his hand and trade quips. He already knew one of them—young Winston Churchill, then a restless MP working his way up the crowded ranks of his party.

At thirty-two, Churchill was slender, pale, and still in possession of a relatively full head of reddish brown hair. Though he was only a junior minister in the Colonial Office, he acted with all the confidence of some-one who knew he would be running things sooner or later. "These are my views," he had recently written at the end of a long report to his superior, Lord Elgin, who acknowledged them with the curt reply "But not mine."[21]

Twain was familiar with Churchill's self-assured—some would say arrogant—manner. They had met at least twice before—first, at a London party given in the summer of 1899 by the Anglo-Canadian novelist and politician Sir Gilbert Parker; and then, a year later, at a lecture in New York, where Twain had introduced the Englishman to the audience with the words "By his father he is English, by his mother he is American—to my mind the blend which makes the perfect man." (Twain also used this occasion to criticize the imperialist conflict that had helped make the young man famous—the Boer War—though he praised Churchill's brave exploits in the field as a war correspondent and soldier.)

Now, seeing him again at the House of Commons, he seems to have felt instinctively that, with his many advantages and high ambition, the politician was headed for real greatness. As he later noted in a dictation, everywhere he went during his trip he heard gossip about "that soaring and brilliant young statesman, Winston Churchill."[22]

At the House of Commons, Twain kept a relatively low profile. It was a different scene, however, when he went to Windsor on a pleasant Saturday afternoon to attend one of the biggest events of the social season. The great occasion was the garden party given by King Edward VII and Queen Alexandra, with eight thousand guests invited to take tea and stroll the vast lawns that stretched far beyond Windsor Castle's turrets and towers. Even dressed like other men in the traditional frock coat and silk hat worn on such occasions, Twain stood out. Before the day was over he managed to upstage everyone, including the royal couple.

"Mark Twain was admittedly the most popular man present," wrote the London correspondent of *Harper's Weekly*. "As he drove from the station to the castle he was kept incessantly bowing in response to the delighted cheers of the crowds. . . . Half the notable men and women of the land hurried across the lawns to welcome him."[23]

Summoned to the royal pavilion, he spent almost a quarter of an hour chatting with the king and queen. Gazing over the scenery, he spoke of his admiration for Windsor and "its beautiful grounds," then offered to buy the castle. When the king good-naturedly declined to sell, Twain feigned disappointment. Later, he said it was only a rumor that he had tried to acquire the property, and added authoritatively, "I started it myself."[24]

Though he enjoyed teasing the king, he was well aware that it was a great honor to receive so much attention from the royal couple. Part of him could laugh at the pretensions of royalty, but another part was in awe of all the history they represented. Noting Twain's fascination with England's past, Howells was to recall that his friend "felt passionately the splendor of the English monarchy, and there was a time when he gloried in that figurative poetry by which the king was phrased as 'the Majesty of England.' He rolled the words deep-throatedly out, and exulted in their beauty as if it were beyond any other glory of the world."[25]

Given the importance of Twain's visit, the American ambassador—Whitelaw Reid—decided that a special tribute to the author was in order. Accordingly, he hosted a large party for Twain at Dorchester House in Park Lane. But he was motivated more by etiquette than sentiment. In fact, the ambassador must have been one of the few Americans in England who didn't like Mark Twain.

There had been a bitter disagreement between the two men decades earlier, when Reid was editor of the *New York Tribune,* and Twain was an ambitious young writer trying to make the transition from popular humorist to novelist. Believing Twain's literary work was overrated, Reid had given a lukewarm response to the author's first novel—*The Gilded Age,* co-written with Charles Dudley Warner. When Twain realized where he stood with the powerful editor, he turned against him. For many years, each man had made a point of avoiding the other. Even after Reid moved away from journalism into politics and diplomacy, relations between them remained frosty, and now neither was happy to see the other in London. Twain didn't think their relationship would change "until Satan wants one of us and the New Jerusalem the other; the final result is not in our hands, but each of us thinks he knows how it will be."[26]

To complicate matters, both men were supposed to receive honorary degrees at Oxford on the same day. Knowing how things stood between the pair, Henry Rogers—who was touring Europe and was briefly in London—joked with Twain that "W.R." was the kind of person to "hog" all the limelight.[27]

But there was not much chance of that. Though Reid had served as ambassador to France, and had run unsuccessfully for vice president with Benjamin Harrison in 1892, his fame was no match for his old adversary's.

For proof of that, the ambassador needed only to observe how Twain was regarded by both the American and English guests who came to Dorchester House for the embassy party in his honor. Everyone wanted to hear what Twain had to say, especially the group of reporters waiting just beyond the door. They arrived with him and would leave with him. As soon as he emerged from Reid's party, they swarmed around him and followed him home. None of them was interested in a diplomat. But they couldn't get enough of Twain.

They were amazed at his energy. Though it was midnight when he left the party, he insisted on walking back to his hotel. One journalist wrote that the famous American was demonstrating considerable physical endurance for a man of his age: "Let it be stated that he stood—stood, not sat—for an hour and a half after dinner, smoking and talking, and then walked home three-quarters of a mile to his hotel." At the end of this long night of shadowing his subject, the weary journalist concluded that the author would "rather smoke than sleep."[28]

One of Twain's daily habits caused a minor sensation at his hotel. Since his arrival, he had been getting up at eight to visit the Bath Club across the street from Brown's. Each morning he went down to the lobby dressed only in a bathrobe and slippers. He then strolled over to the club and enjoyed a Turkish bath. Accompanying him at a discreet distance was Ralph Ashcroft, who had apparently been unable to talk him into wearing something more appropriate in public than a "white bathrobe with a beautiful, pale, convalescent blue stripe running all down it."[29]

The proper ladies and gentlemen of Mayfair who caught a glimpse of Twain's bare legs as he walked out of the hotel were shocked. Some stared in disbelief, others laughed. Soon these daily outings were being reported in both British and American papers. The hotel manager was apologetic, explaining to the press that "a great man like Mark Twain must be allowed to do as he pleases."

When reporters caught up with the author one morning after his return to the hotel and asked whether he understood that people were not used to seeing elderly men in bathrobes on the streets of London, he affected innocence and shrugged.

"I simply wanted to take a bath," he explained with a straight face, "and did the same thing I'd often done at the seaside. London is a sort of seaside town, isn't it?"[30]

Though the incident was soon forgotten in London, the headlines in New York provoked some indignant criticism from well-mannered Americans who thought Twain was giving his country a bad reputation. It was the old question of propriety again. A letter writer signing herself "An American Woman" complained to the *New York Times* that the famous humorist was a national disgrace:

> As a reasonable American I should like to know what treatment would be meted out to any Englishman behaving in a like manner in the Waldorf-Astoria. . . . Every newspaper in the city would howl its indignation at the insult offered our beautiful city,

especially if it occurred, as it has done in London, during the season. Is it any wonder our manners are sometimes called into question?[31]

This was the kind of criticism that Clara and Isabel Lyon had feared. And, indeed, they were mortified when they saw the press reports of Twain's public appearance in his bathrobe. "We never can tell what he will do next," Lyon fretted. Clara was so alarmed that she cabled a terse warning: "Much worried. Remember proprieties." Unrepentant, her father responded cheerfully, "They all pattern after me."[32]

Lord Curzon leads the way as Twain joins the procession to receive his honorary degree at Oxford University.

SEVEN

A Yank at Oxford

For twenty years I have been diligently trying
to improve my own literature, and now,
by virtue of the University of Oxford,
I mean to doctor everybody else's.

Mark Twain[1]

. . .

JUST BEFORE NOON on Wednesday, June 26, a procession of some three dozen distinguished gentlemen and scholars left the Hall of Magdalen College and followed an indirect route through the streets of Oxford to the university's ornate seventeenth-century theater in nearby Broad Street. At the head of the group was the lean, august figure of George Nathaniel Curzon—a member of the Irish peerage and the eleventh viceroy of India. He had resigned his imperial office in 1905, but was still a vigorous, youthful man in his forties and wasn't ready to accept a life of ease in retirement. A former student and fellow at Oxford, he had recently been elected chancellor of the university, and on this warm and windy day in early summer, he was making his first major appearance in his new position.

Though he considered himself a progressive politician who had governed India with efficiency and fairness for six years, he liked old-fashioned pomp and ceremony and was happy to trade his modern suit and tie for an antique academic costume that included a heavy black gown with gold trim. Fond of fancy dress during his time in India—where he insisted with amusing eccentricity that his subordinates attend formal events in knee breeches rather than "take refuge in the less dangerous but irregular trouser"—he looked perfectly at ease walking beneath the old weather-stained towers and domes of the college buildings in his white ruffled neckerchief, silk stockings, buckle shoes, and knee breeches.[2]

Several paces behind him was a white-haired gentleman who appeared rather less comfortable in an academic gown of scarlet and gray. An early dropout of the frontier educational system of Hannibal, Missouri, Mark Twain couldn't help but feel a little out of place wearing the ceremonial outfit of a doctor of literature at one of the world's great universities. He hadn't attended a school of any kind since his early teens, and the ones he had known were mostly one-room establishments staffed by country teachers with little training and no time for ceremony.

At some point during the day's events, a press cameraman took a photograph that captured perfectly all the old-fashioned pomp of the procession. Seeming the very embodiment of aristocratic confidence, Curzon appears at one end of the picture striding purposefully ahead in his costume adorned with various emblems of his high station, and assisted by two pages wearing tricornered hats. On the other side of the photograph Twain can be seen awkwardly smoothing his unruly hair and tugging at his gown, the dark mortarboard riding uneasily on his large head. He is definitely the odd one in the picture, the self-made American who—like his fictional Yankee Hank Morgan—appears to have wandered back in time and is suddenly forced to do his best to cope with the inexplicable rituals of the Old World.

When the procession left the spacious grounds of Magdalen College, the spectators lining the street helped to lighten the formal atmosphere by bursting into loud cheers. At first, it seemed as if they were giving a general welcome to each of the grand men in gowns who had been selected to receive honorary degrees at the day's convocation. Besides Mark Twain, there were several other world-famous figures in the procession whose mere appearance in public could cause tremendous excitement.

Among the most popular were Rudyard Kipling—who was walking directly behind Twain—and General William Booth of the Salvation Army, whose long white beard made him look like a biblical patriarch. Also prominent in the procession were Prince Arthur of Connaught; Henry Campbell-Bannerman; the foreign secretary, Edward Gray; the sculptor Auguste Rodin; and the composer Camille Saint-Saëns. The rest of the group included more than a score of well-respected leaders in the fields of science, medicine, history, law, and religion.

But it soon became clear that all the enthusiastic cries and applause were directed at one man only. Realizing that the crowd's attention was focused on him, Mark Twain beamed with satisfaction. He waved and smiled as the noise grew louder, easing into his usual manner of walking, which a friend once described as "the rolling gait of a sailor." The spectators were ecstatic. Writing afterward to Jean, he said that he "prodigiously enjoyed" every moment of the town's spontaneous tribute to him. "I am glad I came, dear heart, very glad indeed."[3]

From his vantage point in the procession a few feet away from Twain, Rudyard Kipling looked on in wonder, amazed at the outpouring of affection. "All the people cheered Mark Twain," he observed. "And when they weren't cheering and shouting, you could hear the Kodak shutters click-clicking like gun locks."[4]

Both men were surprised by the energetic way that the spectators showed their feelings. As Kipling described it, "The street literally rose at him—men cheered him by name on all sides. Americans begged him to look at them on the grounds they were from such and such a state. Whole detachments of Englishmen shouted: 'good old Mark,' and he took off his mortarboard and smiled and waved his hand and seemed perfectly happy. It was glorious."[5]

Kipling took enormous pleasure in Oxford's enthusiastic response to a fellow author whom he had long admired. The two were friends and had known each other for almost twenty years. In 1889, as an ambitious writer of twenty-three with tremendous energy but relatively few publications, Kipling had made a pilgrimage to Twain's summer home in Elmira, showing up unannounced on his doorstep after searching the town for anyone who could tell him the whereabouts of Mr. Samuel Clemens. When he reached the right address, the earnest, bespectacled

Kipling not only received a warm welcome from his hero, but was asked to stay for a while and talk. It didn't seem to matter that his small collection of work was then completely unknown to Twain.

"Well, you think you owe me something," the older author had said as they shook hands, "and you've come to tell me so. That's what I call squaring a debt handsomely."[6]

Still in awe of his friend, Kipling made a point now of hanging back a step or two during the procession, allowing Twain to have the triumphant moment all to himself. He wouldn't have had it otherwise, he later said, for he was determined to "enjoy Oxford's delight in [Twain] and his delight in it."[7]

When they finally reached the round hall of the university theater, its tiers and galleries were filled to capacity, and both undergraduates and faculty were eagerly stirring. One by one the honored guests entered the theater to receive their degrees and to hear Lord Curzon commend their achievements in Latin. The rowdy undergraduates cheered for their favorites and shouted out impertinent but good-natured remarks about the ceremony, making so much noise that few could hear the Latin readings, much less understand them.

While he waited his turn outside, Twain grew restless and took a break to smoke under an old archway. He wasn't sure what he was supposed to do when his name was called, but he was prepared for anything. On his arrival in Oxford, one of his hosts had asked him in a clipped accent, "Come to Jesus?" Though that invitation had given him pause, he had accepted it. "I thought I was in for a revival meeting or something of that sort, but, being polite, I made no objections. Nevertheless, it was a great relief to find that my host meant Jesus College, where I had a mighty fine time."[8]

When his turn came to enter the university theater, he went in with Kipling, and the audience gave what all observers from the press agreed was the loudest reception of the day. "The great ovation was reserved for Mark Twain, who was the lion of the occasion," the *New York Times* correspondent wrote. "Everyone rose when he was escorted up the aisle and he was applauded for a quarter of an hour." Another reporter described this long ovation as a "veritable cyclone." According to Kipling, "even those dignified old Oxford dons stood up and yelled." As for the center of all this attention, Twain had joked at the time of his arrival in Britain that he would show the university "what a real American college boy looks like." Now he stood tall and soaked up the adulation while he let everyone feast their eyes on the white-haired wonder "boy" they were about to honor.[9]

When the crowd finally settled down, Curzon stepped to the rostrum and made the day complete for his guest by delivering in Latin a long sentence that sounds suitably grandiose even in English: "Most jocund, pleasant, and humorous man, who shakes the sides of all the circuit of the earth with your native merriment, I, by my authority and that of the entire university, admit you to the honorary degree of doctor of literature."[10]

At the end of the ceremony, a large group of undergraduates descended on Twain and practically carried him through the streets to the chancellor's luncheon at All Souls College. When he was able to break free and catch his breath, he looked around and found himself in the company of the student editor of a college newspaper. The student gathered his courage and requested a short interview. Though Twain was feeling overwhelmed by all the excitement of the day, he agreed to answer a few questions. But first he needed to ask one of his own.

"Where is the nearest urinal?" inquired the new doctor of literature.[11]

· · ·

VARIOUS CELEBRATIONS FOLLOWED Twain's appearance in the university town, and he held up well throughout his stay. At one luncheon he was approached by the maharajah of Bikanir, who was dressed in traditional finery that immediately caught Twain's attention.

"Have you bought Windsor Castle yet?" the maharajah asked pleasantly.

"No," Twain answered, "but I'd like to buy your clothes."[12]

Though Oxford was probably not ready for a Twain clad in Indian silks, the town seemed to him an ideal place for showing off. The day after he received his degree, he attended a special celebration that offered him the chance to watch the greatest display of costumes he had ever seen. Both town and gown came together to stage the Oxford Historical Pageant, a colorful production held in a meadow bordering the Cherwell River.

A covered grandstand for five thousand spectators was erected for the occasion, and Twain sat with Kipling in the royal box. (Since no one from the royal family attended, Twain and Kipling "represented Royalty as well as we could in a sudden and unprepared way without opportunity for practice.") From their privileged spot in the front row of the grandstand, they had not only a clear view of the action, but also one unobstructed by anything modern. All they could see in the distance was a timeless scene of woods and fields and the river.[13]

For the next four hours Twain was enthralled by what he witnessed, never moving from his seat as he watched one large group of costumed performers after another reenact epic scenes from Oxford's history, beginning with events in the eighth century and ending with the eighteenth. The authentic look of each scene made Twain think that he was watching real history unfold before his eyes. During a mock battle between the Cavaliers and Roundheads, the fighting was so spirited that when it was over and Cromwell's men passed in triumph before the grandstand, the spectators hissed. For a writer who had spent years trying to bring English history to life in such works as *The Prince and the Pauper* and *A Connecticut Yankee in King Arthur's Court,* it was a joy to sit back and see things of his imagination assume such enchanting forms.

"It was a fairy dream," he wrote excitedly in a letter to Jean. "Hundreds on foot & hundreds on horseback . . . lit up all the grassy stretches with kaleidoscopic movement & color, [and] made all the grand opera's efforts at the spectacular seem poor & small & cheap & fictitious."[14]

Inspired, he continued reflecting on the experience for weeks, as though what he had seen was a vision of art and life in perfect harmony. It led him to make one of the more poetic comments of his later years, saying of the pageant: "The birds were not disturbed by it, but fluttered along with it and seemed to enjoy it as much as anybody. And the swans in the river were undisturbed by all the life and color and gayety, but acted as if used to it, and unconsciously took their part in and added to the beauty and joy of the picture."[15]

The images were still vivid in his mind several months later when he added a chapter to one of his old manuscripts—a work that is now known as *No. 44, the Mysterious Stranger.* In chapter thirty-three he created a spooky procession of ghostly figures—marching skeltons representing famous figures from many historical periods—who magically appear out of nowhere and then suddenly vanish. "The dead passed by in continental masses, and the bone-clacking was so deafening you could hardly hear yourself think. Then, all of a sudden 44 waved his hand and we stood in an empty and soundless world."

. . .

By FRIDAY THE 28TH the excitement had finally worn him out. He was in need of a quiet day of rest before returning to London, where he had agreed to address a large gathering at a Saturday night banquet given by the lord mayor.

Then, without warning, disaster struck—or so it seemed at the time to a weary Mark Twain.

The trouble came in the form of a short, stout woman of about fifty who was the reigning queen of popular fiction in Edwardian Britain. Marie Corelli, whose real name was Mary Mackay, wrote breathless tales of romance and historical drama with heavy doses of mysticism and dark religious desire. She churned out a new book almost every year. Her most recent work—*The Treasure of Heaven*—had sold 100,000 copies on its first day of publication in 1906. Readers found her stories so spellbinding that they tended to forgive her frequent stylistic breakdowns and absurdly elaborate descriptions. When a male character in her novel *Thelma* sneezes, Corelli describes it as the "cornet-blast from that trifling elevation of his countenance called by courtesy a nose."

With good reason, the critics routinely savaged her. But she considered herself a kindred spirit of Shakespeare and made her home in Stratford-upon-Avon, where her money and fame helped to establish her as one of the town's leading figures. Pompous and vain, she was constantly trying to raise her standing in the literary world by cultivating the support of other writers. But most of the good ones who knew her work were appalled at her awful prose and couldn't fathom her appeal. "From the way she writes she ought to be here," Oscar Wilde is reported to have said from the prison cell where he was serving a two-year sentence for acts of "indecency."[16]

Unfortunately for Twain, she decided that being seen with him would be good for her, and temporarily put aside her general prejudice against Americans, whom she considered "the trickiest and most unscrupulous people on earth." In this case, her own trick was to make Twain think that she wanted to be friends. They had met briefly in the early 1890s in Germany, when her commercial success was just beginning. She had been gushing and overbearing. He had been peeved.[17]

But now, after his warm welcome in London and Oxford, he was in such a good mood that he did something he would almost immediately regret—he agreed to have lunch in Stratford on Saturday the 29th with Marie Corelli. There was possibly another reason why he accepted her invitation. Her name was associated in his memory with a minor moment in his daughter Susy's last years. He explained the connection to a friend in 1897, when he turned down an earlier chance to see Corelli, saying that his old mental images of Susy's life—even the seemingly trivial ones—were still too painful to revisit. "It would move me too deeply to see Miss Corelli. When I saw her last it was on the street in Homburg, & Susy was walking with me." The memory had nothing to do with Twain's opinion of Corelli. It was simply that seeing her would bring back the sentimental moment. Though its effect had been too powerful for him ten years earlier, he may have welcomed it now—at least, at the outset.[18]

Ralph Ashcroft was given the job of arranging the rail travel from Oxford to Stratford, and then on to London. But when he reported that such a journey would take up a good part of the day, Twain knew he would have to cancel the lunch. He wrote to Corelli and said that his time was too short, and that he couldn't come to see her after all. If he traveled to Stratford, he explained, he would get back to London with only an hour or so to spare before having to deliver his speech. That would leave him so exhausted that he might "arrive at the Lord Mayor's banquet in a hearse."[19]

His letter left her unmoved. She refused to change her plans and blithely dismissed his concerns, explaining that she had already invited other guests and couldn't disappoint them.

"Consider my side of the matter a little," she said. "I have invited Lady Lucy and two other ladies, and three gentlemen; to cancel the luncheon now would inflict upon them the greatest inconvenience."

Twain tried reasoning with her, but the only side of the question she could see was her own. He couldn't find a graceful way out. Further complicating matters, she had alerted the press to her plans, and they were coming to Stratford in force to report on his visit. If he failed to show, she was sure to make a great fuss and spoil the otherwise perfect coverage of his stay in Britain. It was "a hopeless task," he reluctantly concluded, "to persuade a conscienceless fool to mercifully retire from a self-advertising scheme which was dear to her heart."[20]

So, with great reluctance, he set off for Stratford at the appointed time. To his distress, he found on his arrival that Corelli had organized a series of events throughout the town and was expecting him to give three or four short speeches before lunch. Enraged, he dug in his heels and insisted that the only thing he was going to do was eat and be on his way. He spoke so forcefully that even she was momentarily taken aback and didn't protest.

Her one public triumph of the day came when she tricked him into inspecting her garden and led him through a small gate to a yard where she had positioned more than fifty pupils of the local military school to greet him and to clamor for a speech. Cornered, he obliged with a few remarks, recalling for the benefit of the "budding warriors" his brief service in the Civil War as a Rebel militia leader who waged a successful campaign of "persistent retreating." Told that the mayor of Stratford wanted to award him civic honors, he politely explained that his visit was solely "a personal one to Miss Corelli." Conveniently, a man from *The Times* of London was there to report on the event, and the beaming hostess made sure that her name would appear in the paper.[21]

At lunch, she was all smiles and full of cheerful small talk. He was grim-faced and seething. When she stood and gave a little speech, toasting him with her glass of champagne, he thanked her but made no effort to reciprocate, staring at her in sullen silence. At the first opportunity, he bolted.

Though he may have felt that the visit lasted several hours, he was in and out in only two hours and fifteen minutes. There was no problem getting back to London in time for the banquet. All the same, he was furious and made sure that he recorded his fury for posterity in one of his dictations. What was so regrettable about his encounter with Corelli, he complained, was that she had forced him to act contrary to his true nature, which—compared with hers—was positively angelic. "In any other society than Marie Corelli's," he insisted, with his usual talent for exaggeration, "my spirit is the sweetest that has ever yet descended upon this planet from my ancestors, the angels."[22]

· · ·

As MUCH AS THE DAY in Stratford irritated him, it was the only incident of its kind during his trip. Everyone except Corelli seems to have treated him with the greatest deference and courtesy. A few days of rest at Brown's helped to restore his good humor. By the following Saturday—with only a week left in his stay—he was ready for a little mischief and decided it was time to break Clara's rule and make his first London appearance in his white suit. He chose to do it at a familiar place—the Savage Club, whose boisterous membership of bohemian gentlemen had always given him a warm welcome in the past, beginning with his first dinner as their guest in 1872. Among these friendly "Savages," he felt that his rebellion against the sober tones of formal dress would receive a sympathetic response.

After explaining that he had been under orders from his family "to refrain from white clothes," he told the club that the breaking point of his obedience had finally been reached, and that he could no longer resist wearing his favorite suit on English soil. With a show of mock humility, he thanked the Savages for indulging his weakness. "In these three or four weeks I have grown so tired of grey and black," he told them, "that you have earned my gratitude in permitting me to come as I have."[23]

Of course, the club was delighted to feast their eyes on a sight that the rest of the country had not been given the pleasure of witnessing. And, as it turned out, this was to be both the first and the last time that he wore the suit in England. This fact caused not inconsiderable disappointment, especially during his stay in Oxford, where the students had been expecting him to appear in his famous garb and had shouted to him, "Where is your white suit?" when he stepped forward to receive his degree from Curzon.

Regardless of what he wore, he was always easy to spot wherever he went in England. And many Londoners kept an eye out for him. One journalist gave his readers a helpful alert: "I do not know whether Mark

Twain has brought his famous white suit with him. But in any case, if in the course of the next few days you see on the streets of London a man with a vast mane of gray hair, blue eyes challenging beneath heavy, puckered brows, a grizzled mustache veiling a mouth of equal strength and sensitiveness, with a fine steadfast conquering look about him, and a drawl of incomparable softness—take off your hat to him with reverence, for he is Mark Twain."[24]

Even those Londoners who saw him on the street and were unsure of his identity seemed to realize that he was an American who was famous for something. One day in Regent Street an older woman came up to him and took his hand warmly, saying, "I have always wanted to shake hands with you." Twain paused and gave her a quizzical smile.

"So you know who I am, madam?" he asked.

"Of course, I do," she answered eagerly. "You're Buffalo Bill."[25]

Except for an excursion to Liverpool, he stayed in London for the last half of his trip, primarily visiting old friends. One evening he found time to take a restful break by retiring to a quiet corner of an old pub in Fleet Street. In a cozy corner by a fireplace he spent a couple of hours enjoying a simple meal with his old friend—and the actor Henry Irving's dutiful associate—Bram Stoker, whose genial company he had enjoyed off and on for twenty years, and whose one great book—*Dracula*—includes an allusion to Twain's maxim "Faith is believing what you know ain't so." (Professor Van Helsing, the fearless vampire hunter, mentions "an American" who defined faith as "that faculty which enables us to believe things which we know to be untrue.")[26]

Over meat pies and beer—and out of the limelight—the normally reserved and serious Stoker could let down his guard and allow his Irish wit and charm to shine. The two writers shared an interest in dreams and ghost stories, and spent their time together trading spooky tales of witchcraft like a couple of boys sitting around a campfire on a dark night. There was also a very practical side to the author of *Dracula*—whose primary occupation for more than a quarter of a century was managing Irving's Lyceum Theatre in London—and Twain liked discussing business matters with him. His advice was uncommonly reliable. It was also fun to listen to his gossip. He knew all the famous people in the theatrical world, and many of their secrets.

The brightest star in that world was George Bernard Shaw, and when Twain finally had a chance to see more of him, he was delighted with the experience. He went to Shaw's home for lunch on July 3, and the two spent much of their time exchanging compliments. Charmed by what he later called Twain's "complete gift of intimacy," Shaw felt that they had known each other for years. The playwright was still pouring out praise when he penned a note to his new friend almost immediately after their lunch was over, declaring, "The future historian of America will find your works as indispensable to him as a French historian finds the political tracts of Voltaire. I tell you so because I am the author of a play [*John Bull's Other Island*] in which a priest says, 'Telling the truth's the funniest joke in the world,' a piece of wisdom which you helped to teach me."[27]

Twain had a less successful—though not unpleasant—encounter with another famous playwright. During a dinner at the Garrick Club, he noticed that J. M. Barrie was seated nearby. But the creator of *Peter Pan; or, The Boy Who Would Not Grow Up*—which had opened on the London stage three years earlier—was so shy that he kept to himself most of the evening. Only five feet tall, he was reserved with nearly everyone, but he was so much in awe of Twain that he could hardly speak. They had met a few times before, and on each of those occasions Barrie had demonstrated the same pattern of behavior—he would listen raptly to Twain, start to say something, and then a distraction of one kind or another would draw attention away from him, and he would silently melt into the background and leave.

Though Twain saw this as nothing more than an acute case of shyness, Barrie had another explanation. It was his impression that there was an elusiveness in Twain's manner that made it difficult to engage him. As the playwright would admit many years later, he didn't quite know how to react to Twain's coy humor: "I see myself getting closer and closer to him as he neared the point of what he was saying; then his voice fell and he turned his face away from me, and his one hope seemed to be that I should not catch his meaning. He always appeared to be pained in a gentle lovable way if his listeners smiled, and it almost broke him up if we laughed."

The inability of the two writers to establish a closer relationship was as frustrating to Twain as it was to Barrie. "I have never had five minutes'

talk with him that wasn't broken off by an interruption," Twain complained privately. "I should like to have one good unbroken talk with that
gifted Scot some day before I die." But it was not to be. After Barrie made
his quiet getaway from the Garrick that night, the two never saw each
other again.[28]

What is particularly unfortunate about this failure to connect is that
there was obviously so much for the creator of Tom and Huck to discuss
with the man who invented Neverland and its gang of Lost Boys. Twain
had seen the New York production of Barrie's play in 1905 and had
praised its transcendent vision of a child's world. "It breaks all the rules
of real life drama," he had told reporters after seeing the play, "but pre-
serves intact all the rules of fairyland, and the result is altogether contenting to the spirit."

In fact, it was so "contenting" that it inspired him to make a revealing
declaration to the press that is both poignant and whimsical: "The long-
ing of my heart is a fairy portrait of myself: I want to be pretty; I want to
eliminate facts and fill up the gap with charms."[29]

Now, two years after saying those words, he may have felt that he had
briefly realized his wish during this trip to England, where he had received so much acclaim, and where he had felt such pride in his appearance as a "doctor" wearing the colorful gown of an ancient university.

On July 10 — three days before he was scheduled to sail home — Twain
traveled to Liverpool for his last major public appearance in England.
The long rail journey to the northern seaport was made less onerous by
the fact that he traveled from London in a special car belonging to the
Prince of Wales. He had his own bedroom and was able to nap in royal
comfort on the way up. At the station in Liverpool he was met by the lord
mayor and was provided an honor guard of a dozen burly policemen.
After a twelve-course banquet in the town hall for two hundred people,
he took the podium and gave one of the best speeches of his life.

The most stirring part was the conclusion in which he borrowed an
old seafaring anecdote and embellished it to suit his own circumstances.
It was the story of two ships — a little coasting sloop with an insignificant
cargo of vegetables and furniture, and a massive sailing vessel loaded
with riches from India. When the two ships pass in waters off the coast of
New England, the "self-important" captain of the small ship calls out to

the larger one, asking it to identify itself. In a booming voice, the cry comes back, "The *Begum of Bengal,* a hundred and twenty-three days out from Canton—homeward bound! What ship is that?"

Humbled, the captain replies, "Only the *Mary Ann*—fourteen hours out from Boston, bound for Kittery Point—with nothing to speak of!"

During his long stay in England, Twain explained, he had sometimes wondered whether he deserved all the adulation showered on him. At such times he felt "properly meek"—as though he were "only the *Mary Ann.*" But the rest of the time the praise and affection of Britain had so inspired him that he felt he must be "the stately Indiaman, plowing the great seas under a cloud of sail and laden with a rich freightage of the kindest words that were ever spoken to a wandering alien." As he began to deliver the last words of his speech, his audience sat "spellbound" in silence, according to one observer. In an "uplifted" voice he "sang out the words":

"My twenty-six crowded and fortunate days seem multiplied by five, and I am the *Begum of Bengal,* a hundred and twenty-three days out from Canton—homeward bound!"[30]

These words were greeted with a thunderous cheer, and he left the stage in triumph. The next day he returned to London and rested at Brown's before ending his stay and sailing for home on July 13.

The entire experience was almost enough to give an aging author a new lease on life, and to make him think he should remain in Britain a lot longer. He had felt a powerful spirit emanating from the nation as a whole and was reinvigorated by it. At the end of his visit he boasted to the press that he felt seven years younger.

"If I could stay here another month," he said, "I could make it fourteen." His comment appeared under the headline "Twain Postpones Funeral. Younger Now by 7 Years, He Says, and Changes Mind About Dying."[31]

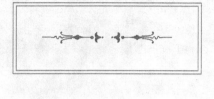

Twain returning from England with a new admirer, Dorothy Quick, an eleven-year-old American girl traveling abroad with her family. She would become a favorite in his group of surrogate granddaughters, or "angelfish," as he nicknamed them.

EIGHT

Young and Old

> At two o'clock in the morning I feel old and sinful,
> but at eight o'clock, when I am shaving,
> I feel young and ready to hunt trouble.
> *Mark Twain*[1]

. . .

WHILE TWAIN WAS ENJOYING his time in England, Isabel Lyon and Clara were feeling miserable at the family's rented summer place in Tuxedo Park, where they were mostly on their own, suffering from boredom and an early heat wave. Clara's accompanist and close friend—Charles Wark—was in and out of the house, helping to entertain her and keep up her spirits. Her singing tour in the spring had left her emotionally exhausted. Some days she didn't want to go anywhere, while at other times she was restless and would fly away at a moment's notice on short trips. The "debilitating" heat wave was so bad that she was desperate to escape it, but was suffering from "listlessness" and couldn't summon the energy to leave.[2]

Lyon wasn't in much better shape. Without Twain around, she was feeling adrift and had developed several nervous aches and pains. The weather only made her feel worse. Each morning "brought renewed heat," she complained, deepening her "terrible sense of loneliness." She stayed busy with her usual duties around the house, and also kept in touch with the builder in Redding, William Sunderland, monitoring his work on the new house, which was progressing slowly. When the heat finally became unbearable, Lyon and Clara suddenly found the energy to do something about it. They decided to escape together on a two-week cruise. It would take them first to Nova Scotia, and then to Newfoundland—a round-trip of three thousand miles.[3]

Undertaking such a voyage on the spur of the moment, when Twain was out of the country, was a bold move. Yet neither woman seems to have had second thoughts about it. They enjoyed each other's company and traveled well together. Indeed, Lyon worshipped Clara almost as much as she worshipped Mark Twain, and was eager to please her. They had pet names for each other—"Lioness" and "Santa" (short for Santa Clara). "What a creature she is, and how beautiful," Lyon commented admiringly in her journal when Clara returned home from giving a concert earlier in the year. On another occasion she raved that it was a "gift" to fall under Clara's "sweet thrall." Unlike Jean, Clara was someone Lyon could admire as the kind of sophisticated and attractive daughter that her King deserved.[4]

There was a particular reason why they could afford to drop everything and sail to such a faraway place. Lyon had authority over the family's checkbook, thanks to a power of attorney granted to her by Twain on May 7. To pay the building costs at Redding, she needed such a privilege. By this point both Twain and Clara thought she could be trusted to keep track of all the family's expenses and to pay them as necessary.

But whether Twain would have approved of their hasty decision to take a two-week cruise is debatable—not so much for financial reasons, but because it left Jean in Katonah without anyone available from the household to deal with emergencies. This was a risk, however, that Clara and Lyon were willing to accept for the sake of their own health. Their low spirits needed reviving, and neither one thought anything bad would happen before Twain returned.

They were wrong. But, as it happened, they were the ones who would soon find themselves in trouble, not Jean. They never made it to Newfoundland, sailing only as far as Nova Scotia before receiving a terrible fright and turning back.

While Twain was resting up in London after his ordeal with Marie Corelli, Clara and Lyon were aboard the passenger liner *Rosalind*. As it entered Halifax harbor on the afternoon of July 1, Lyon was resting in her cabin, and Clara was preparing to go on deck. In twenty minutes the ship was supposed to arrive at its pier. It was a chilly day, with a thick fog hanging over the harbor, so Clara put on her fur coat. Suddenly, a coastal steamer—the *Senlac*—appeared in the mist. Seconds later the two vessels collided.

Clara felt the full force of the crash, which rocked the ship and left a fifteen-foot-long hole in the engine room of the other vessel. She prepared herself for the possibility that she wouldn't survive, later recalling, "I took my hat and put it on, thinking that if matters came to the worst I might as well face it looking as well as I could."[5]

Though the *Rosalind* suffered no major damage, the *Senlac* soon appeared to be in danger of sinking. With its decks awash, the fifty passengers and crew abandoned ship. All managed to escape, scrambling into rescue boats sent out from the *Rosalind*. They left with nothing more than the clothes on their backs. Responding with admirable quickness, Clara helped to organize an effort to care for the shivering survivors, some of whom were soaked to the skin.

The day after the collision several newspaper accounts of the incident mentioned Clara's good work, noting that she had removed her fur coat and wrapped it around a woman clad only in a wet blouse and skirt. She was praised for remaining calm at a time when many of the other passengers on both ships panicked and caused confusion. But the unsettling experience of seeing women passengers drenched in the cold Canadian waters made her change her mind about continuing the voyage to Newfoundland. She and Lyon decided to return to America as soon as possible. "She says she has had enough of the sea," one report said of Clara.[6]

The news in the case of the *Rosalind* was not so much that a tragedy had been averted, but that a famous man's daughter was involved in the rescue. It was front-page news in the *New York Sun* and other papers. As usual, the headlines identified Clara not by her own name but as "Mark Twain's daughter." Lyon was also mentioned as a passenger, which immediately gave rise to rumors back in New York. Press reports soon appeared with fresh speculation about her position in the family.

An enterprising reporter managed to track her down in Halifax, where she and Clara were staying for a few days while waiting for another ship home. Catching her off guard, the journalist asked bluntly if she and Twain were engaged to be married.

Lyon's face must have passed through several shades of red as she tried to compose herself, searching for the right words to make a carefully measured reply. "I hope that you will contradict the report you have mentioned" was her stiff response. "I am so glad that I saw you in order that I might thus be able to give this unqualified denial."

She emphasized that the relationship was more professional than personal. In a *Washington Post* version of the report, her presence in Halifax was explained as simply the result of doing her job—she was looking after her employer's daughter while he was out of the country: "Miss Lyon said that Miss Clemens had been ill, and they were on their way to St. Johns, Newfoundland, but since the collision they had decided to abandon the Eastern part of their trip. . . . Miss Lyon, although she has recently been the secretary for Mr. Clemens, acted in the same capacity for the late Mrs. Clemens. . . . On account of her attention to detail and her ability to keep track of engagements she has been invaluable to Mr. Clemens."[7]

Predictably, an American correspondent in London approached Twain at Brown's Hotel and asked what he thought of the story. He wasn't pleased. Confronted with the question of whether he intended to wed Lyon, he was "speechless." He had just returned to the hotel after a late night and wasn't ready to discuss such a personal matter. Instead he insisted on giving his response in writing. Going to his room, he sat down and wrote two sentences. Then he sent them to the reporter waiting in the lobby. There was nothing ambiguous, coy, or forced about his reply.

"I have not known, and shall never know, anyone who could fill the place of the wife I have lost. I shall not marry again. S. L. Clemens."[8]

There were bound to be further complications for all concerned as long as Lyon's service to the family was more like that of a close relation than of a mere secretary. Outsiders were naturally suspicious that the family secretary was preparing to assume the part of the family matriarch. For someone like Clara, who cared so much for "proprieties," it is odd that she failed to see how others could easily misinterpret her growing friendship with Lyon and jump to conclusions. By taking her along on the voyage, she had inadvertently done more to stir up gossip than Twain's supposedly reckless act of strolling down the street in his bathrobe. As one press report explicitly stated at the time, this new gossip and the Canadian voyage were linked: "Miss Lyon was with Twain's daughter when the latter proved herself a heroine . . . in Halifax harbor on Monday. The engagement rumor is believed to have grown out of this incident."[9]

Basking in his own success, Twain didn't criticize Clara for her trip, but teased her about his own supposedly exemplary behavior. On the day before he sailed home, he wrote her, "I have been most mannerly & etiquetical. I have returned *every* call—card-calls by card, delivered by myself; personal calls in *person*. . . . Everybody has been very affectionate, & you will be spiteful & jealous."[10] Of course, his way of dealing with their rivalry was to make light of it, and this was one of those times when Clara probably didn't appreciate his sense of humor.

Instead of returning to New York with Lyon, Clara traveled on her own to Boston and then stayed for a short time in Norfolk, Connecticut, where she took refuge in another one of her rest cures. In New York, Lyon prepared for Twain's return. She planned to meet him at the pier. But Clara decided that it would be impossible to go home so soon. She was content to let Lyon welcome her father back without her.

· · ·

RETURNING TO AMERICA on the *Minnetonka*—a sister ship of the *Minneapolis*—Twain ran into the same kind of trouble that Clara and Isabel Lyon had encountered on their trip. After just two days at sea, his ship became enveloped by fog in the early morning hours and collided with a fishing schooner. Both vessels survived the accident and remained seaworthy, but there was confusion aboard the liner at first, and the captain ordered everyone on deck for possible evacuation. Most of the passengers were sleeping at the time of the accident and emerged from their cabins still wearing their nightclothes. Just as the lifeboats were being lowered, however, the captain called off the alarm, having determined that the hole from the collision was above the waterline and repairable.

A great sense of relief ran through the various groups of passengers standing on the foggy deck in their robes and pajamas. A moment later any remaining tension vanished completely as the passengers noticed something that brought wide smiles to their faces. Trying to suppress their laughter, they pointed to a figure in a white robe and slippers wandering like a sleepy ghost among them with his white hair sticking out in all directions from his nightcap. It was such an amusing spectacle that the crowd soon forgot about the collision and began asking each other questions about various aspects of Twain's sleeping attire. As one of the onlookers later recounted, "Almost as soon as the news was made known that the danger was over a stage whisper went round that Mark Twain was clad in pink pajamas. Another report was that they were blue, and another was that while they were pajamas all right they were yellow."

It was left to Ralph Ashcroft to clear up the pajamas question. "I am sorry to disappoint you," he solemnly informed the curious passengers, "but as a matter of fact Mr. Clemens doesn't wear pajamas at all but a night shirt." Despite this explanation, some passengers suspected that the real cause of the confusion was that Twain had mistakenly donned his scarlet Oxford gown in the darkness and had been wearing it under his robe.[11]

Some passengers were so frightened by their close call that they slept fully dressed every night of the voyage thereafter. While the ship ran at reduced speed so the crew could make repairs, Twain decided to let the outside world know that he and his fellow passengers had survived their brush with disaster in good shape. Taking advantage of the ship's new wireless telegraph system, he sent a brief report to New York, announcing that the damage was "very slight" and signing his message, "All well, MARK TWAIN." Later, he gave an honest explanation of why he had wired the news. "It was not that I knew anything much about it," he said, "but because I wanted to give the impression that I did."[12]

When the ship sailed into New York harbor on July 22 under a bright sky, the crowd at the pier was surprised to see that the damage from the accident was more serious than Twain's brief message had indicated. As the *New York American* reported, "A long wicked looking scrape on the starboard side of the *Minnetonka,* a jagged hole and several bent plates told of her narrow escape in a fog by collision with an English bark." But when reporters scurried aboard the ship and began bombarding Twain with questions, he refused to take the accident seriously, preferring instead to joke about the way he was dressed when the alarm had sounded. "My costume was a model of propriety and modesty compared to some that I merely glanced at in passing. Of the collision I saw nothing, because I dressed very leisurely. I was disappointed because I felt that I should have been notified beforehand."[13]

He tried to keep his responses light and fanciful, so he ducked most of the serious questions and fired up his wit to produce a steady stream of droll answers. It was a bonanza for the reporters, who were given more than enough memorable quotations to go around. As he rattled off his funny answers, a chorus of laughter periodically erupted from an admiring group of women passengers standing nearby.

He announced right away that he expected the press to address him properly. "Doctor Twain, if you please," he said solemnly, tipping the black derby he was wearing with his white suit. "That is the only title I am using now."

Asked whether he had any interest in tasting a new cocktail named after a recent political scandal, he answered that he was "like the girl in a show I saw before going to England, I'll do anything that won't make me blush. However, I'd like to see anybody make me blush."

When he was informed of a recent rumor concerning the Missouri cabin where he was born—it was supposedly for sale—he fired back, "It is about time it was. It has been burned down four times."

On the subject of whether he understood the British sense of humor, he boasted that he was now an expert on it, saying that he was "the proud possessor of two senses of humor, British and American. Next to my degree my new sense of humor is the most sensible thing that happened to me on the trip."[14]

Twain enjoyed the attention so much that he was sorry when it was time to go. In reply to a question about his age, he sounded like a man who still had many years of fun left in him.

"At two o'clock in the morning I feel old and sinful," he said, "but at eight o'clock, when I am shaving, I feel young and ready to hunt trouble. There is this about old age, though—every year brings one a new accumulation of privileges, a greater capacity for enjoyment."[15]

He was happy with the welcome he received from—among others— Isabel Lyon and his editors at the *North American Review* and Harper's. But Clara's absence was conspicuous. She was still in Boston, where Charles Wark had joined her, and where her health had yet to improve. Whatever reason she gave for missing this proud moment—when her father's fame had soared to new heights on both sides of the Atlantic—he couldn't help being disappointed. But he would have understood why she was reluctant to appear at a crowded event that meant posing for yet another photograph captioned "Mark Twain and his daughter." Even some newspapers were beginning to question "the gratuitous press notices that Miss Clara Clemens is receiving on the strength of being Mark Twain's daughter." Such notices might have done some good if she had wanted a career on the popular stage, but they didn't impress the serious lovers of classical music whom she desperately wanted to cultivate. She feared that few of those people would ever take her seriously as long as they were constantly being reminded that she was the daughter of a "funny man."[16]

. . .

TWAIN DIDN'T NEED to think twice about how to spend his first day back home at 21 Fifth Avenue. He went straight upstairs to his billiards table and began taking practice shots until Paine was able to join him in the evening. As soon as they had finished exchanging greetings at the door, he motioned his biographer inside and said, "Get your cue."

Although Paine was looking forward to hearing the details of Twain's long trip, and wanted to report on his own interviews and other research he had been doing, his host insisted that such things could be discussed later. Having been away from his cherished table for more than a month, Twain wanted to concentrate on the game.

And so, for the rest of that warm summer night, they said very little to each other that didn't pertain to billiards.[17]

Absorbed in the pleasures of his favorite pastime, Twain had no idea that a grave crisis had overtaken his dearest friend earlier that day. Henry Rogers had suddenly become seriously ill, and, for a time, it was feared that he might not recover.

It was a Monday, and the businessman had gone to work as usual at 26 Broadway. But during the morning he had started feeling queasy. Then he found it difficult to stand, grew faint, and collapsed at his desk. A doctor was summoned, and soon confirmed what others in the office suspected. It was a stroke. Rogers's face was distorted, his speech had become garbled, and his left arm was limp.

The attack came as a great shock to everyone in the office, but in keeping with their reputation for cool professionalism, his secretary and other subordinates at Standard Oil made a determined effort to remain calm. Fearing that news of the attack would cause a panic on Wall Street, they tried to pretend that nothing was amiss. Quietly, they managed to get him not only out of the building, but out of town. He was whisked away to his son-in-law Urban Broughton's mansion on Long Island, where the best doctors from the city came in a rush and hovered over the patient. No one beyond the immediate family was allowed to see him, and the official story was that he had suffered nothing more serious than a mild case of exhaustion from overwork and the summer heat.

This drama was still unfolding at the time that Twain was cheerfully enjoying his homecoming at the pier. He was only a short distance from the Standard Oil headquarters; yet, because of all the secrecy, it would take several days before he realized that something wasn't right. And when he tried to find out what was happening, he wasn't told the truth. On a business visit to 26 Broadway, Isabel Lyon was given the impression by the dutiful Katharine Harrison that the powerful executive wasn't seriously ill at all, and would soon return to work.

"Good," Twain wrote to Rogers, after receiving this misleading report, "I was uneasy at first."[18]

In truth, Rogers remained in a bad way for weeks and was moved in late July from New York to his mansion in Massachusetts, where doctors hoped that the familiar surroundings would help in his recovery. It wasn't until the middle of August that Emilie Rogers finally gave Twain a version of events that was closer to the facts. Her husband was improving, she said, but admitted that "he had really been in worse shape than we have cared to acknowledge to anybody." She added that Henry had spoken of him often and was missing "Old Mark."[19]

Gradually, Rogers would regain enough strength to enjoy many more hours in Twain's company, but he would never make a complete recovery. The effects of the stroke would linger for the remainder of his life. It was a great blow that in an instant took away some of the pirate's swagger.

Even after he knew the truth, it was hard for Twain to accept that the man he had always regarded as a tower of strength was as vulnerable to physical shocks as anyone else. Though he knew well enough how hard Rogers worked and played, he seemed to underestimate the pressures that his friend was under, especially during the first half of 1907. The combined burdens of building the Virginian Railway and defending Standard Oil in antitrust proceedings had proved too much even for Rogers, and his health had suffered under the strain. For months, he had been bombarded with subpoenas, and there was talk that the many civil suits being brought against the big oil trust would be followed by criminal indictments against the directors themselves.

At the very time that Rogers fell ill, Standard Oil was on the verge of losing an important case in federal court, and a stiff penalty was expected. Only twelve days after Rogers suffered his stroke, the verdict in this case was announced. On August 3, United States district judge Kenesaw Mountain Landis (the future baseball commissioner) ruled against Standard Oil from his bench in Chicago, finding that it had accepted illegal rebate payments from a railroad transporting its petroleum products across state lines. He wanted to impose a criminal punishment on the directors of the trust, declaring that they were in the same position as someone "who counterfeits the coin or steals letters from the mail." But the law allowed him to hand down only a fine, so he made it a hefty one.

Angered by the "studied insolence" of the officers and lawyers of Standard Oil, Judge Landis required them to pay the government $29,240,000. The *Washington Post* called it "the greatest monetary punishment in the history of American jurisprudence."[20]

Because the gravity of his friend's illness was not explained to him until after Judge Landis ruled against Standard Oil, Twain's first reaction to the verdict was to make light of it. He probably shared the widespread assumption that the penalty would be reduced on appeal. In fact, much to the consternation of President Roosevelt, it would be revoked a year later. Perhaps hoping that he and Rogers would soon find a way to laugh about the massive fine, Twain wrote in his notebook that it reminded him of the June bride's comment after her wedding night: "I expected it but I didn't suppose it would be so big."[21]

Such levity was just the medicine that Rogers needed, and the world's most celebrated humorist was eager to administer a large dose as soon as possible. In early September, Rogers was given permission to receive visitors and to take short trips around his hometown of Fairhaven. Except for a slowness in his speech and some stiffness in his movements, he appeared to be doing much better. His four grown children, their spouses, and his nine grandchildren gathered at the Fairhaven mansion to lend their support to his recovery. Twain was invited to join them.

"I am hoping to see you here in Fairhaven," Rogers told his friend in a letter dictated to a secretary. "I have been on the loaf for seven or eight weeks, and think I will stay. Am due in New York after a time for law suits, but what is the need of being in a hurry?"[22]

Encouraged by Rogers's unusual willingness to remain "on the loaf," Twain came for a visit on September 17, sailing up from New York on a regular passenger steamer. He remained at the mansion for three days, making himself at home and doing his best to entertain Rogers, who was delighted to have his old friend back at his side. Staying at the mansion was like staying at a large resort hotel. Built in the Queen Anne style on twenty-five acres near the sea, it had almost twenty bedrooms and a central tower with an observation balcony fifty feet high.

The two old friends were soon spotted driving around town together in a small electric car with Rogers at the wheel, his features pale and drawn but his eyes full of determination. He was a little absentminded, however, and forgot to set the brake and turn off the engine when he stopped to get a newspaper at a local shop. As Rogers walked away, the wheels slowly rolled forward while his passenger was still sitting in the car.

It took Twain a few moments to realize what was happening. The top speed of the electric engine was only six miles an hour, so the vehicle was merely crawling along. But when he finally noticed its movement, he didn't try to steer or apply the brake. According to a reporter who witnessed the scene, "Mark Twain looked over one side, then he slid across the seat and looked over the other, and then he furtively looked at the lever. He reached for the lever, but drew his hand back uncertainly. It was obvious he was very uncomfortable and would have swapped his place for the wheelhouse of a Mississippi steamboat if the alternative had offered. The runabout continued to hitch along and Twain concluded to desert. He fled to the sidewalk and went into the newspaper store."

With a childlike air of innocence, he explained to Rogers, "She started and I got out."

His friend laughed, then strode down the street in pursuit of the runaway car. Looking almost like his old energetic self, Rogers managed to rescue the machine before it hit anything.[23]

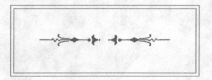

I never write "metropolis" for seven cents,
because I can get the same money for "city."

MARK TWAIN

. . .

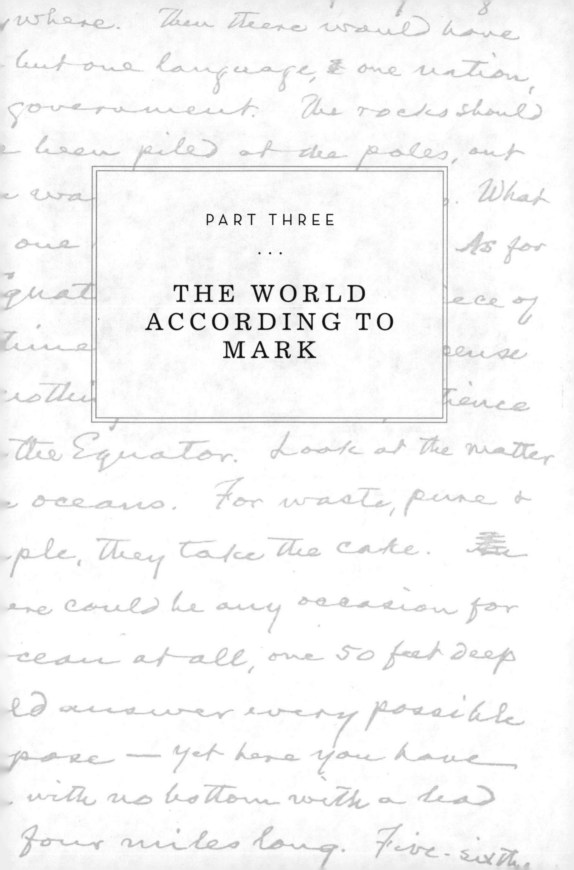

PART THREE

...

THE WORLD ACCORDING TO MARK

Twain assumed that his money was safe inside the vaults of the gleaming fortress of the Knickerbocker Trust Company.

Princes and Paupers

Put all your eggs into one basket—
and watch that basket.
Andrew Carnegie's advice to Mark Twain[1]

. . .

DURING THE HOTTEST PART of the summer Twain spent most of his time at his rented cottage in leafy Tuxedo Park, where he was able to reflect quietly on the exciting events of his English visit. His wealthy neighbors in Tuxedo were generally respectful of his privacy and made few demands. He had an open invitation to all the important social events of the late summer, yet no one seems to have pressured him to attend any of them. He went out often, however, mostly to house parties in the afternoons and the occasional dinner. Everything usually came to a standstill when he entered a room, and only gradually picked up again as the guests watched him find a comfortable place where he could hold court among his admirers.

He sometimes traveled to neighbors' houses in a "jigger," one of the small black auto taxis that served Tuxedo. But usually he preferred to wander the shady lanes of the resort in the back of an open horse-drawn carriage. The scenery along the thirty-mile network of roads included not only lawns and mansions but also long stretches of untouched countryside. With cigar in hand, he would point the driver in the direction he wanted to go and lean back to enjoy the ride as the horse went at a leisurely pace in the drowsy summer afternoon.

At home, he tried to spend part of each day working on his autobiography. Using notes that he and Ashcroft had kept during their English visit, he dictated long passages describing his impressions of the trip, then carefully revised the stenographer's copy. To get in the mood one day, he put on his Oxford gown and posed for photographs on the wide porch that wrapped around the house. In his dictations he lingered over the high points, proudly recounting the enthusiastic treatment he received in London and everywhere else he went. But he was at his best when he began cutting down to size the figures of Ambassador Whitelaw Reid and fellow author Marie Corelli, describing all their faults with the kind of brutal honesty that posthumous publication made possible.

It wasn't until the end of October that Twain gave up the house in Tuxedo Park and returned to the old place on Fifth Avenue. Though he was sorry to leave Tuxedo's peaceful scenery behind, he missed the energy and excitement of city life. In fact, on quiet days in the country when he was alone for any length of time, he sometimes wondered whether he really wanted to make his permanent home in a rural area. He worried that very few people would want to visit him at the new house in Redding, and that the neighbors there wouldn't be nearly as interesting as those in Tuxedo.

At one point in August, when construction of the new house was going slowly and the cost was rising, he almost decided to scrap the whole thing. But John Mead Howells talked him out of it, explaining that the financial penalties for canceling the contract with the builder would be too high. Isabel Lyon also urged that the construction continue. Of course, she didn't want to see all her hard work on the project come to nothing. But she had another reason for wanting to see the house completed. Just before he went to England, Twain had given her a ramshackle cottage and several acres at the edge of his property in Redding. Though the old house needed extensive work to make it inhabitable, Lyon considered it a great prize. She looked forward to making the "Lobster Pot" — as the cottage was called — her own little haven. It was her reward for giving Twain such devoted service.

To her relief, once she and John Howells had voiced their opinions, there was no more talk of postponing or abandoning work on the new house. Twain stopped thinking about it and resigned himself to spending at least $45,000 for a place that initially was expected to cost much less. Part of the problem was that transporting heavy wagonloads of material uphill to the site was difficult, and bad weather often caused delays. But with $51,000 sitting in his account at the Knickerbocker Trust Company, he didn't doubt that he could pay the bills.

· · ·

IT WAS ON THE RECOMMENDATION of Henry Rogers and Katharine Harrison that Twain had deposited most of his cash at the "white marble palace" housing the Knickerbocker's headquarters in Manhattan. (James Stillman's much larger National City Bank served Rogers's needs.) With 21,000 depositors, and more than $60 million on deposit, the Knickerbocker paid high dividends and was known as "the rich man's savings bank." Designed by Stanford White in the style of a Roman temple, its headquarters looked impregnable, with towering pillars guarding either side of a narrow entrance. Its executives were seen as above reproach, and its address at Thirty-fourth Street and Fifth Avenue was considered one of the most prestigious in the city. Standing next to it on one end was the old Waldorf-Astoria hotel (replaced almost twenty-five years later by the Empire State Building), and on the other was the tall building that housed one of Twain's favorite businesses — the Aeolian Company, the makers of his beloved orchestrelle.[2]

Not even the normally astute Rogers seems to have doubted the reliability of the Knickerbocker Trust Company, but as depositors would soon discover to their horror, there was corruption at the top in the person of the company's ambitious president — a beefy, bearded man of fifty-six named Charles T. Barney. A familiar figure in the New York business world, Barney was related by marriage to the powerful Whitney family and knew everyone in high society. But he was also known on Broadway for the fast company he kept, enjoying late-night parties that used to include his good friend Stanford White before the architect was gunned down by the jealous husband of his former lover, Evelyn Nesbit.

Having made a lot of money early in his career from real estate deals around Manhattan, Barney was now trying to make a lot more money on Wall Street. He had developed a habit of quietly using private loans from the Knickerbocker to buy and sell property through various cronies, who would then split the profits with him. In this way, he amassed a fortune of $7 million. But in the early autumn of 1907, he overreached when he took the biggest risk of his life and loaned several million dollars of his depositors' money to a group of Wall Street speculators trying to make a killing on inflated shares in a shady mining operation called the United Copper Company.

This stock market scheme was similar to the one Henry Rogers had employed a few years earlier with Amalgamated Copper. In fact, the mastermind behind the United Copper Company was a young, Brooklyn-born mining investor named Frederick Augustus Heinze, who was an old enemy of Rogers. The two men had spent the better part of a decade fighting for control of Montana's vast copper reserves. Together with Senator William Clark, Heinze had used bribery, extortion, and violence in an unsuccessful effort to drive Amalgamated Copper out of Montana. His methods were so tough that eventually he alienated even Senator Clark and was left to continue his battle alone. Undaunted, he filed a hundred lawsuits against Amalgamated in courts where he had already bribed the judges. To rid themselves of this formidable adversary, Rogers and his associates had finally been forced to buy out Heinze's mining interests at a cost of over $10 million. With this money, Heinze moved to New York in 1906 and started a new career as a stock market speculator.

The aggressive young millionaire quickly surrounded himself with several powerful business partners in New York, including Charles Barney. In his plan to whip up a bidding frenzy for shares in the new United Copper Company, Heinze brazenly copied Rogers's old techniques, using secret deals, dubious loans, and selected leaks of insider information to lift the stock's price. He must have believed that he could play the game even better than his erstwhile foe. But whereas crafty Rogers had timed his tricks in the market perfectly and had emerged with a huge profit from Amalgamated Copper, Heinze and Barney and their other partners failed spectacularly. In a two-day period in mid-October 1907 they suffered combined losses of $50 million when the price of their stock dropped from $62 a share to $15.

When his fellow officers at the Knickerbocker Trust discovered that Barney had lost millions on bad loans to Heinze and others, a board meeting was hastily called and the reckless president was forced to resign. But after news of his ouster reached other financial institutions in the city, messengers were sent racing to the company the next morning with stacks of outstanding Knickerbocker checks. They demanded immediate reimbursement. In a matter of three hours these messengers withdrew $4 million, which was half the available cash in the company's vaults. Panicked depositors withdrew the other half, and at one in the afternoon on Tuesday, October 22, the Knickerbocker was forced to close its large bronze doors and suspend payment of funds.

When the first news of this trouble reached Twain earlier that morning, he was completely caught off guard. For the last few days he had been quietly enjoying the bright display of fall colors at Tuxedo, and was mesmerized by the reflections in the lake—"sleek as a mirror, & all the brilliant colors of the hills painted on it like a picture." Nothing could have been further from his mind than the risk of insolvency at the Knickerbocker. But as soon as he was made aware of the danger, he promptly telephoned Isabel Lyon, who happened to be at 21 Fifth Avenue preparing the house for his return the next week. He gave her instructions to withdraw all his money immediately.[3]

She hurried to the trust company as fast as she could and was stunned by the sight that greeted her outside. The streets were jammed with cabs, private automobiles, and "finely appointed carriages" belonging to Park Avenue widows and other wealthy depositors living nearby. With "bank books in their quivering hands"—as Lyon later put it—the crowd stood on the wide sidewalk and stared blankly at the Knickerbocker's locked doors. Lyon had arrived too late. Police reserves, called in at the last minute, were standing at the entrance and were trying to hold back some of the depositors who were demanding to be let in. Everyone was told the company had run out of cash and would be closed indefinitely.

"Oh, it's too dreadful," Lyon wrote in her journal that night. "Every penny the King has, fifty-one thousand dollars, is in the Knickerbocker Trust Co. and . . . it has gone crashing into a terrible state."[4]

Many depositors assumed the worst and believed that Charles Barney had caused such enormous damage that they would never get their money back. A few were so despondent that they took their own lives. One man in Mount Vernon, New York, shot himself because he couldn't bear the thought of losing his life savings of $20,000. Isolated from events, Jean Clemens read of the crisis and worried in silence at Katonah, suffering what she later called "the misery of imagining poor Father at 72 losing everything." Clara was on the verge of starting her latest round of concert appearances, and everyone in the family wondered whether the cost would now be prohibitive. Lyon inspected the household accounts and said of Clara's expenses, "I thought they were heavy other years, but this year has exceeded the others, and she has all her plans made for another costly concert tour."[5]

For a few days, not only Twain's financial future but that of the whole nation seemed bleak. The panic spread, affecting many banks and trust companies in New York and elsewhere. By the end of the week, money was in short supply on Wall Street and share prices were falling. Political leaders called for calm, and the secretary of the treasury came up from Washington to confer with worried financiers. In the city's pulpits clergymen urged their congregations to "exercise the grace of patience." Speaking at a special mass for New York businessmen, Archbishop Farley declared that he wanted to "allay the panicky sentiment" among depositors by publicly announcing, "I have confidence in the solvency of the banks."[6]

Charles Barney reacted to all this upheaval by retreating behind the doors of his Park Avenue brownstone, where he watched as indignant depositors gathered outside almost daily to demand the return of their money. Legal suits were filed against him, and old friends deserted him. Facing ruin—with a personal debt of more than $2 million—he lost his nerve. In November he rose one morning and raised a gun to his head. But at the last moment his hand was shaking so much that he fired a shot into his lower body, blasting a hole in his abdomen. As a result, he lingered in great pain for several hours before dying during an emergency operation to save his life. He left behind a wife and four children.

"Doctor, I did it myself," he said on his deathbed. "I could not stand the pressure any longer. I alone am responsible."[7]

· · ·

DESPITE TWAIN'S EFFORTS to avoid financial disaster a second time in his life, the author seemed once again to be in deep trouble. He had been blindsided by the crooked dealings of a banker he didn't even know. If ever there was a time when he had reason to curse his luck, this was it. After all his success of the summer, he was suddenly facing the prospect of a staggering loss. There was no federal deposit insurance in those days, so the possibility was great that he would never see any of his savings again.

Yet throughout the crisis he refused to believe all hope was lost. When Lyon saw him after her failed effort to retrieve his funds, she was surprised to find that he was holding up well. In fact, she thought he looked "brave and cheerful." His relatively good mood also impressed Paine, who had come to believe that "the smaller things of life" often upset Twain more than the big problems. As the biographer would later write of his subject, "He often met large calamities with a serenity which almost resembled indifference."[8]

In this case, however, he was anything but indifferent. From the start, he busied himself with plans for salvaging his finances. With Ralph Ashcroft's help, he intended to use every legal means to recover his cash, lobbying his case both directly to the company's officers and behind the scenes with state regulators. He also decided that, if necessary, he would sell some of his remaining stocks and bonds to pay off the cost of the Redding house.

Though he had entrusted his cash to the Knickerbocker, his other investments in various securities were substantial, and some of them were under the safe management of Rogers's office at the Standard Oil Building. However great his disappointment in the Knickerbocker, he knew that he could survive this setback. For his immediate needs, he was able to rely on his royalty income from Harper's, which was guaranteed under his contract to be at least $25,000 a year. (By way of comparison, Howells's contract with Harper's paid him $10,000 a year, and he didn't ask for a raise until 1910.)

It can also be assumed that Twain was privately counting on Rogers to use his influence to help the trust company recover its losses and reopen. The ailing oil baron was still letting subordinates handle day-to-day business operations; but, by late October, Rogers was well enough to oversee the general affairs of his empire and to set new plans in motion. Many of his rich associates and rivals had already made a quick decision to join forces in an effort to restore order to the banking system after the Knickerbocker's collapse. The leaders of this effort were J. P. Morgan and John D. Rockefeller, who raised millions from private and public sources to prop up dozens of beleaguered banks. A large part of this rescue fund came from their own deep pockets.

"You may not know it, but Morgan and myself stood behind something like seventy banks in New York during the panic," Rockefeller would boast to a United States senator in 1908. "Now, that was a pretty nice thing for two such very, very bad men to do, wasn't it?"[9]

Indeed, thanks largely to the behind-the-scenes efforts of the tycoons, calm was slowly restored to the financial markets. In a matter of a few months the Knickerbocker was able not only to reopen but to resume payments to its depositors, including Twain. In the end, despite all the turmoil, he didn't lose a penny. He had survived a close call, however, and it was impossible to forget that the whole episode had caused enormous disruption and distress in the lives of thousands of people.

Some of J. P. Morgan's critics claimed that he had secretly engineered the whole crisis in order to take advantage of panic selling on Wall Street. The "group of financiers who withhold and dispense prosperity," said Senator "Fighting Bob" La Follette of Wisconsin, "deliberately brought on the late panic, to serve their own ends." If so, Morgan's balance sheet didn't show it. In 1907 his American companies suffered a loss of $21 million. What is closer to the truth is that the financial system almost collapsed because it was so poorly organized and loosely governed. It was ripe for exploitation on a grand scale. If Morgan and others had not intervened, the crisis would have been much worse. To bolster public confidence, Rockefeller had claimed that, if necessary, he would use half of his personal fortune to stabilize the troubled banks, telling the press that his supply of securities was more than ample for the job. "I have cords of them, gentlemen," he had said, "cords of them."[10]

It is astonishing how much damage was done by Heinze, Barney, and their associates. They undermined faith not only in New York banks, but in the economy itself. The few weeks of uncertainty and confusion were enough to create a national business slowdown that would last for months. Their scheme also laid bare some of the worst aspects of the buccaneer capitalism that Rogers represented. Though the Standard Oil millionaire liked to think that his Wall Street tricks hurt no one but his less capable competitors, the clumsy plans of Heinze and Barney showed that such tricks could backfire and harm many innocent people. (Unlike Barney, Heinze stood his ground and fought to restore his fortune, but his hard work—and heavy drinking—would take a toll on his health. In 1914 he died of cirrhosis of the liver at the age of forty-four.)

Upton Sinclair—whose scathing criticism of the meatpacking industry in *The Jungle* had made him famous in 1906—was one of the radical voices in America who denounced the financial crisis as an example of how much the whole nation was at the mercy of a few rich men. His novel *The Moneychangers,* which came out in 1908, is set against the backdrop of the Knickerbocker troubles and is a passionate attack on the ways in which finance and speculation were being used to create powerful monopolies. When a gullible character in the novel expresses surprise that a great New York banker (a fictionalized version of Charles Barney) is also known as "a daring speculator," a cynical friend replies, "When you have been in New York awhile, you will realize that there is nothing incompatible in the two."[11]

Though his acquaintance with Twain was slight, Sinclair wanted his support in publicly denouncing "capitalist greed and knavery." He was hoping to boost the chance for real reforms by enlisting the help of "the uncrowned king of America," as he dubbed the older writer. But in the case of the Panic of 1907, the general question of corruption in American capitalism interested Twain less than corruption at the Knickerbocker. Asked by the *New York World* to reflect on his blessings at Thanksgiving, he used the opportunity to lash out at the trust company: "For years it has been a rule with me not to expose my gratitude in print on Thanksgiving Day, but I wish to break the rule now and pour out my thankfulness; for there is more of it than I can contain without straining myself. I am thankful—thankful beyond words—that I had only $51,000 on deposit in the Knickerbocker Trust, instead of a million; for if I had had a million in that bucket shop, I should be nineteen times as sorry as I am now."[12]

Twain's feelings on any subject were never fully engaged unless he could personalize the matter. Whether the subject was imperialism or religion or capitalism, he was at his best when he was able to reduce broad issues to a single target on which he could concentrate his scorn, as in the case of his attacks on Mary Baker Eddy. Though an individual financier could easily earn his condemnation, Twain was in no position to endorse Upton Sinclair's general dislike of Wall Street. After all, he was an inveterate speculator himself—not to mention the closest friend of Hell Hound Rogers, whom he was never tempted to blame in any way for his troubles at the Knickerbocker.

In fact, what continued to anger Twain—even long after his savings were restored at the trust company—was that Charles Barney's loan officers had earlier refused to lend him money for his own effort to make a quick killing in the stock market. Writing on Twain's behalf in November, Ralph Ashcroft told the company's directors: "What seems to have rankled him most is that, a few days before the suspension, he wished to buy $50,000 of a certain stock and asked the trust Co. to loan him $25,000 of this money on his notes, taking the stock as collateral for the loan. He was informed that the Trust Co. did not care to do this. His balance at that time was about $50,000, and he seems to think that the directors of the Company were loaning this and other depositors' money on collateral of doubtful value, and refusing to make legitimate loans of the character he requested."[13]

In his rage at the Knickerbocker, Twain seems to have overlooked the fact that its officers had done him a great favor by refusing his loan request. Under any circumstances, it would have been unwise to bet his savings on the stock market, but he simply couldn't resist the temptation to roll the dice when he thought he couldn't lose. In this respect, he had a lot more in common with the unfortunate Barney than he might have cared to admit. If his loan had been granted, he would have been entering a market that was about to take a steep dive. He could easily have ended up losing thousands even if the Knickerbocker had been able to resume regular operations.

Though Twain had a hard time accepting that he was a bad judge of financial risk, his troubles with the Knickerbocker reminded many people that he had a long history of throwing good money into bad businesses. Shortly before the trust company reopened, a witty columnist at the *Washington Post* observed, "One good way to locate an unsafe investment is to find out whether Mark Twain has been permitted to get in on the ground floor." Of course, Twain liked to point out that his money troubles would be fewer if people didn't have a habit of cheating him. At times he seemed almost proud of the fact that he had done business with so many dishonest people, as though that proved his financial problems were mostly the fault of others. "Why, I have been swindled out of more money than there is on this planet," he told a reporter at the end of the year.[14]

· · ·

As CHANCE WOULD HAVE IT, three days after the body of Charles Barney was laid to rest Twain had an important appointment to keep in the poorest and most congested part of the city, where he was the unofficial host of an unusual theatrical benefit. Because the evening had been planned weeks ahead, it was simply coincidence that his troubles with a rogue banker who had thrown away millions were closely followed by an event involving scores of children whose families could barely afford to clothe and feed them. For Twain, there was no inconsistency in risking thousands of dollars on the stock market one day and raising thousands for the poor the next.

Though everyone of his class knew that the gulf dividing rich and poor in New York was vast, very few of the rich ever bothered to take a hard look at life on the other side, much less to extend a helping hand. On this evening in November Twain went to do both, and he took with him one of the wealthiest men in the world.

At the urging of a young drama teacher, he had invited Andrew Carnegie to attend a special performance at a children's theater on the Lower East Side. Sponsored by the Educational Alliance—a settlement house at the corner of Jefferson Street and East Broadway—the drama teacher's large company of child actors was drawn from the families of

Jewish immigrants living in some of the neighborhood's worst tenements. One of the teacher's declared aims was to use the magic of playacting "to counteract the evil and sordid influences" of the tenements, where crime was a growing problem, and where overcrowding was so bad that it was common to find a family of eight or more living in a four-room apartment and sharing a small bathroom with another family on the same floor. "The architecture seemed to sweat humanity at every window and door," observed British novelist Arnold Bennett after he toured the neighborhood.[15]

Living conditions on the Lower East Side so appalled some visitors that they looked down on the area as an alien world beyond help from outsiders. But Twain warmed easily to the immigrants—whom he refused to stereotype. He was well aware of the horrific conditions that had forced many of them to flee their homelands in Eastern Europe. For several years he been angrily denouncing the Russian government's brutal treatment of its people and had publicly declared his support for the czar's overthrow. He was especially incensed by reports of Jewish massacres and bitterly criticized Russian Christians and the czar for their "bloody bestial atrocity."[16]

Eager to help the immigrants in a practical way, he found a good opportunity in the Educational Alliance, whose large five-story building was a beacon of hope to many in the neighborhood. It gave assistance and instruction to thousands of people, offering classes to anyone who wanted to learn English or a dozen other subjects, and providing reading rooms, lecture halls, and a theater to those who wanted a stimulating cultural experience or simply a brief escape from the darkness of the tenements. The actor Zero Mostel, who took art classes at the Alliance in the 1920s, recalled it as an oasis of open spaces: "The Alliance gave me a new life—I had never seen such *big* rooms before!"[17]

The organization's drama teacher was a hardworking idealist in her thirties named Alice M. Herts. She had little money and no permanent home for her children's theater, but she found her first important benefactor in Mark Twain, who gave her permission to produce a stage version of *The Prince and the Pauper.* Though the work's suitability as a drama for young actors was obvious, Herts also knew that the story about a poor child changing places with a rich one would resonate with both her cast and audience. It was easy for people on the Lower East Side to identify with the poverty suffered by "the Pauper" Tom Canty in Twain's story, and to believe that the wealthy residents of Manhattan's Millionaires' Row— only six miles uptown—existed in a kind of dreamworld as far beyond their reach as the palaces of Tudor England.

The child actors had staged their first performances of the play in April 1907. Accompanied by Clara and William Dean Howells, Twain had attended one of the matinees, paying the standard ten-cent admission fee for an ordinary seat among the audience, most of whom were children. At the intermission he had taken the stage to say how much he admired the production, which included elaborate sets, realistic costumes, and two accomplished girls playing the parts of Prince Edward and Tom Canty.

"I have not enjoyed a play so much, so heartily, and so thoroughly," he told the crowd, "since I played Miles Hendon twenty-two years ago. I used to play in this piece with my children, who, twenty-two years ago, were little youngsters. One of my daughters was the Prince, and a neighbor's daughter was the Pauper, and the children of other neighbors played other parts. But we never gave such a performance as we have seen here today. It would have been beyond us."[18]

After the play was over, Twain had gone backstage and signed copies of the program for the cast. One of the boys who met him was Samuel Chotzinoff, who would later become a music critic and the head of classical programming for NBC radio. He never forgot how quickly Twain's warm manner put the young actors at ease: "Dressed all in white, his wavy hair a yellowish white, he looked pleasantly old and vividly handsome. . . . I had expected him to behave somewhat haughtily, as I would have done in his position. But he spoke to us as equals."[19]

Twain had also taken this opportunity to chat with the teacher about the future of her theater company. "His deep interest was immediate and unbounded," Herts recalled. "After seeing his play he responded enthusiastically to a request of the players to give a special evening performance for his friends, in the hope that some wealthy person or persons might be interested to suitably subsidize this unique and practical method of providing the best means of entertainment for young men, women, and children."[20]

All summer long, Herts and the young actors rehearsed, hoping to make their special performance for Twain's friends as perfect as possible. True to his word, the author issued dozens of invitations to the event and didn't allow anything—not even the ongoing negotiations with the directors of the Knickerbocker Trust—to interfere with his plan to attend the play at its appointed time: eight o'clock on Tuesday night, November 19, 1907. "I must stop making November engagements," he wrote at the end of October. "Of the five or six already made I can excuse myself from all but one—Nov. 19th."[21]

Making sure that Andrew Carnegie attended wasn't easy. Having sold his steel empire to J. P. Morgan for $300 million in 1901, Carnegie was so absorbed in his second career as a philanthropist and opinion maker that he kept on the go constantly and had little time to spare for anything but the biggest causes. In October he was in Europe, and for much of November he was in Washington, conferring with Roosevelt and various cabinet secretaries on the Panic and other matters. In New York he was besieged by old business associates who were in financial trouble, and who wanted advice and loans. With most of his own money in gold bonds earning a steady 5 percent, Carnegie had little reason to worry about the security of his vast fortune and was eager to make pronouncements on the reckless financial habits of others, giving a talk in which he denounced the American banking system as "the worst in the civilized world."[22]

With his busy schedule, Carnegie might easily have decided that the last thing he needed to do was spend an evening at a children's theater on the Lower East Side. But it is a measure of his respect for Mark Twain that he accepted the invitation to watch the play. Though the two saw each other only occasionally, and were never close, Twain was always fascinated by the other man's success and ambition, and charmed him by appearing to be one of the few who didn't take his great wealth seriously. After the steel business was sold, one of the first begging letters the tycoon received was from Twain. Carnegie was so delighted by its irreverence that he later reprinted the letter in his *Autobiography*. "Dear Sir and Friend," Twain wrote. "You seem to be in prosperity. Could you lend an admirer a dollar & a half to buy a hymn-book with? God will bless you." In a postscript Twain requested, "Don't send the hymn-book, send the money; I want to make the selection myself."[23]

"Dear Sir and Friend," began one of Twain's letters to
steel magnate Andrew Carnegie. "You seem to be in
prosperity. Could you lend an admirer a dollar & a half
to buy a hymn-book with? God will bless you."

Such joking helped to disguise Twain's frustrations over his inability
to interest Carnegie in various financial ventures. In the early years of
their relationship he tried unsuccessfully to persuade Carnegie to invest
in the Paige typesetter. Explaining to the wily businessman the wisdom
of putting money into something besides steel, Twain cited the old advice
about not keeping all your eggs in one basket. "That's a mistake,"
Carnegie shot back. "Put all your eggs into one basket—and watch that
basket."[24]

By 1907, Carnegie's annual income was at least $10 million, yet Twain
knew that getting him to donate even a small amount to the children's
theater might prove difficult. Carnegie thought nothing of turning down
charity requests from even his closest friends when the cause didn't
strike him as sufficiently worthy. But Alice Herts particularly wanted the

chance to show off her actors to the world's richest philanthropist, so Twain did his part by making sure that Carnegie was indeed in the audience when the curtain went up.

On the night of the performance there was an air of excitement that extended far beyond the stage of the Educational Alliance. Twain had assembled a dazzling guest list, and when people in the neighborhood learned of some of the names, a large crowd began to gather outside, hoping to see some of the rich and famous arriving in evening dress at the main entrance. According to the *New York Tribune*, there were so many people on the street that the police had "their hands full in keeping the enthusiastic residents from storming the building." Besides the white-haired figures of Twain and Carnegie, other important guests attending were Governor Charles Evans Hughes; U.S. senator Chauncey Depew; District Attorney William Jerome; Police Commissioner Theodore Bingham; President Charles Eliot of Harvard; the conductor of the New York Symphony, Walter Damrosch; the nation's most famous war correspondent, Richard Harding Davis; and the financier and longtime patron of the Educational Alliance, Jacob Schiff.

Many of these dignitaries brought their wives, who were bundled in furs and glittering with jewelry. It was a sell-out crowd of seven hundred. In the lobby the guests paraded past a line of young footmen, and backstage the children told each other they were going to perform before an audience of kings and queens. On the street, the ten-cent tickets to the play went for as much as twenty dollars. Twain was so busy mixing with his guests that one observer said he "seemed to be everywhere at once."[25]

Paine attended and recalled the event as "a gala night." He was astonished by the quality of the performance, later remarking of the young actors, "So fully did they enter into the spirit of Tom Canty's rise to royalty that they seemed absolutely to forget that they were lowly-born children of the ghetto. They had become little princesses and lords and maids-in-waiting, and they moved through their pretty tinsel parts as if all their ornaments were gems and their raiment cloth of gold." A newspaper critic also liked the performance, praising it for upholding "the best standards of amateur acting," and for achieving in the stage management "a deftness that was professional."[26]

Twain was so pleased with the occasion that when he rose to make a brief speech, he looked out on the crowd and noted proudly that "as ambassador of the children" he had managed to give them an audience that represented "the hearts and the brains of New York." He urged everyone present to support not only Alice Herts's work but also the grander project of establishing a children's theater "in every public school in the land." As he explained in an interview the next day, the benefits of such an organization were not limited to the children, but extended throughout their communities. "They rehearse their parts in the homes, and the plays become known to every one of the immediate family and acquaintances. So you see, this education is an education for all the people of the East Side."[27]

If the children and their teacher were expecting that Carnegie would shower riches on them as a reward for their performance, they were mistaken. Though he had given small grants to the Educational Alliance in the past, he decided not to become a patron of the children's theater. That job was taken up by a much less famous man who was also one of Twain's invited guests and a close friend. Impressed by the talent and high spirits of the young actors, the publisher Robert Collier agreed not only to fund the acting company but to help pay for the construction of a larger theater with classrooms included. Meanwhile, he offered his own house as a quiet place for occasional meetings and rehearsals. When Twain— who accepted the title of honorary president of the organization—shared the news of Collier's generous offer to the children, they burst into a "joyous" dance and began chanting, "Oh, we're to have the new theater."[28]

It didn't surprise Twain that the old steel baron failed to back the project. He knew very well that Carnegie preferred giving money to libraries rather than playhouses, and that a mere children's theater was not likely to look as imposing as a new library with the Carnegie name attached to it. The self-importance of the man both amused and annoyed Twain. Two weeks after going to all the trouble of getting Carnegie to attend the special performance at the Educational Alliance, a frustrated Twain used one of his autobiographical dictations to say what he really thought of the rich man's celebrated acts of philanthropy. "The world thanks Mr. Carnegie for his libraries," he growled, "and is glad to see him spend his millions in that useful way, but it is not deceived as to the motive." For Twain, the motive was obvious—pure vanity. "He has bought fame and paid cash for it; he has deliberately projected and planned out this fame for himself; he has arranged that his name shall be in the mouths of men for centuries to come."

After years of suppressing his irritation with Carnegie's highly selective generosity and overblown pride, he seized the occasion of this dictation to launch a wholesale attack on everything he didn't like about the man, including his diminutive frame. "In truth Mr. Carnegie is no smaller than was Napoleon; he is no smaller than were several other men supremely renowned in history but for some reason or other he looks smaller than he really is. He looks incredibly small, almost unthinkably small."

Twain's acid tone is unmistakable here and suggests that he was thinking of moral as well as physical stature. No doubt one reason the business titan was looking smaller to him now was that, despite all the great man's millions, he had refused to support a group of poor but talented children who had tried their utmost to impress him. In contrast, Robert Collier—a busy publisher in his early thirties whose fortune was dwarfed by Carnegie's—had risen to the challenge. And, what is more, Collier kept quiet about it.[29]

Unfortunately, despite Twain's best efforts, the children's theater failed. In the end the job simply proved too much for young Alice Herts. She was overworked, and her nerves seemed to have been strained by the anxiety of preparing her company for their big performance in November. Disputes arose between her and some of the older boys and girls, especially after she dismissed one of her assistants—the actress Emma Sheridan Fry, a favorite among the children. Her health quickly declined, and in early 1909 she decided that she could no longer continue running the theater. As she would later explain, "I was taken gravely ill, suffering from a breakdown from overwork, and was obliged to submit to an enforced rest."

Without her at the helm, there was no one who could keep the company going, and it had to be disbanded before its new home could be built. To the keen disappointment of the young players, the company was never revived. Expressing a sentiment that Twain also must have felt, Paine remarked in his biography, "It seems a pity that such a project as that must fail. The Children's Theater exists today only as history."[30]

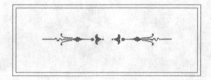

EXTRACT FROM
CAPTAIN STORMFIELD'S
VISIT TO HEAVEN

"His literature grew less and less and his life more and more,"
William Dean Howells wrote of Twain's final years. One of the few
books Twain published in this period is an enchanting story he
had been working on for almost forty years—the afterlife
adventures of a crusty old sea captain trying to make his peace
with eternity. Among other things, Captain Stormfield doesn't
care much for his wings and halo "size 13," and tries to hide them
in a cupboard.

TEN

To Heaven and Back

Try it once, and see how heavy time
will hang on your hands.
Mark Twain on eternal life[1]

· · ·

IT WAS A MATTER OF PRIDE with Andrew Carnegie that he no longer had to work for his money. It had been his ambition to become a great ironmaster, and after he had built up the world's largest steel company, he decided to sell it and spend the rest of his life distributing the riches as he thought best. "Never to make another dollar was my resolve & I've kept it," he boasted. Preaching this gospel was easy when you had a vault full of gold bonds. But it wasn't a message that Twain could take to heart.[2]

Though he and Carnegie were the same age—both men turned seventy-two in the last week of November 1907—Twain knew only too well that a complete retirement from the literary business was impossible. He still worried about his earning power, not only because he was so bad at managing the money he had, but also because it was impossible to make an accurate assessment of his worth. After all, the source of his greatest wealth lay in literary property that would soon begin falling into the public domain unless Congress changed the copyright law. His demands for reform were partly fueled by the knowledge that stocks and bonds were so poorly regulated while copyright was limited to a period that could easily expire before the author did.

He was keenly aware that time was running out for such early works as *The Innocents Abroad* and *Roughing It*. With "a touch of regret," he told a reporter that his first books would begin to "fall" quickly after 1911, "for they will reach their 42d year." The new copyright legislation that he had promoted on his visit to Washington in 1906 was still working its way through Congress, but if it became bogged down and seemed likely to die, he had a backup plan. It involved using large portions of his autobiographical dictations as inserts in future editions of his books. By adding enough fresh material to old works, he believed that they might earn new copyrights. It was a clever but awkward scheme. "On each page," he explained, "a rule will be run about two-thirds of the way down the page, and below these lines will be printed the autobiography."[3]

Because his autobiography was so important to his long-term plans, he wasn't inclined to invest his time in any other major work. At his age, he didn't understand why he should have to write new novels when he had written several that were popular enough to go on making money long after Carnegie's steel plants had crumbled to dust.

Though he was proud of his art, he was also proud of his career as a literary entrepreneur and couldn't help being fiercely protective of his creations. His friend Kipling, who knew how passionately Twain felt on this issue, wrote sympathetically of his position: "What I saw with the greatest clearness was Mark Twain being forced to fight for the simple proposition that a man has as much right to the work of his brains (think of the heresy of it!) as to the labour of his hands."[4]

For the time being, there was nothing else Twain could do for his cause but to wait for his friends and supporters in Congress to do the right thing. Meanwhile, aside from working on the autobiography, he was generally content to confine his literary efforts to tinkering with some of his old unpublished manuscripts, revising here and there or making small additions. One of the oldest was "Captain Stormfield's Visit to Heaven," a story about the afterlife adventures of a fearless sea captain. For almost forty years he had been trying to finish it, having begun it around 1868. Once or twice a decade he would pull out "that rusty old manuscript," work on it a little, and then put it away again. It began life as a simple burlesque of a conventional heaven ("a mean little ten-cent heaven about the size of Rhode Island"), but grew more serious as the years went by. The main setting also expanded considerably. "I built a properly and rationally stupendous heaven," Twain boasted.[5]

He was tempted to abandon the story as unpublishable, but could never bring himself to throw it away. "I have overhauled my literary stock and transferred some of it to the fire," he said in 1906, "but 'Stormfield's Visit' always escaped."[6]

Perhaps what kept his interest in the story alive for so long was an awareness that the title character had the potential to become one of his more memorable creations. Even in the incomplete tale, Stormfield emerges as a compelling, epic figure, making his entrance in grand fashion—speeding toward heaven in a ghostly stream of light and picking up friends along the way, who include a Jewish father weeping for his lost daughter, a wayward Presbyterian who died a suicide, and a former slave. His old skills as a seafarer seem to help him sail through the galaxies faster than everyone else, and he soon leaves his friends behind, moving so swiftly that he races against comets for fun and beats all of them except a giant one headed to hell with a load of brimstone.

Captain Stormfield is heroic as well as funny, assessing the merits of heaven with the keen eye of a seasoned mariner who isn't easily intimidated by all its power and glory. He is pleasantly surprised that he didn't go to the other place. "I judged I was going to fetch up in pretty warm quarters when I got through," he says of his flight across the universe before it drops him at the foot of the pearly gates. After he gets his wings and a halo "size 13," he finds that he doesn't care much for them, and says so, complaining that they weigh him down. He soon quits wearing them. "I've tucked mine away in the cupboard," he explains when another angel asks about his wings.[7]

Though in 1907 Twain was still searching for a proper conclusion to his hero's adventures, he was able at least to reap some profit from the manuscript when he sold two chapters to *Harper's Monthly*. Initially, his publisher George Harvey was reluctant to bring out a story about heaven in "a secular paper like the Magazine." He thought the story was "too damn godly" and returned the manuscript to Twain, who made light of his disappointment. "Mr. Clemens is crying," Isabel Lyon told Harvey, "but he's going to bear it for your sake & the magazine's."

For a while Twain was content to have the whole story stand as a section of his autobiography and to let some future editor figure out how to adapt it for publication. He even dictated a brief explanation of its genesis, recalling that he was inspired to write it after getting to know a heavily tattooed, Bible-quoting, bewhiskered old sea captain named Ned Wakeman, whose ship had carried Twain from San Francisco to Central America in 1866.[8]

At the outset of that voyage Wakeman had demonstrated his incomparable seamanship by safely steering the vessel through a storm so rough that many on board thought they wouldn't survive the passage. Afterward Twain wrote that he was delighted to be traveling with Wakeman at the helm, describing him as a "portly, hearty, jolly, boisterous, good-natured old sailor." He liked the fact that the captain was quick not only to take action but also to speak his mind. They had many talks during the voyage, and Twain came away with great respect for a man who lived large and feared little. In some ways they were alike. What he later said of Wakeman could also apply to him: "He was a lovable man when people pleased him, but a tough person to deal with when the case was otherwise."[9]

In the captain's tall tales and extravagant personality, Twain could see the potential for a literary gold mine. In *Roughing It* he used a little of that gold to create a brief chapter featuring "Ned Blakely," a sea captain who dispenses quick justice to a white bully suspected of killing a black sailor. With a Bible in one hand and a rope in the other, Captain Ned performs the execution himself after urging the culprit to repent: "Lad, you are about to go aloft and give an account of yourself, and the lighter a man's manifest is, as far as sin's concerned, the better for him. Make a clean breast, man, and carry a log with you that'll bear inspection."[10]

The idea of sending such a character to inspect heaven was irresistible, especially since it originated with the character himself. During a long conversation with Twain in 1868, Wakeman revealed that he had already been to heaven. A firm believer in miracles, he was convinced he had been given not just a vision of the next world, but an actual tour of it. Amused, Twain listened "attentively" to the tale and took notes. Over the years, as the author struggled to create a publishable version of the story, Wakeman's language and other rough edges were softened. As a result, the character of Captain Stormfield emerged as more righteous than profane, and therefore less complex than the original. The problem of finishing the story seems to have been complicated by the difficulty of balancing the comic aspects of Stormfield's celestial tour with Twain's more serious efforts to question traditional Christian thinking.

Though the criticism of religion in the chapters submitted to George Harvey is relatively tame, there are several moments of sharp satire. The hierarchy of angels and saints is said to resemble the structure of a tyrannical regime: "This is Russia—only more so." The concept of eternal rest is ridiculed with the remark "Try it once, and see how heavy time will hang on your hands." And when Stormfield mistakenly lands in a part of heaven reserved for souls from other planets, his fumbling effort to explain the importance of Earth makes both his planet and Christianity look unimpressive: "I'm from the world. . . . You may know it from this— it's the one the Saviour saved." (As the captain later learns, Earth appears on heaven's maps as an insignificant speck called the Wart.)[11]

According to Isabel Lyon, one aspect of the story that especially fascinated Twain was the challenge of plotting a course for Stormfield's long flight to heaven: "He dipped again into astronomy (always a beloved subject with him) when he was revising the old ms. 'Captain Stormfield's Visit to Heaven' which carried the captain through the regions of the stars; for he wanted to be reasonably sure of his route." But because the story is essentially a tale of time travel, looking into the next world caused Twain much more trouble than did the process of looking backward in *A Connecticut Yankee in King Arthur's Court*. Though old tales of Camelot offered a long list of specific things to parody, heaven presented a more elusive target, and Twain struggled to bring it into focus. He didn't give up, however, revising the story yet again in 1909, when he agreed to publish a version of the still disorganized and unfinished manuscript as a small book.[12]

A preview of the work was made possible at the end of 1907 when, on reflection, Harvey reversed himself and published a small part of it. He must have decided that the "godly" aspects of the tale made it suitable at least for the Christmas issue of *Harper's Monthly,* where the first of two installments appeared under the title "Extract from Captain Stormfield's Visit to Heaven." Its publication was low-key, with no illustrations to accompany it in an issue otherwise replete with them. But it received a generally favorable response from readers, who liked its gentle humor. "If there were any readers who found it blasphemous, or even irreverent," Paine noted, "they did not say so." Discussing the story with his biographer, Twain confessed that his feelings about the hereafter were mixed. On the one hand, he was so attached to the logic of this world that it seemed ridiculous to accept the "childish notion" of an afterlife. "And yet," he told Paine, "I am strongly inclined to expect one."[13]

· · ·

SOME OF TWAIN'S ADMIRERS have expressed regret that he didn't allow himself to address controversial subjects more forcefully in works that appeared during his lifetime. In 1902 a young Danish admirer sent Twain a letter praising the sharp satire on small-town greed, arrogance, and complacency in the long story "The Man That Corrupted Hadleyburg." But he asked why the author had not written more works like it. Twain replied that he had always wanted to express himself more freely, but that he had erected long ago "a wall across my Nile . . . damming my feelings and opinions behind it, and trying to caulk the leaks." Still, leaks sometimes broke out, he explained, and "The Man That Corrupted Hadleyburg" was the result of one of them. He claimed that the reason for damming his Nile was simple: "I have put this restraint upon myself and kept it there all these years to keep from breaking my wife's heart."[14]

Protecting Livy's soft heart may have been one reason, but it wasn't the only one. She didn't tame the wild Westerner. He tamed himself and—fortunately—he didn't do a very good job of it. After all, there were a lot of "leaks" in his career, and the one that produced the blistering portrait of American society in *Huckleberry Finn* was more like a deluge, giving that book a seething undercurrent of rage. It is still true, however, that his preference throughout his career was to take the measure of that turbid undercurrent while riding comfortably in the mainstream.

He was especially proud of "The Man That Corrupted Hadleyburg"—which was written in 1898 and first published in 1899—because it was almost twenty thousand words of Mark Twain on the loose, jeering in free flow at a community pretending to be "honest and upright" but full of corruption at the core. Not long after reading his Danish admirer's praise for the work, he told Isabel Lyon that "he was so glad he had lived long enough to be able, & fearless enough, to write just what he knew to be true: that 'every man has his price,' and that Hadleyburg had given him his chance to show it up, and [that] Harpers were willing to publish it."[15]

Though Lyon believed that part of her work as Twain's secretary was "to protect him from himself"—trying to prevent "the indiscretions that Mrs. Clemens was always warning him away from"—she couldn't help wondering in her own old age, long after his death, "Where would the great exuberance of him have taken him, had it not been throttled—or directed? Would it have burned out? Suddenly? Leaving only a smoldering heap of ash which might perhaps be lighted again to burn dimly for a short time only?"[16]

She didn't have an answer. Her questions suggest a strong suspicion that had he escaped the confines of polite society and moved perhaps to a bohemian neighborhood in Paris—scorning the genteel comforts of Hartford or Fifth Avenue—he would have written even more powerful works than "Hadleyburg." But her tone also seems to suggest another question—"At what price?" As she well knew, he was a social creature, not a loner. In some sort of bohemian solitude he might have ended his days as a bitter crank, stewing in vitriol and losing touch with both his comic self and his own humanity. In that event, of course, he wouldn't have been Mark Twain any longer, but somebody else who didn't laugh so easily and didn't wear white.

In one of his last comments on the pen name he chose for himself, he emphasized its meaning as a safe point, the very mention of which in his river days used to fill him with relief after navigating in murky shallows. Recalling in 1909 the long-ago time when he piloted steamboats, he spoke of the fear that would grip him on occasions when the current was less than twelve feet deep. Vividly, he described the "deck-hands who used to heave the lead for me and send up on the still night air the 'six—feet—scant!' that made me shudder, and the 'M-a-r-k—*twain!*' that took the shudder away."[17]

He didn't see himself as an outcast, but as a dissenting insider with a wide subversive streak. As he discovered in his boyhood, it was fun to run away and revel in the sweet joy of freedom, but much more interesting to live in town and see how many rules you could break without getting caught.

. . .

REACHING ABOUT FIFTEEN thousand words in length, the two installments of "Captain Stormfield" in *Harper's Monthly* earned Twain almost $5,000, which helped to ease his financial worries while he waited for the Knickerbocker Trust to restore his savings. When it became clear that he wouldn't suffer any significant loss from the crisis, he used the magazine money to pay for a music room at his new house. Isabel Lyon instructed the builder to add it on the second floor of the corner loggia, whose high arches were designed to frame broad views of the countryside. A proper Italian villa—even one in Connecticut—isn't complete without a loggia, and the one John Mead Howells created was inspired by an example from a Medici home near Florence. It was one of the best parts of the new house, and by adding a spacious music room above it, Twain was clearly making an effort to please Clara, who couldn't seem to decide whether she wanted to live with her father or in a place of her own.

After spending most of the summer apart from him, Clara had finally returned to 21 Fifth Avenue in the fall, briefly sharing the house with her father before taking off again to do a concert tour in New England. One reason that she came back to New York was to perform at a small theater in her father's neighborhood. On a Saturday night in early November she sang for a friendly audience at the Young Women's Christian Association, then located at 7 East Fifteenth Street, only a few blocks from Twain's house. Interestingly, she performed a number that must have been dear to her father's heart, Joan of Arc's aria "Adieu, forêts" from Tchaikovsky's *The Maid of Orleans*.[18]

In the week before the event, she rehearsed every day at home. Twain was so pleased to have Clara with him again that he made it possible for Jean to come down from Katonah to join them for a day. It had been a whole year since they had all been together in the city, but Jean's condition now seemed so much better—she had suffered no serious attacks in the last seven months—that it was considered safe for her to pay a short visit.

Her homecoming went well, though Jean was now thoroughly fed up with life at the sanitarium. She wanted desperately to get away for good and was begging for a change. "Dr. Peterson insists on my staying here for a while at least," she had written in her diary the month before. "I feel as tho' I could not <u>endure</u> the place another week. It is ghastly." Not unsympathetic to her feelings, Dr. Peterson was considering other options for her care, and her one-day reprieve from the sanitarium was no doubt meant to keep up her spirits until the new place in Redding was finished or another temporary home could be found. For his part, Twain continued to defer to Peterson's judgment, whose success with Jean's case seemed beyond question. "How fortunate it was that fortune put you into his hands," Twain said of the doctor in an October letter to Jean. "He expects this improvement to go right along."[19]

But Jean no longer cared whether staying in Katonah was good for her or not. She just wanted out, and after a year of following orders at the sanitarium, she was ready for a change of any kind. Coming to the old townhouse on Fifth Avenue didn't help to lighten her mood. It only reminded her of how much she missed her freedom and her family, especially when she listened to her sister rehearse. After she was back in Katonah, she wrote admiringly of Clara's talent, "My sister sang for me several songs & one oratorio (in Latin) that she will use in her tour. Her voice was really wonderful."[20]

Though Clara's performance at the YWCA in November was little advertised and was billed as part of a larger charity event, it served a valuable purpose as a trial run for a much more important event. Both Jean and Twain seem to have been unaware of how much was at stake in Clara's rehearsals for her upcoming tour. After singing in so many small places, she was finally ready to take a great leap and face the largest and most sophisticated audience of her career. This momentous event was scheduled for the end of the month, when she was booked to appear before at least a thousand people at Chickering Hall in Boston's Back Bay.

On the night of the concert—Tuesday, November 26—all her hard work paid off. Accompanied by pianist Charles Wark and the young Boston violinist Marie Nichols, she gave the best performance of her career. She was composed and confident, and earned warm praise from the local press. The *Boston Globe* called her singing "delightful," and the *Transcript* declared, "Clara Clemens's voice may without exaggeration be termed unusually beautiful and individual." The *Globe* didn't even bother to add that she was Mark Twain's daughter. For once she had the spotlight in a big city entirely to herself, and she made the most of it, delighting the audience not only with her voice but also with her appearance.

Instead of wearing the kind of demure gown most people expected to see at such events, she took the stage in an outfit almost as striking as one of her father's white suits—a Grecian-styled dress "of brocaded Japanese silk with inserts of lace on the bodice and flowing sleeves." Her charm and beauty entranced many in the audience, including one reporter who remarked, "The personality of Miss Clemens became a potent factor in her performance. There is the evident impression of a personal spell."[21]

This was the effect she had been striving for, and the triumph reinforced her desire to advance her career to the highest levels of professional music. Almost immediately she started planning a spring tour of the South and a round of summer concerts in Europe. As part of the promotional campaign for these tours, the claim was soon advanced that her success in Boston was "decisive" evidence of her popularity in "Eastern cities." Of course, this was a considerable overstatement, but having proven to herself that she could impress an audience in a cultural bastion like Boston, she was eager to test her talent in other large cities and to aim for the day when she could make her name in New York. Suddenly, that day seemed to be approaching faster than anyone had expected.

Meanwhile, her father tried to accustom himself to her long absences, and to refrain from interfering in her career. And he continued paying most of her bills despite a growing awareness—partly fueled by Isabel Lyon's worries—that Clara was spending money too freely. Whatever his daughter's faults, he couldn't help but admire her perseverance, though his pride in her accomplishments was always tinged with a little envy. "In the matter of dethroning me you will find you've got your work cut out for you, my dearest," he had written her in September, giving his usual teasing a defiant tone.[22]

During the various short periods when Clara and her father happened to be together at the Fifth Avenue house in late 1907 and early 1908, she tended to behave more like a guest than an integral part of the family. She seems to have finally accepted that it was useless to make him abide by her rules for domestic life, and that she could never manage his household. With her career absorbing more of her energy and attention, she now had the perfect excuse to drop in and out of his life at will.

It also left her no choice but to continue letting Isabel Lyon control all the day-to-day demands of family affairs. Though her father would always miss her when she was away, and would always welcome her warmly when she returned, it became clear now that she was enjoying a full life of her own and wasn't likely to be a regular presence at his side again.

As Christmas approached, Jean received the good news from Dr. Peterson that she was hoping for—his permission to leave Katonah. His plan was to send her to a cottage in Greenwich, Connecticut, where she would live with another one of the doctor's female patients, Mildred Cowles, and Mildred's sister Edith. As a companion and nurse for Jean, Peterson hired a young Frenchwoman, Marguerite Schmitt. It was a risky arrangement because the doctor knew that a sanitarium was the safest place for Jean, and he still felt that she should remain in one. It was also obvious that she couldn't bear to remain where she was, and that she had made her wishes very clear to her father.

But if Peterson found it acceptable to move her to Greenwich, why not to 21 Fifth Avenue? Though Jean preferred a small town or a country setting, surely she would have been better off living in the short term at her father's townhouse with his various servants than in a Greenwich cottage with strangers. The answer is that Isabel Lyon had led Peterson to believe that neither she nor Twain were prepared to care for Jean at home. Presumably, she gave old age as Twain's excuse. Hers was that, as a delicate woman of small stature, she was ill-equipped to control a much younger woman whose epileptic seizures left her fearing for her own safety.

Writing in her journal at the beginning of October after a visit to Peterson, Lyon had declared decisively, "Jean must never live with her father again, because her affection might easily turn into a violent and insane hatred and she could slay, just by the sudden and terrible and ungovernable revulsion of feeling." Dreading the possibility of having to supervise Jean at home, Lyon had now convinced herself that the young woman was not merely subject to violent outbursts but was downright homicidal. She even came to believe that Peterson shared her view.

But with the exception of Lyon's words, there is no evidence that Peterson accepted that Jean's disease made her dangerous to others. At Katonah, his favorite therapy for Jean involved intense work in the crafts shop, where her most recent project was an intricate carved figure of herself playing tennis. If Peterson had really shared Lyon's prejudice, it would have been dangerous therapy indeed to leave Jean in possession of sharp carving tools and mallets for hours at a time.[23]

Twain didn't have any idea that Lyon was so afraid of his daughter — nor that she was firmly set against Jean's return under any circumstances. She tended to tell him only what she thought he wanted to hear. But by confiding her fears to Dr. Peterson, she was making it almost impossible for Jean to return. As long as Lyon was in charge of Twain's household, the doctor had little reason to feel confident of Jean's care at home, and every reason to believe that both father and daughter would be better off living apart.

As for the patient herself, she wasn't inclined to question the reasons for her move to Greenwich. She was simply grateful for the change. After she received the good news from home on Christmas Day, she wrote Nancy Brush, "My joy is indescribable."[24]

(*Left*): Evelyn Nesbit's name was made infamous by the scandalous tales that emerged from her husband's two trials for the so-called Crime of the Century. (*Right*): After spending an hour discussing sexual freedom with the outspoken novelist Elinor Glyn—who later coined the phrase "the It girl"—Twain observed, "It was one of the damnedest conversations I have ever had with a beautiful stranger of her sex, if I do say it myself that shouldn't."

ELEVEN

Manhattan Melodrama

I, like all the other human beings, expose to
the world only my trimmed and perfumed and carefully
barbered public opinions and conceal
carefully, cautiously, wisely, my private ones.

Mark Twain[1]

. . .

WITH ALL THE GOOD MATERIAL he was collecting on his subject, Albert Bigelow Paine was growing increasingly confident that he could produce the kind of epic biography Twain was expecting. The only major problem so far was that he was having to spend a lot of his own money on the research for the book. Though Twain was generous whenever they were together, the biographer was expected to pay his own way to such places as Elmira, Hannibal, Hartford, and other far-flung locations. With a family to support and a modest income, he needed to keep his expenses low until he could finish the book and begin earning royalties. It helped that he was good at economizing. When he went up to Hartford for a few weeks to do interviews and collect documents, he enlisted the help of kindly Reverend Joseph Twichell, asking him to find a respectable board-inghouse where he could stay at a reasonable price. He was happy to have the Reverend's recommendation of an establishment run by a Miss Ryan, who offered room and board for as little as nine dollars a week.[2]

But Paine was such a hard worker that he didn't mind taking on extra work to keep his finances in order. Even by his demanding standards, however, the additional job he accepted in 1908 was almost too much, and would surely have overwhelmed many others in his position. Early in the new year he was contacted by a wealthy Texan looking for an established writer who could tell the story of the state's most famous lawman, a fifty-six-year-old captain of the Texas Rangers named Bill McDonald. Grizzled and lean, with a commanding voice and steely gaze, McDonald had made his name in the 1890s by almost single-handedly bringing order to the wild region of the Panhandle, where he and a dozen subordinates were responsible for enforcing the law in an area the size of West Virginia.

Captain Bill arrested so many cattle rustlers and train robbers that a gang formed with the sole purpose of killing him. When three of the gang confronted him on the street in his hometown, he held them off in a bloody gunfight, killing the leader and scattering the others despite suffering wounds to his arms and shoulder that forced him to cock his gun with his teeth before he could return fire.

Besides his courage and his talent with a six-shooter, McDonald was also celebrated for his extraordinary ability to put down riots and disperse lynch mobs. The story was often told of the day he received a dispatch from Dallas asking him to bring his company of Texas Rangers to the city to stop a riot. When he arrived alone at the train station, the nervous mayor asked, "Where are the others?" To which Captain Bill replied, "Hell! Ain't I enough? There's only one riot."[3]

One of McDonald's old friends was Colonel Edward House, an influential political figure in Texas who would later become important in national politics as President Woodrow Wilson's closest adviser. It was House who contacted Paine with the suggestion that he write the legendary lawman's biography. As House later admitted, Paine wasn't his first choice. Initially, he invited William Sidney Porter—otherwise known as O. Henry—to do the book as a collection of twelve stories, "each representing some incident in Bill's life." But in a twist worthy of a tale by

O. Henry, House's letter went astray and didn't reach its recipient for weeks, by which time Paine had been contacted and had accepted the job. When the letter finally came to Porter, he gave an enthusiastic response, saying he would do it as "a labor of love," but he was too late, and House had no choice but to turn him down.[4]

Incredibly, Paine was able to continue working on his biography of Twain while also writing 100,000 words on McDonald. In less than a year he would manage to finish the entire job, submitting his completed manuscript to the publisher at the end of 1908 after interviewing Captain Bill at length and researching a great many old newspaper articles and official documents. For Paine, this exciting tale of Western adventure was so good that he couldn't pass up the chance to tell it. And he could easily justify the project as both a potential moneymaker and good practice for creating the more complex narrative of Twain's life.

He was thrilled when the chance soon arose to introduce his two subjects to each other. Not long after agreeing to do the book, he was able to coax McDonald into coming to New York to be interviewed. The old lawman showed up at the New Amsterdam Hotel in his cowboy boots and Stetson, a six-shooter under one side of his coat and an automatic pistol under the other. "I explained to Paine," House recalled, "that Bill had to carry his artillery in this way to be thoroughly ballasted—that he would have difficulty in walking without it."[5]

Predictably, Captain Bill didn't feel comfortable in crowded Manhattan after all his years of roaming the empty Panhandle. Automobiles in particular seemed to put him on edge. As he was being driven around the city, he growled to the driver, "Look here, you'll get me killed, yet, in a place like this. I don't know the game." He cheered up after a visit to Coney Island, where he happened to witness a street brawl and was able to break it up and send the dazed thugs home with a warning to behave themselves.

Before he could get away from New York, he accepted an invitation to dine at 21 Fifth Avenue. Twain was curious to take the measure of the man whose life was temporarily commanding the attention of their shared biographer. It wasn't easy to predict how they would react to each other. For one thing, McDonald wasn't much of a conversationalist, having always preferred action to words. He also wasn't the easiest man to entertain because he had no interest in cigars or alcohol—indeed, he avoided stimulants of any kind, including tea and coffee.

Impressed by Captain Bill's self-discipline, Paine had asked why he followed such a strict regimen. "Well, you see," came the reply, "sometimes I have to be about two-fifths of a second quicker than the other fellow, and a little quiver, then, might be fatal."[6]

Though the dinner at No. 21 went well, there was a little tension between the host and his special guest at the beginning of the evening. Twain seems to have felt that he had something to prove to the lawman, as though their status as legendary figures from the West made them rivals. At least that was the impression created in the mind of Colonel House, who accompanied Paine and McDonald to the dinner. In his memoirs he recalled being treated to the spectacle of Twain trying to outrun Captain Bill on the stairs leading up to the billiards room: "Clemens ran and Bill ran after, as if to catch him, but did not do so. Bill winked at me and said, 'I believe the old man really thinks I could not catch him.' "

At the billiards table, however, Twain had the last laugh. It seems that McDonald's long experience with firearms was a bad influence on the way he handled a cue. "It was amusing," House remembered, "to see Bill sight his cue as if it were a rifle and, three times out of four, send his ball off the table. It entertained Mr. Clemens immensely."[7]

For Paine, having two such colorful characters as subjects was an embarrassment of biographical riches. Since he had the exclusive right to tell each man's story, he didn't need to worry about competition. Given all his advantages, it seemed he couldn't fail with either project. Yet there was trouble ahead. The very fact that he was doing so well in his work and was on such good terms with his subjects was enough to stir up jealousy in the mind of the one person who was spending more time in Twain's company than anyone else—Isabel Lyon.

· · ·

THE NEW YEAR started off badly for Twain's secretary. She came down with the flu and remained in bed for a couple of days at the very beginning of the month. Clara was at home and spent some time at Lyon's bedside, trying to comfort her. But Twain didn't seem to take her illness seriously, and she was hurt when he failed to give her the sympathy she was expecting. It upset her to think that, after all their time together, her well-being meant less to him than his did to her. Though she was constantly fussing over him, he usually showed only a slight interest in her personal affairs.

But such was her devotion to him that she could usually hide her moments of disappointment and bring herself to forgive any perceived slight. Writing in her journal, she complained that he had been rude to her while she was ill, then quickly shrugged it off with the words, "But I do not <u>really</u> care. He had many things on his mind to exasperate him."[8]

In a few days, her flu was gone, and she felt so much better that she had only good things to say about life at No. 21. Grateful for the attention Twain's daughter had shown her, she was overflowing with praise for "dear Santa" (Clara). After listening one afternoon to her perform in the parlor for a small group of friends, Lyon wrote of the experience as though she had been entertained by a goddess, remarking of Clara, "The very air must love to caress her as she passes through it."

Caught up in this rhapsodic mood, she didn't even mind that the enchanted air of the performance carried not only Clara's sweet tones but also the faint sound of billiard balls clicking. "The King," Lyon noted, "didn't come down until the music was over, for he doesn't like a drawing room performance." Now that she was feeling better, she returned to her old habit of uncritical worship. The King could do no wrong, and she was as full of compliments for him as for Clara, calling him "the lovablest creature."[9]

In a few days, however, Twain became the next member of the household to fall ill. He came down with a bad head cold, but tried to pretend it would soon go away. When it didn't, he turned to an old-fashioned remedy—liberal doses of strong whiskey. One night he stayed up late with a quart of Scotch at his side while he played cards with Lyon and Ralph Ashcroft. He didn't go to bed until three in the morning, by which time the cards were scattered over the floor, the quart was empty, and he and his two companions were thoroughly drunk.

The next day—Friday, January 17—he decided that the alcohol was doing its job because he was feeling a little better. To finish the cure, he stayed up late again and drank some more. Lyon couldn't keep up with him this time and went to bed early, leaving him at the billiards table with Paine, who had come from Redding to have dinner at the house and was spending the night. Around two in the morning Lyon got up to check on Twain and found him in bad shape. He was still at the table with his cue in hand, but his cold had returned, and he was "reeling" from the effects of being both congested and intoxicated. She tried to persuade him to get some sleep, and when he refused, she took a seat and said she wouldn't leave until he agreed to go to bed.

At first, Paine stood by in silence. Always an obliging companion to Twain, he seems to have made a valiant effort to help him finish off the new bottle of whiskey. As a result, when Lyon wouldn't leave the room, the usually polite and unassuming biographer did something under the influence of alcohol that he would never have done otherwise. He lashed out at her, ordering her "to clear out." When she held her ground, he didn't know how to respond and left the room in anger. Only then was she able to talk Twain into surrendering his cue and going to bed.[10]

"Mark Twain Sick," a newspaper headline said two days later, "Under Care of Physician at Home." After trying so hard to avoid admitting that he was ill, Twain finally was forced to accept defeat and send for his doctor, Edward Quintard, who prescribed the usual cold remedies of the day, including a mustard bath. Lyon took charge of his daily care, making sure that he stayed in bed, and supplying him with hot food and healthier liquids than whiskey.[11]

His convalescence lasted more than a week, and he wasn't an easy patient. One day a concerned neighbor sent over a dish of extra large oysters from a nearby restaurant, thinking it would make a good meal for him. In the evening a servant took it to his room, but when Lyon came by a little later to check on him, he had already sent the dish back. Didn't he like the oysters? she asked. "No," he answered, "they looked and tasted like a fetus."

One day it snowed, and he felt well enough to go downstairs and sit at the window where he could watch the flakes drift to the street. Worried that too much cold air was coming through the "leaky loose" window, Lyon made sure that he didn't sit too close to it, then wrapped a green afghan over his shoulders. As darkness came and the snow continued to fall, she sat at the orchestrelle and played sad music until he grew sleepy and "gently" went up to bed.[12]

Lyon knew how to calm Twain, but she also knew how to stir him up. While he was feeling weak and out of sorts during his convalescence, she suddenly planted the suspicion in his mind that someone close to him might be taking advantage of his trust. The person she implicated was the man whose drunken outburst a few nights earlier had deeply offended her pride. Apparently, she wanted to do something that would, at the very least, force Paine to think twice before he tried ordering her around again.

So she suggested to Twain one night that his biographer was taking too many liberties with the collection of manuscripts and letters at the house, making copies without asking permission, and borrowing things and not returning them. Moreover, she stated darkly, he was creating a separate collection of his own by persuading Twain's old friends to hand over their correspondence to him.

Of course, Paine was doing all these things. It was necessary to his research, and he had never made a secret of it. Until now neither his methods nor his honesty had been questioned. From the very beginning he had been allowed to dig into Twain's papers without any restrictions, and had even won Lyon's praise for taking the extra time to organize them. In 1906 she wrote of him, "He is doing the very thing that I longed to have some worshipping creature do with Mr. Clemens's papers. . . . He is bringing the mass into order, reducing the great chaos that I have always longed to be able to touch but have never found time for."[13]

In his early months as Twain's biographer, Paine had earned not only Lyon's admiration but also her trust and affection. For a while she had regarded him in a romantic light, heaping praise on him in her journals as a man of great character and promise. She would take long walks with him, and they would often confide in each other. One day she curled up on a couch and listened raptly as he "walked up and down the room, smoking cigarettes and talking about the King and the Biography." He told her of his great ambitions and revealed some of the details of his humble beginnings. She was fascinated to learn that his current wife was not his first. He explained that he had been married once before in Kansas when he was very young. The marriage began "in romance," he told her, but had soon ended in the "tragedy" of divorce.[14]

Over time, as it became clear to Lyon that her friendship with Paine wasn't going to develop into something more serious, she settled into an uneasy professional relationship with him, regarding herself as his equal in their service to Twain. But so different were their jobs and personalities that they soon came to see themselves as rivals, each growing increasingly suspicious of the other. Part of the problem was that Lyon didn't think Paine understood Twain as well as she did. She was convinced that he lacked the kind of passionate nature that was necessary to appreciate the great man's genius. She blamed this deficiency on his Midwestern roots. As she explained many years later, she thought he suffered from "a flat prairie-like vision" that made him incapable of understanding "emotional depths & pinnacles." With evident bitterness, she dismissed his emotions as "thin & fictitious."[15]

On that cold January night when Paine thoughtlessly told Lyon "to clear out," he touched a raw nerve and brought into the open the various tensions between them that had been building for months. After he had gone home to Redding, she seized the chance to teach him a lesson by using her influence with Twain to undermine his work. If her boss had been feeling better, her professed doubts about Paine's trustworthiness might have made little impression on him. But the head cold and the aftereffects of alcohol muddled his thinking and created just enough suspicion to make him worry that his chosen biographer was hoarding papers and hiding the fact from him.

To exert her influence in this matter, Lyon seems to have relied on suggestion rather than accusation. "My anxiety," she wrote at the time, "had projected itself into his mind." But in later years she took a more cynical view of the ease with which Twain's opinions could be manipulated: "Mr. Clemens . . . could always be swayed by the last person coming to build up a prejudice or to break one down."[16]

Whether or not he was easily swayed in this case, Twain wasn't eager to raise the problem directly with his biographer, and allowed Lyon to convey the message that he now wanted more control over his papers. He did, however, dash off a letter on January 22 to Howells, requesting that his friend check with him first before giving any letters to Paine. Noting that he was "sick abed, these days," he didn't hint at any mistrust of Paine, but said that he didn't want to see too much of his private life revealed in a biography that might appear before his death. "A man should be dead," he wrote Howells, "before his private foolishnesses are risked in print."

When this letter reached Howells, he was in Europe and couldn't understand why Twain had sent him such a request. He replied that he had already given some letters to Paine and thought it was the right thing to do. "I saw Paine on such intimate terms with you," he wrote, "that I should not have hesitated to offer him all your letters." Even though Howells didn't know the circumstances that had prompted Twain to write, he felt compelled to put in a good word for the biographer's integrity. He said there was no reason to withhold information from him, declaring forcefully, "I don't think Paine could abuse the confidence put in him."[17]

When Paine himself was told that there were questions about his use of letters and other papers, he was shocked. Then shock gave way to indignation, and he wrote Lyon a powerful letter defending his actions and threatening to abandon the biography if he couldn't command the trust of Twain and his circle.

Given all the time and money he had put into the project, his show of defiance was risky. He told Lyon that she was free to show the letter to both Twain and Clara, but he was probably betting that she wouldn't. His threat to quit seems to have been directed solely at her, whose part in creating the problem must have been readily apparent to him. Essentially, his letter challenged her to back away from a confrontation or accept responsibility for sabotaging the biography.

"If I am to be handicapped by concealments, and opposition, and suspicion of ulterior motives," he wrote her; "if I am to be denied access to the letters written to such men as Howells and Twichell; in a word, if I am to become not the biographer but simply a biographer—one of a dozen groping, half-equipped men, then I would better bend my energies in the direction of easier performance and surer and prompter return."[18]

Such a statement seemed to demand an immediate answer. But Paine's future as the biographer would take some time to resolve. Though tempers soon cooled and peace was restored on the surface, Lyon's relationship with him suffered permanent damage. As for Twain, as soon as he was his old self again, he was able to smooth over any differences and continue his relationship with Paine as before. He had grown too close to him to do otherwise, and had no evidence of wrongdoing to justify a break in their friendship.

. . .

WHILE STILL RECOVERING in his sickbed, Twain dictated a letter to a beautiful woman he had recently met. She was Elinor Glyn, an English author in her early forties whose racy novel *Three Weeks* was causing a sensation on both sides of the Atlantic. When the American edition appeared in September 1907, it received rough treatment from literary critics, who derided its sentimental romanticism, and from moralists, who condemned its sympathetic treatment of an adulterous affair between an older woman and a younger man. But ordinary readers loved it and made the novel a runaway hit, with sales averaging fifty thousand copies a month during the fall and winter.

As a writer, Elinor Glyn wasn't much better than Marie Corelli. But apart from sales figures and a fondness for purple prose, they had little in common. Whereas Corelli had a talent for making a fool of herself in public, Glyn managed her celebrity status with wit and great confidence. Her own family background was solidly middle-class, but she was so stunningly handsome that she never had any problem gaining entry to the upper levels of English society. Though married and the mother of two children, she didn't care much for domestic life and spent her free time pursuing love affairs with various aristocrats.

When she came to New York in the fall of 1907 for a long visit to promote *Three Weeks*, she brought along several trunks full of clothing and sixty pairs of shoes. Reporters outdid each other trying to come up with adjectives for her physical features. One referred to the "glorious halo of her hair," and another described her in a black gown with a hat that cast "delicate shadows on her white skin, red golden hair and dark eyes." Most observers agreed that the contrast between the rich color of her hair and the fairness of her complexion was the most striking aspect of her appearance, especially when she wore gowns with low necklines that revealed a bosom of "snowy amplitudes," to use one biographer's phrase. In

Three Weeks the heroine, who resembles Glyn, is described as having a complexion as white as "a magnolia bloom."[19]

Twain's first encounter with this remarkable woman was suitably dramatic. It took place at the end of 1907 while he and Isabel Lyon were attending a private dinner hosted by the producer Dan Frohman in the luxurious upstairs ballroom at Delmonico's Restaurant on Fifth Avenue. At the beginning of the event everyone's attention was focused on Frohman's young wife, the popular actress Margaret Illington, who made a grand entrance wearing a new gown that accentuated her statuesque figure. "But, suddenly," Lyon would recall, "she was eclipsed by a woman with milk-white skin, tawny red hair & green eyes; her gown a sea-green soft silk & she wore a strange oriental chain, as her only ornament."[20]

Neither Lyon nor Twain recognized the mysterious beauty, but her arrival created such a stir that the question of her identity was quickly answered when other guests began pointing and whispering, "Elinor Glyn."

Anyone who had seen a newspaper in the last few weeks would have known the name. Though it was Glyn's novel that had made headlines first, the novelist had also become a subject of controversy. Indeed, as Twain later said of her, "She has come to us upon the stormwind of a vast and sudden notoriety." One week she outraged New York literary critics by calling them "idiots." A few weeks later she became involved in a public feud with a women's club called the Pilgrim Mothers. Some of its members had been rude to her at a luncheon, condemning her as a wicked person whose open attitudes toward sex were a threat to marriage and the family. Refusing to accept such treatment, Glyn had gone to the press and entertained them with ridicule of the "preposterous" Pilgrim Mothers, declaring that the group "really reminded me of a lot of sparrows chattering under the eaves."

Shocked by Glyn's unladylike willingness to fight back, one member of the club commented, "I thought she was a high-class Englishwoman — but I didn't know she had claws."[21]

Those claws were fully retracted on the December night that she met Twain at Delmonico's. At the end of the dinner she rushed to his side and sweetly requested a private meeting at a time and place of his choosing. She gave the impression that she had some urgent business to discuss with him, yet he was wary of her intentions and declined her offer, making polite excuses. Not one to give up easily, she wrote him a note pleading to see him, and he reluctantly agreed. One afternoon near the end of the month she arrived at his door and was greeted by Isabel Lyon, who showed her into the parlor and then went upstairs to tell Twain that his visitor was waiting to see him.

When he joined Glyn, they sat down together on a large divan, and Lyon left the room. But the secretary took a last glance on the way out and would always remember what an extraordinary pair they made. "I have a mental picture of them as they sat there," she wrote thirty years later. Twain was "in his usual pure white," and Glyn wore a dress of "brown velvet, with soft sables slipping from her shoulders," and a small hat "banded with the same fur." They looked like actors in costume waiting for the curtain to go up. And both seemed to know from the start that afterward they would create their own versions of what had transpired between them.[22]

Each was impressed with the other's appearance. Glyn liked Twain's "white silky hair" and his "fresh face." Staring into his eyes, she decided that they resembled those of a child who looks "out on life with that infinite air of wisdom one sees peeping sometimes from a young pure soul." A youthful look was also something Twain found in her face and figure, expressing disbelief when he learned that such a "faultlessly formed and incontestably beautiful" woman had a fourteen-year-old daughter.

But he wasn't under any illusions about her character. Ambitious and opportunistic, she had come to enlist his support for her book. He guessed as much from the start, so he wasn't surprised when she admitted it. What drew her to him, she explained, was his reputation as an unconventional thinker who seemed to enjoy exposing hypocrites. Having read his attacks on the sanctimonious Mary Baker Eddy, she considered him just the man to defend her novel against its moralistic critics. Because he was so "very brave," she said, she would be proud to have him as her champion. Such praise from a beautiful woman wasn't easy to resist, yet Twain later insisted that it didn't affect him, admitting only that it might "have beguiled me when I was very very young."

All the same, he must have been beguiled a little, because he stayed on that divan chatting with her for an hour and a half. In fact, he had al-

ready gone to the trouble of buying her novel and reading it from cover
to cover. In their conversation he showed a detailed knowledge of the
story, especially the seduction scene in which the heroine and her young
lover agree to abandon convention and to obey only the laws of nature.
"They get to obeying them at once," Twain later said of Glyn's characters
and their desires, "and they keep on obeying them and obeying them, to
the reader's intense delight and disapproval."

The most controversial scene in the novel featured the heroine
demonstrating her sensual nature to her lover by lying on the floor and
passionately rubbing her body against a tiger skin. It marks the point in
the story at which, as Twain said, "business begins." Many contemporary
readers found the scene shocking not only because it was unashamedly
erotic but also because a woman had dared to write it. In the end, though,
Twain rightly surmised that most readers would feel torn between "delight and disapproval." The lighter side of this conflict found expression
in a memorable verse by an anonymous wit of the period:

Would you like to sin
With Elinor Glyn
On a tiger-skin?
Or would you prefer
To err
With her
On some other fur?[23]

Though Mark Twain and Elinor Glyn only talked about sin, they did
so with remarkable candor. For ordinary men and women of the time, it
was inconceivable that questions of sexual desire, seduction, and adultery could be openly addressed in polite conversation. Yet, as Twain noted
proudly afterward, he discussed these matters with "daring frankness" in
his talk with Glyn, "calling a spade a spade instead of coldly symbolizing
it as a snow shovel." Even so, the experience was more than a little un-
nerving for him at his age: "It was one of the damnedest conversations I
have ever had with a beautiful stranger of her sex, if I do say it myself
that shouldn't."

He told her that he shared her sympathy for the lovers in her novel.

They weren't to blame for following their desires, he said. They were only "obeying the law of their make and disposition," which meant that their Maker was the real one to blame for the trouble. Twain had held such a view for a long time and had discussed it at length in an unpublished portion of his autobiography. "God ingeniously contrived man in such a way," he had said in a dictation two years earlier, "that he could not escape obedience to the laws of his passions. . . . [And is] beset by traps which he cannot possibly avoid, and which compel him to commit what are called sins."[24]

Glyn was thrilled to hear that Twain understood her point of view, and she promptly asked him to declare his support in print. But he refused, explaining that society wasn't ready for an open debate on sexual morality, and that he didn't want to be dragged into such a debate. When she protested that it was his "duty" to speak out, he answered that in such cases his opinions were his own, and that he didn't have a duty to share them with anyone.

Their exchange was friendly, and they parted on good terms. But Glyn didn't want to take no for an answer, so she prepared some notes of their conversation and sent a typed copy to Twain for his approval. It arrived just as he was getting ready to go on one of his quick trips to Bermuda, and though he had many other demands on his time, he read it carefully and gave her his opinion.

"If you had put upon paper what I really said," he wrote on January 24, "it would have wrecked your type-machine. I said some fetid & overvigorous things, but that was because it was a confidential conversation. I said nothing for print. My own report of the same conversation reads like Satan roasting a Sunday school."

In fact, her account wasn't so different from his, but he was trying in a humorous way to impress on her that his words belonged to him and that he didn't want to lend them out for a cause that wasn't his. At the same time, it was obvious that she was determined to make their conversation public, and Twain didn't expressly forbid it. He may even have been secretly hoping that she would. You didn't discuss sex for an hour and a half with Elinor Glyn and expect her to keep quiet about it.

But if she ever did speak out and overstate his case or create too much of an uproar, his letter was fair warning that he wouldn't admit to anything in a report he didn't write. No matter how much merit he may have found in her views, he wasn't in the business of helping her sell books or reforming moral attitudes. "I am not here," he told her, "to do good—at least not to do it intentionally." And with those words, Twain let the matter rest—for the time being.[25]

. . .

As BOTH GLYN AND TWAIN were well aware, January 1908 was a particularly difficult time in New York to take a public stand in favor of greater sexual freedom. It was the month in which the question of guilt in the most notorious sex scandal of the young century was being decided in a Manhattan courtroom. On the last day of the month a jury began deliberating the fate of Pittsburgh millionaire Harry K. Thaw, who was undergoing his second trial for committing what the newspapers called "the Crime of the Century." All the talk of romantic intrigue in *Three Weeks* was nothing compared with the tales of violent passion recounted in Thaw's sensational case.

He was charged with murdering famed architect Stanford White, shooting him on a warm night in June 1906 at the rooftop cabaret of Madison Square Garden (a structure designed by White himself). The crime occurred in full view of the audience while a group on stage performed a musical number called "I Could Love a Million Girls." Without any warning, Thaw approached White's table and fired three times, pointing the pistol so close to the architect's face that he left it blackened by powder burns.

In the first trial Thaw's attorneys argued that their client had become enraged after learning that his new bride—twenty-two-year-old Evelyn Nesbit, a former model and showgirl—had been seduced by White when she was single and still in her teens. They claimed that this past wrong had led Thaw to kill White in a fit of temporary insanity. Though the trial lasted more than two months—allowing the defense ample time to paint a detailed portrait of the wealthy architect as an unfaithful husband and a debauched middle-aged playboy who preyed on young girls—it ended in a hung jury. It wasn't until the beginning of 1908 that officials were able to commence the second trial.

Like most New Yorkers, Twain followed the case in the newspapers, but his knowledge of the facts went far beyond what ordinary people knew. The chief defense attorney in the second trial was Twain's friend Martin Littleton, who lived across the street from him and would often come over in the evening to play billiards or chat. Paine was present on some of those occasions and recalled that Littleton—a garrulous Texan—enjoyed discussing the case with Twain: "It was most interesting to hear from him direct the day's proceedings and his views of the situation and of Thaw."[26]

To save his client from the electric chair, Littleton argued that Thaw's fit of insanity wasn't an anomaly, but was part of a lifelong struggle with mental disease. Despite the fact that Thaw's mother had said in the first trial that there was no history of insanity in the family, Littleton managed to produce a mountain of evidence to the contrary. The defendant, he told the jury, suffered from "a clear case of insanity born in generations before him and still existing." The lawyer's talent for turning a phrase was one of the things that Twain admired about him, and it seems the jury also found his words impressive. The second trial ended with a verdict of not guilty by reason of insanity, and Thaw was sent to a mental institution instead of to a prison cell for life or the electric chair.

Besides defending Thaw, Littleton went out of his way to speak up for Evelyn Nesbit's reputation, which had suffered considerable damage in the first trial. Published accounts of her affair with White were considered so salacious that President Roosevelt had wanted to prohibit them from being sent through the mail. For the rest of her life, Nesbit would be remembered as a rich man's sexual plaything. She was called "The Girl in the Red Velvet Swing," a reference to the fact that White kept a large swing at one of his elaborately equipped love nests and liked to have a nude Evelyn sit in it while he pushed her higher and higher.

But in the closing argument to the jury, Littleton portrayed her as little more than a child when White began taking advantage of her, and he lamented that there was no "guiding hand" to protect her from the predatory designs of the older man. It is tempting to think that he may have rehearsed this argument with Twain earlier, for it reflects a similar view expressed in the author's autobiographical dictations. Twain firmly believed that Nesbit was the victim of a remorseless seducer who used age and experience to exploit her innocence. And he was disgusted by the

Mark Twain's good friend and New York neighbor Martin Littleton (left) served as defense attorney in the second trial of Harry K. Thaw (right), who was accused of shooting architect Stanford White in a jealous rage. White was the former lover of Thaw's wife, Evelyn Nesbit.

fact that the public seemed to derive a voyeuristic thrill from her ordeal. Moreover, he worried that graphic reports from the courtroom might incite more men to prey on vulnerable young women.

In October 1907 he wrote, "Although we do not allow obscene books and pictures to be placed on sale either publicly or privately, or sent through the mails, we exploit our Thaw trials in open court and place the lust-breeding details, per newspaper and mail, under the eyes of 60,000,000 persons, per day, young and old, and do not perceive the curious incongruity of it. A 'wave of crime' quite naturally and of necessity follows, throughout the land, resulting in hundreds and hundreds of atrocities that come to light, and those of thousands that are concealed, out of shame, by the victims and their friends, and do not reach the light."[27]

Oddly enough, if it had not been for his friendship with Littleton, Twain might have been required to be part of the jury selection for Harry

Thaw's second trial. In her journal entry for Saturday, January 4, Isabel Lyon noted that Littleton had visited No. 21 that night and had revealed that the name of Samuel L. Clemens was on the list of prospective jurors ("Mr. L. said that the King's name had been down as a juryman for the Thaw trial"). Thanks to Littleton, the name was removed.

In the Thaw case, Twain was probably the last man in New York who should have been considered for jury duty, and it wasn't simply because of his celebrity or his friendship with the defense attorney. Another factor came into play. As it happened, he and Evelyn Nesbit had a mutual friend. Among the many men who had been attracted to her when she was a young showgirl in New York was Robert Collier.

In a memoir she wrote in the 1930s Nesbit affectionately recalled the attention paid to her by "Bobby" Collier when he was a young man-about-town and she was a fresh-faced beauty in her late teens. Many of the rich men who chased after her were old enough to be her father, but Collier was just eight years her senior, and not only treated her with respect but was so infatuated with her that he asked her to marry him. He wrote her love poems, showered her with gifts, and even offered to send her to art school in Europe, telling her that she was wasting her time in show business.

His offer wasn't an empty gesture. As he demonstrated to Twain in the case of the children's theater, he was a generous man. He was constantly helping his friends, and sometimes the results were remarkable. He changed the life of his college roommate, Condé Nast, by giving him a job at *Collier's Weekly,* where Nast learned so much about the business that he was soon able to strike out on his own and take charge of a struggling periodical called *Vogue.* (Robert Collier also gave Mark Twain's nephew, Samuel Moffett, a well-paying job at his company.)

It isn't clear how close Collier's relationship with Nesbit became, but over dinner one night it reached a decisive point. Looking at her "with absorbed, tender eyes," as Nesbit recalled, he tried to explain how "seriously fond" he was of her. She assumed that he was leading up to a proposal, yet she refused to take it seriously. Already under the spell of Stanford White, she resolved not to encourage Collier. The decision to spurn his effort to make her his wife was something she would regret for the rest of her life.[28]

Handsome, athletic, and fun-loving, Collier was one of the most eligible bachelors in New York. Upton Sinclair—who published some of his research for *The Jungle* in *Collier's Weekly*—described the young publisher as "a picture of health, florid and jolly, a polo-player, what is called a 'good fellow.'" Like Twain, he had a boyish spirit and loved games. He certainly knew how to have a good time and was famous for his elaborate parties with humorous themes.

At one attended by Twain in 1908, he hired a couple of ballrooms, decorated them to look like Spanish palaces, then staged a midnight ballet for his guests in which the dancing was done by several chorus girls, half a dozen trained dogs, and the prima ballerina of the Manhattan Opera House. So many taxis were used to transport the girls and the dogs to the party that the neighbors became alarmed and called the police, who barged in expecting to find "some terrible doings," but who went away laughing at the innocent celebrations. After the ballet, the dogs ("Collies for Collier") roamed free, and one was later seen eating ice cream at the table where Mark Twain and Ethel Barrymore were seated. The festivities lasted late into the night, and the next day Twain reported that he "enjoyed it thoroughly till 4:05 A.M., when I came away with the last of the rioters."[29]

Restless and impulsive, Collier didn't need much time to recover from Evelyn Nesbit's rejection. Not long after his disappointing dinner with her, he threw himself into a whirlwind romance with a twenty-one-year-old Newport heiress—Sarah Van Alen. They wed a few weeks later in a hastily arranged ceremony announced only three days before the event. He continued to keep in touch with Nesbit, however, and would remain her loyal friend long after the Thaw trials ended. Though not many people were aware of Collier's personal interest in Nesbit, it was widely known that he played an important part in promoting her modeling career. After all, it was his magazine that had published her best-known portrait, *The Eternal Question,* a line drawing by Charles Dana Gibson in which her long, luxuriant hair is made to resemble a question mark.[30]

During the Thaw trials it was in the interests of both Collier and Nesbit to keep quiet about their friendship. The prosecuting attorney was keen to prove that doe-eyed Evelyn wasn't as innocent as she looked, and that Thaw didn't deserve the jury's sympathy for trying to defend his wife's honor. The aim was to demonstrate that her honor wasn't worth defending because she had been involved with "dozens of men." According to Nesbit's memoir, detectives worked the sidewalks of Broadway for days trying to dig up details about her past relationships, offering money to showgirls and stage-door Johnnies for incriminating information.[31]

Regardless of whether Collier had been merely an admirer or a lover of Nesbit, his reputation would have suffered if the prosecution had decided to drag his name into the trial and to present him as another rich playboy like White. He was spared that ordeal, but only because Ethel Barrymore's good-looking younger brother gave the prosecution a much better target. In court John Barrymore was revealed to have had a long and passionate relationship with Nesbit. He was portrayed as a lusty young man who was obsessed with the model, but who had been driven out of her life by a jealous Stanford White.

Expecting to be called as a witness, he managed to avoid appearing at the trial by pretending to be ill. At the outset of the proceedings, he had been advised by a friend to "get sick quick" and had retreated to a clinic in Maine, from which he sent word that he wasn't well enough to travel. He said he was "threatened with pneumonia."

Unable to get his hands on the actor, the district attorney asked in frustration, "Who goes to Maine in February to combat pneumonia?"

As soon as the trial ended, Barrymore made a quick recovery, but the newspapers had already printed numerous allegations against him, including the claim that "Mr. Barrymore was a little bit crazy."[32]

It is easy to see why Twain took an interest in the Thaw case. Having Martin Littleton, Robert Collier, and Ethel Barrymore as friends, he was in a good position to know some of the personal histories behind the headlines, and to see how much trouble could be stirred up when a big scandal revealed the enormous discrepancy between what people said in public and what they did in private. How much he knew of Collier's relationship with Nesbit isn't clear, but he may have learned more about the case from the well-versed defense attorney than from anyone else. Throughout the trial Littleton always seemed to be one step ahead of the prosecution, partly because the Thaw family had enough money to employ private detectives to do their own investigation of witnesses.

Even if Twain had been willing to join Elinor Glyn's crusade for sexual candor, it's unlikely that he would have made a good spokesman for it. He liked joking about sex or satirizing the guardians of public morality, but he didn't have much experience explaining the passions and complications of sexual relationships. In his books romantic love is usually a vague sentiment that inspires either mild respect or good-natured mockery. In *A Connecticut Yankee in King Arthur's Court,* Hank Morgan's relationship in Camelot with young Sandy gets both treatments. When Hank falls in love with her, his feeling is described as "a mysterious and shuddery reverence." Yet, after they marry, the great joke on her is that she innocently names their child after the cry that Hank often utters in his sleep—"Hello-Central," a reference to his lost love from nineteenth-century Connecticut, the telephone operator Puss Flanagan.

Twain once told Isabel Lyon that he wasn't good at writing plays because they required a "love element" that he found difficult to handle. As Lyon put it, "He never knew what to do with the woman."[33]

In a few months he would discover—not entirely to his surprise—that his protests had not deterred Glyn from making their conversation public. She wanted to keep readers talking about her and *Three Weeks* for as long as possible. What she wrote about him, and how he responded, are subjects for another chapter. But, in the meantime, it is worth noting that when she said goodbye to America in the spring, some members of the press were already weary of her efforts at self-promotion. The *New York World*'s photo of her boarding the *Lusitania* for England shows her figure only from behind, with the caption "Thanks for back view of Elinor Glyn," and the headline "Mrs. Glyn Goes Away from Here, but She Threatens to Come Back."[34]

On visits to Bermuda, Twain enjoyed the hospitality of Mary Peck (center, with her arm around Twain), who is shown here at her home on the island with other guests, including Henry Rogers (far left) and Isabel Lyon (far right).

TWELVE

Tourist Trade

It's doubly tainted: taint yours, and taint mine.

*Mark Twain, answering a question
about the "tainted" wealth of H. H. Rogers*[1]

. . .

"In BERMUDA A SICK PERSON gets well in 3 days, & strong in a week," Twain wrote on a quick visit to the island in late January 1908. "You only need the Bermuda air to make you weller than ever you were in your life before." In his estimation, the warm climate promptly cured what was left of his winter cold and made him feel as good as new again. When he returned to New York in a few days, he decided that one winter escape to Bermuda wasn't enough. He wanted to go back at the end of February and take Henry Rogers with him. It would do them both a world of good, he said.[2]

To his delight, Rogers agreed. As the *Wall Street Journal* had reported in January, Rogers was starting to look like his old self again and had resumed his busy routine at the office. "Mr. Rogers," the paper noted, "shows a remarkable improvement in health over the last several weeks." By the middle of February, he was sufficiently pleased with his business affairs to decide that he didn't need to risk overworking himself again. He could afford to take a few weeks off and tend to his health.

Though many businesses were still struggling to recover from the financial turmoil of October and November, Standard Oil was awash in money, showing a record profit of nearly $90 million at the end of 1907. Despite the fact that the federal government was continuing to work methodically in the courts to break up the business, the petroleum giant was making so much money that the *Wall Street Journal* joked there must be a new economic phenomenon at work—the "prosperity of the prosecuted."[3]

And so it was big news on Wall Street when Hell Hound Rogers let it be known that various associates and assistants would be overseeing his millions while he and Twain went off to Bermuda to relax for a while. One reaction was disbelief. Given Rogers's fondness for secrecy, there was some suspicion that the trip was merely another one of the tycoon's elaborate tricks. It was easy to imagine that he might want rivals to think he was on a remote island while he hatched some new business scheme elsewhere. Perhaps fueling this suspicion was the fact that even though he owned one of the world's largest and most powerful yachts, he was going to leave it behind and travel with Twain on the regular steamer to Bermuda. (In fact, it was a much safer plan, since the voyage could be very treacherous in late winter.)

When Rogers boarded the *Bermudian* in New York on the cold Saturday morning of February 22, he wasn't surprised to find several reporters eagerly waiting to witness his departure with Twain and to quiz him about his intentions. Wearing a black derby and a matching overcoat with a rolled-up newspaper shoved into the pocket, he met the press on deck. But with the exception of giving an upbeat forecast for the economy, he didn't offer much information because Twain came to his rescue and distracted the questioners with a lot of jokes.

"Well, I see that we're discovered," Twain said. "That's what I get for being in bad company."

Rogers laughed and told his friend, "Well, you've got no edge on me. Some of my methods may be bad. The public says so, at least. But they are no worse than your jokes."

It didn't take long for the two friends to begin sounding like a vaudeville act. "Two Jokers; One Deck" was the clever headline that one paper gave to its report of the Rogers-Twain routine.

"I'm going because Mark is paying my fare," Rogers announced, adding, "I'm broke again."

"Yes," said Twain, playing along, "I'm paying his fare, but I'm $2 shy. I'm going to shake him down for that $2 when we get out to sea."

"That's one of his jokes," Rogers shot back, "but it isn't worth $2, is it?"

"You don't mean to say," a reporter asked Twain, "that Mr. Rogers has had grave reverses of fortune, do you?"

"Yep. Rogers hasn't any more money than the Swiss navy has ships. I'm the good Samaritan in this affair."

"Why are you going to Bermuda, then?"

"Oh, just to keep old Rogers here straight. He's a sly one, is Rogers, and he needs a chaperon. If he behaves himself, maybe I'll beat it back to New York in a few days after we inflict our celebrated persons on the citizens of Bermuda."

When Rogers mentioned that he might stay away for three weeks, Twain managed to spice up the conversation with a reference to another celebrated person he knew—the unforgettable Mrs. Glyn.

"Yes," Twain chuckled, "Rogers is going to make three weeks of it and write a book."

"Not that kind," Rogers responded promptly.

When reporters asked the pair to pose for photographs, they obliged, but not before Rogers stipulated that he would do so "only on the condition that Twain will promise not to pick the photographer's pocket when the cloth is over his head."

Twain took a few puffs of his cigar before responding, "I'm rather particular about who poses with me."[4]

In one of the surviving pictures of this occasion, Twain is looking upward with a bright-eyed expression, his face bathed in light and appearing as innocent as an angel while one hand opens up Rogers's overcoat, presumably to reach inside and find the two dollars he wanted.

Despite all their joking, it is obvious from the photograph that illness had taken its toll on Rogers, whose body may have been on the mend, but whose face looked haggard. Isabel Lyon, who had been invited to join the trip this time, thought that he looked like "a grey feeble man" when he boarded the ship. Some of the journalists also remarked on his weak appearance. As one observed, "The captain of the Rockefeller industries was somberly clad in black, and made a rather dismal figure beside the radiant humorist."[5]

Bantering with the reporters was fun for Twain, but he was also anxious about his old friend's health and didn't want him to be pestered by anyone asking tough questions. The pair's comic routine was so good that most of the newspapermen soon forgot about more serious matters. That was not the case, however, with the earnest reporter from the *New York Tribune,* who complained afterward that he had wanted to "talk seriously on financial matters," but "neither traveler would do aught but joke."[6]

Though it was true that the voyage was primarily for pleasure and had no hidden purpose, Twain had been around Rogers long enough to know that he liked to safeguard his privacy as much as possible. The proud businessman wouldn't have wanted to admit even the possibility that his health was still weak or that it might be improved by taking a long vacation. It was better to keep everyone guessing about his real intentions, and to remind the world—as Twain took the trouble to do—that Rogers was "a sly one" who kept his cards close to his chest.

· · ·

ARRIVING IN BERMUDA at the height of the tourist season, Twain and Rogers found that though their rooms had been held for them at the crowded Princess Hotel, they weren't together on the same floor, and neither of them had much space. Twain complained that his room "was intended for a cigar box, in fact it <u>was</u> a cigar box once." But the mood at the hotel was so festive, and the views across the harbor so beautiful, that it was easy to put up with a little inconvenience and enjoy the stay. Rogers had no complaints, though he was slow to drop his formal manner and adopt the easygoing spirit of the island. One day, as Twain watched his friend walking toward him in the hotel's large dining room, he teased him for maintaining such a stately air in a place meant for relaxation.

"There he comes, looking just like Gibb's Lighthouse," said Twain, referring to a local landmark, "stiff and tall, turning his lights from side to side."[7]

To chip away at some of his friend's reserve, Twain took him to a base-ball game. It was an unconventional affair, not least because it was played at Richmond Ground, the home field of the Hamilton Cricket Club. The American game was played between teams from the two largest hotels, the Hamilton and the Princess.

"Mark Twain was a champion of the Princess nine," one observer re-ported. "He sat in the front row of the grandstand, and there was not a good play nor a bad one which escaped him. When he was particularly pleased with something the Princess team did he would subside, after ap-plauding it in a cloud of smoke which rolled from a big, black cigar. Several times he puffed so hard as to almost obscure his white-flannelled figure and silvery mane."

Unfortunately, all the excitement was too much for Rogers, who ap-peared to be a little shaky as he left the grandstand at the end of the game. The next day he felt much better, however, and was ready to ex-plore more of the island with Twain, who seemed to be on the go all the time, traveling around each day in carriages or donkey carts. At the end of the first week, when everyone was preparing to attend the Princess Hotel's regular Friday night ball, Lyon summed up Twain's first few days of activity with the comment, "The King drives out, and he walks out, and he is gay and young and full of a new and splendid life."[8]

While Twain and Rogers were busy enjoying themselves, Lyon made a new friend among the guests at the hotel. She was a tall, dignified woman named Elizabeth Wallace, who was about the same age as Lyon. Highly educated and fluent in Spanish and French, Wallace was on leave from her job as an associate professor of French literature at the University of Chicago and had been staying at the hotel with her mother since the first of the year. She entered easily into a friendship with Lyon, and they began spending much of their time together. They went on shopping ex-peditions, took afternoon tea with other ladies at the hotel, and sat on the veranda watching the sailboats while Wallace read to Lyon from her un-published memoir of a year spent in Paris.

Twain approved of Wallace, whom he described in one of his dicta-tions as "a bright and charming lady with a touch of gray in her hair." Fascinated by Twain after meeting him on his short visit the month be-fore, she was now amused by his comings and goings with Rogers. "It was

On their visit to Bermuda in early 1908, Twain and Henry
Rogers became fond of "our beloved Betsy," as they came to call
Elizabeth Wallace, a charming and sophisticated professor of
French literature at the University of Chicago.

always a mooted question," she reflected a few years later, "whether Mr.
Rogers took care of Mr. Clemens or Mr. Clemens of Mr. Rogers. It was a
question that they took much delight in unsettling."[9]

When Wallace adopted Lyon's habit of referring to Twain as the King,
he was flattered, but didn't want Rogers to feel slighted and therefore
suggested an equally regal title for him—the Rajah. Everyone laughed
when the two men began referring to each other by their respective titles,
but the joke must have given the greatest pleasure to Twain. No doubt it
pleased him to pretend that he and Hell Hound were a couple of royal im-
postors who, in another life, might have been rapscallions like the King
and the Duke in *Huckleberry Finn*. (Of course, Rogers's critics would
have argued that the millionaire was already a pretty convincing rapscal-
lion.)

On Bermuda, however, the pair's schemes were rather tame. Early on,

Wallace was asked to participate in one that Rogers called the S.L.C. Life-Saving Society. After breakfast one day he solemnly explained to her that because of Twain's "guileless and unsuspecting nature" strangers were always trying to take advantage of him and to monopolize his time. Protecting the writer from such "annoying relationships" was Wallace's job as the newest member of the S.L.C. Life-Saving Society. At the first sight of some "doubtful party" trying to engage his interest, she was expected to approach Twain and say, "Pardon me, but Mr. Rogers is looking for you, and would like to speak to you immediately." Otherwise, Rogers explained, his friend's "kind heart" would never allow him to get away. (Though he was slow to warm to most people, the millionaire took an instant liking to Wallace, calling her "our beloved Betsy.")[10]

After two weeks on the island Twain had no doubt that his friend was doing much better. On March 10 he remarked, "Mr. Rogers is improving so decidedly that he has stopped talking about going back home—so I am hoping & expecting to keep him here until April 11." Rogers certainly needed all the energy he could muster to keep pace with Twain, who was full of plans. "We are having very lively times every day," Twain exulted.

Indeed, they never seemed to lack things to do. Together the old friends roamed the grounds of the island's military garrison and watched the British troops parade in their red coats, inspected the coral reefs in a glass-bottomed boat as guests of Bermuda's governor, sailed to Agar's Island to tour the large aquarium, made themselves conspicuous as they took daily drives through Hamilton in an open carriage, went to picnics and band concerts, and played billiards and late-night card games in the hotel parlors.

"I am now so strong," Twain wrote in a burst of enthusiasm, "that I suppose I could pull up one of these islands by the roots & throw it half way to New York. In fact I know I could."[11]

· · ·

TWAIN'S GOOD SPIRITS were tested one day when he and Rogers were invited to have lunch at Shoreby, a small estate not far from the Princess Hotel. Their hostess was planning to serve a dark stew made of three kinds of meat, hot peppers, and spicy seasonings.

It was at Twain's request that the dish was served. In his good mood he seems to have misjudged his ability to digest it and had cheerfully asked his hostess, whose cook was famous for the potent stew, to prepare a big kettle of it.

"Rogers, did you ever eat West Indian pepper pot?" Twain had asked when the subject of the meal first came up.

"Not knowingly," his friend replied.

"Mrs. Peck," he had said to their hostess, "some day invite poor Rogers here to eat pepper pot." The invitation was promptly extended and just as promptly accepted by Twain on behalf of himself and his friend. The stew had to cook for three or four days, so by the time the lunch took place the number of guests had increased to almost a dozen, and included Wallace and Lyon.

When the big kettle was carried to the table, only a few of the guests seem to have known what was in store for their taste buds. "It possesses an apparently mild flavor until you have half finished your dishful," Wallace later wrote of the pepper pot. "Then it begins to burn insidiously, first your tongue, then your palate, then your throat, until you feel gently aflame."

It didn't take long for everyone's eyes to begin watering, and many of the guests soon found the tears cascading down their cheeks. Neither Twain nor Rogers wanted to let the other think he couldn't stand it, and both bravely continued eating.

After a long silence at the table, Twain dried his eyes and said slowly, "This would be a very good dish if it had a little pepper in it."

"We all smiled humidly," Elizabeth Wallace recalled, "and furtively wiped our eyes."[12]

The trials of eating pepper pot were offset by the pleasure of spending time with the charming hostess. During his previous visit to Bermuda, Twain had enjoyed getting to know Mrs. Mary Peck, an attractive American in her mid-forties who often spent the winter on the island. She was married to a wealthy businessman she didn't love whose life revolved around his woolen mills in Massachusetts, and who didn't care for Bermuda. A free spirit who felt stifled in New England, she shocked the high-minded people in her husband's hometown by her unconventional habits and modern ideas. "Woman Seen Smoking on East Street" was the headline in the local paper after she dared to light up a cigarette in public.

In Bermuda she found more acceptance, though the island's wives kept a close eye on their husbands when she was around. Known for her "frank courting of susceptible males," she regularly attended the weekly balls at the Princess and Hamilton hotels, where she loved to dance and flirt and show off her fine figure in the latest fashions.[13]

She took an instant liking to Twain, regarding him as a sweet "old dear" whom she could spoil with affectionate attention. It was hard for even the most upright of men to ignore her tender looks and soothing words. One woman said that Mary Peck used her pretty voice "caressingly though lazily," and that she had an "absorbing way of listening to the words of wisdom uttered by *a man.*" The warmth of her feelings toward Twain is evident in a photograph taken when he came to Shoreby for lunch with his friends. Everyone is standing on the wide porch of her home, with Rogers posing stiffly at one end and Isabel Lyon looking small and insignificant at the other. In the middle is the hostess—dressed all in white like Twain—with her arm around his shoulder and a coy smile on her lips. Another woman in the background whose face isn't visible also has a hand on the shoulder of the author, who has the look of a contented pet.[14]

In New York Twain might have been more reserved around a woman like Mary Peck, but in Bermuda he could let down his guard and enjoy being the occasional object of her attention, especially since he knew she had no designs on him. As he had discovered on his previous visit, she seemed far more interested in another man—someone of her own generation, a quiet, bookish fellow who had begun making solitary trips to the island to escape the pressures of his job as the head of an Ivy League university. He was Woodrow Wilson, of Princeton. Only fifty-one at the beginning of 1908, he had served as the university's president for almost six years.

Wilson had met Mary Peck on his first holiday to Bermuda in 1907. She caught his eye one day when she hurried past his table in a gold lace dress as he sat eating alone at his hotel. After they were introduced at a party a short time later, Wilson quickly fell under her spell, and hated to

leave her when it was time to return to Princeton. On the last day of his
stay he dropped by her house to say goodbye, but she had already gone
out, and he left a note that reveals the depth of his great attraction to her
despite its stilted tone. "It was with the keenest disappointment that I
found you not at home this afternoon," he wrote. "It is not often that I can
have the privilege of meeting anyone whom I can so entirely admire and
enjoy."[15]

At the beginning of 1908 he returned to the island with the intention
of spending as much time with her as possible. It was at this point that
Twain showed up on his first visit of the year, and Wilson was initially
jealous of the author. They didn't know each other well, though they had
met a couple of times a few years earlier and shared a mutual friend in
George Harvey, who was an early supporter of Wilson's political ambi-
tions. When Mary Peck postponed an appointment with Wilson to greet
Twain's ship at the waterfront, he wasn't happy. "Now I am cut out by
Mark Twain!" he complained. "He arrived on the boat this morning, and
Mrs. Peck at once took possession of him."[16]

He didn't have any cause for worry. She soon made it clear that he had
captured her heart. As she would remind him several years later, when
they were coming to the end of their affair, "You have been the greatest,
most ennobling influence in my life. You helped me to have my soul alive
and I am grateful." All the same, they made such an unlikely couple that
rumors of their affair wouldn't be taken seriously for years. Theodore
Roosevelt burst out laughing when it was suggested that the relationship
could be used against Wilson in the presidential election of 1912. "You
can't cast a man as Romeo," he said, "who looks and acts so much like an
apothecary's clerk."[17]

The son of a Presbyterian minister, Wilson was tormented by strong
desires that he worked to suppress for most of his life, cultivating a public image as a man of high ideals and superior moral character. With his
bland face, fastidious manners, and solid reputation as a loyal husband
and the father of three daughters, he seemed beyond reproach. But meeting seductive Mary in the relaxed atmosphere of Bermuda opened the
emotional floodgates and allowed him to reveal the passionate side of his
nature. With her, he said, he "lost all of the abominable self-consciousness
that has been my bane all my life." She made him feel "perfectly at ease,

happily myself, released from bonds to enjoy the full freedom of my mind."[18]

Wilson's fascination with Mary Peck must have been obvious to Twain during his first trip of 1908, for the visiting academic quickly managed to become a regular guest at her home as well as her escort to the hotel balls. (Wilson always declined to dance, appearing content to sit in the gallery and to guard Peck's fan or scarf while she glided across the floor with someone else.) In due course he and Twain became better acquainted and grew to like each other. Among Wilson's many talents, the most impressive for Twain may have been his skill at the billiards tables in the parlors of their hotels. The university president loved the game almost as much as Twain did and considered himself an expert. "I have seen a good deal of him," Wilson said of Twain. "He seems to like being with me. Yesterday Mrs. Peck gave him a lunch at her house and gathered a most interesting little group of garrison people to meet him. He was in great form and delighted everybody."[19]

With his Oxford degree, Twain was now in a position to shoot the breeze even with an Ivy League president and never feel at the slightest disadvantage. He also didn't see any need to drop hints that Princeton might want to add to his collection of sheepskins. After his experience in Oxford, nothing else could measure up. Besides, whenever Wilson began sounding too academic, he left Twain cold. The writer was easily bored by any professorial pronouncements on political or economic subjects.

The two men did see eye to eye, however, on one local issue of political concern and joined forces to campaign for it. They launched an effort to save Bermuda from what they perceived as a dire threat to its tranquillity—the proposed importation of automobiles. At the time, the colonial government was trying to decide whether to allow a limited number of people to own motor cars, and the members of the House of Assembly were almost equally divided on the question. The future American president couldn't resist adding his voice to the debate, having found that one of the things he liked best about Bermuda was bicycling for miles in complete safety along its peaceful roads. "There is only one automobile in Bermuda," he had noted on his first visit, "and that, I was delighted to learn, broke down almost immediately after arriving here."

Though Twain was a lot fonder of automobiles than bicycles, he agreed that the noisy machines would do more harm than good on the tiny island. Wilson prepared a petition expressing support for the anti-automobile faction in the House of Assembly, and Twain signed it. Before it was published in the local paper, 109 other guests at the two major hotels had added their signatures to the document, which warned that tourism might be the first casualty if the island suffered an invasion of motor cars. The opening put the case succinctly: "We, the undersigned, visitors to Bermuda, venture respectfully to express the opinion that the admission of automobiles to the island would alter the whole character of the place. . . . The island now attracts visitors in considerable numbers because of the quiet and dignified simplicity of its life. It derives its principal charm from its utter detachment from the world of strenuous business and feverish pleasure in which most of us are obliged to spend the greater part of our time."[20]

Alienating tourists was the last thing the colony wanted to do. The opinions of such famous American guests as Twain and Wilson mattered a great deal, and the petition may have helped to influence the debate. In April 1908 a ban on automobiles passed the House of Assembly by the narrow margin of fifteen to fourteen. Though it was a small triumph for a man who would soon be using his powers of persuasion on the world stage, the ban had a long-lasting effect on life in Bermuda. It remained in force for the next thirty-eight years.

Wilson's copy of the petition was still among his papers at his death in 1924, and many decades later the meticulous editor of those papers—Arthur S. Link—noticed a shorthand notation in Wilson's hand on the back of the petition. When it was deciphered, Link found that it was the beginning of a love letter. "My precious one, my beloved Mary," Wilson wrote, and then stopped, apparently deciding that even disguised in shorthand such a personal message shouldn't be continued on the back of a petition.

But Wilson didn't work hard enough to hide his love for Peck. Rumors of their affair began to circulate in 1908 and would become a source of great worry after he entered politics two years later. Though Theodore Roosevelt didn't put any faith in those rumors, many others did, jokingly referring to Wilson as "Peck's bad boy." By the time he ran for reelection to the presidency in 1916, the affair would be behind him, but that wouldn't stop his political foes from trying their best to use it against him. As Mary herself later claimed, a Republican operative offered her as much as $300,000 for her two hundred letters from Wilson, but she refused and always insisted that she had been nothing more than a good friend. When Wilson's first wife—Ellen—died of kidney failure in 1914, there was some gossip that she had actually died of a broken heart after learning of the affair.[21]

In the years after Ellen's death Wilson was increasingly plagued by guilt over his relationship with Mary, saying that it belonged to a time "of folly and gross impertinence in my life." But when Twain set foot in Bermuda for the second time in 1908, his new friend Woodrow was still in the exuberant stage of loving Mary and was willing to do almost anything in order to be with her, even if it meant sitting down at her table to share a steaming kettle of pepper pot with one of America's most notorious robber barons, Henry Rogers.[22]

In the memoir that she wrote in her seventies, Peck recalled that Wilson was reluctant to dine with a member of the "money-trust," but that he had done so to please her, and that he enjoyed the company, though not the dish. "He had a sensitive digestion," she wrote, "which was accustomed to rebel suddenly if displeased." The passage of more than twenty-five years, however, had played tricks with her memory, causing her to confuse a meal she served to Twain and Wilson with the one she served to Rogers and Twain. But she was right in remembering that Wilson had been willing to meet Rogers at her place. In fact, he spent the last day of his winter vacation waiting for him and Mark Twain to come over for a visit. A storm came up, however, and it rained all afternoon. At short notice they couldn't find a closed carriage to take them over to Shoreby. And, of course, there were no automobiles available.[23]

And so, even though Twain and Wilson would see each other again in Bermuda, Rogers missed his chance to meet the future president of the United States, the very man—as fate would have it—who in 1913 would sign into law a measure dreaded by all robber barons: the federal income tax.

· · ·

ONE DAY AT THE PRINCESS HOTEL, as Twain and Elizabeth Wallace were walking down one of its long corridors, he suddenly began hopping and skipping, and then broke into a run. When a door to one of the guest rooms opened, he dug in his heels and came to an abrupt halt before resuming his progress in a stately walk more appropriate to his age. Though Wallace was amused that he would want to put on this act for her sake, she could also see how eager he was to prove that a few weeks in Bermuda had taken years off his age. It was one thing to have the heart of a boy, but the longer he stayed on the island, the more he seemed to relish acting like a boy.

She saw another example of this on a Sunday night when she heard a soft knock at her door and opened it to find him motioning her to step quietly into the corridor. "Hush," he cautioned, not wanting to rouse her mother in the adjoining room. "Can't you run away and have a game of cards?"

When she answered that her mother wouldn't approve of her playing cards on a Sunday, he responded like a mischievous schoolboy trying to tempt a good girl to break the rules.

"Play hookey," he whispered, "she'll never know."

A moment later the well-behaved middle-aged professor was following Twain to the card table downstairs, unable to refuse his invitation to sin. "Closing the door," she later wrote, "we escaped down the hall, with a well-simulated thrill of adventure, while . . . Mother remained sweetly unconscious of the perfidy."

Henry Rogers didn't feel neglected when Twain was busy entertaining Wallace or others, and he didn't show any sign of wanting to go home before April. "This was the very place for him," Twain said of Henry in a letter to Emilie Rogers at the beginning of March. "He enjoys himself and is as quarrelsome as a cat." Emilie herself arrived on the island in the middle of March and soon began organizing activities to keep her husband entertained. Sometimes Twain joined them, and sometimes he wandered off to find other amusements.[24]

While many adults bored him with their polite small talk or tiresome efforts to impress him, he was overjoyed whenever he fell into the company of some worshipful young girl on the island who could make him feel young again. What he wanted was the kind of attention he had enjoyed as the young father of three affectionate girls, and the kind of companionship that he had hoped to enjoy with those daughters in his old age. Death had taken Susy from him, frustrated ambitions had undermined Clara's relationship with him, and illness had separated him from Jean.

He had no grandchildren to turn to, yet he knew that he had "reached the grandpa stage of life," and felt deeply the need for something that he had spent much of his literary career celebrating—the high spirits of youth. It was a comfort to him not only to share in those spirits with a willing friend, but to see the world again through a young person's eyes—especially those of girls who seemed to him the ideal of innocence, ones "to whom life is a perfect joy and to whom it has brought no wounds, no bitterness, and few tears."[25]

During his two winter visits he made friends with several girls who either lived on the island or were staying at his hotel. It wasn't uncommon to see him riding around town in a donkey cart driven by one of these girls or to find him spending the afternoon telling one of them tall tales on the hotel veranda. He was aware that his conduct prompted more than a few raised eyebrows, but he meant no harm and did none. He certainly never overstepped the bounds of propriety that Clara and others tended to worry so much about. "Consider well the proportions of things," he liked to say to the girls. "It is better to be a young June-bug than an old bird of paradise."[26]

Elizabeth Wallace accompanied him on his donkey cart excursions with a bright-eyed twelve-year-old from New York named Margaret Blackmer. As a teacher, Wallace was fascinated to see how easily Twain was able to understand a young person's point of view, and how he could adopt it without appearing to be condescending. One reason that he was so much fun to be with, she concluded, was that he had not lost what most adults eventually lose—a child's sense of wonder and freshness. When she shared his company with Margaret, she found that his influence was stronger than ever: "All pretentious wisdom, all sophisticated phrases, all acquired and meaningless conventions were laid aside, and we said what we meant, and spontaneity took the place of calculation."[27]

Walking along the beach one day with the girl, Twain picked up a small shell and gently separated the two halves. Giving her one, he said that if they met again at some distant time in the future, and she looked so different that he couldn't recognize her, she only had to produce her half of the shell to prove her identity. Margaret was charmed by the idea and agreed to keep the shell in a safe place. But, for Twain, the fun of this arrangement wasn't to be had in the distant future.

The next morning, when he saw her in the hotel dining room, he went up to her with a sad face and pretended not to recognize her, insisting that she looked like "my Margaret," but was somehow different. As he turned to walk away, she cried out for him to stop and "triumphantly" produced her half of the shell. Twain beamed with pleasure, taking satisfaction from the scene because it was spontaneous on her part and cleverly theatrical on his.

"The child could not have enjoyed this thrilling little drama more if we had been playing it on the stage," he later remarked in an autobiographical dictation. "Many times afterward she played the chief part herself, pretending to be in doubt as to my identity and challenging me to produce my half of the shell. She was always hoping to catch me without it, but I always defeated that game—wherefore she came at last to recognize that I was not only old but very smart."[28]

Unlike so many adults, Twain paid careful attention to what children said and took their words seriously. It was a pleasure for him simply to sit and listen to the unpremeditated way that most children spoke, and to take note of their unexpected turns of phrase and inventive twists of syntax.

His habit of doing this had paid rich dividends earlier in his career in the case of his now famous encounter with an African-American boy he nicknamed "Sociable Jimmy." As Shelley Fisher Fishkin has argued in her groundbreaking study *Was Huck Black?*, the style and substance of the boy's comments to Twain may have provided a model for "the distinctive voice of Huck Finn." He met the boy—whose real name was probably William Evans—after giving a lecture in Paris, Illinois, at the end of 1870. Evans lived next door to the local hotel and was sent to Twain's room to serve him dinner. The author engaged young Evans in conversation and was amazed by the extraordinary flow of speech that came from the boy as he made himself at home in the room, relaxing in an armchair with his legs thrown over one arm and discussing how his "Pa used to git drunk," and how the hotel owners hated cats and drowned them, and why the town wasn't larger—"Some folks says dis town would be considerable bigger if it wa'n't on accounts of so much lan' all roun' it dat ain't got no houses on it." Twain considered the boy "the most artless, sociable, and exhaustless talker I ever came across," and was so captivated by his words that he tried to write them down as accurately as possible and later declared, "I think I could swing my legs over the arms of a chair & that boy's spirit would descend upon me & enter into me."[29]

Part of the secret of Twain's literary success was his skill at capturing in print what he made a point of studying and celebrating in person—the magical spirit of childhood. Though his literary powers had diminished in old age, he never lost his fascination with the things that make Huck such a compelling character. When he was around young people, he became a genteel version of the Missouri boy that still lived within him, which helps to explain his teasing but affectionate manner toward girls.

· · ·

BESIDES ELIZABETH WALLACE, there was another person in Bermuda who closely observed Twain's interactions with children on the island, and who put her impressions on paper. She was Marion Schuyler Allen from Belmont, New York, whose husband, William, was the American vice consul in Hamilton. They lived only a short walk from the Princess Hotel, and their thirteen-year-old daughter, Helen, liked going there to watch the fancy balls. One evening toward the end of Twain's long stay on the island, Helen met him at the hotel and invited him to come over to her place the next afternoon.

When he arrived at Bay House, as her home was known, he found that she was still at school, and that her mother was just leaving to do some shopping in town. For most of her life Marion Allen had been an admirer of Twain's work, and had always considered herself lucky that years ago she had caught a glimpse of him at a distance in upstate New York. Now he was standing in front of her, and she didn't know what to say to him. When he broke the silence by offering to go shopping with her, she accepted, but was in awe of his presence the whole time. She couldn't quite believe that her childhood hero was at her side while she went about her daily routine in the shops of Hamilton.

They both enjoyed their afternoon together, and when Helen returned from school, she found that her mother and Twain were already acting like old friends. In fact, Marion had discovered in her conversations with Twain that the Allen family had old connections to Livy's family in Elmira. William Allen's mother—who was then in her eighties and lived in her own house on the island—had known Livy and the rest of the Langdon family many years ago.

"Was it not a strange coincidence?" Marion later wondered.[30]

Marion made Twain feel that he was almost like family, and gave him to understand that her home would always be open to him. So, for the last few days of his stay in Bermuda, he was often in the company of the Allens and their daughter. He spent his last full day on the island swimming with Helen in the shallow waters at the foot of Bay House. Isabel Lyon took pictures of the two splashing about in the placid bay. In one shot Twain can be seen showing off to Helen by arching his back to dive under the surface like a porpoise. He loved the pictures and later sent her copies after boasting to her in a letter that it took several days and "5 separate and distinct soapings & scourings" to get all the salt out of his hair.[31]

On future trips to Bermuda, Bay House would become like a second home to Twain. Surrounded by thick hedges of oleanders, "the low, rambling, white stone house" was two hundred years old, and stood at the end of a cedar-lined drive. It was a comfortable house, with a big fireplace for rainy days, and a wide porch for shade on sunny days. There was ample room for a guest or two.[32]

Twain's friendship with Helen and her parents would deepen with each visit. Marion would never lose her admiration for him. The more she saw of him, the more she liked him. Though Helen was a strong-willed daughter who often found herself at odds with her parents, her mother was impressed from the beginning at how much patience and kindness Twain showed toward the girl. Young people "attracted and inspired him," she recalled. "He could be himself with them, a simple lovable man, childlike in his ingeniousness; also they were the best of shields from the too [demanding] grown-ups."[33]

Twain's use of the seashell to forge a bond with Margaret Blackmer seems to have given him the idea that each girl who became his friend

Twain became like an adopted member of the family at Bay House in Bermuda,
where he often stayed as the guest of the American vice consul, William Allen,
whose wife, Marion Schuyler Allen, was a great admirer of the author's work.
Here Twain is shown in 1908 swimming with the family's teenage daughter,
Helen.

should have a similar token. While he was in Bermuda he found a lapel
pin with the figure of an angelfish in enamel, and decided that it made the
perfect gift because the small creature was the most beautiful thing
swimming in the waters of the island.

He bought several of the pins and began sending them to the various
girls in a newly established club he called the Aquarium. Margaret and
Helen were among the first "angelfish," along with two American girls he
had met on his trip to England, eleven-year-old Dorothy Quick and
sixteen-year-old Frances Nunnally. Other girls would be added to the
Aquarium over the next two years, including one of Paine's daughters
and one of George Harvey's. Twain was immensely proud of the group,
calling them "gems of the first water." Among other things, he wanted to
make sure that each of them became experts in the pastimes that really
mattered—billiards, card games, and storytelling. Sometimes he called
himself the Admiral of the group, and sometimes its slave or shad.[34]

On Saturday, April 11, Twain's long holiday in Bermuda finally came to an end as he and his party boarded the ship for their return home. The six-week stay was one of the most enjoyable periods of his life, but Isabel Lyon was beginning to fret about their absence from America and was anxious to go home. If they continued to stay in Bermuda, she wouldn't be able to superintend the final stages of construction on the Redding house. Rogers was also eager to return to his business affairs. He had put up with about as much relaxation as a man of his restless energy could endure. But Twain seemed pleased with the result, saying that his friend was now "rather steadier on his feet than when he went away."

The weather had been mild for most of their stay, but on the way home they ran into a final blast of winter as they approached New York. The ocean churned, the ship began "pitching heavily," and a great wave suddenly crashed over the decks, drenching Twain while he was in the middle of recruiting another girl to join his Aquarium.

"I was standing on the main deck aft," he said on his arrival in New York, "in the company of Miss Dorothy Sturgis, sixteen years old and from Boston. As we were watching the line take up its slack a beautiful blue comber broke on the rail and 'soused' the two of us from head to foot."

Asked if he and his friend had suffered any injuries, he said no. But then he added with his usual air of innocence, "I never knew the ocean was so wet before."[35]

Safely separated by patriotic bunting at a police parade in New York City, Twain looks to his right as Cardinal Logue looks in the opposite direction.

THIRTEEN

Farewell, Fifth Avenue

I have made all the noise allotted to me,
and now I intend to be quiet.

Mark Twain[1]

. . .

As much as he had enjoyed Bermuda, Twain was glad to see New York again and was even inclined to think better of his old house after being away for so long. On his first night back, he admitted that the house was looking "homelike and inviting," and that he was "not sorry to be in my own bed again." More important, he was overjoyed to be reunited with his billiards table and to spend half the night playing with Paine, who was back in favor and seemingly content to act as if their relationship had never been under any strain. Though her long holiday had done little to soften her resentment of the biographer, Isabel Lyon did her best to be cordial and sat in the billiards room until nearly midnight, chatting amiably with neighbor Maud Littleton, the wife of Harry Thaw's attorney.[2]

Now that spring was here, Twain returned to his habit of taking long walks in the afternoon, and Paine was often invited to come along. During Twain's absence in Bermuda, his biographer had been conducting research in Hartford, and was full of questions. There was ample time for discussion because their walks up Fifth Avenue sometimes took them as far as Andrew Carnegie's mansion on Ninety-first Street (now the Cooper-Hewitt Museum), which was about five miles from Twain's house. On their way back they liked to rest on a bench in Central Park or at the Plaza Hotel, where the doorman knew Twain well and would greet him warmly. One Sunday when they went walking in the morning and turned back early at the Plaza, Paine suggested they hurry home to avoid the "throng" leaving St. Patrick's Cathedral, the Brick Church, and other places of worship along their route.

Twain objected, saying simply, "I like the throng." Obviously, his long absence from the crowds of New York had made him eager to bask in their adulation again.

At a leisurely pace, he led the way back and timed things just right, weaving through hundreds of people pouring onto the sidewalks after services had ended. "Of course," Paine later said of the episode, "he was the object on which every passing eye turned, the presence to which every hat was lifted."[3]

He took this game one step further on the last Wednesday in April, when he made a special trip to St. Patrick's Cathedral to witness an extraordinary spectacle involving six thousand children selected from the city's parochial schools. The archdiocese was celebrating the centenary of its founding, and the excitement was so great among the Catholic faithful that huge crowds were turning out at every event. Half a million attended a Saturday parade that lasted two and a half hours, and that almost ended in disaster when a large crowd seeking a blessing from Cardinal Logue, the primate of Ireland, surged toward the reviewing stand. Hundreds of police on foot and horseback were needed to hold back the crowd and prevent a stampede. Fortunately, the only problems at the "Children's Day" event on Wednesday were relatively minor ones— hundreds of spectators blocking the sidewalks, and a traffic jam caused by all the horse-drawn carriages and automobiles arriving at the same time from dozens of schools scattered throughout the city.

The six thousand children were coming to attend a solemn pontifical mass celebrated by Cardinal Logue. The boys were dressed in black suits with flags in their lapels, while many of the girls were all in white with gold sashes. Inside the great cathedral the tightly packed congregation was made up entirely of children—except for an elderly white-haired man who had managed to gain admission by special permission.

As a newspaper article reported the next day, "Six thousand and one children, the odd one being Mark Twain—the youngest of them all—filled St. Patrick's cathedral to-day. . . . Mark Twain, with his flowing white hair and wearing a light gray suit and hat, said he was one of the children. He pleaded his love for the little ones, and a special seat was arranged for him near the altar. The humorist explained that he had lived through the period of manhood and had relieved himself of its limitations when he passed the threescore and ten milepost. To-day, he said, he was back with the children, and he seemed to be happy."

Under the circumstances the text of the day's sermon—"Suffer the little children to come unto me"—seems to have been appropriate in more ways than one.[4]

Though he wasn't wearing his famous suit, Twain must have felt that he couldn't pass up the chance to join a ceremony in which so many girls were arrayed in white. While he was admiring the spectacle, he may have also been enjoying the secret thrill of being a lapsed Presbyterian among so many thousands of innocent Catholic schoolchildren. He was clearly the lone goat in that vast flock of sheep.

For much of his early life he had been inclined to view Catholicism with "enmity," to use his own word. As he confessed in *The Innocents Abroad,* "I have been educated to enmity toward every thing that is Catholic, and sometimes, in consequence of this, I find it much easier to discover Catholic faults than Catholic merits." His fault finding was usually directed against the Church as an institution rather than against any individual Catholic. In *A Connecticut Yankee in King Arthur's Court* Hank Morgan blames the Church for undermining individual rights in order to expand the privileges of prelates, kings, and aristocrats, and believes that this "poison" of favoring rank over personal achievement has remained in "the blood of Christendom" from the Middle Ages to his own "birth-century." Reflecting on the unquestioning reverence for rank in King Arthur's Britain, Hank says, "There you see the hand of that awful power, the Roman Catholic Church. In two or three little centuries it had converted a nation of men to a nation of worms."[5]

Yet the spring of 1908 found Mark Twain taking a seat not only at mass in St. Patrick's Cathedral, but also at Cardinal Logue's side in another event a few days later. The occasion was a parade on May 9 honoring the New York Police Department, and both the cardinal and the writer were among a small group of dignitaries given front-row seats at the reviewing stand next to Madison Square Park. In the middle of the platform was a wooden pole covered by red, white, and blue bunting, and on either side of this thin divide sat Twain and the cardinal. They must have presented a strange sight to the five thousand policemen who marched past them on Fifth Avenue, with Twain dressed in black for a change and the cardinal upstaging him in scarlet biretta and shiny pectoral cross.

When reporters asked why he was wearing black, the author joked that he was wearing a disguise in an effort to avoid being recognized by the police. He was careful to add, however, that he was a great admirer of the brave men of the force. "I've always liked the police, but I suppose that's because they've always seemed to take such a deep, abiding interest in all that I do."

Before the parade started, the newspapermen had noticed that Twain seemed to be getting along well with the cardinal, who was often seen laughing as they talked. When Twain was later asked about their conversation, he gave a slightly creative reply: "I found his eminence a very nice old gentleman. He told me he had read my books. He didn't say that he approved of them, but I didn't need to have him tell me that. He looks like an intelligent man, so I take it for granted he approves of high class literature."[6]

Twain's mellow attitude in matters of religion didn't last long. Having been caught conversing with a cardinal in public, he may have felt that he needed to make amends by sharing with the world something of his own ongoing quarrel with God. An occasion for doing so presented itself just five days after the police parade. He was invited to speak at a dinner following the dedication of City College's new campus on St. Nicholas Heights, overlooking Harlem. Though good citizenship was supposedly his topic, what he really wanted to discuss was religion and public life.

It was the kind of address that might have caused serious trouble for him if he had delivered it to a pious assembly of provincial worthies on a

Sunday afternoon. But his City College crowd was much better suited to his purpose. It was made up of young alumni and faculty who had come down to the Waldorf-Astoria for a late-night dinner after celebrating all day on campus, and by the time Twain rose to speak at eleven o'clock, they were in such high spirits that they greeted him with a raucous toast, "lustily" shouting that he was "first in war, first in peace, and first in the hearts of his countrymen." Drink had made them merry, and nobody was inclined to contradict anything the old boy wanted to say.

So, after a few preliminary remarks about citizenship, Twain suddenly began to explain why he didn't think America had any business using "In God We Trust" as a motto: "There is not a nation in the world which ever put its faith in God. It is a statement made on insufficient evidence. In the unimportant cases of life, perhaps, we do trust in God— that is, if we rule out the gamblers and burglars, and plumbers, for of course they do not believe in God. If the cholera or black plague should ever come to these shores, perhaps the bulk of the nation would pray to be delivered from it, but the rest of the population would put their trust in the Health Board of the City of New York."[7]

This was the kind of thing that he often said in private. In fact, in December he had made it the subject of one of his dictations, declaring boldly, "It is not proper to brag and boast that America is a Christian country when we all know that certainly five-sixths of our population could not enter in at the narrow gate." If America is a Christian country, Twain said in the privacy of his study, "so is hell." Indeed, because of the demanding entrance requirements to the other place, he assumed that hell must be "the only really prominent Christian community in any of the worlds."[8]

What prompted his criticism of "In God We Trust" was the popular uproar that had followed President Roosevelt's decision in November 1907 to eliminate the motto from a new issue of ten-dollar and twenty-dollar gold coins. After designing the coins, the sculptor Augustus Saint-Gaudens had told Roosevelt that the motto needed to be left out because it would mar the beauty of his work, creating an "inartistic intrusion." Roosevelt agreed, but later claimed that his reason for doing so was to avoid the sacrilegious association of God and Mammon. This excuse was widely ridiculed, especially by those who wanted the motto restored. But in his December dictation, Twain had a different reason for dismissing Roosevelt's excuse, saying, "That is just like the President. . . . He is very much in the habit of furnishing a poor reason for his acts while there is an excellent reason staring him in the face. . . . The motto stated a lie. If this nation has ever trusted in God, that time has gone by."[9]

If Twain had inserted more comments from his private dictations into his speech at the Waldorf, some in his audience might eventually have sobered up and shouted objections. But he said just enough to make his point, and then softened it with a couple of well-placed jokes before letting it go. The motto, he jested, should at least be revised to say, "Within certain judicious limitations we trust in God." If that couldn't be made to fit, then he suggested that the government simply "enlarge the coin."

As soon as he was finished speaking, he made a quick exit, perhaps thinking it wasn't wise to linger after expressing his honest opinion of America's relationship with God. "With a long cigar in his mouth," one paper reported, "he hastened from the dining hall, pausing at the door to say: 'I have an important engagement at a quarter of eleven.' It was then 11:45."[10]

His subject, however, couldn't have been more relevant. The day before he gave his speech, the Senate passed a new act requiring the motto to appear on coins in accordance with a custom dating back to the Civil War. Six days later, a humbled Roosevelt signed the act into law in an effort to put the contentious issue behind him. Most Americans wanted the motto to be a permanent fixture on every coin. In pulpits across the land, the idea of excluding it had been denounced. One group of Presbyterian ministers had warned that the Panic of 1907 illustrated why the nation must put its faith in God instead of "in trust companies and banks." And some journalists had joked that if a new law wasn't approved, the country might soon see coins featuring a Teddy Bear with the inscription "In Theodore We Trust."[11]

The day after he gave his speech Twain saw parts of it printed in some of the New York papers, and at first these excerpts worried him. He wasn't sure cold type could convey his efforts at comic relief. "If only the reporters would not try to improve on what I say," he told Paine. "They seem to miss the fact that the very art of saying a thing effectively is in its delicacy, and as they can't reproduce the manner and intonation in type

they make it emphatic and clumsy in trying to convey it to the reader."
But, of course, this was the risk he took in going public with thoughts
that he usually tried to keep private. For Paine's benefit, Twain took
one last shot at the subject, saying that the earlier troubles of the
Knickerbocker Trust had made him wonder "how many were trusting in
God" to restore their savings.[12]

· · ·

AFTER A FEW WEEKS of having fun in the public arena, Twain turned
his attention to his big move to Redding, which was set for the middle of
June. Despite his hopes that the new house would give Jean and Clara a
family home as good as or better than the one they had lost in Hartford,
neither of his daughters would be with him when he moved in. In fact,
Jean was now living 250 miles away. After giving up on Katonah at the
end of 1907, she had not done well at the house in Greenwich where Dr.
Peterson had arranged for her to stay. She had experienced several
seizures within days of leaving Katonah, where she had been free from
such attacks for nine months. Without nurses and doctors routinely
checking on her, it took a whole day for her to realize what had been happening. "I had bitten my tongue," she recalled, "and that aroused some
very slight suspicions, but I didn't know I had been ill five times."[13]

If proof was needed that the sanitarium had been good for her, this
was it. But she was determined not to return there and managed to get
through the winter and early spring without suffering another setback.
With the arrival of warm weather, however, Dr. Peterson worried that her
condition might grow worse if the summer heat became too intense. He
advised that she and her housemates—the Cowles sisters and Marguerite
Schmitt—should spend the summer in Massachusetts at a cottage on
Cape Ann. Having vacationed there on several occasions, he knew the
area well and thought the cool sea breezes would be good for Jean.

In April Isabel Lyon went up to the old fishing port of Gloucester and
found a pleasant cottage for Jean to share with her friends. It was located
in the fashionable area of Eastern Point, where there were usually a number of summer homes available for rent. Two or three good-sized hotels
stood along the shore of the rocky peninsula, including the rambling old
Hawthorne Inn. Several large houses built by wealthy New England fam-

ilies were scattered over the area, and nestled among them were more modest homes and studios for the artists who came every summer to paint seascapes. A Harvard sophomore by the name of Thomas Stearns Eliot sometimes came up from Cambridge during his summer holidays to stay at the vacation home his father built at Eastern Point a decade earlier. In fact, T. S. Eliot was so fond of Cape Ann that he would later write a moving meditation on its rough beauty in "The Dry Salvages," one of the poems in his *Four Quartets*.

Despite the many attractions of the area, Twain was worried that Jean would resent being uprooted and wouldn't like living in a place so far away. As always, he thought it was best to accept whatever Dr. Peterson recommended. "I must help Dr. Peterson in his good work," he wrote Jean, "& not mar it & hinder it by going counter to his judgment & commands." But he feared that she might feel too isolated at Eastern Point. He had a couple of anxious days in mid-May, waiting for her to settle into the new place and wondering whether she would like it. To his relief, she was so pleased with Eastern Point that, as he later put it, she couldn't "find adjectives enough to express her delight in it." Responding to the good news, he confessed, "I had a growing fear—founded upon nothing— that you would feel the other way about it. I am unspeakably glad that it pleases you, and now I hope & believe you will have a happy summer."[14]

The "salt-laden air" and the easy life among the summer visitors to the peninsula brought a quick improvement to Jean's health. She ate heartily, slept well, and spent most of her days exploring the area in a leisurely fashion. "I am out-doors—with exception of meal-times—all the time," she wrote her father on May 26. In addition to going on long drives, she said, "I sleep out, I sit out on the rocks, [and] I take my cold baths out." Dr. Peterson asked a local colleague to keep an eye on her, but for much of the time, she was free to do as she pleased. Marguerite Schmitt was usually at her side, and they thoroughly enjoyed each other's company. (It was a different story with the Cowles sisters, who had turned out to be a troubled pair, and with whom Jean was trying to have as little to do as possible.)

A leading figure in the social life of Eastern Point was the painter Cecilia Beaux, whom Jean knew through Richard Watson Gilder and his family. Beaux made a point of getting to know Jean better, extending an open invitation to visit her at Green Alley, her charming house a short walk away. It was airy and comfortable, and was surrounded by one of the finest gardens on Cape Ann. Both Jean and Cecilia Beaux encouraged Twain not merely to pay a visit in the summer—as he planned to do—but to come and stay in the area for a long period. "She asked me to tell you from her," Jean wrote of Beaux in a letter to Twain, "that if you came up here, she hoped you would stay for some time, [and] that you would find the place quiet & that you should not be disturbed."

A contemporary description of Beaux's property in summer makes the area sound as idyllic as anything in Bermuda. The "shell-colored cottage" was hidden from the road by a thicket of tupelo trees and stood at the end of a narrow path shaded by interlaced branches and lined with wild flowers. Covered by vines, climbing roses, and clematis, the two-story house had a brick terrace with a wide view over the lawn, which sloped toward the sea, and was bordered by "clumps of larkspur" as blue as the bay.[15]

Grateful to be in such an environment, Jean had only praise for Dr. Peterson's decision to send her there. She was more convinced than ever that Katonah had been a mistake and wouldn't give the sanitarium any credit for helping her. But she didn't blame Peterson for trying it in her case. She disliked Dr. Sharp so much that she made a distinction between the administration of the sanitarium and the treatments prescribed by Peterson. "I can say but little good of the place, even today," she wrote of Sharp's establishment in May, but "of Dr. Peterson's treatment, I cannot say enough."[16]

For Clara, May 1908 was also an eventful time. Half of it was spent preparing for her first overseas tour. The plan was for her to sail to England in the middle of the month and then to spend the summer performing and sightseeing in various parts of Europe. During her father's long stay in Bermuda, she had been appearing in small concerts in New York and in much larger ones in several cities in the South and the Midwest. Her most important performance took place in Atlanta on April 2. Billed as "Miss Clara Clemens, Contralto, Daughter of Mark Twain," she sang at the Grand Opera House on Peachtree Street.

Her reviews were generally good, and she passed some along to her father, who continued to give her encouragement. "You are coming along, dear, you are coming along. You are getting splendid notices, & I am aware that you deserve them. It makes me very glad." But she was on the move so much that her father couldn't keep track of her half the time. "I don't know where you are," he wrote her three days after her appearance in Atlanta, "but you are drifting professionally around somewhere, I suppose—& hope."[17]

By the time she had finished her tour, Clara was in such a nervous state that she didn't know whether she would be able to travel to Europe. Her spring concerts were supposed to have provided valuable preparation for her London debut, but the traveling and the rehearsals wore her down, undermining her confidence. When she returned home to New York, she made life difficult for Isabel Lyon, whose help she needed in planning the trip overseas. Her moods were so volatile that one day she would tell Lyon to continue making preparations for the voyage, and the next day she would consider canceling the whole tour. Nine days before Clara was supposed to sail, an exasperated Lyon complained in her journal, "Santa is never sure for 24 hours if she will be able to make this trip to London. . . . My days are terrible."[18]

At the same time Lyon was also trying to prepare for the move to Redding and to make sure that the new house would be ready for its owner. The burden was too much for one person, but she tried to hide the strain, suffering in silence rather than disappoint her boss or risk a falling out with her "dear Santa Clara." One weekend in early May she almost reached her breaking point. Clara was being especially unreasonable, complaining not only about the upcoming tour but also about Lyon's plans for decorating the new house.

"Headache. So ill all day," Lyon wrote, "for I wept without control for hours last night, because I was exhausted, and the fact that Santa misunderstood all my efforts, in working over the house. My anxiety over the finishings, my interest in my search for the right thing for the King's house has all been misinterpreted, and the child says I am trying to ignore her."[19]

Lyon wanted everything to be perfect and dreaded the thought that Clara and her father might not like the finished house. As the builder's son, Philip Sunderland, would recall, Lyon was uncompromising in her determination to get everything just right: "We had the whole interior finished, painted white, and Miss Lyon decided she didn't like it. The house was supposed to look like an Italian villa; she felt we had made it look like a New England colonial place. She said what it needed was a dark stain—so we did the whole place over again in the dark stain."[20]

Though the emotional tension kept Lyon in a constant state of misery, she continued to humor Clara and to maintain her composure around her. Because Clara took so long to reach a final decision about her travel plans, Robert Collier's help had to be enlisted at the last moment to book tickets and to make all the necessary arrangements for her and the three people she was taking along—her accompanist and friend Charles Wark, the violinist Marie Nichols, and the family housekeeper Katy Leary. It was an enormous relief for Lyon when Clara and her party boarded their ship in New York and sailed for London on May 16. Largely unaware of the difficulties that Clara had been causing at home, Twain wrote her a cheerful note while she was at sea, sending it ahead to her hotel in London. He wished her good luck with her debut, telling her, "Dear heart, I hope everything will come out exactly as you would wish." He also made a point of adding, "Robert Collier did certainly do well by you. He is a dear."[21]

On her arrival in London, Clara was asked by a reporter why she had not brought her father with her. As politely as possible, and with a light touch, she explained that she preferred not to be upstaged. "I had him with me for two years in America, accompanying me, but I found he was so anxious to get on the platform and make a speech before I had finished singing, and the people seemed to want to hear him so much, that I thought it safer to leave him behind."[22]

· · ·

WHILE CLARA WENT OFF to conquer new worlds, her father set aside a whole day to think up a new name for Autobiography House. He was bothered by the fact that the original name wasn't likely to make much of an impression on the general public, and, of course, his ambition in most things was to get the world's attention and keep it.

So he set himself a challenge. He needed to find a name that would meet four conditions: "I wanted a name that wasn't use-worn; & wouldn't resemble any other house's name, either in this world or Sheol; & couldn't be copied by anybody; & would at once suggest me to anybody hearing it uttered or seeing it in print."

In other words, he wanted a name for the house that was as memorable as the one under which he had chosen to write his books. At the beginning of June he sent a letter to Clara in London and headed it with the words "Summer-address, INNOCENCE AT HOME, REDDING, CONN." He liked the nice twist on the title of his *The Innocents Abroad,* but he also thought the name was in keeping with his public image as the Man in White, eternally youthful and pure of heart. "Many populations will think it describes me," he said of Innocence at Home, and then added in a spirit of modesty, "but I do not wish to seem to know that."[23]

From the moment the name came to him, he began looking forward to people discussing its significance just as they discussed his habit of wearing white. The fun of answering questions on the subject would come from being coy about it. As he confessed to Jean, the name was "susceptible of more than one interpretation." But Clara had no interest in this sort of game and would later insist on a different name. For the time being, however, she was preoccupied with her tour and let the subject drop. Everyone else, however, seemed to like Twain's choice, and he took pride in using it as his new address.[24]

As he waited for the day of the big move, he invited nearly everyone he knew—young and old—to come out and pay him a summer visit once he was settled in Redding. He wanted the house to be full of friends all the time and planned to record the comings and goings in a formal guestbook. On the chance that he might want to have an automobile for transporting his guests to and from the local railroad station, Robert Collier offered to pick out one of the latest models and have it delivered to the house. But Twain continued to resist having a car of his own, especially since he had no intention of learning how to drive. "The chauffeur would be expensive," he reasoned, "we shouldn't use the thing often, for I mean to walk, not ride; we should have to build a garage—an unsightly one, no doubt. And so, there's not going to be any mobile."[25]

Two friends who seemed especially eager to be among the first to stay at the new house were the young actresses Billie Burke and Margaret Illington. In 1908 they were two bright stars on the American stage, and both were devoted admirers of Twain. Whenever Burke was invited to

"You were especially born to love and be loved, and be happy," Twain wrote Margaret Illington, whose friendship he valued and whose Broadway career he followed closely.

dinner at No. 21, she was quick to drop what she was doing and race to his door. As Burke recalled in her autobiography, "I thought nothing of making a trip to New York from either Boston or Philadelphia after the show if he had invited me to one of his charming little Sunday night dinners."[26]

When Margaret Illington learned that Twain was planning to make the billiards room of Innocence at Home the headquarters of his Aquarium Club, she insisted on becoming an official angelfish, despite the fact that she was twenty-six and married. When Twain laughed off her request, she staged an elaborate prank to change his mind. About a month before he moved to Redding, Twain invited Illington and her husband, Dan Frohman, to a Sunday night dinner and was amazed when he went to the door and found her playing a new part solely for his benefit.

"She was dressed for 12 years," Twain later remarked, "& had pink ribbons at the back of her neck & looked about 14 years old; so I admitted her as an angel-fish, & pinned the badge on her bosom. There's lots of lady-candidates, but I guess we won't let any more in, unless perhaps Billie Burke."

If Twain was expecting some more actresses to show up at his house in costumes similar to Illington's, it was probably a good idea that he made producer Frohman an officer of the Aquarium Club. On the membership roll he listed him as "legal staff," just below Clara's designation as "Mother Superior."[27]

Obviously, he was no longer worried that life in the country would be dull. But in the event that he failed to persuade enough people to visit him "up-country," as he liked to call Redding, he was prepared to come back to No. 21 for short periods in order to see friends or to appear at some worthy public function. He wasn't ready just yet to give up the old townhouse for good, and had already extended the lease to run until the end of the year. But he was convinced that it was time to take a long break from the bright lights of Manhattan, and he even claimed that he wouldn't mind if his days as a prominent figure on the social scene were over. "The burden of city life is heavy upon me," he declared a few weeks before boarding the train to begin his new life in a place he had never seen.[28]

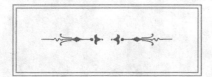

A serious card game on the terrace of Twain's new home in Redding, Connecticut, with "angelfish" Dorothy Harvey (center) and the daughters of biographer Albert Bigelow Paine.

FOURTEEN

Connecticut Yankee

> We float buoyantly upon the summer air a little
> while, complacently showing off our grace of form
> and our dainty iridescent colors; then we vanish with
> a little puff, leaving nothing behind but a memory.
>
> *Mark Twain*[1]

. . .

AFTER MONTHS OF HARD WORK, Isabel Lyon was finally ready to show off the house she had helped to create in the Connecticut woods. She sent word to Twain in New York that he could come up on Thursday, June 18. Many of the furnishings at No. 21—including the huge orchestrelle—had already been shipped to Redding. A few kittens and a tough old alley cat adopted earlier by Twain were given a new home at the villa and were allowed free run of the property, with tiny bells around their necks to warn the local bird population of their arrival.

Twain was so eager to see the house that he barely slept the night before. He was out of bed in the morning at an hour that rarely saw him stirring—six o'clock. His train wasn't scheduled to depart until late in the afternoon, but he was shaved and dressed and ready to go before breakfast. Paine was with him and managed to keep him entertained until it was time to leave. "I am conscious of a steadily augmenting great curiosity to see what the house looks like," he said. The area around Redding, he had been told, was "as beautiful as Tuxedo," but he doubted the claim was true.[2]

Wearing his white suit and a Panama hat, he took a cab to Grand Central with his biographer at his side and boarded the four o'clock train on the New Haven Railroad for the sixty-mile trip to Redding. It was a sunny afternoon, and on the way he sat by the window enjoying the view of the countryside while he chatted with Paine's daughter Louise, who was returning home from her boarding school on Long Island. As the train neared its destination, he assumed a benevolent, princely air toward the porters and other railway workers helping to transport him to his palace. Passing a large handful of silver coins to Paine, he gave instructions that sounded faintly Elizabethan: "Give them something—give everybody liberally that does any service."[3]

At the little station three miles from his house, a crowd of local people waited patiently to welcome him to the neighborhood. They were mostly simple farmers and tradespeople, and had no experience of staging a big reception for a famous man. Lacking proper signs or banners, they did the best with what they had, decorating their horses and wagons with ribbons and roses. Some carried copies of Twain's books, hoping for an autograph, while others held their children's hands and tried to explain why an important man was coming to live among them.

It wasn't easy to explain. Everybody had taken note of the new house as it rose above the treetops on the heights of Diamond Hill, but most people had trouble understanding why anyone with so much money would build a big house far from the main road in woods overlooking their modest homes. They marveled at the news that a professional architect had designed the house. As a local man would later remark, nobody in Redding "had ever needed an architect." They were a little fearful that Twain would go up the hill to his house, see what a "lonesome" spot it occupied, and take the next train back to New York, never to return.[4]

These old-fashioned Connecticut townsfolk were too reserved to cheer when Twain arrived at the station, but they did wave and nod in a friendly fashion. A few gathered enough courage to approach him and shake his hand or to offer their books for signing, while others brought their children forward to be photographed with him. Some of the women took the liberty of adorning his horse and carriage with maidenhair ferns and pink roses.

It was six o'clock when he left the station, but the sky was still bright at that time in mid-June, allowing him a good view of the wide fields and dense woods bordering the road into town. He passed the Saugatuck River, and a little farther on Paine pointed out the brook near his own cottage where the trout fishing was ideal. Then the carriage turned into the lane that led up to the villa, where Isabel Lyon, Claude the butler, and the rest of the staff stood at the door waiting to greet him. After his carriage cleared the stone gates of the estate, he caught his first glimpse of the house as he came up the long gravel drive.

The sturdy walls of the two-story villa were covered in a soft gray stucco beneath a low roof of stained shingles. At regular intervals the lower floor had tall arched windows, allowing light to fill the rooms in a way that was never possible at No. 21. There was a wing at each end, with the sun porch—or loggia—occupying the ground level of the wing closest to the drive. The front entrance had a small covered porch and the drive came right up to it, so that it was possible to arrive by carriage and step quickly indoors.

Paine and the others stood back and watched anxiously in silence as Twain entered the house and began to look around. As they were all aware, it had been more than a decade and a half since he had stood under a roof he could call his own. He hesitated in the spacious front hall, then walked slowly into the dining room, where the tall French windows had been left open to draw his attention to the view. Stepping onto the terrace, he looked down on his wide lawn with its elegant avenue of cedars leading to a pergola, and then gazed out over the green expanse of rolling hills that stretched as far as the eye could see.

"How beautiful it all is!" Paine overheard him say. "I did not think it could be as beautiful as this."[5]

As he toured the rest of the house, he was amazed by the sheer size of the place. It was much larger than its simple front suggested. A big living room forty feet long dominated the first level and was expected to serve as the social center of the house, with a prominent space reserved for the orchestrelle. In addition to the dining room, this floor also included a kitchen, a small study, and—of course—a large billiards room where

Twain could circle the table with lots of room to spare in every direction. Upstairs, there were six bedrooms and the "Nightingale's Cage," Clara's suite that included her music room and an ornate sleeping balcony over the loggia. There were also four smaller bedrooms for the servants.

From a distance the house may have looked like something that belonged in old Tuscany, but inside it had all the latest conveniences. There was a steam plant for warming the rooms in winter and for providing a steady supply of hot water in all seasons. The estate had its own spring-fed reservoir capable of holding eight thousand gallons of fresh water. This served not only the kitchen and bathrooms, but also a small laundry and ice house. The house was illuminated by gas lights connected to the built-in acetylene plant, which could power two hundred separate fixtures throughout the villa. (For big houses in rural areas, acetylene was then considered an efficient and powerful way of illuminating large spaces.)

Isabel Lyon and John Howells had worked hard to create a home that would please Twain from the start, and they succeeded beyond all expectations. Before the day was over the proud owner announced his verdict: "It is a perfect house—perfect, so far as I can see, in every detail." He was tempted to believe that the villa had always been there, waiting for him. As he told John Howells, it looked "native & at home among these Yankee woods & hills."[6]

After dark the house began to fill up with neighbors and friends coming to congratulate Twain and to look over the rooms. Food was served, and then everyone was treated to a fireworks display that sent rockets soaring over the back lawn and down into a distant pasture, scattering horses and cattle. The master of the pyrotechnics was a local farmer who was new to the area, but whose relationship with Twain went back many years. He was fifty-eight-year-old Dan Beard, who had recently left New York after working in the city for a quarter of a century as an illustrator and writer. In 1889, Twain had chosen him to illustrate *A Connecticut Yankee in King Arthur's Court* and had been thrilled with the results, calling his pictures "charming & beautiful," and declaring, "Beard got everything that I put into that book and a little more besides."[7]

Though they had kept in touch over the years and had worked together on other books, most notably *Following the Equator*, it was only by chance that they moved to the same small town in Connecticut. Beard was already busy pursuing his next great passion—teaching frontier skills to "boy pioneers" in an organization he called the Sons of Daniel Boone, the forerunner of the Boy Scouts of America—and his little farm was part of his effort to perfect his own outdoor talents. The future national scout commissioner was in the middle of painting an old chicken coop on the afternoon that Twain arrived in Redding, but his neighbors talked him into putting down his brush and taking charge of the fireworks. He never bothered to change clothes, so he was embarrassed when Twain learned he was responsible for the colorful explosions and invited him inside to thank him and offer him a drink.

"My face and hands were blackened with powder," Beard would recall, "and my clothes stiffened with that peculiar shade of red paint only to be seen on farm buildings in rural districts. Thus arrayed, I stood in the middle of the floor while my genial old friend and new neighbor proposed a toast to me."[8]

Twain was bursting with pride in his new house and couldn't wait to spread the news of his joy. "I like the house ever so much," he wrote Jean the next day, "& I like the deep quiet, after tumultuous New York. I arrived at 6 p.m., yesterday, & Paine & Ashcroft & I played billiards until mid-night and had a good time."[9]

He told Clara that he had never lived in a better house. He even went so far as to find fault with their old home in Hartford, which was ordinarily a sacred subject beyond criticism. "The Hartford house was a lovely home, but the architect damaged many of its comfort-possibilities and wasted a deal of its space. The New York house is a roomy and pleasant home, but it is sunless, not beautiful. This house is roomy and delightful and beautiful, and no space has been wasted. The sun falls upon it in such floods that you can hear it."

In his letter to Clara, who was then enjoying the limelight of her English tour, Twain made a special effort to needle her for her absence. First he told her that her suite was "the prettiest feature of the whole house," then he teased her that it might not be available if she stayed away too long. "I expect to move into it when it is finished and furnished," he threatened. "No, I will lodge angel-fishes in it."

She knew not to take such bluster seriously, but she may have felt jealous of Isabel Lyon's unqualified success with the house, especially given their recent disagreements over the final details. Her father was extravagant in his praise for the secretary's good work. "Miss Lyon has achieved wonders," he wrote Clara. "There isn't a discordant note in the whole place."[10]

He was trying to persuade his daughter that the house was one they could be proud of, but he knew that her own pride would make it hard for her to enjoy the gift he was offering—a new home to rival, if not surpass, the one of her youth. Unfortunately, the more he did for her, the more she was reminded of his success and of her struggle to earn fame on her own. Even while she was in London, where her father's name was so revered, she felt the need to complain about the burden of always being identified with him. In an interview she gave to the English press, she made no mention of the new home her father had built or the fact that he was paying her travel expenses. But she was eager to explain, as a reporter later put it, "the tribulations which face the daughter of a celebrity."

Some of her comments in London were published in the Sunday *New York Times* just four days before Twain moved to Redding. The article was accompanied by a recent photo of father and daughter playing cards at No. 21. To her English interviewers, Clara tried to speak lightly of her predicament, joking about "the glaring injustice of having to go about labeled 'Mark Twain's daughter' when I am doing my best to pursue a musical career." But she wasn't able to suppress the occasional hint of real resentment. Recalling awkward parties she had attended at her father's side, she said, "At social gatherings graced by his presence my existence was on the level of a footstool—always an unnecessary object in a crowded room."

Though she was trying to be witty, her remark sounds hollow in print and gives the impression that she was trying to be cruel. No doubt Twain was annoyed when he read it, but he never bothered to rebuke her for it. He didn't begrudge her the right to make such a complaint, and mere words couldn't alter his affection for her. Their conflict of wills was serious, but their verbal sniping at each other often sounded worse than it was.

Try as she might, Clara couldn't hope to match her father's wit, and she knew it. For one thing, strangers kept reminding her of the fact. As she lamented to the English press, she often felt at a disadvantage meeting new people because they "expect me to be 'bright' and amusing."

Yet she had spent so much time around her father that some of his sly humor rubbed off on her, and sometimes—if she didn't force it—she could almost sound like him. Asked in London to explain her father's fondness for white clothing, she gave an answer as amusing as any of Twain's previous explanations. "Father's white suit is another of my trials," she said. "I have always believed that the reason he took to wearing it is that it soothed him and reminded him of bed."[11]

. . .

Paine's old new England saltbox stood at the foot of Diamond Hill, only a short walk from Twain's villa, so it was now a simple matter for the biographer to go up the hill in the afternoon or evening and spend time with his subject. When the weather was good, as it often was that summer, they would take long walks together, rambling miles from home on winding lanes or down narrow woodland paths. Twain loved exploring the steep ravine below his house where there was an old stone bridge, a waterfall, and a small cave. He boasted that a strenuous hike in his new neighborhood wasn't too demanding for him "after my long tramps up and down Fifth Avenue to show my clothes."[12]

In the daytime his favorite lounging place at home was the loggia. It had a domed ceiling, tiled floor, comfortable wicker furniture, and cool breezes. He liked sitting there with guests and playing card games, usually Hearts, or spreading out on a chaise longue by himself and reading. "The loggia was lovely," one of his servants recalled, "and Mr. Clemens used to sit out there in the summertime and have the sun glare at him from all sides; and he seemed happy and contented." At the close of day he would stand under the arches and watch the sun disappear behind the hills. "As for sunsets," wrote a visiting journalist, "Mr. Clemens proved to me that he gets them in their full splendor from the loggia."[13]

After dark, he would sometimes return to the loggia to admire a sky unspoiled by city lights. He enjoyed sharing his knowledge of astronomy with guests, pointing out constellations and explaining the concept of a light-year. He was also fond of speculating on a time far in the future when the sky would be dotted with fast airships and spaceships. Staring up at the stars from an archway, he told Isabel Lyon, "Oh, I suppose that a hundred years from now people will be sitting in these very arches to watch the airships go by."[14]

Because the house stood on a breezy hillside, the summer heat wasn't oppressive, and insects weren't usually a problem. Whenever a pesky fly dared to trouble his peace on the terrace or inside the loggia, the new lord of the manor regarded the intrusion as a personal insult. One morning while he was having his breakfast outdoors, a fly bothered him for so long that he stared at it with fierce indignation and growled, "I'd rather have a rank old prostitute around than one fly."[15]

The only creatures whose behavior never seemed to trouble him were his cats, who were pampered and spoiled. They were even allowed to interfere with the billiard games. Two of the more adventurous kittens—Danbury and Sinbad—liked to get on the table and bat the balls around. During games they would sometimes position themselves over a pocket and take swipes at incoming balls. Instead of reprimanding them for disrupting his sacred pastime, Twain would carry on with his play and would expect his guests to do the same. While a cat occupied a pocket, the normal rules were temporarily suspended.

The general routine of the house was informal and relaxed. Nobody was expected to show up for breakfast at a fixed time or place. Guests could come and go as they liked as long as they showed a proper regard for the beauty of the place and the genial company of their host.

There was a constant stream of guests that summer. Their names began to fill up the pages of the guestbook, which was usually kept on a table in either the front hall or the living room. Such devoted admirers as Robert Collier and George Harvey showed up with their wives, and there always seemed to be at least one angelfish coming or going, often accompanied by a relative. But there were also visits from old acquaintances who had not seen much of Twain in recent years. One day the great muckraking journalist Ida Tarbell came to pay a call, bringing with her Richard Watson Gilder's sister, Jeannette, who was also a writer. Tarbell had a house on the outskirts of Redding and wanted to welcome Twain to the neighborhood. She avoided raising the subject of her old investigations into the corrupt business methods of Standard Oil and was content merely to chat with Twain about his charming house. "It was a pleasant company," Lyon wrote after the visit, "and the King approves of those 2 fine old girls. They love the house with its mellow colorings, its 'mouth-watering' colorings, as Jeannette Gilder calls it."[16]

In her autobiography Tarbell recalled that Twain was so eager to show off his house that he once employed the local butcher to make sure that everyone in Redding received an invitation to one of his parties. To a few of his old friends in New York, he wrote little notes trying to entice them to pay a visit. "You wouldn't have to play billiards until three in the morning," he wrote Henry Rogers's attractive young daughter-in-law, Mary, "unless you felt a little dissipation like that would do you good." Despite the isolation of the place, he reassured her, "It isn't lonesome here, and I don't intend that it ever shall be. . . . The friends come and go, right along—laps and slams—the new visitor getting into the old visitor's bed before it is cold."[17]

He invited almost everyone in Henry Rogers's family to "bring a trunk" and stay for a while. He even asked the formidable Katharine Harrison at the Standard Oil headquarters if she wanted to come for a weekend, and she promised to do so. But Rogers himself was preoccupied for most of the summer with the job of completing his Virginian Railway and wasn't able to visit Redding. Twain was eager to show his old friend the new house and was disappointed that he couldn't persuade him to put everything aside and spend a few days enjoying the pleasures of Innocence at Home. To Emilie Rogers he wrote, "I wish you and Mr. Rogers had elected to come here for a few weeks' rest, for this is the very quietest place outside the dungeon of St. Peter and St. Paul; no strangers, no crowds, no fashion." As an added incentive, he promised that if they came he would "learn bridge, and entertain you, and rob you."[18]

One member of Twain's Aquarium was a frequent guest because she lived in the neighborhood and was able to walk up at short notice to entertain other angelfish coming from out of state. "What a lovely place he made of it," Louise Paine said of Twain's house in an interview fifty years later, "and how we used to enjoy visiting him there. . . . I could walk there easily, but other 'Members of the Aquarium' came with their parents or governesses to stay for weekends or longer, and he taught us all to play Hearts and, with infinite patience, to manage billiards cues. He never made us feel that he was an elderly man whose good manners included being kind to children. On the contrary, he seemed to be having such a genuinely good time himself that age differences were forgotten."[19]

As a general rule, the house didn't have any pictures on the walls.

Twain said that he wanted the tall windows to serve as frames for the views outside, which were much better than any artist could capture on canvas, he insisted. He said that the house offered "what you might call a feeding view, for every time you look away across the hills and vales you see some new point of interest to feed upon and enjoy."[20]

The walls of the billiards room, however, were an exception to his ban on pictures. Because the room was the "Official Headquarters of the Aquarium," it was lined with photographs of the young members and a few drawings of real angelfish from Bermuda. The only other place in the house with a picture on the wall was Twain's own bedroom, where he kept a portrait of Jean.

The Aquarium headquarters contained a list of club rules and regulations. They didn't amount to much, however, because in his capacity as Admiral, Twain created so many loopholes that almost every clause was open to review or revision at his discretion. A parody of the restrictions that other clubs of the period liked to impose on members, the list creates bogus obligations of a kind that no other club would propose—such as one encouraging the angelfish to engage in conspiracies (but only on the condition that they "give notice to the Admiral & tell him what it is about. Except when the proposed conspiracy is against the Admiral himself; in that case notice must be given to the Official Legal Staff"). The document also includes dire warnings of criminal prosecutions for members who engage in "conduct unbecoming an Angel-Fish," with stiff penalties for such crimes as bribery or the failure to answer letters from the Admiral. It is all written in the same spirit of fun as Twain's famous "Notice" at the beginning of *Huckleberry Finn*, which threatens that any reader "attempting to find a plot" in the novel will be shot.[21]

Because he had the means and the imagination, Twain was able to create the illusion at Redding that he was still the father of young daughters living in a sunny house where everything was arranged to perfection, and where a faithful circle of friends watched over him and amused him. When his angelfish Dorothy Quick and her mother came for a long visit that summer, she found that Twain was now completely at ease in the kind of life he wanted most. "Mr. Clemens was never so happy," she recalled, "as when he had a number of congenial people around him, and he ruled his little household with a kindly despotism." Dorothy was especially impressed by the way that the openness of the house created an impression that it was in harmony with nature. Windows and doors were often left wide open, and when the orchestrelle was playing, the sound flowed in all directions, drifting over the terrace or into the loggia as if by magic from a passing cloud. Within the limits of the technology of his time, Twain and his guests were able to enjoy a little wonderland of their own that seemed far removed from the rest of the world.[22]

It amused Dorothy that Twain, in his easygoing mood, would have a bath upstairs and then come down to the loggia to dry his hair in the sun, draping a Turkish towel over his white clothes. Freshly washed, his hair would lie flat against his head and make him look like a different man. But after an hour on the wicker chaise longue, his hair was restored to its usual curly mass, and he was ready to start the day. Then he would wander off to the terrace or down to the garden pergola or take his guests on a tour of the countryside and return to the loggia for tea. He liked being outdoors so much that sometimes he wouldn't come in until well after dark. On moonlit nights his white figure on the lawn looked like a ghost's.

One day that summer he came downstairs and found the view from the loggia so entrancing that he didn't mind when he suddenly realized there were no guests to share it with. The scenery had become familiar and comforting, like a friend. "It is a luxuriously lazy & delightful day; & the sun, & the shade, & the far-spreading greenery, & the sumptuous dense foliage, & the soft blue distances, & the gossiping birds make me stay out doors. With myself for company."[23]

It took only a couple of weeks for Twain to decide that the new house was so good that he didn't need to keep No. 21 after all. Ashcroft was asked to negotiate an early end to the lease on the townhouse. Twain wanted to be rid of it and didn't care if he never saw it again. In the future, when he needed to go into the city, he planned to stay with friends like Henry Rogers or Martin Littleton.

Though he was never satisfied with No. 21, he had started to overlook its faults in the first part of 1908, and had almost talked himself into keeping it as his permanent residence, with the Redding house serving only as a summer home. But all that changed after the move. Now that he had experienced a taste of the good life in his new place, he didn't want to live anywhere else. He paid the house the highest compliment when he

wrote Helen Allen about it and said, "My child, it's as tranquil & contenting as Bermuda."[24]

At last, he was certain that he had found a real home again. "It is a
home—unquestionably a home," he wrote Mary Rogers. "I have lived in
only one other house which was able to produce in me the deep feeling
implied by that word; that was the Hartford home." By comparison, No.
21 seemed to him irredeemably inadequate. "It was crude and rude, and
its too pronounced and quarrelsome colors broke the repose of my spirit
and kept me privately cursing and swearing all the time, even Sundays."[25]

Isabel Lyon shared his desire to leave behind their old life on Fifth
Avenue. As she looked back over her years at the house, the sad experiences seemed to dominate her recollections. She had found happiness
working alongside Twain, but also great sorrow in her difficulties with
Jean and Clara. In her journal she wrote, "In that house. . . . I saw Jean in
her convulsions, and I saw Clara in her agony and in her illness, and in
her strugglings with her career and in her hates and fierce lovings, and
while my heart was full of loving for all of them, there was a long, long
lack of peace, and the stairs I climbed were often pitifully weary ones."[26]

At Redding, Lyon hoped she would find the "peace" that No. 21 lacked.
Determined to make sure that everything ran smoothly, she was ready at
any hour to attend to the needs not only of her employer but also his
guests. To some, she gave the impression that she considered the house to
be as much hers as Twain's. Though the original plan was for her to work
at the house during the day and go to her own cottage—the Lobster Pot—
at night, she liked the new place so much that she claimed a spare bedroom for herself and usually stayed overnight. She soon brought her
elderly mother down from Hartford to live at the cottage.

For assistance and emotional support, she was beginning to rely
more and more on Ralph Ashcroft, who was often in Redding despite the
fact that he lived in Brooklyn and didn't receive a salary from Twain. He
had his own work to do in the city, where he dabbled in various minor
investments, including companies that made such ordinary items as
safety pins and shoe insoles. But Twain had grown so accustomed to having him around that he didn't question why a man of modest means
would want to serve him for no pay. He liked to think of Lyon and
Ashcroft as a devoted pair working together for the sole purpose of mak-

ing his life easier. His hospitality and the pleasure of his company were their reward.

"Miss Lyon is extravagantly fond of the place," Twain wrote Helen Allen, "& so is Ashcroft. Ashcroft comes up every Friday & stays over Sunday."[27]

To make the Lobster Pot more comfortable for her mother, Lyon hired a local builder—Harry Lounsbury—to renovate parts of it and paid him about $2,000. Twain would later loan her another $1,500 to cover the cost of additional work, and he planned to turn that loan into a gift in a year or so. What she failed to tell him, however, was that she had already used his money to pay for the first renovation. She knew how much he hated deception of any kind, yet with his checkbook under her control, she couldn't resist the temptation to begin fixing up her cottage at his expense, slipping her bills in with his.

Because $2,000 was a relatively small sum in his annual budget, he wasn't likely to notice how it had been spent, and she must have considered it a reasonable reward for all the work she had put into the main house. For at least a year she had been in the habit of taking small amounts of cash from the household accounts to buy clothes and other minor items for herself, and the ease of doing this may have emboldened her to pay Lounsbury from Twain's checkbook.

Part of the problem was that her place in his life had never been clearly defined. If he considered her only a household secretary, then he had every reason to assume she would not use his money as though it were her own. But he had come to expect a lot more from her, and it isn't surprising that she began to want more for herself. Having done so much to make his house comfortable, she didn't want to neglect her own. And because she was expected to entertain his friends, and to accompany him on social occasions, she wanted to look her best. She told Twain about some of these extra expenses, but he didn't pay much attention to her spending habits and assumed that now and then she would buy a few things for herself when she shopped for him or Clara. But he expected her to be open and responsible about it. Instead she overspent and tried to hide it. It was a big mistake, and would later cost her dearly.

· · ·

BEFORE MOVING TO REDDING, Twain had reluctantly agreed to attend a public event in Portsmouth, New Hampshire, at the end of June. Getting there would involve several hours of travel on a railroad he particularly disliked, and the event itself would bring him into close contact with a person he couldn't stand. But he agreed to go because it was a ceremony to honor his old friend the poet and novelist Thomas Bailey Aldrich, who had died the year before. Lilian Woodman Aldrich, his widow, had established a museum in the writer's boyhood home near the wharves in the old Puddle Dock section of Portsmouth, and had invited hundreds of people to the dedication, including such important literary figures as Twain and William Dean Howells.

Because the house was the original of the one where the fictional Tom Bailey lives in Aldrich's best-known work, *The Story of a Bad Boy,* the author's widow assumed that it would become a shrine for his admirers. But after almost forty years in print, the novel had lost much of its popularity—unlike the major work it had influenced, *Tom Sawyer*—and some people wondered whether the museum would attract many visitors. Twain was one of those who thought it would soon go bust. "Aldrich was never widely known," he said in one of his dictations. "His fame as a writer of prose is not considerable; his fame as a writer of verse is also very limited." A museum devoted to Aldrich, Twain said, wouldn't attract enough visitors even in the heart of a large city, much less in a place as small as Portsmouth. "A memorial museum of George Washington relics could not excite any considerable interest if it were located in that decayed town."

But Twain thought it was his duty to attend the dedication. He had known Aldrich since the early 1870s and had been fond of his company, largely because of their shared sense of humor. "When it came to making fun of a folly, a silliness, a windy pretense, a wild absurdity," he recalled, "Aldrich the brilliant, Aldrich the sarcastic, Aldrich the ironical, Aldrich the merciless, was a master." The wife, however, was the opposite. Self-important and self-righteous, Lilian Aldrich took everything too seriously, including her husband's modest reputation. Twain never had any use for her. He considered her "a strange and vanity-devoured, detestable woman," and declared privately, "I do not believe I could ever learn to like her except on a raft at sea with no other provisions in sight."[28]

And now that her invitation to the new museum was going to force him to leave his newfound paradise at Redding and take a slow train to a "decayed" town, he was seething with resentment and determined not to enjoy the trip. "It is possible," he admitted to himself, "that I would never be able to see anything creditable in anything Mrs. Aldrich might do."[29]

To add to his misery, Isabel Lyon talked him out of wearing his white uniform to the ceremony, saying that it wouldn't be appropriate at an event honoring the memory of a man who had died so recently. The weather on the way up to Portsmouth was hot, and Twain squirmed uncomfortably in his stiff black clothes while he rode in a sooty old carriage of the Boston and Maine Railroad. He regarded the line as one of the worst in the business, which was saying a lot, and later claimed that he spent the whole journey swallowing cinders.

According to Paine, who accompanied him, Twain "was silent and gloomy most of the way." By the time they arrived in Portsmouth, the heat was sweltering, and no one came to welcome them. Lilian Aldrich had been at the station earlier, but had taken off in her "sumptuous and costly" automobile, as Twain described it, to drive the governors of Massachusetts and New Hampshire directly to the ceremony at the town's Music Hall. Twain and his biographer had to walk.[30]

As one of the speakers, Twain was obliged to occupy a prominent place on the stage. For two hours, he stared at the audience and sweated in the "suffocating" heat while one dignitary after another rose to praise Aldrich in solemn tones. He was scheduled to speak last. When his time came, he was so fed up with the dreariness of the event that he pocketed his prepared remarks and decided to pay a different kind of tribute to Aldrich, one that would be more appropriate to his old friend's love of irreverent humor.

Striding to the podium, he pulled out a big white handkerchief. Without saying a word, he slowly ran it across his forehead and put it away. Then he pulled it out a second time to wipe his cheeks. Still silent, he started to put it away again, but brought it back up to his neck and began dabbing at the sweat.

"Poor Tom! Poor Tom!" he exclaimed finally in a sad voice. "I hope— he isn't—as hot—as I am now."[31]

It is not known how the widow reacted to this bit of comic relief, but the rest of the crowd welcomed it, and Twain responded by launching a vigorous denunciation of the black clothing he was wearing and of the "lugubrious custom of having tailors to help us mourn for the dead." Besides, he declared, this was no time for sad reflection. Aldrich wouldn't have wanted it. "He had been a man who loved humor and brightness and wit." Accordingly, Twain spent the rest of his time entertaining his fellow "mourners" in the only way he thought proper, delivering what he later described as "twelve minutes of lawless and unconfined and desecrating nonsense." They loved it. "The audience," Paine recalled, "that had been maintaining a proper gravity throughout, showed its appreciation in ripples of merriment that grew presently into genuine waves of laughter."[32]

· · ·

IN THE END Twain had more fun playing the "bad boy" in Portsmouth than he wanted to admit, and he certainly enjoyed lambasting Mrs. Aldrich afterward in his autobiographical dictations. Moreover, the journey had a side benefit that especially pleased him. Because Jean's summer home in Gloucester was just fifty miles down the coast from Portsmouth, he and Paine were able to stop there for a visit on the return to Redding.

To his delight, he found that Jean was living comfortably in a "very pretty cottage" and glowing with robust health. She had made good use of the new freedom allowed her in Gloucester and was now more active than she had been in years. She and her friend Marguerite had even taken up sailing. As a result of spending many hours in and around the water, she looked tanned and fit. Paine agreed that this new life by the sea had done wonders for her. "We were charmed & surprised," Twain said later, "to see how well she was, how sound & vigorous in mind and body."

On the spot he decided that Jean was ready to come home. To him, it seemed that her months of seclusion had finally given her enough strength to overpower her disease. And now that he knew what a peaceful and sunny place his new house was, he thought that Redding could do as much for Jean's health as Gloucester.

He assumed that Dr. Peterson would object to the idea and argue that Jean would find life at home too stressful. But given how much her condition had improved, he didn't see how living at his beautiful and spacious house could cause a relapse. Of course, he wasn't aware that Lyon had been telling the doctor for months that Jean's return under any conditions would be too upsetting for all concerned. It had been easier for him to accept the doctor's orders when Jean was being treated at the sanitarium, and when he was living on busy Fifth Avenue. But now it didn't make sense that she should stay away from home.

At last he was ready to act. He quickly thought of a plan that might satisfy Peterson. On his walks around Redding, he told Jean, he had seen a vacant farm for sale, and thought the old house could easily be fixed up to accommodate both her and Marguerite. That way Jean could live under her own roof, yet be close enough to visit him. Over time, he reasoned, she could prove beyond a doubt that the doctor's worries were unwarranted and take her rightful place at his side. Jean responded enthusiastically to this plan, saying that she had always wanted to live on a small farm.

Seeing her happiness, Twain believed that at last there were good reasons to be hopeful about her future. He said that he would tell Isabel Lyon to get in touch with Dr. Peterson right away. They would ask his approval for Jean to "come home at once," and then buy the farm and fix it up. Even though father and daughter spent only a few hours together in Gloucester, the visit raised their spirits and made them think they would soon be reunited in Redding.[33]

When Twain arrived back home on July 2, he took Lyon aside and "in an outburst of enthusiasm" shared the good news about Jean's health. The secretary seemed to share his joy, but as he vaguely sensed at the time, there was—as he later put it—"frost upon her raptures." In fact, she was deeply unsettled by his sudden proposal to move Jean to Redding and began talking him out of it, gently explaining that the house he had in mind wasn't suitable for Jean and couldn't be improved without a great deal of work. Besides, she cautioned, they shouldn't interfere with Dr. Peterson's successful efforts, but wait for him to decide when Jean was well enough to come home. It didn't take long for her to kill his enthusiasm, and by the end of the night she had planted so many doubts in his mind that he decided to abandon the plan. He was too exhausted from the long trip, with all its emotional ups and downs, to think clearly, and once again found himself feeling defeated by the complications of his daughter's illness.[34]

Before going to bed he wrote a painful letter to Jean, calling off the move and explaining that he had been wrong about the farmhouse. He was no longer sure what the best course of action was, except to continue the one plan that seemed to be working—her doctor's. "I am disappointed, distressed, & low-spirited," he wrote, "for that dream of yours and mine has come to nothing. . . . I wish I could situate you exactly to your liking, dear child, how gladly I would do it. And I wish I could take your malady, & rid you of it for always. I wish your mother were here; she could help us."[35]

The next morning he took out his frustrations on Lilian Aldrich by beginning the first of a series of autobiographical dictations that slowly and methodically piled ridicule on her character, her museum project, and her dreary dedication ceremony. He knew that his attacks were excessive and admitted as much in the dictations, but he needed some way to vent his anger, and the subject of her vanity was fresh in his mind. It also gave him a chance to demonstrate once again his peerless ability to position his target in one part of a sentence and blast it in the next. "She is one of those people who are profusely affectionate," he said, "and whose demonstrations disorder your stomach."[36]

After a few days of making Mrs. Aldrich pay for her sins, Twain felt happier. Gradually, he returned to the mellow condition he had enjoyed before going to Portsmouth, and he vowed not to leave his cool haven for the rest of the summer. Visitors continued to come and go, and he was cheered by the growing chorus of praise for his house from both guests and neighbors. By the end of July he was feeling so much better that he rarely had a bad word to say about anything. In Gloucester, Jean was continuing to enjoy her summer by the sea, and seemed happy to stay there for the rest of the season. Her upbeat letters took away some of his disappointment at failing to bring her home and made him think she was better off to stay put for the time being. "Go on with your boating, dear Jean," he wrote, "& have the very best times you can!"[37]

Though Lyon was successful at preventing Jean from coming home for the summer, she knew that the shore of Eastern Point would lose its appeal as soon as the weather turned cold. By September, she would need to find another place to send Jean or risk having her at Redding. A solution came to her when she heard of a medical professor in Berlin— Hofrath von Reuvers—who was supposedly achieving great results in his work with epilepsy patients. Actually, Dr. Von Reuvers's treatments were no better than Dr. Peterson's, but Lyon probably exaggerated their effectiveness in order to create a good excuse for sending Jean abroad. She knew that a long stay in Germany wasn't something Jean would object to. After all, Jean was fluent in the language, and she had enjoyed living in Berlin with the rest of her family when she was eleven. If Lyon wanted an effective way to keep father and daughter apart for another year, sending her to Germany made sense.

Working quickly in August and early September, Lyon won Dr. Peterson's approval of the trip and made the necessary arrangements for Jean to sail to Germany with Marguerite and a maid on September 26. Such haste to get her out of Gloucester before the end of the month should have aroused everyone's suspicions. But Lyon handled the trip in a way that made Jean think she was following the wishes of her father and her doctor, while Twain was led to assume that Jean and Peterson had come up with the idea.

"Jean goes to Germany . . . to be placed under a famous specialist in Berlin," Twain wrote Mary Rogers in August. "And she is glad, for she likes Germany and the language."[38]

In fact, Jean wanted to spend the winter in Redding, and was apprehensive about taking such a long journey, telling Lyon, "I'm scared." But the secretary convinced her that Germany was the better option. It must have occurred to Jean that by going so far away from home, she would finally be able to enjoy the kind of freedom that she had so often dreamed about in Katonah. Though life in a big city wasn't what she preferred, she realized that all kinds of new opportunities would be available to her there, including the possibility of romance. "I am wildly excited at the idea of going abroad again," she told Nancy Brush in August.[39]

Lyon arranged everything so quickly that Jean was on her way to Germany before either Twain or Peterson could give the plan more thought. On the day of departure Lyon wrote in her journal, "Jean, pathetic & wan, sailed at eleven today on the Pretoria." At the very least, Twain might have asked why Jean was well enough to make a transatlantic voyage and to live in a large European capital, but not to come to Redding and sleep in her own bedroom. It wasn't logical that only nine months after leaving the safe world of the sanitarium she would be sent thousands of miles from home to live independently in Berlin for the sole purpose of receiving occasional treatments from a doctor she had never met. But Twain seemed to think the risks were worth taking. No doubt he hoped that, with the help of the new doctor, Jean could finally achieve some lasting control over her disease. As Lyon shrewdly calculated, the promise of a cure was the best excuse for keeping Jean on the move and far from home.[40]

· · ·

ON THE FIRST WEEKEND in August, Twain was jolted by sad news about his nephew—and nearest male relative—Samuel Moffett. At forty-seven, Moffett was a reasonably successful man with a long career in journalism that had included jobs in both the Hearst and Pulitzer organizations. He was the only son of Twain's sister, Pamela, and was born in St. Louis when his uncle was still plain Sam Clemens, a steamboat pilot on the Mississippi. Partly because of his uncle's influence, he had landed the best job of his career at *Collier's Weekly* in 1904, becoming a senior member of the editorial staff. He bought a house in the New York City suburb of Mount Vernon, where he lived comfortably with his wife, Mary, and their two young children. Then tragedy struck on Saturday morning, August 1, 1908, as he and his family were beginning their vacation on the New Jersey shore at Sea Bright.

Eager to go into the ocean, Moffett quickly changed clothes on his arrival and ran down to the beach. Despite being warned by his hotel manager that the surf was dangerously high, he plunged right in. "I'll be all right," he told the manager. "I'm a fairly strong swimmer." Not long afterward, he was heard crying for help, and a lifeguard dashed out to rescue him from the waves. But it was too late. As his wife watched, his lifeless body was carried to the beach, where a doctor from the hotel pronounced him dead.[41]

Though Twain was not especially close to his nephew, they were always on good terms, and his death was a great blow. It pained him to know that the death was witnessed by Mary Moffett. "It is the most heartbroken family I have seen in years," he said after attending the funeral in Mount Vernon on Tuesday. Once again dressed in black, he suffered in the heat during the services, and on the train journey there and back.

Fortunately, Robert Collier took charge of the funeral arrangements and had "a splendid motor car" waiting to take Twain from the station to the funeral, which made the ordeal a little easier. But it took its toll, and when he returned to Redding, he was exhausted.[42]

On Thursday night he felt ill and had trouble staying on his feet. He went upstairs to retire early, but while he was getting ready for bed, he staggered into the bathroom and vomited. Isabel Lyon heard his groans and came immediately. She managed to get him into bed, but was so worried about his condition that she couldn't sleep. For most of the night she watched over him. At dawn he claimed to be feeling better and said, "Well, I *did* have a clearing out." Then he sat down and began smoking a pipe as though nothing had happened. (Much as he loved his cigars, he also had a large collection of pipes and liked to smoke them in bed.)[43]

Though he refused to take this episode seriously, Lyon insisted on calling Dr. Quintard. A few days later Twain admitted in a letter to Livy's sister, Susan Crane, that he had been ill, and that his doctor had told him to avoid leaving home again until the weather was cooler. After describing the pitiful scenes at the funeral, he told her, "I came back here in bad shape, & had a bilious collapse, but I am all right again, though the doctor from New York has given peremptory orders that I am not to stir from here before frost."[44]

This "bilious collapse" made Lyon worry that Twain was headed for something worse. She couldn't bear the thought of losing her King and resolved to work even harder to keep him healthy and at peace in the house she had prepared for him. She saw this as a sacred undertaking and believed she now had a trusted ally with whom she could share the burden—Ralph Ashcroft, or "Benares" as Twain nicknamed him. (In one of Twain's favorite plays, Charles Rann Kennedy's *The Servant in the House,* the Bishop of Benares creates a convincing disguise for himself as a butler.) On August 8 Lyon wrote in her journal, "Benares and I have a moral obligation now in looking after the King. I shall not leave him for an hour unless Benares or another as good is here to look after him, and together we must uphold him in our spiritual arms."[45]

Ashcroft managed to win her confidence that summer by siding with her against Paine. In July he had come to her room and told her that Paine was spreading rumors about her. When she asked what kind of rumors, he replied that the biographer claimed she was addicted to drugs and was becoming increasingly unstable. The truth was that she had been trying to hide an increasingly serious drinking problem, not a drug addiction. As Ashcroft was aware, the ample supply of liquor in Twain's house had always been a temptation for her, but of late she had found it more difficult to resist and was sneaking drinks to her room at night. Lyon was aghast at the idea that anyone would accuse her of taking drugs, but she was flattered when Ashcroft echoed her words of indignation. He soon made it clear that he was on her side in other matters as well, including the question of whether her hard work was properly appreciated by Clara.

The more they talked that summer, the closer Lyon and Ashcroft became. Convinced they were the only ones who could protect Twain, they decided to work together to make sure no one else would exert more influence over him. But they worried about what might happen to them if he died suddenly. Lyon feared that her own meager income—not to mention her comfortable life in Redding—would be taken from her within weeks, if not days, of his death. As for Ashcroft, he had invested a lot of time in helping Twain, and was increasingly anxious to get something solid in return.

They couldn't count on Clara's support. She was too caught up in her own life to give any thought to their futures. And dealing with Jean was never under consideration. Ashcroft shared Lyon's view that Jean was mentally unbalanced, and that she must be kept away from home at all costs.

It was obvious that they needed to make some long-term arrangement to secure their privileged positions. He emphasized that point to Lyon, but was careful to dress it up in high-sounding words that made him sound less calculating.

Aware of her weakness for vague romantic sentiments, he tried to explain his ambitions as noble and selfless. She was easily charmed by his inflated rhetoric and accepted without question "his sweet philosophy that we must pay for what we have. And to hold so great a treasure as the King means that the price one must pay can never be too high a one. It will be a high one. But to know that you know the King is to send big roots down to support your tree."[46]

This kind of talk so bedazzled Lyon that she decided to open up and tell Ashcroft more about her own desires and fears. At some point, she shared with him one of her most closely held secrets about Twain's household. In the days when she and Clara had been on closer terms, she had learned that Clara's friendship with her accompanist, Charles Wark, had turned intimate. They were not only in love, but were hoping to marry. The purpose of Clara's summer tour of Europe wasn't merely to advance her career. It was also a way to give her almost four months with Wark in places far removed from the prying eyes of the American press.

As soon as they left England and began to move around the Continent, the couple lived almost like husband and wife. To pay their way, they relied on Lyon to send money each month from Twain's checkbook. The secretary rarely sent enough, however, so it became Wark's job to write flattering notes asking for more.

Ashcroft could have guessed all this. But the big secret Lyon revealed to him was that Wark was a married man. Clara was doing her best to hide that fact. Even her tour manager—R. E. Johnston—was kept in the dark about it, as he later acknowledged. Yet the truth wouldn't have required too much sleuthing to uncover. On October 10, 1903, Dr. R. Heber Newton—a well-known liberal clergyman in Manhattan—had married Charles E. Wark and Edith Cullis in the chantry of Grace Church, only a few blocks from 21 Fifth Avenue. The *New York Times* carried the announcement.[47]

Why the married couple had grown apart in just a few years isn't clear. They didn't divorce until 1912, but in the summer of 1908 Clara seemed to believe that the wife would agree to end the marriage in a year or two. Meanwhile, she shared her secret with only a few close friends, looking to them for support and lamenting the need for subterfuge. Even after her disagreements with Lyon in the spring, she continued to confide in her. From Europe, she wrote in June: "Dear old W. is more wonderful all the time but I can't bear the many many months still that separate us from freedom and frank expression of the truth."[48]

The affair had begun in earnest during the previous summer, when Clara and Wark spent several weeks together in Boston. The secrecy that surrounded the relationship helps to explain why Clara was often so tense during this period, and also why she worried so much about a scandal in the family, projecting onto her father the fears she must have harbored about herself. If Twain suspected that the relationship between his daughter and her accompanist was romantic, he kept quiet about it. But nobody bothered to tell him the young man was married. If he had known that, he would have found himself in a real quandary.

On the one hand, as he had confided to Elinor Glyn, he didn't consider adultery a sin and believed lovers of any type couldn't be blamed for following their natural impulses. On the other hand, he knew only too well that his liberal sympathies wouldn't do him or Clara much good if a scandal erupted and society turned against them. The great irony is that while he had been worrying earlier in the year about Elinor Glyn dragging his name into the controversy over *Three Weeks,* his own daughter was engaged in an affair that had the potential to cause him much more grief. Clara was taking the chance that her father would wake up one day and read in the papers that his daughter, the well-known contralto, was seeing a married man. The risk of bad publicity was enormous, given the amount of press attention lavished on Twain and his circle. In 1908 it was the kind of thing that could sink careers and family reputations.

In fact, only two days before the singer returned home from Europe, someone did attempt to stir up a scandal. On Monday, September 7, a compromising rumor was planted in an otherwise innocuous newspaper report about Twain's decision to give up his old residence on Fifth Avenue. The article appeared that morning on page one of the *New York World,* and by evening it was also on the front page of the *Washington Times* under the title "Mark Twain Quits Gay Old New York." After noting that the only objects remaining in the house were a few chairs, a small table, and some pictures, the article said that Clara and Charles Wark would soon arrive in New York after "some months" in Europe, and that Clara would be giving a party at No. 21:

> With these scant furnishings, however, Miss Clemens will give a reception in her old home on Saturday to her many friends. It is expected that at the reception her engagement to Mr. Wark will be announced. After his daughter's marriage, a friend of Mr. Clemens said yesterday, the novelist will be virtually alone; and this, it was said, influenced him strongly in deciding to make Redding his home throughout the year.

Of course, Clara couldn't announce her engagement to a married man, and it is unimaginable that such a proud woman would consider holding a reception of any kind in a vacant house. Whoever planted this bogus information was attempting to throw into question the whole nature of her relationship with Wark. It was an open invitation to others to come forward and to correct the record by pointing out the damaging fact that Clara had spent the summer abroad with another woman's husband.

Who was this anonymous "friend of Mr. Clemens" willing to pass along inflammatory rumors to a newspaper? Only a small number of friends knew that Twain was giving up the townhouse, and most of those didn't know that it was now practically empty. In fact, only Ashcroft and Lyon, the Littletons, and perhaps one or two others were in a position to know both facts. When the article appeared, Lyon was at 21 Fifth Avenue collecting the last of the family's belongings. The first person to alert her to the story was Ashcroft, who knew exactly where to reach her. "There is a report in the paper today that Santa is engaged," she noted in her journal on September 7. "Benares telephoned to me the paragraph in the World about Santa."[49]

Lyon seemed genuinely surprised by the story and was quick to refute it when reporters showed up later in the day seeking comment. Indeed, it is unlikely that she was the anonymous source. She was not yet so alienated from Clara that she would have wanted to harm the young woman's reputation, not to mention Twain's.

Ashcroft, on the other hand, felt nothing but contempt for Clara. He detested her "prima donna" attitude and thought her summer abroad was an enormous extravagance. When he had been busy earlier in the year helping to safeguard Twain's money in the Knickerbocker Trust, she had shown little interest in her father's financial affairs and had continued to spend lavishly on herself and her friends. Ashcroft resented that he was expected to manage Twain's money wisely, while Clara was rarely subject to any financial discipline. Her spendthrift ways were forgiven by her father, who believed that she was "like all the artist breed, & like myself— foggy in matters pecuniary."[50]

But now, having won the confidence of Lyon, Ashcroft was in possession of a secret that could ruin Clara. After months of lurking in the background of Twain's life, he finally had an opportunity to create an advantage for himself, and he seized it by planting the false story in the press. If he could diminish Clara's power and influence at home, he had a good chance of securing his future as Mark Twain's trusted friend and business partner. It was an audacious ploy, but he knew from experience how easily the press could be used to spread almost any story associated with Twain. The author himself would later become convinced that Ashcroft had planted several false stories about him in the press, including one that Isabel Lyon was going to become the next Mrs. Clemens.

When the article about Clara and Wark appeared in the *World,* no one suggested that Ashcroft was the source. But Lyon must have realized it soon enough. And, at first, she was reluctant to play along. The weight of the evidence suggests that she was only gradually drawn into Ashcroft's schemes and didn't understand the extent of his deviousness until it was too late. She proved as much when she stood at the doorstep of No. 21 and gave such a forceful denial of the engagement story that the reporters went away convinced it was untrue. Thanks largely to her efforts, the story died quickly and Ashcroft's hopes for more revelations were suddenly dashed. "Miss Clemens," one paper said after interviewing Lyon, "had no thought of marriage. Instead it is possible that she may become a grand opera star. Her voice is a contralto of great power and has gained much praise in her concert tour in Europe."[51]

Ashcroft may have been hoping that Lyon would be coy in her denials and leave an opening for the scandal to catch on, but neither her words nor her manner gave the necessary hint. No investigation ensued, and no word of protest came from Mrs. Wark or her friends. After publishing a brief summary of the *World*'s original report, the *New York Times* didn't even bother to check its own archives and question how Charles Wark could wed Clara when he was already married to the former Edith Cullis, whom the paper had meticulously described on her wedding day five years earlier as wearing "a gown of white crepe de chine and a long tulle veil" and carrying "a cluster of white anemones."[52]

In due time Ashcroft would make another effort at spreading rumors about Clara and Wark. He was a cunning man with big plans and was just getting started in his effort to make his friendship with Twain pay rich dividends. But because the initial story failed to catch on, Clara was spared an embarrassing interrogation by the press when she arrived in New York on September 9.

Instead of being ambushed by scandal, she was greeted warmly by admiring reporters. They were intrigued by a message Twain had sent ahead from Redding to be handed to Clara when her ship docked. They watched as she read it with a perplexed look, then waited for her comment.

According to the *New York Tribune*, "As soon as the gangplank was made fast, Miss Clemens received a letter from [Twain], in which he explained that he was bilious and, as his doctor had advised that he stay in Connecticut until the first frost, he thought it advisable not to go to the steamer to meet her.

"Miss Clemens said that, although her father may have known the meaning of what he wrote, she certainly did not know."[53]

Such a remark was typical of Clara's irreverent attitude toward her father's fame. At that moment, however, she had no idea that she had narrowly escaped from a trap that could have tarnished her name and his.

Dutifully, Lyon and Ashcroft were waiting at the Cunard pier to welcome Clara home and to escort her straight to Redding. Paine also showed up for the occasion, but seemed upset about something. It is possible that he suspected either Lyon or Ashcroft of gossiping to the newspapers. "Paine came in pale," Lyon noted in her journal, "and I begged him not to quarrel there. He had no intention of that though."[54]

Whatever was troubling him, he was reluctant to make a scene in public or in front of Clara. As he would later admit to Twain, he was beginning to feel that Lyon's influence in the household was so great he couldn't argue with her or complain about her. He thought that Twain had come to rely so much on Lyon and Ashcroft that any criticism of them would be ignored. And he was right, as Twain would later acknowledge.

"I would not have allowed any one to say a word in criticism of those worshiped pets of mine," Twain said of Lyon and Ashcroft a year later, sadder but wiser. "To every man & woman in this region they were a pair of transparent rascals, but to me they were worthy of the kingdom of heaven."[55]

After surviving the burglary at his home, Twain demonstrates
what he intends to do if another burglar shows up.

FIFTEEN

Breaking and Entering

Anybody can hit a relative,
but a Gatling gun won't get a burglar.
Mark Twain[1]

. . .

ALL THE PUBLICITY surrounding Mark Twain's new life in Redding created interest of a kind the author and his circle didn't expect. The press reports caught the attention of an ex-convict in New York who was on the lookout for promising places to burglarize. A young man with a long criminal history, Henry Williams considered himself an accomplished thief. According to his own account, he had spent several years behind bars—most recently, at the Wisconsin State Prison, where he had been punished at hard labor for stealing from a mansion in Milwaukee.

After studying a picture of Twain's villa in a Sunday supplement, Williams decided that the tall windows on the ground floor would be easy to pry open. He was also attracted by a description of the house as "isolated," and by Twain's boast to the press that the villa now contained all his "earthly possessions." As Williams later acknowledged, "My interest and curiosity were aroused, not so much by the description of the beautiful home as by that of the portable 'earthly possessions.' They appealed to me very strongly."[2]

A smooth talker who had acquired a little learning in the prison library, Williams was well aware that his intended victim was the most famous author in America. He had read at least one of Mark Twain's books and liked it. But the literary charm of the work served merely to remind him that the author was a successful man who could afford to live in a grand showplace. The burglar couldn't resist the temptation to make a quick profit from an unsuspecting rich man who was old and living on a remote hillside. Even the fanciful name of the house—Innocence at Home—seemed to confirm Twain's vulnerability.

For the past year Williams and his partner in crime—Charles Hoffman—had been sneaking out to the New York suburbs at night and burglarizing the new homes of wealthy commuters. They looked for places far from the main roads and waited outside until the residents went to bed. Once they were satisfied that the house wasn't protected by an alarm or a guard dog, they usually entered by forcing open a window on the ground floor. Because they couldn't afford an automobile, they carried their loot away in a large leather satchel and returned to the city on the morning train. They stole cash, silverware, and jewelry, but would occasionally come home with an expensive fur or a painting torn from its frame and rolled up. What they liked best was silverware, especially if it had the Tiffany mark. It was easy to fence and brought a good price.

Tougher and more confident than his partner, Williams seemed to enjoy the dangerous thrill of breaking into occupied houses in the dead of night. He wasn't a big man, but was fearless and scrappy, and in the dark his close-cropped black mustache gave him a menacing look. The police didn't worry him as much as the homeowners. The local forces tended to be small and poorly trained, and were ill-equipped to chase burglars. The outraged victims posed the greater threat, especially when they happened to have a shotgun close at hand. In fact, so many people had taken shots at him in the dark that he always went armed on a job and was prepared to fire back. Whatever the cost, he was determined to avoid another prison sentence.

Only a week after Clara's return from Europe, Williams met with his partner and told him of the easy pickings waiting for them in Redding.

Hoffman liked the sound of it, and they agreed to do the job the next day. On Thursday, September 17, they boarded a late-afternoon train and arrived just after dark. It was a mild evening, with a clear sky, and the road from the station to the town was quiet. As they approached Diamond Hill, they had no trouble spotting the villa. With its bright acetylene lights in full use at dinnertime, it stood out like a beacon. (Twain once said that when there was a light in every window the house looked "like a factory that's running over-time to fill rush-orders.")[3]

Taking cover behind some thick shrubbery, the men watched the house and waited for the residents to turn in. Around midnight, when everything was dark, they emerged from their hiding place and crept toward the villa. Getting inside turned out to be even easier than they thought. Someone had carelessly left a kitchen window unsecured, and it opened with barely a sound.

The burglars headed for the dining room and went straight to the sideboard to steal the family silver. When they found that a locked drawer couldn't be opened without making too much noise, the men picked up the heavy oak sideboard and carried it outside. At a safe distance from the house, they broke open the lock. Discovering about $500 worth of fancy silverware in the drawer, they emptied it into their satchel. Each piece was engraved in Italian script with Livy's maiden name. Of all the "portable earthly possessions" in the house, the burglars couldn't have chosen anything that had more sentimental value to the owner.

Deciding to clean out the rest of the sideboard later, Williams and Hoffman went back inside to search for more loot. They moved boldly from room to room, apparently thinking they could afford to take risks in a house where all the residents seemed deep in slumber. But then Hoffman made a mistake. In the darkness he tripped over a brass bowl. It made a terrible racket and brought a swift response.

"I was awakened by the crash in the dining room," Isabel Lyon recalled in the morning. "I thought at first it was a swinging shutter, but it was followed by a second noise, as if something had tumbled off a table, and I decided that something was wrong.

"I hurried from my apartment, which is just over the dining room, and ran downstairs. . . . The French windows which lead out onto the terrace were open. I crossed the room and looked out onto the lawn. A short distance from the house, almost at the front gate, in fact, I saw the flicker of a small pocket electric light and two figures moving about and rifling the sideboard.

"I screamed for help."[4]

Her cry woke everyone in the house. Lights were switched on, and the butler came running to the front hall with a raised pistol. Stepping onto the porch, Claude pointed his gun in the general direction of the front gate and fired several shots. Fortunately, there was no return fire. The burglars had heard Lyon call out "hello" from the top of the stairs and had escaped through the open French windows before she could come down to investigate. After pausing near the drive to finish loading their satchel, they had left the grounds as fast as they could, the stolen silverware jangling as they raced to the bottom of the hill.

Though Twain was awakened by Isabel's cry, he didn't come downstairs right away. In his drowsy state he imagined that all the noise was coming from a late-night party. As he explained the next day, the gunshots sounded to him like popping corks, and he assumed that his daughter must be entertaining a few friends. "Father didn't get downstairs until ages after it was all over," Clara later informed the press. "And then he came sauntering down at 2 o'clock in the morning, mind you, in a bathrobe, smoking a pipe and asking what all the commotion was about."[5]

His response to the intrusion was more serious than Clara wanted to admit. He couldn't have ignored the gravity of the situation. The family's treasured sideboard lay in shambles on the lawn, Livy's silverware was gone, and everyone in the house was in shock—not least because of the gunfire.

After he learned that no one had been harmed, and that the burglars had fled, he wondered whether there was any way to get the silverware back. Realizing that the burglars would probably try to fence it in New York, he decided to send a personal plea for help to his friend Police Commissioner Bingham. Despite the early hour, he sat down and wrote a description of the stolen items so they could be identified in a search. He couldn't bear the idea of losing the silverware, he wrote Bingham, explaining that it "has great value for me, because of its associations."[6]

Meanwhile, Isabel Lyon had telephoned the builder Harry Lounsbury—who lived nearby—and had frantically pleaded for help. In her nervous state she overstated the loss, telling him, "Burglars have been here and stolen the furniture."[7]

A short time later Lounsbury showed up with the local deputy sheriff, a "big red-faced man" named George Banks. Lantern in hand, Banks searched the grounds, spotted a distinctive shoe print in the flower bed under the kitchen window, and was able to follow the burglars' tracks down the drive and along the country lane leading north to Danbury. Lounsbury went with him, as did another man whose name would later surface in a couple of newspaper stories about the chase. He was Charles Wark, the only guest at the house that night. Perhaps because the press had made no further comment on their "engagement," Clara had assumed it was safe to invite her accompanist to stay overnight in one of the spare rooms. It was bad timing.[8]

The three men followed the tracks for a mile or two and then split up. Convinced that the suspects would try to make their getaway by train, Deputy Banks instructed Lounsbury and Wark to watch the station at Bethel—a little town on the outskirts of Danbury—while he guarded the platform at Redding. In fact, the burglars were already hiding in the woods next to the Bethel station, nervously awaiting the morning train. When it arrived at six, they rushed to the window to buy tickets.

With their large satchel and scruffy appearance, they immediately attracted attention, and were followed onto the train by Lounsbury and Wark. "There weren't many people on it," Williams was to recall of the train ride, "and we were a little conspicuous, I guess. You know how all those trains are—everybody knows everybody else, or pretty close to it. But we were strangers."[9]

During the seven-mile journey to Redding, Lounsbury bravely approached Williams and asked, "Haven't I met you somewhere?" The burglar answered no and made it clear that he had nothing else to say, but after getting a close look at him, Lounsbury knew he had his man. As the train pulled into Redding station, he and Wark got off and alerted Deputy Banks on the platform, describing the suspects and pointing to the car where they were sitting.[10]

What happened next was a fierce gun battle that must have left the mild-mannered suburban commuters wondering whether their train had been invaded by bandits from out West. Backed up by a couple of railway workers carrying clubs, Banks entered the car and made his way down the aisle toward the burglars. When Hoffman saw the men approaching, he ran to the rear of the car. Banks drew his revolver and came after him, but the burglar jumped from the moving train and ran toward a small bridge.

Taking aim, the deputy fired once and hit Hoffman in the leg. He watched as the man stumbled and collapsed under the bridge. Thinking he had finished off the first suspect, he turned and walked back to confront the second, whose escape from the car was blocked by the railway workers.

With a pair of handcuffs in one hand and his smoking revolver in the other, he loomed over Williams and said, "I want you." Then, noticing the satchel, he added, "And I've got you with the goods, too."[11]

Williams later insisted that an angry posse of a dozen men had gathered in the car to help Banks, and that he had felt compelled to shoot his way out. "I was commanded to surrender," he recalled. "Instead of obeying the command, I pulled out my own revolver and began to blaze away at the ceiling of the car to cause a panic if possible. I did not want to kill any one." But this was a story invented afterward to avoid a charge of attempted murder. There was no posse, and neither Banks nor the frightened passengers who ran for cover thought Williams was simply firing harmlessly into the air. In fact, his first two shots were aimed at Banks, and the second tore into the deputy's right thigh. Williams continued to "blaze away" as he backed toward the rear door, and the wounded Banks did his best to return fire. Bullets seemed to be whizzing everywhere as the shots ricocheted in the car.[12]

At this point, according to the *New York Evening World*, "The scared passengers were huddled like sheep in the combination smoker and baggage car forward. Somebody jerked the emergency cord and the train came to a sudden stop."

Thrown to the floor, Williams looked up to see the two railway workers coming toward him with their clubs. He raised his revolver, but when he realized the cylinder was empty, he dropped the gun and lashed out with his fists. The men stood over him and beat him with all their might.

"With blood streaming from his battered head," the *Evening World* wrote of Williams, "he fought like a wildcat. . . . At last, after he had been battered till his face was almost unrecognizable, he shouted, 'Let up, for God's sake. I'm all in.' "[13]

The workers relented and the deputy limped forward to handcuff his assailant. Meanwhile, back at the bridge near the station, Hoffman had been captured by half a dozen local farmers, but only after firing several shots at them. He didn't hit anyone and meekly surrendered when his bullets ran out. Though he was bleeding, he wasn't seriously injured. The deputy's first shot had inflicted only a flesh wound.

By half past seven, a doctor was busy treating the injuries of the burglars and the deputy, and by nine o'clock Justice John Nickerson—who was also Redding's town clerk—was ready to preside over the arraignment of both suspects at the Town Hall. Bandaged and pale, the intrepid Banks escorted his dazed prisoners to the hearing and stood watch over them, despite having—as he said in his old-fashioned way—"a boot-full of blood, begob."[14]

· · ·

NEWS OF THE BURGLARY spread fast, and a small crowd gathered outside the Town Hall to exchange gossip and to take a hard look at the thieves. Dan Beard was allowed inside before the hearing started, and he stared in amazement at the spectacle of two desperate gunmen being held by authorities in a community where crime of any kind was rare. With the eye of an accomplished illustrator, he studied the scene as though it belonged in a novel.

"At the south end of the room there was, on this occasion, a small table, at which the two prisoners, with the gyves upon their wrists, sat waiting their fate. One of them had his head swathed in bandages, and the back of his coat [was] stiff with his own gore. The other, with an insolent smile, was smoking a cigarette. Some kind neighbor had supplied them with sandwiches and coffee. . . . The officials were in the clothes they wore at their farm work, and the doors were crowded with rustics."

As if on cue, the owner of Innocence at Home entered this scene wearing his white suit and approached the thieves. Standing over them, he glared at their surprised faces. Then he made a remark so perfect that he

In the New York papers, Twain was front-page news after two armed burglars invaded his mansion in Redding one night in September 1908.

must have been rehearsing it on the way: "So you're the two young men who called at my house last night and forgot to put your names in my guest-book?"[15]

Taken aback, they stared at him in silence. They had misjudged the old man. He was not a pushover nor was he as innocent as they had assumed. Then, as Williams recalled, Twain "turned upon me and delivered a scathing verbal castigation and lecture on morality, ending by denouncing me as a 'disgrace to the human race.' "[16]

Dan Beard was not the only one in the room who saw this unfolding drama as a series of memorable vignettes. A reporter for the Danbury paper wrote, "The contrast between the white-haired . . . gentleman against whom the men were accused of committing a grave crime, and the coarsely dressed and bloody burglar who sat nearest him would have made an ideal study for an artist."[17]

After administering his tongue-lashing, the author felt better, and his sense of humor returned. "Don't you see where you're drifting to?" he asked. "They'll send you from here down to Bridgeport jail, and the next thing you know, you'll be in the United States Senate. There's no other future left open to you."[18]

This little touch of wit was not lost on Williams, who hoped that Twain's anger would give way to pity. But if he expected a show of mercy, he soon realized that he wouldn't get it. At first, Twain "manifested much interest in the court proceedings," but he quickly became bored with all the legal maneuvering and "asked the justice if he might be excused from the courtroom." Permission was granted, and he left well before both suspects were officially charged with "breaking and entering" and the theft of "goods and chattels of the value of Five hundred dollars." In addition, Williams was charged with the more serious offenses of felonious assault and carrying a concealed weapon. If convicted, he faced the possibility of spending the next thirty years in the state prison at Wethersfield. His bond was set at $2,000, twice that of Hoffman's.[19]

That afternoon, while the burglars were being transported to the county jail in Bridgeport, Twain entertained reporters at his house and made every effort to minimize the seriousness of the crime. He passed around a handwritten statement he was intending to post at the front door for any future intruders. He wrote at the top, "Notice. To the Next Burglar." Below that was a comical sketch of a masked bandit and these words:

> There is nothing but plated ware in this house, now and henceforth. You will find it in that brass thing in the dining-room over in the corner by the basket of kittens. If you want the basket, put the kittens in the brass thing. Do not make a noise—it disturbs the family. You will find rubbers in the front hall, by that thing which has the umbrellas in it, chiffonier, I think they call it, or pergola, or something like that.
>
> Please close the door when you go away.
>
> > Very truly yours
> > S. L. Clemens

"The brass thing," it would seem, was the large bowl that Hoffman had knocked over. But the reporters didn't waste time studying the statement. They were too busy trying to copy it into their notebooks before Twain moved on to make another joke.

Despite his playful attitude with the press, the author understood that most people in Redding weren't in the mood to laugh about the trau-

matic events surrounding the burglary. George Banks was highly regarded in the community, and everyone was relieved that he had survived
the gunfight with only a minor wound. (In fact, Twain made a point of visiting Banks the next day to check on him and to thank him for capturing
the burglars.) Twain was also keenly aware that the crime had rattled
everybody at home except him. As he told Howells a week later, "Not a
woman in this house has had a whole solid hour's sleep since. I mean
Clara, Miss Lyon & all the others. They drop into feverish cat-naps, & at
the very slightest & almost inaudible noises they spring to a sitting pos-
ture. . . . Miss Lyon has kept her bed for the last two days. Clara left for
New York promptly & never wants to sleep in the house again. Miss Lyon
& two of the maids will soon go away for a week & busy themselves with
theatres & other burglar-abolishing restfulness."[20]

Williams and Hoffman undermined the tranquillity that had made
Innocence at Home such an oasis for Twain. His summer idyll had lasted
almost as long as the season itself. He took possession of the house only
three days before the summer began, and the burglars struck three days
before it ended. The isolation and openness that had charmed Twain were
turned overnight into liabilities that unnerved his household. Moreover,
fears of another intrusion threatened to put a stop to the steady flow of
guests. Who would want to spend the night at a remote house that had
been the target of hardened criminals willing to engage in a gunfight
with the law?

Instinctively, Twain relied on humor to save him from being stuck in a
house that everyone else might want to avoid. Right away, he set to work
making a violent incident seem almost like a minor inconvenience. With
his amusing "Notice. To the Next Burglar," he managed to change the way
the crime was reported in the newspapers appearing the next morning.
(He couldn't do much to influence coverage in the evening papers, because they went to press only a few hours after the burglars were captured.) Instead of beginning with the horrific details of the shootout,
many of the major dailies started their stories with Twain's jokes about
plated ware, kittens, baskets, and that "brass thing." The article in the
New York Times didn't give the details of the shootout until the seventh
paragraph, and the headline in the *New York Tribune* made the whole in-

cident sound like a harmless prank: "Mark Twain's Robbers: Humorist Posts Notice on Home Telling Next Ones What to Do."

To the reporters who interviewed him at home, he pretended that he had always wanted to be friends with burglars, and that he was sure they wouldn't want to harm him. As the *New York World* reported, "Mark Twain said he was very, very glad to receive burglars—that he had always found them to be the most amiable people, and that he had had so much experience with them in his lifetime that he had come to like them greatly." He charmed the New York correspondent of the *Baltimore Sun* by complaining that he had not been burglarized enough: "A few years ago, Mr. Clemens was sorely disappointed when burglars broke into the houses on each side of his, but ignored him entirely. He said at the time he did not know what offense he had given to the Burglar's Union to cause them to treat him with such marked and persistent contempt."[21]

Twain's funny stories about the crime were a big hit. "So Glad they did not steal you," wrote one of his amused angelfish—Margaret Blackmer. For many readers around the world, the great Mark Twain burglary soon became merely another entertaining adventure in the humorist's life. The stuff of terror was transformed into comedy. "By the letters which are arriving now," Twain observed in early October, "I find that [the "Notice: To the Next Burglar"] has traveled through the European newspapers, and as it had already traveled through the American ones I think that the most of the burglars of this world have read it and will see the wisdom of allowing themselves to be guided by it."[22]

Just to be on the safe side, however, he borrowed Claude's pistol, stood near the spot outside where the intruders had entered, and posed for a photograph to demonstrate how he would shoot a burglar who overstepped the bounds of proper criminal behavior. Dressed in white and holding a cigar in one hand, he is leaning forward and pointing the gun with a look that seems both intimidating and hilarious. No burglar could be sure whether the author would actually shoot him or merely attempt to disarm him with laughter.

To his friends, he also boasted that he planned to install a burglar alarm and was thinking of acquiring a bulldog or two. But to those who lived under his roof or in the neighborhood, all the comic remarks and promised improvements in security didn't lead to the necessary "burglar-abolishing restfulness." Clara and Katy Leary retreated to an apartment in New York on Stuyvesant Square—about a mile east of their old home on Fifth Avenue—and were reluctant to spend more than a few hours at a time in Redding. "Clara has the shudders every time she thinks of that night," Twain said. Near the end of September, all the servants in the house—including Claude—informed their employer that they were quitting. Catherine, one of the Irish maids, complained of nightmares. She said that every night she saw herself being attacked by "a swarm of masked burglars" who riddled her body with bullets. On October 8, Twain wrote, "The servants came to bid me good-bye, at 11. They gave notice a week or ten days ago, still frightened to death about that burglary."[23]

Undaunted, he instructed Lyon to hire new servants and said he would be happy to replace them with simple, hardworking people from rural Connecticut. "We think we shan't need city servants at all," he wrote Emilie Rogers. "I don't like them anyway: they have to have facilities all the week for going to hell, and facilities every Sunday for grafting their way into the other place." He continued urging Henry and Emilie to pay him a visit, but now they were understandably reluctant to do so, though they would never have admitted it. Burglars or no burglars, he didn't want to take no for an answer. "Dear me, I wish you two would come here, and right away! and look at the foliage. Can't you? Won't you? <u>Will</u> you?"

He made it clear to everyone that he wasn't going to run away, but would stay put in Redding and would try to carry on with the same kind of life he had enjoyed before the burglary. And, if necessary, he would do it alone. He hired a contractor to install glass doors in the arches of the loggia so that he could spend time there in cold weather. "We can sit there with our knitting," he wrote young Dorothy Quick, "& watch the snow-storms."[24]

In spite of his professed affection for the burglars, he looked forward to seeing the pair convicted on all charges. The trial was set for early November, and he planned to attend. But while he waited for his chance to testify against the culprits, a journalist came to the house with news that someone else was stealing from him. In this case what had been taken was his most valuable possession—his words. Ignoring his stated wishes, Elinor Glyn had recently published a short pamphlet in London giving her version of their conversation about her best-selling novel. Charles Meltzer, an Oxford-educated critic employed by the *New York American*, obtained a copy of the pamphlet and took it to Redding to get Twain's reaction.

After leafing through it, he told Meltzer, "It looks like the [same document] she showed to me the time I told her it was a quite extraordinary piece of misreporting. . . . I am afraid she wants another advertisement of her book." He avoided discussing his views on adultery, saying the subject wasn't "a wholesome one and its discussion is much more likely to do harm than good." But he admitted that Glyn's book had "uttered a very large truth," and he didn't deny that he sympathized with her point of view. Though her indiscretion irritated him, he agreed that she had correctly conveyed the "substance" of what he had said. Where she had gone wrong, he explained to Meltzer, was in "making me talk in the first person, when she could not by any possibility reproduce the words I used, since she did not take me down in shorthand."

He had warned Glyn before that she was putting words in his mouth, but now her determination to quote him directly made him feel that she was acting more like a burglar than a fellow writer, "borrowing" Mark Twain for her own purposes and making him speak in a language that wasn't his own. "She put into my mouth humiliatingly weak language," he complained to Meltzer.

In his view that was a serious crime. Entering his home and running off with his persona was a lot worse than stealing the silverware. If society had agreed with him, he probably would have wanted Elinor Glyn to be tried along with Williams and Hoffman. He might have been tempted to say as much to Meltzer, but he decided that launching a full-scale attack on Glyn wasn't worth the trouble. "He was more deeply, profanely annoyed than is indicated in . . . the statement which he gave to Mr. Meltzer," Isabel Lyon later wrote.[25]

It is also possible that he wanted to avoid a public battle with Glyn because of a suspicion that sex scandals were no longer a subject to be addressed merely in the abstract. He may have been giving more thought to Clara's relationship with Charles Wark, which underwent a sudden change after the burglary. Clara seems to have been rattled by the fact that two major New York papers—the *Times* and the *Tribune*—

mentioned Wark's presence at Twain's home when it was burglarized. Though the earlier rumor about an engagement had been quickly put to rest, she knew that more gossip could begin circulating if her name and Wark's continued to be linked in the press. As a precaution, she tried to avoid being seen with him in circumstances that might arouse suspicion.[26]

About three weeks after the burglary, Twain noticed an example of her new behavior. He had invited Captain Daniel Dow, whose Cunard liner had brought Clara and Wark back home from Europe, to spend a weekend in Redding. Ashcroft met the captain in New York and rode with him on the train to Connecticut. But Twain was intrigued to learn that "Clara followed in a later train, & Wark in a still later one." It would have been obvious to Isabel Lyon that they were taking separate trains to avoid attracting attention. How much significance Twain read into these travel arrangements isn't clear. In the photographs that were taken of him clowning with Captain Dow that weekend (he called him "the loveliest darlingest Irishman that ever was"), he is flanked by Clara, Wark, and Ashcroft, and they all seem to be enjoying themselves.[27]

But by the time the burglars were tried in November, Twain must have realized that Clara and her accompanist were making an effort to avoid appearing in public together, for both declined to attend the trial. What he made of their decision, he didn't say, though the strangeness of it couldn't be overlooked, especially when Paine and Ashcroft agreed to accompany him instead. On November 10 he walked into the Danbury Courthouse with these two friends who had not been present on the night of the burglary, while back in New York two witnesses to the crime, Clara and Wark, kept out of sight.

Had the couple decided to come along, they would have observed a dramatic spectacle, beginning with the prisoners entering under heavy guard and confronting once again the man they had tried to victimize. "The small room was crowded with spectators and with witnesses for the state," Henry Williams recalled. "The most noticeable and distinguished person in the room, naturally, was neither the judge nor the sheriff, but the humorist, Mark Twain, wearing a dark suit instead of his customary light-colored clothes for this serious occasion."[28]

The prosecutor was so respectful toward the author that he insisted on referring to him throughout the proceedings as Dr. Clemens. The thieves didn't stand a chance, and their New York lawyer knew it. The defense attorney pleaded with the judge to reduce the number of armed officers standing guard over the prisoners, saying that the sight of them would prejudice the jury. His request was denied. "They are believed to be desperate men," explained the *New York Times*.

Watching the defense attorney in action, Twain decided that he didn't like him, later referring to him in private as "a bushy-headed, truculent-looking animal from the criminal haunts of New York." On the witness stand, Twain was asked to identify some of Livy's silverware found in the burglars' possession. He made such a sympathetic figure that the defense attorney promptly advised his clients to avoid a jury verdict and to cut a deal with the prosecution.[29]

In court the next day both defendants entered guilty pleas. As a result, they received reduced sentences. Hoffman was ordered to serve four years at the state prison, Williams was given ten. "For the first time in all my years of wrongdoing," Williams later admitted, "the defiant spirit seemed to leave me, and a feeling of unutterable hopelessness and despair took possession of me."

Because of good behavior, Williams would spend only eight years behind bars, leaving prison in 1916 with just four cents in his pocket and a heavy set of books under his arm. It was the four-volume edition of *Mark Twain: A Biography,* by Albert Bigelow Paine—a Christmas gift from the publishers.[30]

· · ·

LARGELY IN RESPONSE to the burglary, Twain decided to change the name of his house. After the servants quit and Clara moved out, he realized that his wit and good cheer wouldn't be enough to make others feel safe under his roof. He needed to make some bold moves to show everyone that he had no intention of allowing members of the Burglar's Union to visit him again. Instead of merely joking about putting in an alarm system, he had one installed in October and immediately began claiming that it was the most powerful system ever invented.

Referring to the possibility of another burglary, he told a group of townspeople in late October, "Now we are prepared for these visitors. All sorts of alarm devices have been put in the house, and the ground for half a mile around it has been electrified. The burglar who steps within this danger zone will set loose a bedlam of sounds, and spring into readiness for action our elaborate system of defenses. As for the fate of the trespasser, do not seek to know that. He will never be heard of more."[31]

In view of his well-known fondness for the latest gadgets, he must have been hoping that at least a few people would take his remarks seriously enough to create rumors of their own concerning his elaborate security measures. His purpose was to dispel the notion that his home was still as vulnerable as it had been in September. But no matter how much he exaggerated the power of his new defenses, he couldn't make the place sound well protected as long as it continued to be known as Innocence at Home. He needed a new name suitable for a house owned by an unpredictable genius who was supposedly creating a hidden electrical barrier to protect it.

On the very day in October that Clara moved into her New York apartment, Twain wrote Jean in Berlin that he was changing the villa's name to Stormfield. It was a brilliant substitution, but he gave Clara the credit for suggesting it. She had never liked his choice of Innocence at Home and had been thinking of other possibilities before the burglary. Now that there was a real incentive to make a change, both father and daughter agreed that Captain Stormfield—the courageous celestial mariner—should lend his name to the embattled house.

The new name seemed appropriate in more ways than one. As he had seen during his four months at the house, its position made it a magnet for the heavy storms that sometimes swept over the hills from the sea. "It is set so high," he explained to Jean, "that all the storms that come will beat upon it, there being no obstruction." Also, he couldn't forget that the money he received from the magazine publication of Captain Stormfield's adventures had been used to pay for Clara's rooms over the loggia. And so, with good reasons to support the change, he gave his house its third, and last, name. A new supply of stationery was ordered with the simple heading, "Stormfield, Redding, Connecticut."

Because Jean had been spared the experience of being burglarized, Twain tried not to make the name change seem the necessity that it was. Instead he pretended that he didn't care one way or the other about it, and that he was simply indulging Clara's wishes. Jean must have been puzzled by all this fuss over the name of a house she had yet to see, but one that was supposedly built with her future in mind, and that included a bedroom reserved for her. In fact, she was enjoying her new life in Germany and was beginning to think her future might lie there. Though her German doctor didn't seem to be doing much for her, she believed that she was continuing to get the better of her disease. She was developing an active social life in Berlin, attending concerts and going to dances. By the end of the year, she would be convinced that it was better for her to stay in Germany than come back to America and wait once more for permission to live in the house her father was now calling Stormfield.

Though it was supposed to frighten burglars, the name wasn't one to inspire confidence in the minds of potential guests. Worried that it might frighten away some of his angelfish, Twain hastened to inform them that the change had been made simply to give the house a different public image. He insisted that it didn't mean his view of it had turned gloomy. "The house has two names," he wrote. " 'Innocence at Home' for the Aquarium girls, and 'Stormfield' for the general public." There was a conspiratorial pleasure to be had from this arrangement, but he also could take satisfaction from knowing that even the new name wasn't what it seemed. Whereas burglars might find it intimidating, he could still regard it in the same light as Innocence at Home—a clever term connecting his work with his life.[32]

While he was trying to reassure his angelfish that the old name had not been discarded, a guest arrived whose younger self had served as the model for the most famous example of female innocence in his fictional work. She was his childhood sweetheart from Hannibal, Laura Hawkins Frazer, whom he had portrayed as Becky Thatcher in *Tom Sawyer* and *Huckleberry Finn*. She was now a seventy-year-old grandmother living in Hannibal who—as chance would have it—had chosen this moment to make a rare journey back East. For years, Twain had not been sure of her whereabouts. It wasn't until 1902, during his last visit to Hannibal, that they reestablished contact. When he moved to Redding, she was one of the friends he invited to stay at the new house. And now, in the middle of October, she was standing at his door, gray and plump, but still as cheerful and affectionate as the Laura who used to live across the street from him in the 1840s. She didn't seem to be aware of the burglary, but it wouldn't have changed her plans. Given her frontier upbringing, she was no more inclined than Twain to be spooked by such things.

Clara came up from New York that day just for the chance to meet her. When she opened the door, she threw her arms around Laura and said, "I know you. . . . Father has told me about you. You are Becky Thatcher."[33]

Young Sam Clemens had begun his relationship with Laura by showing off. She never forgot her first glimpse of the "barefooted boy" who "came out in the street before our house and turned hand-springs, and stood on his head, and cut just such capers as he describes in Tom's 'showing-off' before Becky." As a boy, he had only his charm to display. But now, as the owner of Stormfield, he was able to lead Laura on a tour of the kind of palace they might have imagined for themselves in childhood. The evidence of his success was extraordinary, and though her own means were modest, she didn't think his attitude toward her had changed at all.[34]

"It was a wonderful visit," she recalled several years later. "Mr. Clemens took me over Stormfield. It must have been a tract of three hundred acres. We went through the fields . . . and across a rustic bridge over a little rushing brook which boiled and bubbled among the rocks in the bed of a great ravine, and we sat down under a rustic arbor and talked of the old days in Hannibal when he was a little boy and I a little girl, before he went out into the world to win fame and before I lived my own happy married life. Mr. Clemens had that rare faculty of loyalty to his friends which made the lapse of fifty years merely an interim. It was as if the half century had rolled away and we were there looking on the boy and girl we had been."[35]

In a sense, Laura was the original angelfish. The girls whose pictures lined the walls of the billiards room were merely variations of her at the age when she was young Sam's ideal of girlhood. She had captured his heart in the same way that Becky captures Tom Sawyer's. Fresh from playing soldiers with his friends, Tom passes "a lovely little blue-eyed creature with yellow hair plaited into two long tails, white summer frock and embroidered pantalettes." Instantly, he forgets other girls and his triumphs as a playground general. "The fresh-crowned hero fell without firing a shot," Twain writes of Tom.

According to Laura, Sam's infatuation with her was so innocent that when they were together she often forgot he was of the opposite sex. She "liked to play with him every day and all day long," she said. "Sam and I used to play together like two girls." She remembered him as "gentle . . . and kind of quiet, and he always did have that drawl. He was long-spoken, like his mother."[36]

It is remarkable how much of that innocent, fun-loving boy remained inside the aged author. Though Laura visited him at a time when he might have complained bitterly about the pitfalls of fame, he said nothing on the subject and was as enthusiastic as ever about his life in Redding. The villa and the wooded hills in their bright autumn colors seemed the perfect setting for renewing a friendship begun so long ago. When Laura was ready to leave, he handed her a gift that confirmed her importance in his life, and that hinted at her influence on his imagination. It was his framed portrait inscribed "To Laura . . . with the love of her earliest sweetheart."[37]

A few months after moving into his new house in Redding, Twain changed its name, calling it after his fictional character Captain Stormfield.

SIXTEEN

The Mark Twain Company

It's my opinion that everyone I know
has morals, though I wouldn't like to ask.
Mark Twain[1]

· · ·

HAVING DECIDED TO KEEP his permanent residence in Redding, Twain looked around for a way to give something back to the community. He settled on the idea of helping to start a public library. If Carnegie could build hundreds of them across America, Twain reckoned that he could at least establish a small one somewhere in his new hometown. In October 1908 he became the first president of the Redding Library Association and informed its members that "by and by we are going to have a building of our own." To the surprise of Dan Beard and a local retired businessman named Theodore Adams, Twain suggested that one of them should donate the land for the library. (Adams accepted the challenge and gave the town a convenient site on the main road below Diamond Hill.) For his part, the author said he would donate books from his own shelves and would collect money for the building fund by hosting several charity events. He also intended to impose a visitor's tax at

Stormfield for the benefit of the library. "Every male guest who comes to my house," he declared, "will have to contribute a dollar or go away without his baggage."[2]

Some of his neighbors may have doubted his sincerity in this matter, especially after he spent most of his speech to the library association joking about his burglars instead of explaining how to pay for a new building. But in the coming months he would raise thousands for the library, persuading all sorts of people to donate to the cause, including Andrew Carnegie himself, who gave $500. In addition, Twain put aside for the library more than 1,500 books from his own collection, selecting works of biography, fiction, history, poetry, science, self-help, and travel. He got rid of old novels he never liked, including several by George Eliot ("I can't stand George Eliot, & Hawthorne & those people; I see what they are at, a hundred years before they get to it, & they just tire me to death"). But he also contributed copies of many works that he treasured, such as *Alice's Adventures in Wonderland* ("the immortal Alice," as he called her) and Thomas Macaulay's *History of England* ("A library can not justly be called dull which has that in it"). At the top of his list of donations was a copy of the Bible. The books he donated would form the core of the holdings at Redding's Mark Twain Library, as it would eventually be called. (In 1911 it opened at the site provided by Theodore Adams and is still going strong in the twenty-first century.)[3]

In late November, Twain invited practically the whole town to come up to Stormfield for a library benefit. He was the featured speaker and charged twenty-five cents admission. Chairs were borrowed from the undertaker and placed in rows from the living room to the loggia. By the time Twain rose to speak, there was standing room only. One man walked five miles to be there.

In the audience that afternoon was Twain's companion from his last visit to Bermuda, Elizabeth Wallace. A guest at Stormfield for a few days, she suddenly found herself playing hostess at the benefit performance, but was happy to help out. She was amused by the old New England farmers who sat up front and remained so quiet and serious. They were reluctant to make themselves comfortable in a stranger's house, she recalled, and "held on grimly to fur overcoats and fleece-lined jackets."

Looking down on the expressionless faces of these farmers, Twain tried his best to make them laugh.

"Once in a while stern features would relax for a moment," Wallace remembered, "but the effort seemed to hurt, and the muscles would become fixed again." Twain had better luck with the younger generation at the back, "who suffered from occasional apoplectic outbursts." Wallace had the impression that the older people enjoyed listening to their famous neighbor's jokes, but that they considered it unseemly to laugh. "They were proud . . . proud almost to sinning, of their illustrious fellow-townsman, and they would have shouted with laughter, if only they could."

At the end of the talk, which lasted an hour and a half, they responded with generous applause and lingered afterward to acknowledge Twain's generosity with silent handshakes, appreciative nods, and simple words of praise. When the crowd was gone, Twain discussed his performance with Wallace and offered a good excuse for the silence in the front rows. "They weren't used to laughing on the outside," he explained.

The event raised only a modest amount for the library, but the real point of it was to show the town that Twain wanted to be a good neighbor, and that he intended to be active year-round in the life of the community. Though he had rubbed shoulders with some of the richest and most powerful people on earth, he considered it a privilege to open his home to "100 of the sterlingest farmers & their families encounterable anywhere" and to spend a cold November afternoon entertaining them in white.[4]

No one was happier to see Twain enjoying Redding than his biographer. "I confess I had moments of anxiety," Paine was to recall, "for I had selected the land for him, and had been more or less accessory otherwise." It's a tribute to Paine's understanding of his subject that he picked a place Twain liked so well, and that he did it without the advantage of showing him the area first. "I did not really worry," he was to write, "for I knew how beautiful and peaceful it all was; also something of his taste and habits."

Indeed, even when the frosts came and the hills turned brown, Twain lost none of his enthusiasm for the look of the place. "Although the beginnings of winter are here," he wrote a few days after the library benefit, "&

the trees are more or less bare, the landscape is still astonishingly beautiful."[5]

Perhaps fearing that the coming winter might be too harsh, Paine tried to interest him in taking a break from Redding to see other scenic parts of America. One suggestion was the Grand Canyon.

"I should enjoy that," he replied, "but the railroad journey is so far, and I should have no peace. The papers would get hold of it, and I would have to make speeches and be interviewed."

When Paine suggested a disguise, Twain showed no interest in hiding his famous face, and didn't think it would work anyway. "I might put on a red wig and false whiskers and change my name," he said, "but I couldn't disguise my drawling speech, and they'd find me out."[6]

The idea of staying at home was more appealing now because he finally had a home where he was content to stay. For a good part of his life he was a wanderer and had already seen much of the world. Before marrying Livy, he had been on the go almost constantly. Besides his adventures in the Mississippi Valley and in the mining towns of California and Nevada, he had traveled from one end of the Mediterranean to the other, climbing to the top of Mount Vesuvius, touring Egypt's pyramids, and swimming in the Sea of Galilee. After his marriage, he had lived for extended periods in the European capitals of Berlin, London, Paris, and Vienna, and had visited such faraway places as Australia, India, and South Africa. Despite the often formidable difficulties of travel in his time, he covered a lot of territory and saw many of the world's wonders.

But now there was nothing that fascinated him more than Stormfield. After taking Elizabeth Wallace on a tour of his land on a "bright, crisp, cold day" in November, he told her, "I never want to leave this place. It satisfies me perfectly."[7]

One Sunday in early November he spent an hour "drifting about the ground-floor noting the enchantments." In room after room he studied the way the sunlight played on various objects, observing how a copper vase glowed on a black mantel, and how a gleaming vase of red flowers in the dining room was "reflected like a miniature sunset cloud in the polished dark-wood of the table." As he gazed outside at his avenue of cedars, they looked to him like thrones, "graceful, symmetrical, beautiful." With winter approaching, he was grateful that these evergreens would continue to provide flashes of color on the landscape throughout the season. "If I should plant trees they might die and wound me," he wrote poignantly, "but these will still be green & lovely & full-flushed with life when I have been dead a century."[8]

· · ·

ABSORBED IN THE PLEASURES of his new home, Twain failed to heed the signs of a worsening conflict between Clara and Isabel Lyon. Under strain for several months, the relationship between the two women fell apart soon after Clara moved into her New York apartment. Having been left on her own to run a household disrupted by the burglary, Lyon resented Clara's unwillingness to stay and help, especially since so much money and effort had gone into making the Nightingale's Cage as comfortable as possible. At the end of October she was still struggling to complete the changeover from the old group of servants to the new one. On October 20 she wrote Samuel Moffett's widow, "We have been busy fitting in new servants to take the place of those who think they were frightened away by the burglars." As her tone suggests, she didn't have much sympathy for anyone in the household who had run away, and that included the privileged daughter.[9]

Yet Clara kept coming back to Redding for short visits, usually accompanied by Katy Leary. Each time she acted as though she—not Lyon—was the mistress of the house. The two women began getting into arguments over minor problems related to the servants, meals, or furnishings, and they soon dropped any pretense of friendship, trading increasingly nasty insults behind Twain's back. After one especially traumatic argument, Katy Leary watched Clara storm away and then whispered to Isabel, "She hates you, and don't you forget it."[10]

It didn't help that Clara's worries about her relationship with Charles Wark may have made her suspect Lyon of spreading rumors about it. On October 26 Lyon bitterly complained in her journal that her very soul was being destroyed by Clara's antagonism. She was up to her "ears in mud," she wrote, "the mud of criticism—no, misunderstandings fired by C.C." Her only consolation was that Ashcroft shared her feeling of being misunderstood, for Clara had also begun insulting him. "Benares went hurtling away to day," Lyon noted on the 26th, "glad to get clear of the mud."

Lyon told herself not to be disheartened, but to bear the criticisms patiently and to rise above them for Twain's sake. "I'm a coward to not know that mud can clarify things in time, and can build a foundation from which I'll be the better able to see the King." At this stage, she was still hoping to settle her differences with Clara in a way that wouldn't upset Twain or harm his reputation. She regarded Ashcroft's support as crucial. "I am unafraid, for always there is Benares to be near me, and to help me."[11]

But Ashcroft wasn't impressed by her idea of passive resistance. He wanted direct action to strengthen his position in the event that Clara ever gained the upper hand. Having failed to interest the press in her relationship with Wark, he decided to try an even bolder plan. For months, he had been waiting for the right moment to make his relationship with Twain pay, and now he saw a chance to gain control over not just some of the author's wealth, but all of it—from the copyrights to Stormfield itself. Less than three weeks after "hurtling away" from the petty bickering in Redding, Ashcroft prepared a breathtakingly comprehensive document allowing him the power to manage every penny of Clara's inheritance. The trick was to get Twain to sign the document without giving him the chance to understand its significance.

Ashcroft had spent enough time with Twain to know that such a trick wouldn't be hard to pull off. The author had come to place so much trust in him that he treated him like a member of the family. Ashcroft had worked hard to win that trust, always looking for ways to please the older man. In August Twain had noted, "Ashcroft plays the orchestrelle for me a great deal; & he has improved so much that if I am out in the loggia & don't see him I think it is Miss Lyon. And he plays good billiards now. Not as good as Col. Harvey or Mr. Paine, but better than formerly." Ashcroft even began wearing white suits like Twain's. Walking around Stormfield in their identical dress, they might easily have been mistaken for father and son. Ashcroft was always eager to be of service, no matter how small the job. When Twain idly remarked one day that "it would be nice to have some gorse around the place," Ashcroft raced back to New York and "combed the city for seed."[12]

Having worked closely with Twain during the troubles at the Plasmon Company and the Knickerbocker Trust, Ashcroft knew how imprudent and confused he could be in business matters. He may even have heard Twain comment on his general inability to understand contracts and keep track of their requirements. It was a common complaint. "I am a pretty versatile fool when it comes to contracts, and business and such things," Twain had observed in 1904. "I have signed a lot of contracts in my time, and at sometime I probably knew what the contracts meant, but six months later everything had grown dim and I could be *certain* of only two things, to wit: One, I didn't sign any contract. Two, the contract means the opposite of what it says."[13]

On Saturday, November 14, Ashcroft took advantage of Twain's carelessness to get him to sign a document extending the power of attorney granted earlier to Isabel Lyon. The new arrangement included Ashcroft as one of the author's "true and lawful attorneys" and included a long list of privileges in the kind of legalese that Twain often preferred to ignore — "to sell, assign and transfer any and all stocks, bonds and mortgages belonging or which may at any time belong to me; to change any or all of my investments and to make any investment of any or all of the moneys belonging to me; to draw checks or drafts upon any banks, banker or Trust Company. . . ." And on it went, covering every possible way that Twain's wealth could be used, and making sure that Ralph Ashcroft and Isabel Lyon possessed the authority to control all of it.[14]

True to form, the author later would say that he couldn't recall signing this document. When it was shown to him in the late spring of 1909, he surmised that Ashcroft had slipped the paper in among ones he had read and approved, and that he had signed it without realizing what it was. In retrospect, he couldn't believe that he had been fooled so easily, sarcastically describing the document as "a stately one, a liberal one. . . . By it I transferred all my belongings down to my last shirt, to [Ashcroft and Lyon], to do as they pleased with. . . . Ashcroft had had this fraudulent document placed on record in New York, just as if it had been a deed."[15]

In fact, because Justice John Nickerson at the Redding Town Hall was familiar with the author's signature, and with Ashcroft's privileged standing at Stormfield, he notarized the document without the author being present. Ashcroft was then able to file it in New York, and to put it away in Twain's safety deposit box at the Liberty National Bank in Manhattan. With such a document on record, it wasn't necessary for Ashcroft to raid the Twain treasury right away. He simply needed to move the assets into a company where his power would be strong enough to oppose Clara's, and where he could enrich himself in a quiet way over time.

Not by coincidence, he was busy in November organizing such a firm. For much of the summer and fall he had been discussing with the author a plan to make the name of Mark Twain the property of a corporation. Ashcroft's idea was that the company would use licensing rights of the author's name to control publication of the works even after the copyrights had expired. It was an effort to make Mark Twain a brand and to sell books and other items under that name for decades to come. "When this name is the property of a perpetual corporation," Ashcroft later explained to the press, "Mr. Clemens's heirs will be in a position to enjoin perpetually the publication of all of the Mark Twain books not authorized by the Mark Twain Company."[16]

The author praised Ashcroft for coming up with this idea, calling it "a stroke of genius." He gave it his full blessing and was so enthusiastic that he didn't bother to study it carefully. Like the Paige typesetter, it looked better on paper than in practice. Was it realistic to assume that the courts would allow copyright law to be circumvented so easily? When his copyrights expired, wouldn't publishers be able to thwart his scheme by issuing books under Sam Clemens's name instead of Mark Twain's? If the author had insisted on getting answers to such questions before plunging ahead, he might have saved himself a lot of trouble. When the press later raised just one of these questions, Ashcroft couldn't provide a good answer. As the *New York Times* reported, "Mr. Ashcroft was not prepared to say at present whether the incorporation of the Mark Twain name would prevent any publisher, after the expiration of copyrights on the books, from printing the books under the name of Samuel L. Clemens. He said that this was a matter for the courts to decide." If the courts didn't rule against the plan, declared the *New York Sun,* "We fancy that it would not be long before the Legislature intervened."[17]

Twain seemed to be the only one who took Ashcroft's plan seriously. Some newspapers treated it as an excuse to make jokes. "Mark Twain, Incorporated is all well enough," remarked the *Washington Times,* "but everybody hopes it may never become Mark Twain, Limited." The *Washington Post* had fun imagining a board meeting run by the author and his most famous characters, with Huck Finn and Hank Morgan making speeches while the Jumping Frog croaked his approval. After the business matters had been discussed, the paper said, "The corporation then shook its own hand and adjourned."[18]

Ashcroft knew that Twain would approve of the new firm because he understood how much the copyright issue meant to the author. By promising him a way to protect his books forever, he misled him into creating a business whose chief beneficiary was meant to be—as Twain later put it—"Ashcroft, disguised as the Mark Twain Company." At the end of December, when the incorporation papers were filed in New York, S. L. Clemens was named as president, but the real control lay in the hands of the secretary-treasurer, Ralph Ashcroft, who also had the satisfaction of knowing that Isabel Lyon would serve as one of the directors.[19]

With stunning speed, Ashcroft was able to turn the tables on Clara, leaving behind his humble position as the author's unofficial business manager to become an officer in a corporation in which he controlled the purse strings, and to which he could begin quietly transferring Twain's money and property. After setting this plan in motion, it had taken him only two months to create the legal and financial structure that would put him in charge of Clara's inheritance. She didn't know it yet, and that was the way he meant to keep it until either his hand was forced or her father died. In the event of Twain's death, he had the power to seize control of the company because—through some trickery or the author's own carelessness—the stock certificates in the firm were fully negotiable. Twain had endorsed them before asking Ashcroft to store them in the safety deposit box.

As Twain later realized, this foolish act made it possible for Ashcroft to convey the ownership to himself in a completely legal way. "It would have been difficult for a court to find any objection to it," Twain was to write in retrospect. "The Mark Twain stock was worth a million dollars, & the other stuff about two hundred thousand. . . . The children would have been paupers. However, I didn't die."[20]

Asked in her old age whether Twain had liked Ashcroft, Isabel Lyon replied, "Yes, very much. . . . He was a great help in every way. . . . But all the time he was laying his own plans." Lyon's mistake was to allow herself to be drawn into them. He couldn't have done much at Stormfield without her cooperation, and he knew it. So he found her weak spot and exploited it, just as he did Twain's. Because she was hungry for affection, it was easy for him to go from being her confidant to her lover. While he was busy winning Twain's trust, he was also seducing Isabel, and she fell completely under his spell. After devoting her best years to the service of others, she thought she saw a chance to have a life of her own with a bright, hardworking man determined to move up in the world. The fact that she was forty-four and he was only thirty-three didn't seem to concern her. Not long after the Mark Twain Company was established, she wrote a friend in Hartford that she was so much in love with Ashcroft she couldn't "live without this dear & wonderful man."[21]

In the weeks immediately following the burglary Ashcroft would sometimes sneak down to Lyon's room after dark and spend the night with her. Twain didn't realize this was going on, but the servants did. As he was later told, some of the servants had heard a loud noise one night and had gone for help to Ashcroft's room, fearing another break-in. But they didn't find him there. What they discovered was an empty bed that had not been slept in, and they soon figured out that he was in Lyon's room.

Lyon's devotion to Ashcroft inevitably led her to betray Twain's trust. Until November 14, 1908, she had been able to convince herself that she was always trying to do what was best for him. In her efforts to undermine Paine's credibility or to keep Jean at a safe distance from home, she could tell herself that she was helping Twain by protecting him from, on the one hand, an overambitious biographer, and on the other, a supposedly unstable daughter. Even when she used his money to renovate her house or to buy a new dress, she could justify it on the grounds that improving her image was also good for his. No doubt Ashcroft told her that his own plans were also designed to safeguard Twain's interests (and theirs) by preventing spoiled and reckless daughters from squandering their father's fortune. But Lyon was too intelligent not to realize that Ashcroft was taking advantage of Twain by getting him to sign a power of attorney that went far beyond any reasonable requirement. Yet she turned a blind eye to it because her loyalty to Ashcroft was now greater than her loyalty to Twain.

She was upset by her betrayal, and it showed. For reasons that Twain couldn't have understood at the time, she had a nervous collapse on November 14 and spent the day suffering silently in bed.

...

ON A MONDAY MORNING in December two young men arrived at Stormfield for a short visit. One was Archibald Henderson, George Bernard Shaw's biographer and Twain's fellow passenger on the voyage to England the year before. The other was a bearded twenty-six-year-old photographer whose work was much in demand on both sides of the Atlantic. Though he was a native of Massachusetts, Alvin Coburn felt more at home in England, where he had been a frequent visitor since he was eighteen, and where his talent for photography had earned him many admirers, including Shaw and Henry James. The playwright called the young man "one of the most accomplished and sensitive artist-photographers now living," and had posed for him several times. Having become acquainted as a result of their mutual friendship with Shaw, Henderson and Coburn were now working on a new project together, and it was this job that brought them to Mark Twain's door.[22]

Because his earlier offer to write a full-scale biography of Twain had been rejected, Archibald Henderson planned to write a shorter study that would focus more on the career than on the private life. Without giving his consent to this new idea, Twain decided that it would do no harm to be photographed for the book and to have an informal chat with Henderson. Perhaps because it would annoy Paine, Isabel Lyon was happy to welcome this rival biographer to Stormfield and went out of her way to make his visit a pleasant one. She even took Henderson and Coburn down to her own small cottage to show it off. "Such rich, darling folks do come here to see the King," she wrote on December 21. "Today Prof. Archibald Henderson and Alvin Langdon Coburn came.... We had a charming day with plenty of talk & Hearts & a walk down to my house."[23]

Twain relaxed with Henderson in the living room, sharing random stories about his life, including a recollection of Livy's efforts to make him a more serious writer. "After I had written some side-splitting story," he told his guest, "something beginning seriously and ending in preposterous anti-climax, she would say to me: 'You have a true lesson, a serious meaning to impart here. Don't give way to your invincible temptation to destroy the good effect of your story by some extravagantly comic absurdity. Be yourself!" For the sake of Livy's memory, Twain was inclined to say that she had been right. But he disproved the point every day in his refusal to let high moral purpose deflate his impish, irreverent free spirit. The problem wasn't that he lacked seriousness, but that almost everyone else had too much of it.[24]

The three dozen photographs taken of Twain on this visit reveal more of the author than anything he said to Henderson. About twenty of Coburn's pictures were taken in the living room, billiards room, and Twain's bedroom, and the rest were shot outdoors in the garden pergola. Most show Twain in conventional poses, standing erect in his white suit or Oxford gown, playing pool or relaxing in bed wearing a colorful dressing gown. But several of the outdoor shots capture the playful side of the author and look more spontaneous.

The snow helped. Several inches had fallen over the weekend in the first storm of the season, turning the grounds into a sparkling white backdrop for Coburn. After the servants shoveled the walkways, he and Twain went down in the early afternoon to the pergola, where the photographer positioned his tripod at the edge of the brick terrace and began shooting as the author roamed among the pergola's stately columns or paused beside one to strike a pose. With his hair tucked under an ill-fitting cap, a dark overcoat flapping at the sides of his white uniform, and a crude walking stick under his arm, Twain looked like a giant snowman come to life. Coburn photographed him from the side and the rear, catching him in motion as the author retreated behind one pillar or strode between two with a cigar in the corner of his mouth.

Enjoying the chance to show off, Twain kicked up his heels and almost broke into a dance as he circled the empty basin of the low fountain that stood in the middle of the pergola. Then, seized with an idea, he pointed to a small pedestal at the center of the basin where a statue was supposed to go at some later date. "Why should not I be the statue?" he suggested proudly.

Coburn liked the idea, answering, "Why not indeed!"

"So he mounted the pedestal," the photographer was to recall, "cigar in one hand and staff in the other, an erect and dignified figure. The sun shone on the background of snow-mottled yew trees, and thus was made a unique picture of Mark Twain as a living statue."[25]

To make sure that all went well, Isabel Lyon and Ralph Ashcroft waited at the edge of the pergola and watched Coburn work. Lyon had a small camera with her and took a few shots of her own, while Ashcroft tried to stay warm wearing only a thin overcoat with a white suit that matched Twain's. Coburn didn't mind having them around and was happy to take a picture of Ashcroft standing with Twain and Henderson by the empty fountain.

An amiable man, Coburn was easy to work with. He had a knack for putting his subjects at ease, and for encouraging them to reveal their inner selves. George Bernard Shaw trusted him so much that he revealed perhaps more than the world wanted to see, posing in the nude as "the Thinker." Thanks to introductions from Shaw, Coburn was able to photograph many other literary figures, including H. G. Wells and W. B. Yeats. After only a short acquaintance with Coburn, Henry James was sufficiently impressed to offer the young photographer the commission of a lifetime, hiring him to provide the frontispiece of each volume in the collected edition of his works.

In 1906, James had sent him to Paris and Venice to photograph places associated with his novels. On a similar assignment in London he had accompanied him for long periods as they walked the streets in search of suitable scenes. In Coburn's presence, James was uncommonly relaxed and informal. On one scouting expedition in London, the photographer thought that James acted more like a schoolboy than a distinguished novelist. He never forgot the image of the great man happily sharing Bath buns with him as they walked home after a long day of work.

While he was at Stormfield, warming himself by a roaring log fire after dinner, Coburn showed his host some of his recent portraits of famous literary and artistic figures. It was obvious that the young man was an expert at his craft. Such ability always fascinated Twain. Though the author may not have been aware of it, Coburn was already being singled out by critics as a master of technique. As early as 1904 a New York journal of photography had praised him as a "very promising talent" who "has solved various pictorial problems which even would set a Stieglitz or a Steichen thinking." Like his mentor, Alfred Stieglitz, Coburn was a pioneer of color photography, having learned the new autochrome process shortly after the Lumière brothers introduced it in Paris in 1907. "I have the color fever badly," Coburn had confided to Stieglitz later that year.[26]

About the time that autochromes first appeared in Europe, Twain had chanced to remark to Dorothy Quick that a photograph of her wearing some fanciful costume would look better if only "there was such a thing as color photography so that those rich reds and that heavenly shade of turquoise blue need not be lost." Now, to his delight, one of the best of the early color photographers was a guest in his home. Coburn came prepared to use the new process at Stormfield and shot two autochrome portraits of Twain indoors. They turned out brilliantly, even though the long exposure time meant that the author had to hold his pose for about twenty seconds without moving a muscle. He wore his academic gown in one of the pictures, and the scarlet cloth still looks dazzling.[27]

A courteous guest, Coburn repaid Twain's hospitality by making a point of losing to him at cards and in a game of billiards. As he recalled in his autobiography, "An important rule of the household, which was secretly imparted to newly-arrived guests, was that the host must always win, but by the narrowest margin so as not to be too obvious." At the billiards table, he was fascinated by Twain's fervent desire to win and wondered why such an ordinary game should matter to a man of such great importance in the world. But as he watched the author taking so much pleasure in every successful shot, he decided it was more fun to lose to him and to watch his face light up than to beat him and see his look of disappointment. "He wanted to win so eagerly that it was a positive pain for him not to do so," Coburn observed. "To see his intensity and determination as he leaned over the table, his face pink with excitement, was to understand something of why he *had* succeeded in life."

Pleased with the warmth of his welcome at Stormfield, Coburn came away with the impression that it was a peaceful home where Twain had few cares. Even fifty years later he could still recall "the expression of perfect contentment" on the author's face as they listened to Clara sing a beautiful melody beside the grand piano in the living room. He had not noticed any sign of tension in the household, but he didn't have any reason to look for it, just as he didn't have any reason to think twice about

the guest at Stormfield who played the piano while Clara sang for her father. If he had known more about her career, he might have wondered
why it wasn't Charles Wark instead of a famous foreign musician who
was no ordinary accompanist—Ossip Gabrilowitsch.[28]

· · ·

SINCE HIS LAST AMERICAN TOUR in the winter of 1907, Gabrilowitsch had seen his reputation continue to grow. Impressed by his power
to excite audiences, the Boston Symphony Orchestra had invited him to
return to America and serve as its featured soloist for a short tour in late
1908. The highlight of that tour took place only a few weeks before
Coburn's visit to Stormfield. It was a concert at Carnegie Hall on
December 3. Gabrilowitsch gave a strong performance of Rachmaninoff's
Second Piano Concerto and won some of the best reviews of his career.
The *New York Sun* praised him for his "singularly charming style," and
the *Times* said of him, "He is an artist who has steadily grown greater
since his first coming to this city some years ago, and his art is now bear-
ing its full fruition." His performance was described as "full of power, of
delicacy, of all imaginable contrast . . . admirably seconded by the orchestra."[29]

With this triumph behind him, and with several solo appearances
scheduled in the coming year—including a recital in Carnegie Hall on
January 10—Gabrilowitsch needed a quiet place in the country where he
could relax during the holidays, and where he could have the use of a
good piano. He was invited to stay at Stormfield, apparently because
Clara had decided it was more sensible to renew her relationship with
this rising star of the music world than to continue her risky affair with
Charles Wark. By the end of the year the rumors about that affair had become too widespread for Clara to ignore. Even old family friends in
Hartford were gossiping about her, and it appears that she was warned of
this by Reverend Joseph Twichell. At some point in late November or
early December, she quit seeing Wark, abruptly ending both their affair
and their professional relationship.

After his brief but passionate fling with Mahler's wife, Ossip may
have thought that courting Clara again was his safest bet. But, as he
would discover, she was still uncertain of her feelings about him, waver-

ing between love and friendship. Even during his stay in Redding over the holidays, she felt free to leave him at Stormfield for short periods while she went back to her apartment in New York.

On New Year's Eve day he and Twain were the only ones left in the house. Isabel Lyon had gone to New York on business, but before leaving she had asked Twain to be on his best behavior. She was afraid that the two temperamental artists might get on each other's nerves. Specifically, she urged Twain to avoid cursing in his usual exuberant way. But he was having too much fun indulging in various outbursts of "profanity and rage and pleasure over the morning mail," and didn't care what anyone else thought. "I tell the King that Gabrilowitsch hearing such wondrous blasts of cursing will be afraid to stay," Lyon noted in her journal. "The King likes just such suggestions and blasted forth another volley of cursing."[30]

There was little chance that he would frighten the pianist, who had learned long ago that the moods of the Clemens family were volatile and unpredictable. Obviously, these qualities held some appeal for Gabrilowitsch, who couldn't seem to stay away from the family. It had now been ten years since he had first fallen under Clara's spell, and despite all his success and artistic growth, she still held some strange power over his emotions that kept him pursuing her no matter how elusive she seemed. At this point in his career, with New York at his feet, he didn't need to be waiting around for Clara to make up her mind about him. But the applause of his audiences and the praise of the critics weren't enough to make him abandon an obsession that his teacher Leschetizky had long ago defined as "Delirium Clemens."[31]

Early in his stay at Stormfield he was given a chance to prove to Clara that he had lost none of his devotion to her. On the very morning that Coburn and Henderson arrived at the house, there were dramatic reports in the New York papers that Ossip had saved Clara from certain death in an accident the previous day. It was difficult to overlook the story. It appeared on the front pages of both the *Times* and the *Tribune,* and was soon picked up by the wire services and published nationwide. "Miss Clemens Hurt," said the headline in the *Boston Globe.* "Says Her Escape Was Marvelous," reported the *Washington Times.*

According to the press, Ossip and Clara went for a sleigh ride around Redding on Sunday morning, December 20. About three miles from home, as they were going uphill on a narrow country lane, their horse bolted when it was frightened by "a wind-whipped newspaper." Ossip wasn't able to control it and the sleigh overturned, throwing Clara to the side of the road but leaving her dress tangled in the runner. Just to the right of her was a ravine and a drop of fifty feet. As the horse began to drag the sleigh and Clara toward the edge, Ossip ran forward and grabbed the animal's head, pulling it back to the road and holding it fast until Clara could free herself. He performed this feat despite having sprained his ankle when the sleigh overturned. Though his injury was "painful," he was able to comfort Clara and drive her home. Besides suffering from shock, she was unhurt.[32]

It is difficult to imagine how someone with Gabrilowitsch's slight build and delicate hands was able to regain control of a horse in the snow at the top of a hill. With a sprained ankle, he must have had a hard time staying upright on the slippery incline. It isn't clear who reported the accident to the newspapers, but the only witnesses were Ossip and Clara, and the press accepted the story without question. Nobody came forward with any corroborating evidence, and the incident isn't mentioned in family documents or in Coburn's account of his visit to Stormfield. But, to reporters, the tale of a damsel in distress and a heroic rescue by a romantic Russian pianist was simply too good not to print.

There is evidence to suggest, however, that the accident never happened or was simply a minor mishap. Among Coburn's photographs taken the next day is one that includes a full-length shot of Gabrilowitsch. He is posed beside Isabel Lyon's cottage, which she had volunteered to show Coburn and Henderson. Wearing buckled overshoes and standing normally without any assistance, he doesn't look like a man who has recently suffered a sprained ankle. In fact, he was fit enough to have walked all the way down to Lyon's house in the snow with the others.

But why would he and Clara have wanted to invent an accident and pretend that he had rescued her? For one thing, it was good publicity for a man who wanted to fill Carnegie Hall for his solo performance in a few weeks. For Clara, it provided an excellent way of curtailing speculation by gossipmongers that she was going to wed Charles Wark. The same papers that had linked her name to a married man were now obliged to report that she was involved with a perfectly respectable, and very eligible, bachelor. And how could anyone suspect her of wanting to marry Wark when the new man in her life was a dashing young star of the music world who had rescued her from certain death?

There is no doubt that the news reports helped Gabrilowitsch. His publicity agent in New York made sure of that, though as the time of the recital grew closer, the agent hastened to reassure music lovers that the pianist's injury was minor and wouldn't affect his performance. On the morning of the recital the *New York Tribune* reported, "The hands and arms of Ossip Gabrilowitsch, the Russian pianist, are solemnly pronounced 'as good as ever' by his publicity agent, despite his recent experience in a runaway accident with Miss Clara Clemens near Redding, Connecticut. The wrench to his ankle is reported as not severe enough to interfere at all with his playing this afternoon in his recital."[33]

The turnout on January 10 was everything Gabrilowitsch could have hoped for, and the enthusiastic response to his performance was overwhelming. Cast now as a heroic figure in music and life, he was mobbed at the end of the recital and the crowd refused to leave the theater, demanding encore after encore. "The Gabrilowitsch enthusiasts," wrote an amazed critic, "were still clamoring for encores after a two-hour long recital." The pianist gave them three encores, yet they stayed and shouted for more. "Audience Only Leaves Carnegie Hall When Lights Are Put Out," said the headline in the *Times* the next day.[34]

So the episode of the runaway horse served Ossip well, but didn't put an end to the gossip about Clara's relationship with Wark. That problem would continue to haunt her for many months to come, even though she scrupulously avoided any contact with him. Meanwhile, her father must have learned the truth about Wark. When Joseph Twichell visited Stormfield in January, the Reverend probably told his old friend of all the rumors going around Hartford. But there is no evidence that Twain tried to interfere in his daughter's love life by demanding that she stop seeing Wark. Though he grumbled about all her comings and goings, he may not have known what to make of her renewed interest in Gabrilowitsch or the improbable tale of her rescue in the snow. Understanding that she was as stubborn as he was, he knew that there was no point in trying to bend her will to his. Like him, she was a force unto herself.

In the haven that he was trying to create at Stormfield, there wasn't supposed to be any intrigue or scheming or deception. He was explicit on that point, warning against such things in the guestbook, where he had written on the first page these lines adapted from Shakespeare's *Titus Andronicus:*

> In peace and honor rest you here, my guest; repose you here,
> Secure from worldly chances and mishaps!
> Here lurks no treason, here no envy swells,
> Here grow no damned grudges; here are no storms,
> No noise, but silence and eternal sleep:
> In peace and honor rest you here, my guest!

Though he took these sentiments seriously, the people in his home who were closest to him did not. As 1908 came to an end, he persisted in believing that he had found a place of beauty and repose, but all the while envy was swelling and "damned grudges" were growing among Ashcroft, Lyon, and Clara. In the next few months they would create more turmoil than he could bear and make his house seem a "stormfield" indeed. Yet he may have long suspected that some such trouble was brewing under his nose, for his adapted quotation from Shakespeare isn't as comforting in the original as it may have seemed in the guestbook. In the play the words are spoken by the bloodthirsty General Andronicus at a tomb where he is burying his sons who have fallen in battle (Twain replaced "sons" with "guests"), and where he is attended by other sons who have just returned from killing a man.[35]

In December it would have been difficult not to see that something was troubling Lyon, whose nerves were increasingly on edge. More and more, she complained of headaches and would lock herself in her room and ask not to be disturbed. Ashcroft made excuses, saying that she was suffering from overwork. Annoyed, Twain decided that she was just being lazy. "Laziness was my own specialty," he later remarked, "& I did not like this competition."[36]

She was easily upset and always seemed worried that something was going to go wrong. One day Robert Collier sent a note saying that he had found an unusual Christmas present for Twain. It was a baby elephant, and would arrive at Stormfield as soon as a freight car was available to bring it to Redding. Collier also said that a trainer was needed, and that he was going to find one at Barnum & Bailey's winter headquarters in Bridgeport. Instead of realizing that this was one of Collier's harmless pranks, Lyon took him seriously and panicked. Mary Howden—a stenographer who worked for a short time at Stormfield—brought the note to Lyon, who was in bed with one of her headaches. Howden recalled that the secretary read it, then "dropped back on the pillows and indulged in what appeared to be a near-apoplectic fit," asking in a desperate voice, "And where are we going to keep it?"

When Howden suggested that Collier was only joking, Lyon shook her head and said that she knew him "all too well . . . he was a man of his word, and if he asserted that an elephant was forthcoming, an elephant undoubtedly would arrive."[37]

Lyon telephoned and tried to talk him out of it. He managed to keep from laughing and cheerfully pretended that the little elephant would be as easy to manage as one of Twain's cats.

"Put him in the loggia," he suggested. "That's closed in, isn't it, for the winter? Plenty of sunlight—just the place for a young elephant."

"But we play cards in the loggia," she answered. "We use it for a sort of sun-parlor."

"But that wouldn't matter. He's a kindly, playful little thing. He'll be just like a kitten. I'll send the man up to look over the place and tell you just how to take care of him, and I'll send up several bales of hay in advance."[38]

No one at Stormfield seemed to think Collier was in earnest except Lyon, whose worries grew with each new message from him about his efforts to reserve a freight car and to find a trainer. She dreaded the thought that the first Christmas at the new house would be ruined by a rich man's whim. For the first time in years Twain was actually looking forward to the holiday, and was planning to celebrate it in the loggia, which had been decorated in greenery so that it could serve as "a Xmas-present show parlor," to use his words. "It is very comfortable, and very handsome, and is much the showiest room in the house," he said of the newly decorated room. "I haven't seen such a display since the old, old times in Hartford—gone, to return no more."[39]

Two days before Christmas, Lyon was alarmed when a shipment of ten bales of hay, several bushels of carrots, and a few baskets of apples arrived at Stormfield. Then, on Christmas morning, a man claiming to be Professor May, professional elephant trainer, telephoned and asked to look around the place before transporting the animal from the station.

"The day of doom was at hand," Paine later joked in his account of the elaborate prank. Mary Howden recalled that the trainer "was received by the social secretary, also the financial secretary [Ashcroft], who had come out from New York for the occasion; and he solemnly instructed them in the art of entertaining an elephant, told them what the animal liked to eat, how to treat him when he was ill, and which end of him to avoid when he was angry, etc."

Harry Lounsbury had driven the man to the house and had quickly concluded that he was an impostor. In fact, as Collier would soon reveal, "Professor May" was his butler. But Lyon and Ashcroft listened to the instructions and waited anxiously for the man to return with the elephant.

"Lounsbury came back by and by," Paine recalled, "bringing the elephant but not the trainer. It didn't need a trainer. It was a beautiful specimen, with soft, smooth coat and handsome trappings, perfectly quiet, well-behaved and small—suited to the loggia, as Collier had said—for it was only two feet long and beautifully made of cloth and cotton—one of the finest toy elephants ever seen anywhere."

Twain enjoyed the prank and fired off a response of mock indignation, complaining to Collier that the animal had come to life and had insisted on observing Christmas, "and now we have no furniture left and no servants and no visitors, no friends, no photographs, no burglars—nothing but the elephant."[40]

Everybody had a good laugh. But Lyon wasn't laughing on the inside. She felt foolish and depressed. Over the next few days, as she tried to go about her usual duties, her depression deepened. It wasn't helped by the sad pieces that Gabrilowitsch rehearsed at the piano. "I have worked hard," she wrote in her journal on December 30, "but life has lost something vital, accentuated by a minor theme that Gabrilowitsch plays very much. Snow must be coming for the sky looks very big and very grey."

Truth is stranger than fiction, but it is because
Fiction is obliged to stick to possibilities; Truth isn't.

MARK TWAIN

. . .

PART FOUR

...

TEMPEST

Helen Keller visits Twain at Stormfield, January 1909.

SEVENTEEN

Hannibal-on-Avon

I cannot call to mind a single instance
where I have ever been irreverent,
except toward the things which were
sacred to other people.

Mark Twain[1]

. . .

OF ALL THE VISITORS to Stormfield none wrote a more vivid description of the place than a young woman of twenty-eight who was Twain's guest for a weekend in early January 1909. Almost nothing was lost on her, beginning with the "tang in the air of cedar and pine" as her carriage came up the drive, and then the smell of burning logs in the fireplace, and the orange pekoe tea and toast with strawberry jam served shortly after her arrival. Even twenty years later she could still recall the dried wildflowers—cattails, goldenrod, and thistles—adorning vases in the loggia, the distant views of snow-clad hills and stone walls from the icy terrace, the bright spectacle of Twain reading aloud by the firelight in his white suit, the sweet aroma of his favorite desert—apple pie—coming to the table fresh from the oven, and his restless manner at dinner as he got up and paced between courses, talking and gesturing and ignoring his food.

All these things and many more were included in a memoir written in her late forties by Helen Keller, who had famously learned in girlhood that the loss of her sight and hearing couldn't stop her from finding other ways to connect with the world. On her visit to Stormfield, her teacher, Annie Sullivan—the "miracle worker" who had helped her to discover the power of language—was at her side, and enabled her to converse with Twain and to "see" his house by spelling words into her hand. Helen was also amazingly proficient at reading lips with her fingers and could remember conversations word for word. Her "deliberate, measured speech"—as Annie's husband, John Macy, once described it—was difficult for many adults to understand, but not for Twain, who could communicate with her even when her teacher wasn't present. She would "listen" to him by placing her thumb against his throat, her forefinger to his lips, and her middle finger against his nose.[2]

Twain was fascinated by her extraordinary abilities, and was in awe of her confidence and courage. He once called her "the most marvelous person of her sex that has existed on this earth since Joan of Arc," which was about the highest praise he could offer. He was a great admirer of her writing. When her first book—The Story of My Life—came out while she was finishing her degree at Radcliffe, Twain wrote to congratulate her, saying that he was "enchanted" by it. He added that he was especially proud of their friendship, which began when she was fourteen and had remained strong ever since—"without a break, & without a single act of violence that I can call to mind."[3]

They had met in March 1895 at a Sunday luncheon held in Keller's honor at a tall red-brick house in New York on West Thirty-fourth Street. It was the home of Laurence Hutton, an editor and critic who was Twain's friend and one of Helen's early benefactors. Henry Rogers came with Twain, and the two men joined about a dozen other guests in a receiving line to wish the girl well during her stay in New York, where Annie had brought her to study speech at a school for the deaf. The poet Margaret Sangster, who was standing near Twain when he caught his first glimpse of Helen, remembered seeing him "impetuously dash the tears from his eyes as he looked into her sweet face."

Helen had read some of his work and asked him to explain the origin of his pseudonym. After telling her what "Mark Twain" meant to steamboat pilots, he said the name suited him because he "was sometimes light and on the surface, and sometimes—"

"Deep," she interrupted, surprising him with her quickness and intelligence.

She seemed to feel more at ease with Twain than with any of the other guests. He was the only one whose face and hair she examined with her hands in order to form an idea of his appearance. As Laurence Hutton said of him afterward, "He was peculiarly tender and lovely with her— even for Mr. Clemens—and she kissed him when he said good-bye."[4]

At the end of the luncheon Helen astonished all the guests when she shook their hands and addressed them by name as they went out. When he left, Twain had merely patted her on the head, yet she also recognized him. "Perhaps someone else can explain this miracle," he later remarked, "but I have never been able to do it. Could she feel the wrinkles in my hand through her hair?"

He was always intending to ask her for an explanation, but never managed to do it until she came for her first and only stay at Stormfield.

Did she remember him patting her on the head? he asked. She smiled and said yes.

How did she know it was his hand?

"I smelled you" was her honest reply.[5]

She must have found it a pleasing smell because she loved to cling to him and touch his face and feel the power of his voice through her fingers. "His voice was truly wonderful," she recalled. "To my touch, it was deep, resonant. He had the power of modulating it so as to suggest the most delicate shades of meaning, and he spoke so deliberately that I could get almost every word with my fingers on his lips."[6]

It was not generally known that Keller had a great sense of humor, but it was one of the things Twain liked best about her. She could take a joke as well as make one. "If she does not know the answer to a question," John Macy observed, "she guesses with mischievous assurance. Ask her the color of your coat . . . [and] she will feel it and say 'black.' If it happens to be blue, and you tell her so triumphantly, she is likely to answer, 'Thank you. I am glad you know. Why did you ask me?' "[7]

Knowing how much she liked to laugh, Twain was always finding some excuse to tease her. When he showed her to her room on the first night at Stormfield, he told her that if she needed anything, she would find an ample supply of cigars and bourbon in the bathroom. When he gave her a tour of the billiards room, he offered to teach her the game.

She took the bait and replied innocently, "Oh, Mr. Clemens, it takes sight to play billiards."

Not the way his friends played, he answered. "The blind couldn't play worse."[8]

It was the publication of Keller's second major work—*The World I Live In*—that had prompted Twain to invite her to Stormfield. The book—which came out in October 1908—was dedicated to Henry Rogers ("My Dear Friend of Many Years"), who had continued giving Keller financial help after paying her way through Radcliffe. The copy Twain received was warmly inscribed, "Dear Mr. Clemens, come live in my world a little while/Helen Keller." In response, he had said that she must come to his world first, and to bring Annie and John Macy with her. He teased her by pretending to be dictatorial. "I command you all three," he wrote, "to come and spend a few days with me in Stormfield." (As he was well aware, Helen and her teacher were rarely apart. Even after Annie's marriage in 1905, the two women continued living together.)[9]

The highlight of Helen's visit came one evening when Twain read to her from his short book *Eve's Diary*, which had been published three years earlier. He sat in a big armchair by the fire with a pipe in one hand and the book in the other, while she and Annie Sullivan sat in lower chairs beside him. John Macy and Isabel Lyon stood apart and watched as Keller followed the story with an ecstatic expression that turned tearful when Twain read the last line. It was Adam's lament at Eve's grave (as well as Twain's tribute to Livy): "Wheresoever she was, there was Eden." In her journal Lyon described the emotional effect of this reading on both the famous guest and the author: "She quivered with delight, and he was shaken with emotion. Could hardly find his voice again. It was a marvel to behold."[10]

Twain's Eve has a gift for language and prides herself on knowing immediately the correct name for each new thing she encounters. Adam is often at a loss for words. "I have taken all the work of naming things off his hands," she says, "and this has been a great relief to him, for he has no gift in that line. . . . Whenever a new creature comes along, I name it before he has time to expose himself by an awkward silence. . . . The right name comes out instantly, just as if it were an inspiration, as no doubt it is, for I am sure it wasn't in me half a minute before."

When he wrote of Eve's delight in naming things, Twain may have been thinking of Keller's *The Story of My Life*. At several points in her book she recalls the joy of learning the names of things after she had acquired the gift of language just before she turned seven. "I did nothing but explore with my hands and learn the name of every object that I touched; and the more I handled things and learned their names and uses, the more joyous and confident grew my sense of kinship with the rest of the world." Whether or not her story influenced Twain's, she instantly recognized something of herself in his portrait of Eve. In his guestbook, as she was leaving Stormfield, she wrote that she had been in "Eden three days," and signed herself "A daughter of Eve, Helen Keller."

He understood her meaning so completely that he wrote under her entry his own explanation of it. "The point of what Helen says above, lies in this: that I read the 'Diary of Eve' all through, to her last night; in it Eve frequently mentions things she saw for the first time but instantly knew what they were & named them—though she had never seen them before."[11]

In Twain's view, what made Keller such an important figure was not simply that she had learned to communicate in spite of being both blind and deaf, but that, for her, the imagination and the world had become one. Without the distractions of sight and sound, and protected by her devoted teacher, she was indeed the author of "the world I live in," transforming everything around her into a reality only she could imagine. Twain understood that she was the artist of her own life, and he envied the pure state of an imagination unfettered by ordinary perceptions. "A well put together unreality is pretty hard to beat," he once observed, responding to a friend's remark that Keller's "concept of things . . . must lack reality."

In Twain's best book—written long before he knew Helen—Huck and Jim are given a brief glimpse of that miracle of a "well put together unreality." On their raft as it floats down the big river, they enjoy a free life of their own making where the hard realities of poverty and slavery can be forgotten for a while. When Huck says, "It's lovely to live on a raft," he means not only that it's a relief to escape the troubled lands on both banks, but that it's a rare chance to imagine his own world and to live in it. In fact, the boy's satisfaction with this isolated existence is greatest at night when the river is a sea of darkness or when, in daylight, it is a blank canvas with, as he says, "nothing to hear nor nothing to see." At such moments, when he is absorbed in watching "the lonesomeness of the river," he must—like Helen—rely on his imagination to fill the void.[12]

As a way of thanking Annie for helping to bring Helen's imagination to life, Twain handed her a small souvenir just before she left Stormfield. It was a postcard with a picture of him dressed in white, and on the top margin he wrote, "To Mrs. John Sullivan Macy with warm regard & with limitless admiration of the wonders she has performed as a miracle-worker."

It was a kind gesture, but it would take another fifty years for that term "miracle-worker" to catch on as the best description of Annie. Playwright William Gibson liked it so much that he used it for the title of the drama he wrote in the 1950s about Helen and her teacher. *The Miracle Worker* was a Broadway hit and later a successful film. "I like to fall a little in love with my heroines," Gibson told the *New York Times*, "and the title—from Mark Twain . . . was meant to show where my affections lay." When the play debuted, Keller was still alive, but Sullivan had been dead for many years, and her extraordinary work as a teacher was in danger of being forgotten. "This stubborn girl of twenty," said Gibson of the young Annie, "who . . . salvaged Helen's soul, and lived thereafter in its shadow, seemed to me to deserve a star bow."[13]

· · ·

DURING HIS VISIT to Stormfield, John Macy showed Twain a new book on the old question of whether Shakespeare's plays were written by someone else. Macy knew the book's author—a former librarian named William Stone Booth—and thought Twain would be intrigued by its claims that Francis Bacon wrote the plays. At six hundred pages, *Some Acrostic Signatures of Francis Bacon* wasn't exactly bedtime reading, but Twain took Macy's galley proofs of the book to bed with him and stayed up late trying to follow Booth's complex method of deciphering signatures and other clues supposedly hidden in the plays by the crafty Bacon. This nighttime study, Isabel Lyon later noted, didn't work out "very successfully."

Though the book was published by a respectable Boston firm—Houghton Mifflin—it reads like a technical manual written by a mad scientist, with bewildering references and codes scattered everywhere. Many of the acrostics are arranged on the page in diagonal lines, circles, triangles, or zigzag patterns. As one annoyed and frustrated reviewer later complained, "Mr. Booth has eaten of the insane root that takes the reason prisoner." Yet Twain's curiosity was aroused, and he would keep returning to the book in the coming days in the hope of understanding it. He never did. "He confessed that his faculties had been more or less defeated in attempting to follow the ciphers," Paine recalled, "and he complained bitterly that the evidence had not been set forth so that he who merely skims a book might grasp it."[14]

But Booth's strange book was merely the spark that set Twain's imagination going on the larger subject of Bardolatry, which had interested him for decades. Though he admired the plays, he didn't think much of the man from Stratford whom he once called "that third-rate actor who never wrote a line in his life." A born debunker, he had long wanted to explain to the world why he considered Shakespeare the playwright a myth. After discussing the subject with Macy, who encouraged him to write about it, Twain suddenly decided that it was indeed time to air his views. "It always seemed unaccountable to me," he said, "that a man could be so prominent in Elizabeth's little London . . . yet leave behind him hardly an incident for people to remember him by. . . . Not even a distinguished horse could die and leave such biographical poverty behind him."[15]

As someone who was in the process of leaving quite a long biographical trail behind him, he was amazed that in three hundred years no one had been able to produce a single letter or literary manuscript that was indisputably in Shakespeare's hand, or even a book that had belonged to him. For Twain, the vast amount of conjecture needed to flesh out

Shakespeare's life made the Bard resemble a reconstructed dinosaur—"nine bones and six hundred barrels of plaster of paris." Refusing to join "the Shakespearites" or "the Baconians," he preferred to call himself a "Brontosaurian," explaining that even though he wasn't able to say who wrote the plays, he was "sure that Shakespeare *didn't*," and "strongly suspect[ed] that Bacon *did*."[16]

Isabel Lyon was shocked when she overheard Twain and Macy hotly denouncing Shakespeare's authorship of the plays. "You'd think both men had Shakespeare by the throat . . . strangling him for some hideous crime."

As soon as Keller and the Macys left Stormfield on the morning of January 11, Twain started writing the little book that would become *Is Shakespeare Dead?* "There was silence in his room all morning," Lyon recalled. "About noon he came swinging down the hallway to my study, waving some sheets of ms. and read what he had written. . . . It is disturbing. His attack is not gentle, and not very clever. He has Shakespeare in shreds, just where he wants him to be."

Lyon tried to talk him out of continuing the work, saying that readers wouldn't want to see one beloved author attacking another. A few days later Paine also objected. "I was ardently opposed to this idea," he later wrote. "The romance of the boy, Will Shakespeare, who had come up to London and began by holding horses outside of the theater, and ended by winning the proudest place in the world of letters, was something I did not wish to let perish."

But Twain was in no mood to heed the sober advice of his circle, especially after Macy added fuel to the fire by sending him another new book on the authorship question, *The Shakespeare Problem Restated,* by George Greenwood, a British lawyer and Liberal MP. He read it enthusiastically and "splattered" his copy with notes. He told Lyon that he liked the way Greenwood "gets one of those Shakespearian scholars by the tail and twists it." Suddenly, he couldn't wait to twist some of those tails himself. The subject seemed to have awakened in him the freewheeling spirit of his early career, when he loved nothing better than mocking the unquestioned devotion to some revered figure or artistic treasure of the Old World.[17]

The title he gave to his short volume on Shakespeare echoes a question asked in jest in *The Innocents Abroad*. As a way of teasing earnest tour guides in Europe, Twain and some of his companions from the *Quaker City* would often pretend to be much more innocent than they seemed. The aim was to make even the most confident guides react to their bogus question with dropped jaws and bewildered stares. "After they have exhausted their enthusiasm pointing out to us and praising the beauties of some ancient bronze image or broken-legged statue, we look at it stupidly and in silence for five, ten, fifteen minutes—as long as we can hold out, in fact—and then ask: 'Is—is he dead?' That conquers the serenest of them. It is not what they are looking for."[18]

Mark Twain tearing Shakespeare to shreds was not what most readers were looking for, and that was one reason he wanted to do it. He knew it would get him into trouble, but it was the kind of mischief he liked and could handle. If the risks of trying to explode a major religious, moral, or political myth were too great, then the next best thing was to go after a cherished cultural icon, and Shakespeare was at the top of the list. In the wake of such an assault, he might expect an outraged reaction from various critics and professors, but he knew their complaints wouldn't do him any permanent harm.

He was under no illusion that he might change the accepted view of the Bard. For much of the English-speaking world, doubting the existence of Shakespeare the playwright was like doubting the existence of the sun or the moon. "Am I trying to convince anybody that Shakespeare did not write Shakespeare's Works?" asks Twain in his book. "Ah, now, what do you take me for? Would I be so soft as that, after having known the human race familiarly for nearly seventy-four years? It would grieve me to know that any one could think so injuriously of me, so uncomplimentarily, so unadmiringly of me. No-no, I am aware that when even the brightest mind in our world has been trained up from childhood in a superstition of any kind, it will never be possible for that mind, in its maturity, to examine sincerely, dispassionately, and conscientiously any evidence or any circumstance which shall seem to cast a doubt upon the validity of that superstition."[19]

For Twain, the main purpose of his book wasn't to score points in the authorship debate, but to show off his talents for an art he had mastered long ago—the art of irreverence. One of the best chapters is called

"Irreverence," and nicely illustrates why butchering a sacred cow now and then is not only necessary, but sometimes noble. First, however, Twain reminds his readers that most people—including himself—think irreverence is fine so long as it's directed against someone else's sacred cow. "When a thing is sacred to me," he explains, "it is impossible for me to be irreverent toward it. I cannot call to mind a single instance where I have ever been irreverent, except toward the things which were sacred to other people."

During his long career, the art of irreverence had helped him to fight injustice in many forms, including that of racism, but such a powerful weapon can easily be misused, and he doubted that anyone else shared his talent for making such good use of it. "I am the only sect that knows how to employ it gently, kindly, charitably, dispassionately. The other sects lack the quality of self-restraint. The Catholic Church says the most irreverent things about matters which are sacred to the Protestants, and the Protestant Church retorts in kind about the confessional and other matters which Catholics hold sacred; then both of these irreverencers turn upon Thomas Paine and charge *him* with irreverence."

In fact, Twain was such a master of his art that he had even learned how to be irreverent about irreverence. "One of the most trying defects which I find in these Stratfordolaters, these Shakesperoids, these thugs, these bangalores, these troglodytes, these herumfrodites, these blatherskites, these buccaneers, these bandoleers, is their spirit of irreverence. It is detectable in every utterance of theirs when they are talking about us. I am thankful that in me there is nothing of that spirit."[20]

Bardolatry is a mistake not because of doubts about Shakespeare's identity, but because, as Twain suggests, no idol should be so far above reproach that it can't be assaulted with laughter or carefully inspected for feet of clay. Recalling the famous bust of Shakespeare he had seen on a visit in 1873 to Stratford's Holy Trinity Church, Twain provides a helpful example of how to do a suitably irreverent description of an enshrined idol: "The precious bust, the priceless bust, the calm bust, the serene bust, the emotionless bust, with the dandy moustache, and the putty face, unseamed of care—that face which has looked passionlessly down upon the awed pilgrim for a hundred and fifty years and will still look down upon the awed pilgrim three hundred more, with the deep, deep, deep, subtle,

subtle, subtle, expression of a bladder." As this sentence shows, Twain in his seventies had lost none of his ability to lead readers through an elaborate maze of words and then stop them short with a surprising turn of phrase. The fancy rhetoric of the sentence parodies the worshipful style of some Bardolaters until Twain suddenly deflates it by comparing the idol's face to a bladder.[21]

Twain takes his most irreverent swipe at Shakespeare when he compares their literary careers and argues that his has been much better managed. If Shakespeare was Shakespeare, then he didn't properly promote his career, Twain suggests. Instead of making sure that the world knew more about him, the playwright was so careless of his fame that he left behind only "a vague file of chipmunk-tracks stringing through the dust of Stratford." In the years after he retired from the London stage, he should have had ample time to do what Twain was doing in retirement—making sure the world knew what manner of man had created so much great literature.[22]

But the fact that even the people of his own hometown didn't seem to know the details of Shakespeare's career is enough to suggest to Twain that the actor didn't write the plays. To prove his point, he asks readers to consider what would happen if they went looking for information about Mark Twain in Hannibal. "I am away along in life—my seventy-third year being already well behind me—yet sixteen of my Hannibal schoolmates are still alive to-day, and can tell—and do tell—inquirers dozens and dozens of incidents of their young lives and mine together."

As he knew from his biographer's research, there was no end to the number of people who could give you firsthand information about Mark Twain. "On the few surviving steamboats—those lingering ghosts and remembrancers of great fleets that plied the big river in the beginning of my water-career—which is exactly as long ago as the whole invoice of the life-years of Shakespeare number—there are still findable two or three river-pilots who saw me do creditable things in those ancient days. . . . They know about me, and can tell. And so do printers, from St. Louis to New York; and so do newspaper reporters, from Nevada to San Francisco. And so do the police. If Shakespeare had really been celebrated, like me, Stratford could have told things about him; and if my experience goes for anything, they'd have done it."[23]

To the critics who say it's the work that matters, not the author's life, Twain answers that both matter. He wanted the world never to forget what he had done to become a writer, and how he had lived as a writer. His books were not written in a vacuum. They were the products of a man with specific experiences and characteristics, and Twain was as proud of his life as he was of his works. The best passages in *Is Shakespeare Dead?* are not about the Bard's life, but about Twain's. They tell of the ways in which experience has informed his writing. The kind of life he has lived, he says, is reflected in what he writes and how he writes.

In the copy Macy sent him of Greenwood's *The Shakespeare Problem Restated,* Twain wrote, "Did ever a man move the world by writing solely out of what he learned from schools and books, and leaving out what he had *lived* and *felt*?" Of course, what he wanted was a Shakespeare who resembled Mark Twain—a largely self-educated writer of humble origins who came of age in a bucolic river village, and who went off one day to find adventure in wild places, then moved to a big city and used his wit, imagination, and experience to conquer the world, and who succeeded beyond all measure, and who retired from the limelight to savor his triumph and burnish his legacy. Writing *Is Shakespeare Dead?* gave Twain the chance to speculate on the nature of his own posthumous fame. And what he found was reassuring. Though he didn't have a *Hamlet* or a *Macbeth* to his credit, the story of his life was second to none, and the literature that had flowed from it was pretty good, too.[24]

· · ·

IT TOOK TWAIN only two months to finish *Is Shakespeare Dead?* He was in high spirits for much of that time, exulting in the pleasure of "throwing bricks at Shakespeare," as he put it. He dictated some parts of the book, and wrote others in longhand, and was pleasantly surprised at how easily he fell back into the old routine of writing a certain number of words each day. One afternoon, after working for several hours, he came into Isabel Lyon's room to tell her that he had finished writing for the day. He was enjoying the subject so much that he was confident of continuing his flow of thought the next morning without any trouble. "Now," he told her, "I let it rest there; where formerly I would force myself to write two-thirds of a sentence to be my starting point for the next day."[25]

As the book speedily progressed, he became more and more satisfied with his performance, "chuckling" to himself while he reread the latest addition to the manuscript. When he was finished, he went to Lyon and waved the manuscript in triumph, feeling certain that it would be a great success. "He was proud of it," she recalled. But she still had her reservations, and wasn't surprised when the editors at Harper's showed little enthusiasm for the book.

"Harper's did not want to publish it," she later commented, "but they were under contract to print anything he wrote. . . . Col. Harvey said to me: 'Can't you get Uncle Mark <u>not</u> to have these ideas of his made public? His readers are not looking for such matter. . . . They want only the beloved humorous side of him.' "[26]

Twain knew that Harvey wasn't pleased, yet he insisted not only that Harper's publish the book, but also that the firm bring it out as soon as possible. He wanted to make sure it appeared before William Stone Booth's book, which was scheduled for publication in late April. In obedience to his wishes, the staff at Harper's rushed to get the work into print. The manuscript was completed on March 9, and the book was published on April 8, 1909.

The reviews were mixed, and only a few critics seemed to appreciate Twain's comic intentions or his autobiographical slant, despite the book's subtitle, "From My Autobiography." But by the time the reviews appeared, problems at home would give Twain far more serious things to worry about than the reception of his book. He would ignore the critics, with the exception of one outraged British author—George Greenwood.

A Philadelphia lawyer named Thomas B. Harned bought a copy and noticed that several pages of text from Greenwood's *The Shakespeare Problem Restated* were included verbatim in *Is Shakespeare Dead?* Harned was one of Walt Whitman's literary executors, and was well versed in copyright law. He was also on close terms with George Greenwood and was amazed to see so much of his friend's work reproduced in Twain's book. Claiming that these pages offered the best evidence the playwright must have had some legal training, Twain had acknowledged the source and warmly praised it. But in the rush to get his book out, he had failed to identify Greenwood as the author of the borrowed text and didn't personally contact him for permission to quote.

In early May Harned sent Greenwood a copy of *Is Shakespeare Dead?* and wrote on the flyleaf, "This book is a fine boost for your book." But then he asked, "Did Mark Twain get your permission to use your chapter 'Was Shakespeare a Lawyer?' [?] I assume that he did & that you have already got a copy. I send this for full measure." When Greenwood received this gift from his American friend, he wasn't pleased to discover that Twain had taken so much material from him. Angrily, he took a pencil and underscored Harned's comment, "I assume that he did," and then scrawled his response in the margin, "No, he did not."[27]

A meticulous, forthright man, Greenwood decided to fight back against the apparent infringement of his rights, directing his publisher to fire off threatening letters to Harper's. In an effort to embarrass Twain and to create some publicity for Greenwood in America, the publisher—John Lane—wrote to the *New York Times,* complaining of "literary larceny."[28]

Twain should have known not to quote so liberally from a lawyer's work, but it soon emerged that he had, in fact, done nothing legally wrong. After the initial panic wore off at Harper's, the staff consulted the correspondence files and discovered that Lane's firm had been contacted before publication and had given written permission for Twain to use the lengthy excerpt from Greenwood's book. On March 29 a request had been sent on Twain's behalf to the managing director of Lane's New York branch—Rutger Bleecker Jewett, who generously responded that Twain could "quote from Mr. Greenwood's book as much as he pleased." Such a reply was binding and was the only permission needed. The firm had no legal case against Twain in America, yet Lane was upset because Jewett had not cleared the request with the London office. So he and his author decided to shift the blame to Twain and to insist that more credit be given to *The Shakespeare Problem Restated.*[29]

Graciously, Twain apologized for the unintentional omission of the author's name. When the British edition of *Is Shakespeare Dead?* appeared, there was an extra leaf tipped in to advertise "*The Shakespeare Problem Restated,* by George G. Greenwood, MP." And shortly thereafter

Lane ran more advertisements in the trade press that included a blurb from the alleged larcenist himself. Shamelessly, the publisher used Twain's words from a *New York Times* article in which the author had defended himself against Lane's bogus claim of injustice. "In writing my book I took the liberty of using large extracts from Mr. Greenwood's book," Twain told the paper. "I made use of the extracts because of the great admiration which I have for that book." Conveniently, Lane ended the blurb at that point, because Twain's next comment would have made the publisher look foolish. The entire sentence reads, "I made use of the extracts because of the great admiration which I have for that book, and with the full permission of the publishers."[30]

When the dust settled, it was clear that the only harm done was to Greenwood's vanity. And the only reason John Lane encouraged his author to complain was that he saw a chance to sell more copies of a book that had not received much attention up to that point. More amused than annoyed, Twain declared that Greenwood should consider himself lucky. As he mischievously explained to the press, "To have a man like Mark Twain steal portions from another man's book makes that book something extraordinary."[31]

· · ·

TWAIN SEEMED TO ENJOY his brief notoriety as a literary thief. He must have found a comic irony in the exaggerated complaints of John Lane, given that he had struggled for so many years to stop people stealing from his books—especially in Britain, where his work was routinely pirated in the 1870s by the notorious John Camden Hotten (or "Hottentot," as Twain sometimes called him). As a young author fresh from America's wild frontier, he had made far more serious threats against Hotten than John Lane would have dared to use in the more civilized world of 1909. Writing in the London *Spectator* in 1872, Twain had suggested that if Hotten didn't give up literary piracy, he might have to crack his head open: "I feel as if I wanted to take a broom-straw & go & knock that man's brains out. Not in anger, for I feel none. Oh! not in anger; but only to see, that is all. Mere idle curiosity."[32]

By the spring of 1909, however, Twain could afford to take a much less bellicose view of protecting literary property. Congress had finally bestirred itself and done something important for authors. On March 3 both houses passed a new copyright act. Among other things, it extended the term of protection to fifty-six years after the date of publication. It wasn't everything that Twain had hoped for, but he saw it as a good start and was relieved to know that even some of his earliest books would now remain in copyright well into the 1920s. *Huck Finn* wouldn't lose its protection until the beginning of the 1940s.

If the bill had passed only a few months earlier, he might have been less willing to accept Ralph Ashcroft's plan for creating the Mark Twain Company. But even though, as subsequent chapters will show, disentangling himself from Ashcroft's snares wouldn't be easy, he could still take great satisfaction from the fact that Congress had given him and his fellow authors a law they could accept.

To Congressman Champ Clark of Missouri (who would soon become Speaker of the House), he wrote, "I think we've got a mighty good (& lucid) copyright law at last. Hereafter there'll be no complexities to fuss over. Effort can be restricted to a single & simple detail—*extension of the term*. Ten or fifteen years at a time. In the end, the author will be lifted to the rank of the publisher & the shoemaker: he will be the actual owner of his property." Twain was especially proud of the fact that America's new law was better than Britain's existing one. "At last—at last and for the first time in copyright history—we are ahead of England! Ahead of her in two ways: by length of time and by fairness to all interests concerned."[33]

For the first time in his career, he had reason to believe that American law would safeguard his works for many years beyond his death. It made him proud, and he was justified in feeling that he was partly responsible for the new law. Wearing white had paid off. In fact, Paine fervently believed that if Twain had not made such a memorable case for the bill during his appearance at the Capitol in December 1906, it wouldn't have passed for many years to come.

"Champ Clark was the last to linger that day," Paine recalled of Twain's lobbying efforts in 1906, "and they had talked far into the dusk. Clark was powerful and had fathered the bill." Clark himself didn't have any doubt that Twain was the prime influence on the legislation. After its passage, he wrote the author to ask "if the copyright law is acceptable to you. If it is not acceptable to you I want to ask you to write and tell me how it should be changed and I will give my best endeavors to the work. I believe that your ideas and wishes in the matter constitute the best guide we have as to what should be done in the case."[34]

Over time many others would come to see that Twain's eloquent support of copyright reform had made an important difference in the long debate that produced the 1909 act. Almost fifty years after Congress passed the law, the American Bar Association took note of Twain's contribution, praising him in a special resolution adopted at its annual meeting in 1957. Their tribute "recognized the efforts of Mark Twain, who was so greatly responsible for the laws relating to copyrights which have meant so much to all free peoples throughout the world."[35]

· · ·

ISABEL LYON'S LACK OF ENTHUSIASM for *Is Shakespeare Dead?* was partly a reflection of her depressed state of mind throughout the period of its composition. While Twain was gleefully engineering his assault on the man from Stratford, Lyon was often in bed and unable to leave her room. If he wanted to read to her from his manuscript, he would have to go to her room to do it. "Miss Lyon is sick abed these two or three weeks," Twain wrote his angelfish Frances Nunnally in February. "It is a sort of nervous break-down, attributable to too much work & care."[36]

Apparently, what finally pushed Lyon over the edge was the sudden return of Jean from Europe. A few days after Helen Keller's visit to Stormfield, Jean arrived in New York, having been ordered home by her father on the advice of Dr. Peterson. The doctor was alarmed by the news that Jean was receiving a certain medication in Berlin that he considered dangerous, and he told Twain that she should stop seeing her German doctor immediately and return to America. At any rate, that was the reason given to Jean, who was enjoying Berlin so much that she didn't want to come home. But the real reason may have been that both Peterson and Twain feared that her German doctor wasn't supervising her closely enough. As she innocently reported in her letters home, she was living so freely in Berlin that she was staying up "quite late" and had come home from one party in the early morning hours. According to Peterson's view of epilepsy, keeping such irregular hours was a sure path to disaster for the patient.[37]

But Jean's return to America meant that Lyon was once again faced with the problem of keeping her away from Stormfield. In January she had found a rooming house for her in Babylon, Long Island, where there were two live-in nurses. But Jean took an immediate dislike to the place, especially after coming there from her stimulating life in Germany. "The country was as flat as a pan-cake," she later wrote, "and contained nothing but a few bushes and small ponds used as ice-ponds. After Berlin and the varied life and broad interests that one sees over there, it was too much of a come-down."

Finding the place "unendurable," Jean took action. "I hadn't been there ten minutes," she was to recall, "when I telephoned Clara & told her I could not stay there." In response, Clara complained to Lyon, and the ongoing feud between the two women became even worse as each resisted giving in to the other. For the first time, Clara made a serious and sustained effort to find out why her sister wasn't being allowed to live at Stormfield. Lyon offered the usual reason—Dr. Peterson didn't think Jean was well enough. But Clara couldn't believe he still held that view after Jean's four months abroad, and she threatened to discuss the matter directly with Dr. Peterson.[38]

Lyon did her best to keep Clara in the dark, but near the end of January, she lost her nerve and retreated to her bed, using illness as an excuse to avoid any more confrontations. She had a lot to hide and may have thought that if she merely stayed out of Clara's way for a while, the volatile daughter would calm down and turn her attention to other things. But Clara continued to press her case, and on February 23, when Twain was in the last stages of work on his new book, Lyon decided that she couldn't sulk in her room any longer and did the unthinkable—she deserted her King and left Stormfield. She told him that she wanted to go to a hotel and "to have a good long uninterrupted rest."[39]

"Miss Lyon has gone to Hartford for ten days, sick," Twain wrote Jean, whose complaints had been heeded, and who was now on her way to a new house in Montclair, New Jersey, which would prove to be much more to her liking. After moving in, she wrote her father on March 5, "You don't know how glad I am to be here! . . . I really couldn't write you from Babylon, because . . . I didn't want to start complaining as soon as I had gotten back."[40]

But this move wasn't enough to satisfy Clara. Her suspicions about Lyon had been aroused to such an extent that she wasn't going to be content with one or two changes. So while Lyon was in Hartford, Clara went to Stormfield and tried her best to make her father reconsider the trust he had placed in his secretary. She wanted everything out in the open now and explained why she had been feuding with Lyon, and why she didn't like the way the household was being run, and why she objected to the way Jean's illness was being treated. Though she didn't understand exactly what Lyon and Ashcroft were up to, she knew they had too much influence over her father, and she wanted him to see the danger before it was too late. As soon as possible, she insisted, he needed to authorize a complete audit of the family's finances. And she wanted him to deal directly with Dr. Peterson so that a way could be found to bring Jean home immediately.

Having delayed this showdown for months, Clara was so full of anger and frustration that her heated criticisms and demands made Twain think she was exaggerating the problem. Despite his reputation for being impatient and impulsive, he advised patience and moderation in this case. He promised to get a financial report from Ashcroft, but didn't see any reason to have outsiders conduct an audit unless there was some specific evidence of impropriety. He wasn't going to engage in a messy confrontation with Lyon unless he had the proof to back him up. "Not theory, not guess," he told Clara, "but evidence."

Meanwhile, Lyon was pretending to be a semi-invalid trying to regain her strength in Hartford, where she was supposed to be staying at a quiet hotel. In fact, she was living in luxury at the city's best hotel on a busy street downtown. The Heublein wasn't the kind of place a single woman with her salary could afford. It enjoyed a national reputation for the high quality of its rooms—its brochures promised "an Oriental carpet in every room"—and for the superior "cuisine and fine liquors" served in its restaurant. The local company that owned it—G. F. Heublein—was one of America's biggest importers of wines and spirits. As Twain later remarked of her stay at the hotel, she couldn't have had a room "for anything short of ten dollars a day." At that rate, a mere five days would have consumed every penny of her monthly pay.[41]

But Twain didn't want to believe that he had misjudged Lyon. On

March 11—only two days after finishing his book on Shakespeare—he told Clara, "I know Ashcroft & Miss Lyon better & more intimately than I have ever known any one except your mother, & I am quite without suspicion of either their honesty or their honorableness." He made it clear that he was particularly grateful for Lyon's many efforts on his behalf. "She could not have been replaced at any price, for she was qualified to meet our friends socially & be acceptable to them. . . . And she has been a house builder. In this service—a heavy one, an exacting one, & making her liable to fault-finding—she labored hard for a year. I would not have done it at any price, neither would you. . . . She was not trained to business & doubtless has been loose & unmethodical, but that is all."[42]

But Clara had lost any interest in mustering sympathy for a woman she now regarded as her family's enemy. She hired a lawyer to advise her and wanted to enlist Henry Rogers's help in reviewing any figures Ashcroft managed to produce. Her steely resolve in this matter left Twain wondering how he could possibly satisfy her demands without tearing the household apart. He didn't want the dispute to become public, so he tried to persuade Clara to avoid dragging others into it, and was reluctant to seek advice from even his closest friends.

Paine was someone who might have been expected to take Clara's side against Lyon, but just as the conflict was heating up in mid-February, he left on a tour of the Mediterranean to see some of the places Twain had written about in *The Innocents Abroad*. Having put the finishing touches on his life of Texas Ranger Bill McDonald, he was free to spend a couple of months abroad and took his daughter Louise with him on the long voyage. But while they were gone, Paine's wife, Dora, watched the drama unfold at Stormfield and sent reports to her husband. On March 8 she warned him that the domestic turmoil was driving Twain "almost crazy," and said the "poor old man" had told her that the last few weeks "had been h— and if things did not get better he would cut his G— D— throat."

Such news may have made Paine wonder whether he should come home early to rescue his beleaguered subject. But he was probably also grateful that he had avoided getting caught in the crossfire, especially when he read the next piece of news in his wife's letter. Faced with Clara's implacable opposition, Lyon and Ashcroft had raised the stakes by deciding to fight her together as husband and wife. No public an-nouncement had been made, Dora said, but the couple planned to marry very soon. No matter how she looked at it, Dora couldn't make sense of it, especially given the eleven-year age difference between the two. Speaking of Ashcroft, she asked her husband, "What can *he* be think-ing[?]"[43]

It was a question a lot of people would soon be asking.

At his billiards table, Twain contemplates his next move.

EIGHTEEN

End of the Line

Supposing is good, but finding out is better.

Mark Twain[1]

. . .

ON ST. PATRICK'S DAY 1909, Ralph Ashcroft and Isabel Lyon went to New York to pay a visit to the Marriage Bureau at City Hall. The clerk who issued their license said they "seemed happy as larks and treading on air." The following morning they exchanged vows in a short wedding ceremony at the Episcopalian Church of the Ascension, one block from Twain's former home at 21 Fifth Avenue. Popular with several of Manhattan's old established families—including the Rhinelanders and the Astors—the big brownstone church had been the scene of many important weddings. The altar was one of the most beautiful in the city, and was designed in the 1880s by a young Stanford White, who used a golden arch to enclose John La Farge's large painting of the Ascension scene. ("A dim old church, hushed to admiration before a great religious picture," was how Henry James described the interior.)[2]

But on the chilly Thursday morning when Isabel Lyon walked to the

altar wearing a dark dress with a small hat and veil, the church was practically empty, with only a few friends and family sitting in the front pews.
Isabel's mother was there, and Ashcroft's brother John stood at his side as
best man, but conspicuously absent were Clara and almost everyone else
in Twain's circle. The author himself was present, though he didn't look
pleased to be there. Asked by the press to account for the sudden marriage of his secretary and his financial adviser, Twain replied, "A business
association ripened into warm friendship and then grew worse."[3]

A few days earlier, while they were in the billiards room at Stormfield,
Ashcroft had tried to tell Twain why he wanted to marry Lyon. It wasn't
for love or lust, he explained, emphasizing that they were not going to
have children. He said it was simply because she was a vulnerable woman
who needed a capable man to protect her. She believed that he was the
right one to help her, and he agreed. (As Lyon put it in a letter from
Hartford, "I will have one with the right to watch me, & keep me from
breaking down.")[4]

Twain was amazed that a man of Ashcroft's relative youth would accept a loveless marriage. As he later wrote of their conversation, "He told
me frankly & without a blush that he didn't love her, he only wanted to
be in a position to take care of her in her persistent & exhausting illnesses. He knew she got her illness out of a whisky bottle & was drunk a
good half of her time, but I didn't know it. . . . He told me she had proposed the marriage, & had also urged it. It was that day in the billiard
room, & the 'urgency' had seemed to me to translate itself into *compulsion*. This was a justifiable guess, in view of a thousand familiar circumstances, but not as good a guess as I could make now. Now that I know
what they had up their sleeve."[5]

Because in March he was still giving them the benefit of the doubt, he
was simply at a loss to explain why the two would offer such an implau-
sible excuse for marrying. He tried to talk them out of it. He didn't hold
back. "You two are *insane* to think of marrying," he told them; "don't do
it; you will separate within two years." The kind of noble union they had
described to him was foolish, he said, and would never work. The only
conclusion he could draw was that they were ashamed to admit their sexual "compulsion." Trying to lighten the mood, he told Ashcroft, "The first
one that gets pregnant gets fired."[6]

Twain even bet Ashcroft ten dollars to one that Lyon would have children, and continued to believe he was right long after both had left his service. Privately, he noted that the coldly calculating Ashcroft seemed to be stirred by the volatile Lyon: "It is a case of iceberg & volcano, you see; there may be an [eruption], there may be a litter of kitty icebergs—let us wait & see."[7]

When the couple continued to insist that they must get married—and soon—Twain put his objections aside and reluctantly agreed to attend the ceremony. But all the while that he was in the church, he couldn't wait to get out. It was "cold & clammy," he recalled, and Lyon "could hardly have been more sweetly and gushingly . . . girlish." On the way out, a photographer asked the newlyweds to pose with their employer. Ashcroft was all smiles, and Lyon looked demure. But in his haste to leave, Twain ignored the camera and kept his eyes down as he finished buttoning his overcoat. In the published photo he looks more like a passerby than a friend of the bride and groom.

The little wedding party broke up, and the Ashcrofts went straight back to Stormfield with Twain. Isabel wanted to continue her work as though nothing had changed. There were no plans for a honeymoon. It wasn't because of a shortage of money, however. The couple had a ready supply of cash—enough, in fact, to splurge on a twelve-dollar cablegram to Paine, whose travels had taken him at that moment to Egypt. The new Mrs. Ashcroft was eager to make sure that her rival knew of her marriage before he returned to America. She seemed to believe that both Paine and Clara would be less willing to challenge her position at Stormfield now that she had a clever young husband to intercede on her behalf.

Ashcroft was willing to marry Isabel, and to serve as her champion, because he needed her complete cooperation if he wanted to secure control of the Mark Twain Company. She knew too much, and he couldn't risk leaving her free to expose his plans to others. The marriage, Twain later wrote, "was a binding together of conspirators, for protective purposes. Each knew of the other's crimes, & neither was willing to trust the other, ungagged. . . . Otherwise why was he tying himself to her? He didn't want her. He had never proposed to her. He told me so, himself."

Knowing that Clara would continue making trouble for him, Ashcroft wanted to strengthen his position in the household not only by marrying

Lyon but also by persuading Twain to give him a new job with increased authority. The more Clara complained, the easier it was for Ashcroft to insist that Twain clear up any confusion by spelling out his responsibilities. His aim was to make sure that every penny the author earned or spent went through his hands first. Five days before the wedding ceremony, he asked Twain to sign a handful of legal documents. One gave him the power to supervise the writer's "household affairs and expenditures," and another authorized him to manage all business dealings for two years on a commission basis. Two more agreements concerned Isabel, increasing her salary to $100 a month and giving her permission "to compile for publication the manuscript of a book or books to be entitled 'Life and Letters of Mark Twain.' "[8]

It was unlikely that Isabel would ever be able to buckle down and complete an edition of Twain's letters, but she and Ashcroft wanted some way to keep Paine in check, and this was the best they could manage for the time being. It gave them an excuse to withhold letters from him if he tried to give any support to Clara. Simply by saying that she was busy working with certain letters for her edition, she could hold on to them for months and create endless delays for Paine as he tried to complete his own work. But, of course, the couple gave no hint of their true intentions to Twain. In fact, they pretended that Isabel's work on the edition would be an entirely selfless act of devotion to her King. To make Twain believe this, Ashcroft stipulated in the document that Isabel would do the work for free, forgoing any claim on future royalties.

Instead of questioning why Ashcroft was so keen to put so many new agreements in writing, Twain assumed they must be in his best interest. He thought they provided the kind of safeguards Clara was seeking for the family. After signing them he was quick to send her a note of reassurance. "All things in this house are now upon a strictly business basis," he wrote. "All duties are strictly defined, under several written contracts, signed before a notary. All services rendered me are paid for, henceforth."

But more contracts were not going to satisfy Clara. They only made her more suspicious that the Ashcrofts were hiding something. She didn't want to make peace with her adversaries. She was determined to catch them in some act of wrongdoing and to prove to her father that his trust in them was misplaced. Yet he was almost desperate to avoid that kind of upheaval, knowing that it would cause him far more pain than Clara could imagine. The new contracts didn't solve anything, but they gave him some hope that he could preserve his haven at Stormfield a little longer.

"There is no vestige of ugly feeling," he wrote Clara of his new arrangements with the Ashcrofts, "no *hostility* on either side. The comradeship remains, but it is paid for; also the friendship. Stormfield was a home; it is a tavern now, & I am the landlord. . . . Jesus, what a week!"[9]

· · ·

FOR A SHORT PERIOD after the wedding, Stormfield was relatively calm. The Ashcrofts made an effort to seem mild and forbearing, but Isabel was still relying on alcohol to soothe her nerves, and Ralph was continuing to look for new ways to undermine Clara's authority and to dissuade her from challenging his. In the near term, he held the advantage, because in late March and early April Clara was forced to direct her attention elsewhere. Her next big concert was fast approaching, and she needed to devote most of her time to rehearsing. Scheduled for April 13 at Mendelssohn Hall, it would be her first major performance in New York. An audience of at least a thousand was expected, and she knew that many of the city's most influential critics would be there. Anxious to impress, she put together an ambitious program that included numbers by Debussy, Strauss, and Schumann. While she prepared for her important night, her feud with the Ashcrofts was put on hold.

One visitor who was fooled by the deceptive calm at Stormfield was William Dean Howells. On March 23 he arrived for a three-day stay and thought everything seemed fine. Twain looked "tired," but was "full of fire and fun," and the two old friends had "a roaring time." There was no mention of any family troubles, and Howells considered Twain fortunate to have two devoted friends looking after him. "The Ashcrofts," he wrote home, "watch over him with tender constancy." If Howells—the great novelist of American manners—was so easily deceived by the couple, it is no wonder that Twain persisted in thinking they could be trusted.[10]

What impressed him most during his visit was Twain's deep attachment to Stormfield. "Truly he loved the place," he wrote afterward. As the father of the architect, he was delighted by Twain's show of pride in every aspect of the house. It was his first visit, and he was pleasantly surprised by the "beautiful country" surrounding the large and modern home. "In the early spring days," he wrote of his stay, "all the landscape was in the beautiful nakedness of the northern winter. It opened in the surpassing loveliness of wooded and meadowed uplands, under skies that were the first days blue, and the last gray over a rainy and then a snowy floor."[11]

Twain was so eager for company that he urged Howells to build a house in the neighborhood. He even had a lot picked out for him. Though he turned down the idea, Howells was touched by Twain's desire to share Stormfield's charms with sympathetic friends. "Every morning before I dressed," he was to recall of his visit, "I heard him sounding my name through the house, for the fun of it and I know for the fondness; and if I looked out of my door, there he was in his long nightgown swaying up and down the corridor, and wagging his great white head like a boy that leaves his bed and comes out in the hope of frolic with some one."

· · ·

SHORTLY AFTER HOWELLS left Stormfield, Twain had the chance to "frolic" in a big way with Henry Rogers. As Howells put it in a letter home, Twain was "going to Norfolk, Va., with Rogers, to open a railroad." All 446 miles of track on the Virginian Railway were now in place, and new locomotives in West Virginia were ready to begin hauling thousands of tons of coal each day to the massive pier at Sewell's Point on Hampton Roads. To mark the completion of this railroad from the mountains to the Tidewater, Rogers and the civic leaders of Norfolk scheduled two days of festivities at the beginning of April. Once again, Rogers wanted to share the spotlight in Virginia with Twain, who was happy to go back if he didn't have to exert himself too much. The organizers were quick to assure him that he would have an easy time of it, especially at the large formal dinner in Rogers's honor. As Twain noted with satisfaction before leaving home, he wasn't expected to sit through the whole banquet or "come in black clothes." Accompanying him on the trip was Ashcroft, who was content to stay in the background but was determined not to let him out of his sight.[12]

It was raining when the triumphant railroad magnate and his best friend arrived at the docks in Newport on the morning of April 2. Despite the wet weather an enthusiastic crowd of five hundred turned out to greet them, and many were wearing orange badges with the railway's name abbreviated in white letters as "VGN." They were driven to their hotel in a powerful new Rambler automobile, and were given a reception and luncheon at the Board of Trade, where they stood at the entrance of the large green-and-gold clubroom and shook hands with more than a thousand people. "It was a nearer approach to a White House reception than Norfolk ever had before," said one of the state's newspapers, "and when the two distinguished visitors had grasped every hand their palms were quite red."

In the densely crowded room there was so much noise and confusion that some of the local businessmen mistook Twain—who was at the head of the reception line—for Rogers. As they shook his hand, they warmly congratulated him for building such a great railroad, and the author silently accepted their compliments. When everyone was gathered in the clubroom, cries of "Speech! Speech!" came from the crowd. In response Twain mounted a chair, and the room grew quiet.

"My friends," he said, "while I have been shaking your hands I have listened to some very flattering compliments. . . . They went straight to my heart, and I thank you all. I could not help but feel flattered as you passed me and thanked me so sincerely for the splendid railway I had built through your state. I like compliments, gentlemen, and I thank you."

The wave of laughter that swept across the room removed any doubt about the identity of the man on the chair, and the room soon erupted with calls for Rogers to come forward and address the gathering. Taking Twain's place, he kept his remarks short. "Gentlemen, it is my business to build railroads," he said, and then placed his hand on his friend's shoulder. "I employ my orator here to talk about them."

"I have raised my price," Twain said.[13]

Rogers spent the next two days inspecting his new rail yards and coal pier while Twain held court in the lobby of the Lynnhaven Hotel or strolled around downtown showing off his clothes. The big banquet took place on Saturday, April 3, at the Monticello Hotel, and, as promised, Twain was spared the ordeal of sitting through the seven-course meal that included cove oysters on the half shell, broiled guinea hen, fried hominy, baked potatoes, cheeses, cakes, and strawberry frappé. About ten o'clock he strolled into the dining room and took his place next to Rogers at the head table. The speakers that night outdid each other trying to find superlatives for the new railroad and the man who built it. Governor Swanson called the project "the chief event in the history of Virginia since the civil war."[14]

Twain was the only speaker who knew the guest of honor well enough to tease him. "I like to hear my old friend complimented, but I don't like to hear it overdone," he told the audience. He admitted that he couldn't get too excited about a "railroad in which I own no stock." Though everyone else was full of enthusiasm for the coal pier, he dared to make light of it, calling it "that dump down yonder." Rogers laughed heartily when Twain explained that a glimpse of the pier from the sea was enough to make him decline an invitation for a closer look. "I didn't go because I was diffident, sentimentally diffident, about going and looking at that thing again—that great, long, bony thing; it looked just like Mr. Rogers's foot."

Knowing that the other speakers would do nothing but sing the praises of Rogers the railway builder, Twain decided to joke about that subject so he could then speak with perfect seriousness about matters closer to his heart. Everyone knew of his friend's reputation as a businessman, he said, but not many were aware "of that generous heart of his." A man of few words in public, the proud tycoon rarely spoke of his efforts to help others in need. "He is supposed to be a moon which has one side dark and the other bright," said Twain. "But the other side, though you don't see it, is not dark; it is bright, and its rays penetrate."

Growing emotional, the author declared that he was one whose life had been penetrated by those rays of generosity, and he wanted the audience to know the details. "If I don't look at him," he said, "I can tell it now."

Concisely, he described how his publishing firm had failed in the hard economic times of the early 1890s, and how he had become mired in debt. "I was on my back; my books were not worth anything at all, and I could not give away my copyrights. Mr. Rogers had long enough vision ahead to say, 'Your books have supported you before, and after the panic is over they will support you again,' and that was a correct proposition. He saved my copyrights, and saved me from financial ruin."

Though Twain knew how hard Rogers had worked to complete the railroad and to expand his vast business empire, he wanted everyone to know that their friendship was rooted in something that had nothing to do with great wealth or power. It had begun with a simple act of kindness and was sustained by a deep bond of sympathy unrelated to either man's fame. Surrounded by hard-nosed businessmen, Twain wanted to acknowledge a debt he could never repay. If Rogers had not saved him, he said, "I would now be living out-of-doors under an umbrella, and a borrowed one at that."[15]

The next morning Rogers invited Twain to accompany him and other dignitaries on an inspection trip of the railroad all the way to its western terminus in the coalfields of West Virginia. That was asking too much. Though he loved the owner of the rails, Twain still didn't care to ride them if he didn't have to, and politely declined the offer. He chose instead to sail home the following day. But before he parted from Rogers, he requested one last favor, and was careful to do so within earshot of reporters. He asked him to "speak to Manager Johnston, of the hotel, and assure him that Mark was a nice man and probably would pay his hotel bill some time."

Later that morning he decided to liven up his free Sunday in Norfolk by trying out his old routine of loitering outside a church in the hope of attracting attention from the crowd leaving the worship service. In this case he chose the big Baptist church on Freemason Street, a few blocks from his hotel. In no time he was surrounded by admirers and was asked to Sunday dinner by one of the deacons of the church, Dr. Livius Lankford. As a prominent leader of the new Laymen's Missionary Movement, Lankford may have been a little too pious for Twain's tastes, but he accepted the dinner invitation despite being reminded by Ashcroft that they had made another engagement for that hour.

"Guess I am man enough to break it," Twain said, and ambled off to see more of Norfolk.[16]

· · ·

WHEN TWAIN ARRIVED BACK in New York on April 7, he went alone to Stuyvesant Square to visit Clara at her apartment. Her concert at Mendelssohn Hall was less than a week away, and he wanted to make it clear that he intended to be in the audience. Because the event was so important to her professionally, she welcomed all the support she could get, and didn't raise any of her old objections to the possibility that her famous father's presence might overshadow her performance. Even the Ashcrofts were planning to attend, thinking it prudent to be present on the all-important night. Whether she succeeded or failed, they wanted to be among the first to know the outcome and to assess any changes in her mood.

Though she was preoccupied with rehearsing, she had lost none of her desire to be rid of the Ashcrofts, and said as much to her father during his visit. She was more convinced than ever that her family was in danger of losing everything to the couple, who were acting as if they already owned Stormfield. She was appalled at Isabel's "impudence" in openly wearing jewelry that had belonged to Livy. One day she noticed a brooch pinned to Isabel's dress, and recognized it as her mother's. After Clara revealed her indignation with "a pretty decided look," the brooch was silently returned to the cabinet where it belonged. Realizing that she was taking too many risks, Isabel hastened to return other items to their rightful places, including some carnelian beads of Livy's. She also took the precaution of hiding her journals in a "voluminous dress that hung inside out in her closet." In addition, she may have begun destroying at this time certain parts of her journal for 1909. Only a few entries from it have survived.[17]

To Clara's surprise, her father confessed at her apartment that he now had reason to think her suspicions of the couple were well founded. Something had happened during his stay in Norfolk that had shaken his confidence in Ralph Ashcroft. The two men had argued on the night he gave his speech at the banquet, and Clara was the subject of their disagreement. With no definitive evidence to back him up, Ashcroft told Twain that Clara had unjustly dismissed one of the servants at Stormfield. Twain strongly suspected that Ashcroft was lying, and was now able to get Clara's side of the story. She easily demonstrated that the charge was false. She had not discharged anyone. In fact, it was Ashcroft who had frightened the servant into leaving, and who had then tried to blame Clara for it.

All the facts wouldn't come out for a few more weeks, but Twain heard enough from Clara to make him more sympathetic to her view that Ashcroft and his new bride were up to no good. For the first time the author had serious doubts about the trustworthiness of the couple in whom he had placed so much confidence, and those doubts grew stronger as he recalled the younger man's arrogant attitude toward him during their argument. Ashcroft had given the impression that he didn't care whether the truth came out or not. He seemed to think he could make Twain believe anything.

At that very moment, while father and daughter were discussing the incident, the telephone rang. It was Jean calling from the house in New Jersey where she had been living for the past few weeks. The conversation went well, and afterward both Twain and Clara agreed that Jean seemed in unusually good spirits. She was bursting with pride after the *New York Times* had recently published one of her letters to the editor. The topic of the letter didn't have any direct connection to her, but was related to her general sympathy for victims of cruelty. In this case her tender heart was moved by the abuse of a Native American youth living hundreds of miles away from her.

In late March a small band of Creek Indians in Oklahoma had begun an uprising after losing their lands to new settlers. The leader—an elderly chief named Crazy Snake—was wanted for murder, and when deputies captured one of his sons, they used torture to find out where the chief was hiding. "Tell us where your father is," they had shouted to the son after tying a rope around his throat and slowly lifting him off the ground, "or you'll hang there until you die." Running out of breath, the young man gasped for mercy and was finally let down when he agreed to cooperate.

This episode didn't raise much concern in the Eastern press, but it enraged Jean, who responded with a sharp letter of protest overflowing with the kind of indignant sarcasm her father was famous for. The letter appeared on April 5 under the heading "Medieval Torture," and was signed "Jean L. Clemens, Montclair, N.J."

Is it possible that in this civilized land today a Deputy Sheriff can with impunity torture a prisoner? Though the son of Crazy Snake is but an Indian, how is it that the Sheriff could threaten him with death by half hanging him in order to extort revelations concerning his father and his friends? Is such brutality to pass without punishment merely because the prisoner is not a citizen? If we, considering ourselves one of the most civilized nations of the world, permit our officers to make use of the methods of the middle ages—without counting our wholesale robbery of the Indians' lands—then they who make less pretense of being civilized should be expected to murder and burn on all occasions.[18]

After discussing this powerful protest and their telephone conversation with Jean, Twain and Clara once again took up the question of why such a vibrant young woman wasn't living in her own home. With his mind now troubled by misgivings about the Ashcrofts, Twain decided on the spot to shake things up. Clara was given permission to deal directly with Dr. Peterson, and to arrange for Jean to come home as soon as possible. And, with grim resolve, Twain agreed that the time had come to change his relationship with the Ashcrofts.

He would start with Isabel, he confided, terminating her contract after giving her the necessary notice of thirty days. He thought it was best to do this on April 15, avoiding any conflict with Clara's concert on the 13th. Ralph Ashcroft's case would take more time to address because his contracts and his position at the Mark Twain Company made him more difficult to dismiss, and because the author himself wasn't sure how he could run his affairs without his business manager's expertise. But it was clear that Twain had reached his breaking point and was ready to act.

Though Clara wasn't sure how the Ashcrofts would respond, she was glad that at long last her father had seen the light. And she knew that once he had turned against someone, he was unlikely to reverse his decision. He was now able to admit that he had misjudged the Ashcrofts. He had allowed himself to become entangled in what he would later call a "queer & shabby & pitiful tale—to wit, a pair of degraded & sufficiently clumsy sharpers, & I the born ass, their easy victim."[19]

After returning to Stormfield, he tried not to give Isabel any hint that her days in his employ were numbered, but he did reveal his intention to bring Jean home as soon as possible. She didn't take the news well. She panicked, and it showed as she nervously insisted that such a move was impossible. She claimed that Jean was still too ill, and then made her usual argument that the young woman's condition would deteriorate quickly in a busy house where guests were constantly coming and going. Whereas Twain had always taken her objections to heart in the past, he ignored them now and said that he would do whatever was necessary to win Dr. Peterson's approval for the move. In fact, the more Isabel protested, the more convinced Twain became that he was doing the right thing, and that she had been misleading him for years.

Worried that he might prevail, the Ashcrofts took drastic action. They canceled their plans to attend Clara's concert and arranged an urgent meeting with Peterson at Stormfield on the day of the concert, when Twain would not be around to interfere. The idea was to persuade the doctor that Twain's daughters were trying to pressure him into doing something rash, and that the new plan had to be resisted at all costs. Unaware of how much intrigue was swirling around Stormfield, Peterson agreed to the meeting on the assumption that Isabel was simply trying to reinforce her long-standing effort to spare Twain the burden of caring for Jean at home.

Such turmoil in the family didn't help Clara's nerves, and on the night of her big performance she wasn't at her best. The audience at Mendelssohn Hall was large and enthusiastic, and many of the seats were filled with old friends and admirers. They made a great show of support, especially William Dean Howells, whose hearty encouragement prompted one observer to say that he applauded the singer "as if he belonged to a paid claque." At the end of the evening Twain approached the stage and handed his daughter a "huge" bouquet of roses.[20]

But the critics were out in force and were almost unanimous in their opinion that her performance was a disappointment. The New York Times tried to explain the problem without sounding too harsh. "It seems a pity that a singer with as good a natural voice as that of Miss Clemens, who sings with so much feeling, should not use her voice to better advantage. Her tones last night were too often uneven and muffled." Other reviewers were less polite. "Miss Clemens was heard in a recital of songs not long ago," wrote the New York Sun, "and was accorded some critical censure because of her imperfect vocal technique. Her singing last evening was less affected by nervousness than it was on the previous occasion, but it could by no means have satisfied the young woman's artistic aspirations." Some critics bluntly stated that her voice had not been properly trained. One complained that her singing showed "a struggle against a poor method of tone production," and another said that it was obvious "the technical difficulties of her art are not yet fully mastered."[21]

Though there were many compliments for her talents, the verdict of the press was clear: by the demanding standards of America's music capital she was a second-rate performer. Her career never fully recovered from that verdict. She and her father put a brave face on it, and she made an effort later in the year to arrange another tour. But the night of April 13 marked the end of any hope that she might achieve the kind of success Gabrilowitsch had been enjoying. It was a great blow to a woman who had wanted so passionately to outshine the two most important men in her life.

Meanwhile, the Ashcrofts used that fateful evening to make Dr. Peterson believe that sending Jean home would kill Mark Twain. They "dinned lies into his ears," as Jean would later say of their tactics. But the lies may not have been necessary. With the Ashcrofts so adamantly opposed to Jean's presence, Peterson could easily have agreed that his patient was better off not coming home. He always believed that she needed better care than Isabel was willing to provide or Twain could manage, and he still thought the best place for all his epilepsy patients was in the controlled environment of a sanitarium or similar retreat.

When Clara went to see the doctor on April 15, she didn't want to debate the true merits of Stormfield as a home for an epilepsy patient. She wanted action and, after the drubbing she had received from the city's music critics, she was in no mood to be contradicted. Yet Peterson stood his ground and refused to give permission for Jean to be moved. Frustrated, Clara kept insisting that her sister was well enough to come home, and that her father desperately wanted her there. After forty-five minutes of arguing, the doctor made a concession. As Jean later put it, Clara "succeeded in wringing his consent to a one week's trial visit."[22]

While his older daughter was with Peterson, Twain was at Stormfield taking action against the woman who had worked for him for nearly seven years, and whom he had once considered indispensable. He wrote her a note saying that her services were no longer needed and enclosed a month's pay. But he couldn't bring himself to give her the letter in person. Instead a servant took it to her.

Though he had tried not to reveal his plans, Isabel had noticed a change in his manner and wasn't surprised when she received his message. He had said something recently that had made her think the end was coming: "Remember, whatever I do is because of a promise I have made to Clara." All the same, it was hard for her to accept that he could turn his back on her. She had helped him in so many ways and had come to think of herself as the most important person in his life. But she and her husband had underestimated his loyalty to his daughters, and had mistakenly assumed they could manage his life and his estate for as long as they wanted. Flattered by their attentions, he had been lulled into a false sense of security, but now that his mind was filled with doubts, he couldn't carry on as usual.[23]

Isabel decided not to protest her dismissal. She knew it wouldn't do any good to argue with him. It made more sense to wait for his temper to cool, and then to let her husband begin the slow process of negotiating a good settlement for themselves, using as leverage the various agreements they had made with him over the last few months. She knew that, if necessary, her husband could launch a very aggressive campaign on their behalf, and perhaps make Clara regret pushing Twain into action. So she sent him a gentle response. "Thank you so much," she wrote, "for doing in so kind a way, the thing that I have been expecting."[24]

Though firing her was easy, Twain soon realized that ending their relationship would prove more troublesome. After all, she still owned the cottage that stood just beyond his front gate. Even if he could quickly sever Ralph Ashcroft's connection to the Mark Twain Company, he had to face the possibility that the couple would be his nearest neighbors for as long as they wanted to remain in the area, and that every time he left his grounds he would have to pass their house.

Isabel made it clear that she had no intention of leaving Redding. In the ten days following her dismissal, she even made several visits to Stormfield, hoping that she might be able to charm Twain into softening his attitude toward her and her husband. She knew she had to work fast. She didn't want to be in the house when Clara brought Jean home on April 26 to begin the one-week trial visit. But her charm offensive backfired. Twain was infuriated by her visits and received her coldly, writing afterward of his amazement that she "still haunted the place, still infested it with her unwelcome presence, still tried to let on that our relations were as pleasant as ever."[25]

For a time, he worried that she would never go away. It was humiliating to admit that he had allowed her to exercise so much influence over him, and he desperately wanted her to fade quietly from his life. If she refused, he would have a fight on his hands that would create a scandal and ruin any chance of restoring peace at Stormfield. Having allowed himself to become so entangled in the lives of the Ashcrofts, he began to fear they would dog his steps all the way to the grave.

On April 21, at three o'clock in the morning, he was overcome by a wave of despair. The big house was still, and he was sitting up in bed with a book in his lap. It was the first volume of the *Letters of James Russell Lowell,* which he had been reading for the last few nights. Turning a page, he came across a passage in which Lowell recalled a time in his youth when he had contemplated suicide. "I remember in '39 putting a cocked pistol to my forehead," Lowell wrote in a letter of 1866 to Charles Eliot Norton, "and being afraid to pull the trigger, of which I was heartily ashamed, and am still whenever I think of it. Had I been in earnest, why, of course, you would never have had the incomparable advantage of my friendship. But, of course, I was only flattering myself. I am glad now that I was too healthy, for it is only your feeble Jerusalems that fairly carry the thing out and rid the world of what would have been mere nuisances."[26]

In the margin beside this passage Twain wrote, "3 a.m., Apl. 21/09. Down to 'trigger' I am with him, but no further. It is odd that I should stumble upon this now, for it is only two days ago since something called to my mind *my* experience of 1866. . . . I put the pistol to my head but wasn't man enough to pull the trigger. Many times I have been sorry I did not succeed, but I was never ashamed of having tried. Suicide is the only really sane thing the young or old ever do in this life. 'Feeble Jerusalems' never kill themselves; they survive the attempt. Lowell & I are instances."

It is a measure of how deeply this crisis in 1909 affected him that Twain felt obliged to compare it to a period long ago when he had come perilously close to ending his life. At a dark time in the mid-1860s he had told his brother, "If I do not get out of debt in 3 months, —pistols or poison for one—exit me." Though his will to live was too strong to succumb to the temptation of suicide, he longed for some way to make a quick "exit" from the troubles surrounding him at Stormfield.[27]

Much as he loved the place, he might have abandoned it altogether had Jean remained elsewhere. But she was eager to see the house that had been built with her in mind, and to make it her permanent home. And he knew it was his duty to stay put and help. He wanted to end her "exile" by making sure that she and Stormfield were right for each other. That meant putting aside his worries about the Ashcrofts and trying to undo some of the damage they had done. Gathering his strength, he prepared for Jean's arrival and sent her an encouraging note.

"Dear child," he wrote, "you will be as welcome as if it were your mother herself calling you home from exile!"[28]

Seemingly devoted to their boss, Isabel Lyon and Ralph Ashcroft strike deferential poses at Stormfield in this photograph from late 1908.

NINETEEN

Crime and Punishment

*If he thought you had in any way played him false
you were anathema and maranatha forever.*
W. D. Howells on Mark Twain[1]

. . .

AS PLANNED, Jean entered her new home on April 26. She recorded
that fact in the guestbook and wrote something else that made it clear
she didn't intend to leave—she listed Stormfield as her only address. For
the first time in years, she didn't have to worry about any interference
from Isabel. There was no sign of her presence at the house. She had visited Twain a few days earlier, but by the time of Jean's arrival, she had removed the last of her things and would never again cross the threshold.
Twain and his daughter did their best to ignore her cottage whenever
they left the grounds, and she was careful to keep out of sight.

Jean warmed to her new home right away and finished her trial week
in such high spirits that her father decided she must stay as long as she
liked. Dr. Peterson didn't object, and Jean breathed a great sigh of relief,
knowing that she wouldn't have to move again. Twain observed that she

was "so glad to be in her own home once more that she hadn't any words for her gratitude."[2]

To Joseph Twichell, she wrote, "You can't imagine how thankful I am to get back home again, & in this beautiful place, too. . . . I love country life & dislike city life, so that my one & only cause for irritation is the thought of what has happened in the past & the necessity of passing the charming little house still in Miss Lyon's possession every time I leave the house."

She boasted, "I am in better health than for a long time; able at last to be of use to father."[3]

Indeed, her robust appearance impressed Twain so much that he thought she was as strong "as the very rocks." It seemed to him that she had finally managed to get the better of "her cruel malady," and he berated himself for "my own inexcusable stupidity" in ever listening to Isabel's advice. His former secretary had tricked him, he complained, making him an unwitting accessory to the "crime of keeping Jean exiled . . . after she was well enough to live at home."[4]

Of course, Jean's disease was not cured, but both father and daughter wanted to believe the worst was over. Feeling that he had wronged her in the past by agreeing to so many restrictions on her freedom, Twain now went to the opposite extreme and let his daughter do more or less as she pleased. She was given a small farm next to his own property and was allowed, as she put it, "to develop & improve [the farm] after my own desire & ability." And, as she noted with immense satisfaction in her letter to Twichell, she was "permitted once more" to ride her horse whenever she liked.

Making up for lost time, she became a whirlwind of activity. Usually, she was up before seven, and stayed busy until dinner twelve hours later, with only short breaks for lunch and tea. Wherever she went, her constant companion was her new dog, Fix, a German shepherd. She had acquired him in Berlin and spoke to him only in German. At her farm she bought some livestock and poultry, and planted a garden; at home she took over many of Isabel's old duties, answering letters and paying bills. The household affairs were in a mess after weeks of neglect. "I found bills overdue several months," she told Twichell, "& there was plenty of evidence of letters never answered. . . . I have a great deal to attend to but while it seems a pretty large amount some days, when I get things into proper running-trim, I don't expect to find it a burden."[5]

Twain was shocked to discover how careless Isabel had become in the last months of her employment, but was grateful to find that his daughter was willing and able to restore some order to his affairs. "How glad I am that Jean is at home again," he said to himself over and over.[6]

At the end of April Paine returned from his long Mediterranean voyage to find—as he would later put it in a massive understatement—"There had been changes in my absence." Though the change he welcomed most was Isabel's departure from Stormfield, he was also pleased to see Jean living at home. Except for Clara and Twain, nobody was more appreciative of Jean's character than Paine, who always had a good word to say for her. As far as he could tell, her long ordeal had done nothing to undermine her spirit or her appearance. He thought she looked "fine and handsome, apparently full of life and health." He described her as "overflowingly happy" with her busy new routine.[7]

It was easy for anyone who didn't understand her illness to assume that she had made a remarkable recovery, and that she would be able to take care of herself. Dr. Peterson knew better, but his views had been overruled. The more Twain saw of his daughter at home, the more convinced he became that she deserved her new freedom. His anger toward Isabel also grew with each passing day as he continued to brood on his failure to bring Jean home earlier. Every time he saw his daughter return from a day's work on her farm looking strong and healthy he was reminded of how often Isabel had told him that Jean was too ill to live with him.

While her father's resentment of Isabel deepened, Clara was busy trying to prove her suspicion that the Ashcrofts had been stealing from the family and were plotting to steal more money. In the last week of April she won her father's permission to visit Standard Oil headquarters and to ask Henry Rogers's help in conducting a professional audit of the family's finances. Rogers welcomed her warmly, listened to her story, and promptly agreed "to take up the matter" and "straighten it out."

As soon as she had left the office, Rogers dictated a letter to Twain in which he acknowledged that he wasn't entirely surprised by Clara's accusations against the Ashcrofts: "In the last two or three years I had my suspicions of things, which you in your good natured way have over-looked." Like others in Twain's circle, he had hesitated to question a re-lationship to which the author had always seemed so devoted. But he didn't lecture him on the mistakes of the past, and didn't say a word about all the pressing business facing him at the office. He simply made it clear to his old friend that he was ready once again to go out of his way "to serve you, as ever."[8]

With Twain's approval, Rogers invited Ralph Ashcroft to the Standard Oil building and asked him to submit all papers in his possession relat-ing to Twain's business affairs for the last two years. Ashcroft complied, but didn't like having to report to Rogers and feared what the audit would turn up. He complained bitterly to Twain, saying that he and his wife didn't deserve to be viewed with such suspicion after all they had done for him. Clara had treated Isabel in a "ghastly" manner, he said, and he considered it a "poor return for the way in which she has, since Mrs. Clemens' death, looked after you, your daughters and your affairs."[9]

Ashcroft's criticisms only reinforced Twain's belief that authorizing the audit was the right thing to do. A bookkeeper in Rogers's office began a methodical review of the accounts, and a full report was expected by the end of May. Meanwhile, the Ashcrofts waited nervously and made oc-casional efforts to stir up doubts about the mental stability of Clara and Jean. In a letter to Archibald Henderson, Ashcroft warned that Storm-field was no longer the tranquil place of the previous year, but was now disintegrating into chaos, thanks to Twain's "two semi-insane daugh-ters."[10]

Such scurrilous charges may have reached Twain's ear, for in early May he decided that whatever the audit revealed he wanted a quick end to Ashcroft's involvement in his affairs. "The check-books and vouchers which Ashcroft will have to place before your expert," he wrote Rogers on May 4, "are my property, and I would be glad if you will keep possession of them for me, when the inquiry is finished. I don't want them to go back into Ashcroft's hands."[11]

· · ·

ON WEDNESDAY, MAY 19, Rogers rose early, as was his custom, and began getting ready for another busy day at the office. He was going to spend his one free hour in the day having lunch with Twain, who planned to leave Stormfield at mid-morning and take the 10:30 express into Grand Central Station. They intended to discuss the progress of the audit, but mostly they wanted to spend their time talking and joking in their usual manner. Despite his best efforts, Twain had never been able to get his friend to visit him at Redding, so in recent weeks he had been spending more time traveling into town to see Rogers at his home or office. After what he had been through with the Ashcrofts, he needed the companionship of a sympathetic friend he knew he could trust.

But at 6:30 that morning Rogers was alarmed by a numbness in his arms, which was soon followed by a severe headache. He called out to Emilie for help, and she came running to his side. His symptoms were serious enough to prompt her to telephone the family doctor, who promised to come to the house as soon as possible. A short while later, however, Rogers lost consciousness, and by the time the doctor arrived at 7:30, the patient was dead, the victim of a massive stroke.

For the next several hours Emilie was distraught with grief, but at some point in the morning she suddenly remembered that Twain was supposed to have lunch with her husband, and she didn't want him to hear of the death from a stranger. A call was made to Clara at her New York apartment, and she agreed to meet her father at the station and give him the news before he could see a morning paper. At noon, when his train arrived, Clara was waiting for him.

"There is no way to break sad news," she later wrote of the occasion, "so that it does not carry a brutal shock with it. The expression of grief on Father's face was pitiful to behold."[12]

A few newspapermen spotted Twain leaving the station and descended on him. There were tears in his eyes, his hands were trembling, and he was leaning heavily on Clara's arm.

"It is terrible, terrible," he said. "I am inexpressibly shocked. . . . The shock has been too great for me to think of anything to say befitting so great a man as Mr. Rogers. I can't talk any more. Mr. Rogers was as close to me as a brother."[13]

Clara took her father to the Grosvenor Hotel near their old house on Fifth Avenue, and he sat disconsolately in his room trying to fathom what had happened. Paine joined him in the afternoon and stayed at his side for the next two days while they waited to attend the funeral on Friday. "He had a helpless look," his biographer recalled, "and he said his friends were dying away from him and leaving him adrift."[14]

Rogers's fellow tycoons shed few tears when they received word of his death. John D. Rockefeller heard the news while he was playing golf at the Homestead Hotel in Hot Springs, Virginia. After he was finished with his game, he issued a statement reassuring Standard Oil stockholders that the death of the company vice president wouldn't affect the share price. He also couldn't resist taking the opportunity to note with self-righteous pride that he had often warned Rogers to slow down and not to work so hard. "But he was so strong, so powerful," he explained, "that no one could persuade him to cast aside his burdens."[15]

Andrew Carnegie was vacationing in Europe and sent Twain a letter of condolence that was short on sympathy. He was more interested in remarking on his own good fortune. "Gone & only [sixty-nine years old] & here you & I are left & both in good health though older men," Carnegie wrote. "Pity he did not retire years ago. I tell you my Friend no man is fit to meet business conditions in old age. I have seen too many fail.... Never to make another dollar was my resolve & I've kept it."[16]

About three hundred people attended the funeral at the Unitarian Church of the Messiah on Park Avenue and Thirty-fourth Street. Twain was one of the pallbearers. Calling the deceased a "man of clean ideals," the minister emphasized Rogers's many acts of charity and said little of his business dealings. Twain must have found some relief from the sad atmosphere and smiled when Rogers—with whom he had shared a deep fondness for profanity—was eulogized as a man who never "used a coarse, profane or unworthy word."[17]

But afterward, as he stood apart on the sidewalk in his dark suit and top hat, he showed no sign that the service had done anything to ease his grief. In a picture taken by a news service photographer, his face is filled with sadness, and he seems on the verge of tears. He was so broken-hearted that he didn't think he could endure the trip to Fairhaven for the burial service.

As Paine recalled, "He wanted to be very quiet, he said. He could not undertake to travel that distance among those whom he knew so well,

Weighed down by grief, Twain leaves the Manhattan church where the funeral of
Henry Rogers took place in May 1909.

and with whom he must of necessity join in conversation; so we remained
in the hotel apartment, reading and saying very little until bedtime."

As they turned in for the night, Twain broke the long silence with the
mournful words "Mr. Rogers is under the ground now."[18]

Coming so soon after the break with the Ashcrofts, Rogers's death left
Twain feeling as if his whole world had been turned upside down.
Because Rogers was four years his junior, he had always assumed that despite the earlier stroke his friend would be around for many more years,
providing him with the kind of guidance and companionship no one else
could give him. Without that solid source of support, he felt lost.

When someone did him a favor, he often wondered what it would cost
him. "Gratitude is a debt which usually goes on accumulating, like black-
mail," he remarked in a new section of his autobiography intended as a
tribute to Rogers's memory; "the more you pay, the more is exacted. In
time you are made to realize that the kindness done you is become a curse
and you wish it had not happened." But one reason that he had admired

Rogers so much was that his friend never gave any indication of wanting something in return. And, in truth, there was nothing either man could have given the other except friendship. For that reason they were able to behave like true equals, each supreme in his own field with no sense of rivalry or jealousy.

"I often gave him fresh financial ideas, quite uninvited," Twain was able to joke a few months after the funeral, "and in return—uninvited—he told me how to write my literature better; but nothing came of it, both of us remained as poor as ever."[19]

The example of Rogers's noble conduct toward him contrasted sharply with the actions of the Ashcrofts, and led Twain to see them as no better than any of the other scoundrels and adventurers who had plagued him in the past. "All through my life I have been the easy prey of the cheap adventurer," he remarked in his autobiography's discussion of Rogers's death. The method employed by each scoundrel was depressingly similar: "He came, he lied, he robbed and went his way, and the next one arrived by the next train and began to scrape up what was left." As far as Twain was concerned, it was clear that the Ashcrofts were now in the process of trying "to scrape up what was left," and he meant to stop them. Though there was nothing he could do to bring Rogers back, he could teach his two former friends a lesson they would never forget.[20]

. . .

His effort was helped by Ralph Ashcroft's irrepressible arrogance. One day in late May, during a conversation with Harry Lounsbury's son, Ashcroft bragged that he wasn't intimidated by Twain. Now that Rogers was out of the picture, he felt that he had the upper hand once again. "I can sell his house, over his head," he said of Twain, "for a thousand dollars, whenever I want to!" In the little community of Redding it didn't take long for this comment to reach Paine, who promptly repeated it to Twain and suggested that it might not be an idle boast.[21]

A search of Twain's papers soon turned up the comprehensive power of attorney that Ashcroft had placed in the safety deposit box in November. When Clara, Jean, and Paine examined the document, they were stunned by the realization that the business manager possessed the authority to sell not only Stormfield but everything else Twain owned. Two weeks later, Jean wrote an admirably succinct explanation of the discovery. The Ashcrofts, she said, had "so worked Father that he was as clay in their hands & the climax of their actions was the signing of a general power of attorney to *them,* individually and *to*gether, which gave them the power to do *anything* they chose with every sort of property Father now has & might at any time possess!"[22]

On June 2 the couple received a formal notice revoking their power of attorney. Ashcroft made an effort to appear unperturbed by this turn of events, pretending in his response to Twain that the document was of little consequence. "Of course, we both cheerfully acquiesce in your request," he wrote; "in fact, neither of us has used or had cause to use the same recently." But Isabel was frightened and seems to have been worried that Clara might insist that they be charged with a crime. Though she could barely afford it, she wanted to get out of the country and go to Europe as fast as possible. It made sense to stay out of sight for at least several weeks and make sure that they weren't in any legal danger. Her husband still had connections with the London office of the Plasmon Company, and was able to explain away a sudden overseas voyage as merely a business trip.

For good measure, they prepared an excuse for why Isabel needed to accompany him. "Mrs. Ashcroft's health has been seriously undermined," her husband wrote Twain on June 3, "owing to the unjust and unfounded accusations made against her, and she is on the verge of a breakdown. Her doctor orders immediately a complete change. As I have important business to attend to in England, some of which you are acquainted with, we shall probably sail in a few days to be gone about four weeks."[23]

When Twain reported this development to one of his new lawyers in New York—Charles Lark—the attorney contacted Ashcroft and suggested that he stay in the country. Ashcroft denied that he had any plans to leave right away, but on June 9 he and his wife quietly slipped away on a passenger freighter of the Northwestern Transportation Line. It wasn't the kind of ship that someone looking for them might think to search, and in any case it wasn't going to England. Its destination was Rotterdam.[24]

"They had occasion to be frightened," Twain remarked after learning of their departure, "for, as a precautionary measure, Mr. Lark was intending to ask the district attorney of Fairfield county to place Miss Lyon's case before the grand jury for said county & let him summon her."[25]

Though Rogers's death had delayed the formal audit, Twain's lawyers felt confident in mid-June that they had collected enough evidence to prove Isabel had stolen money from her employer. Suspecting that she might stay in Europe for some time, Charles Lark recommended seizing her cottage as one way to recover the lost money. Twain agreed and on June 19 a sheriff's attachment for $3,000 was issued against the house. The announcement of this action in the *New York Tribune* concluded with the terse statement "Mr. and Mrs. Ashcroft are now in Europe."[26]

Twain hoped that his firm response would be enough to make the couple accept defeat in silence and leave him alone. For a few weeks there was indeed peace at Stormfield. In England the Ashcrofts complained to the press, vowing to return and fight for their rights, but it was impossible to tell whether they were in earnest or simply bluffing. Whatever they chose to do, Twain wanted to put his side of the story in writing. If he died suddenly or became incapacitated, his daughters would be able to use his narrative of events as a way of answering any future attacks by the Ashcrofts. But he was also anxious to explain to himself what had happened.

How could he have been so blind to the troubles brewing under his nose? And how would this latest twist in his fortunes be viewed by posterity? Having gone to so much trouble over the last few years to polish his legacy, he was fearful that the much younger Ashcrofts might emerge from obscurity many years in the future and fool the world into believing whatever tales they wanted to spread about him or his family. It was clear that he needed to add even more paper to his bulging stack of autobiographical dictations, but this time he wanted to fill the pages of his story with words written in his own hand. It was the only way to prove that he meant every word of it.

· · ·

THE "ASHCROFT-LYON MANUSCRIPT," as scholars call it, is Twain's last major work. Yet for a hundred years it has remained unpublished. Written at a furious pace over the summer of 1909, the manuscript runs to more than four hundred pages, some of which exist in a very rough state, with many corrections and additions. The handwriting isn't always easy to decipher, and Twain is often sketchy about dates, places, and some of the minor players in the drama. Specialists who have read the work in the Twain collection at the University of California, Berkeley, have generally come away unimpressed. *The Mark Twain Encyclopedia* dismisses it as a rambling collection of petty complaints by a broken-down author who has "lost control over his materials." *The Oxford Companion to Mark Twain* barely mentions it, and one lengthy study by a British scholar complains that it is merely an "intemperate" rhetorical exercise. This seems a polite way of saying it is nothing but one long rant.[27]

As rants go, however, it is a gem. It is the sort of thing Twain always did well, but here there is no attempt to hold back anything, no effort at balance, and no pretense of civility at the start. Twain is hopping mad, and his rage never abates as he slams the Ashcrofts with all the verbal fireworks at his command.

"Where would the great exuberance of him have taken him," Isabel Lyon wondered in her old age, "had it not been throttled — or directed?" It is just as well for her that she never found out, for one answer lies in the pages of the "Ashcroft-Lyon Manuscript," which would have left her trembling in horror if she had ever been allowed to read it. The work is one of the best examples of Mark Twain uncensored, and is made all the more powerful because it deals with two people the author knew so intimately. He knew enough about the Ashcrofts to analyze their motives and describe their faults in vivid detail.[28]

In his manuscript they are portrayed as villains of the first order, a "pair of rotten eggs" who sowed dissension in his family and plotted to rob his daughters of their inheritance. He outdoes himself in inventing terms of abuse for the two, calling Isabel "that little old superannuated virgin," and Ralph "that Liverpool bastard." He says they won his trust by flattering and pampering him. They were "like a pair of anxious & adoring nurses," he writes, "& I couldn't even go to Bermuda, & not even to New York . . . without one or both of them along to see that I didn't catch cold or get run over by a baby wagon. And I liked that nursing & petting & was vain of being a person who could call out such homage, such devotion." As a result, he says, Ralph Ashcroft had become convinced "that he

& [Isabel] owned me body & soul & I couldn't help myself; that all in good time they would be indisputably supreme here."

Their scheme to rob him, he writes, was "so darkly & shudderingly & mysteriously showy & romantic that they must surely have lifted it out of an old-time novel." In fact, it was the "booky" quality of their villainy that seemed to offend him most. It was so "damn *stagey*" that he felt doubly humiliated for not being astute enough to see through it. It galled him to think that a writer of his talents had allowed himself to be turned into a character in a melodrama concocted by two thieves. And, worst of all, the part he had found himself playing so well was that of the gullible old fool.

As a storyteller, he needed to reclaim the narrative and tell it in his own fashion. But no matter how it's told, the story is neither pretty nor simple. And that is perhaps the main reason it has failed to spark enthusiasm among the few who have read it. None of the principals in the tale emerge from it looking good except Jean. Moreover, it isn't easy to unravel the tangled sequence of events that led Twain to turn against the Ashcrofts. And for readers who don't know all the facts, it is tempting to think that he overreacted and allowed a series of minor disagreements to escalate into a nasty, all-consuming feud.

It is true that the money Isabel Lyon spent on herself without asking permission was relatively small in comparison with Twain's wealth, and that she had never received a salary commensurate with her considerable duties. And it was only because of her hard work that Twain was able to enjoy a life of comfort at his new house. When he had been ill, it was Isabel who had taken such good care of him, remaining at his side when no one else was willing to stay with him, including Clara. But it was precisely because Isabel had been so close to him that Twain considered her betrayal to be so serious.

Whether her household accounts balanced or not wasn't the main problem. Rather, it was her willingness to mislead him. She lied not only about money, but also about Jean's condition, Paine's research, and her own relationship with Ashcroft. The great cry of regret in Twain's manuscript is about trust: "I had the most absolute & uncompromising faith in the honesty, fidelity & truthfulness of that pair."

It wasn't just his faith in the Ashcrofts that suffered. It was also his faith in himself. After Livy's death, he had slowly managed to rebuild his life and to reach new heights of fame as the celebrated Man in White who was cheered at home and abroad. At Stormfield, he thought for a time that he had found a paradise where he would be able to rest from his labors and enjoy his success among a circle of adoring friends. His fight with the Ashcrofts destroyed all that, and he knew that he was as much to blame as they were. He had allowed himself to be duped, and in a shabby fashion that left him feeling as if all his pride in his fame amounted to nothing. How could the great Dr. Clemens, with his cherished Oxford gown, have entrusted his future, and his family's future, to the care of Ralph and Isabel Ashcroft?

It was especially painful to admit to himself that he had failed Jean. What had begun as a noble attempt to improve her condition at a reputable sanitarium had degenerated into a selfish effort by Isabel to send her anyplace but home. Twain should have asked more questions of Dr. Peterson, and should have listened with greater care to Jean. But it had been convenient for him to leave the details of her treatment to Isabel, and to accept her word over Jean's.

"It cuts me to the heart, now," he confesses in the manuscript, "to know that Jean made many an imploring & beseeching appeal to me, her father, & could not get my ear, that I, who should have been her best friend, forsook her in her trouble to listen to this designing hypocrite whom I was coddling in the place which should have been occupied by my forsaken child."

Twain's account of the Ashcroft-Lyon debacle is not a "literary curiosity," as one critic has called it, but a powerful, often gut-wrenching effort by a great writer to speak directly to readers about his most personal failings. With its preface addressed "To the Unborn Reader," the manuscript is Twain's last effort to explain himself to posterity. The portrait of the artist that emerges is not that of a petty or mean-spirited man, but of one who wears his passions on his sleeve, and who cares too much about the truth to let it be obscured by half-truths and lies.[29]

It is not the work of a broken-down writer or a bitter one. From beginning to end, it breathes a sense of urgency, as if the author can't wait to share his story. And it isn't lacking in humor. In his efforts to convey his disgust with the Ashcrofts, he is often his old playful self, embellishing descriptions with the kind of exuberance Isabel might have admired in another context:

> Miss Lyon is good company, agreeable company, delightful company, drunk or sober, but there is nothing about her that invites to intimate personal contact; her caressing touch—& she was always finding excuses to apply it—arch girly-girly pats on the back of my hand & playful little spats on my cheek with her fan—& these affectionate attentions always made me shrivel uncomfortably—much as happens when a frog jumps down my bosom.

· · ·

A COUPLE OF YEARS after Twain's death, his sister-in-law, Susan Crane, addressed the Ashcroft-Lyon controversy by observing of Isabel, "How she hastened the good man out of this life!"[30] There is no denying that the controversy took its toll on Twain's health. In June, during a brief visit to Baltimore to attend the high school graduation of his angelfish Frances Nunnally, he felt a sharp pain in his chest while he was resting at his hotel. His biographer, who was accompanying him on the trip, asked if he needed help.

"It's a curious, sickening, deadly kind of pain," the author said.

"Where is it, exactly, Mr. Clemens?"

He pointed to the center of his breast. "It is here, and it is very peculiar indeed."

Thinking that he might be suffering from rheumatism, he asked Paine to bring him a hot water bottle, and that seemed to help. But when the trouble returned a little while later, the biographer suspected it was angina and urged him to see a doctor when they returned to New York. It was the first sign of what Dr. Quintard would later diagnose as "tobacco heart." For Twain, the worst part of it would mean having to cut back on cigars, smoking "only 4 times a day instead of 40."[31]

But it can't be entirely coincidental that his heart trouble surfaced at the height of his feud with the Ashcrofts. Indeed, it grew progressively worse over the summer. By the end of August Twain was drinking "barrels of boiling water to keep the pain quiet," as he explained in an effort to joke about one of his home remedies. His tolerance for the pain was amazing, as his biographer observed repeatedly. "I have seen it crumple him, and his face become colorless while his hand dug at his breast; but he never complained, he never bewailed, and at billiards he would persist in going on and playing in his turn, even while he was bowed with the anguish of the attack."

He would also insist on taking long walks, and wouldn't turn back if the angina flared up. Occasionally, when he was feeling better, he liked to pretend that nothing was wrong with him, and that his only serious health problem was "acute indigestion." As Paine recalled, "There would come a week or a fortnight when he was apparently perfectly well, and at such times we dismissed the thought of any heart malady."[32]

Not wanting to disappoint an angelfish, Twain suppressed any concern about his chest pains during his trip to Maryland and took part in the graduation ceremony at St. Timothy's School for Girls, on the outskirts of Baltimore. If he felt any lingering discomfort, it probably disappeared the moment he walked onto the grounds and found himself surrounded by an admiring group of "kodaking girls," as the local paper called them. "I always like the young ladies," the smiling author declared, "and would go a long way to be in their company."

He delivered an entertaining commencement speech. Wearing his white suit and a big Panama hat, he sat patiently on the stage listening to the other speakers offer uplifting words of wisdom and advice. The last person to speak before him was Edward Martin, a poet from New York whose daughter was one of the graduates.

"I don't know what to tell you girls to do," said Twain when his turn came. "Mr. Martin has told you everything you ought to do, and now I must give you some don'ts.

"First, girls, don't smoke—to excess. I am 73 and a half and have been smoking 73 of them. But I never smoke to excess—that is, I smoke in moderation, only one cigar at a time.

"Second, don't drink—that is, to excess.

"Third, don't marry—that is, to excess."[33]

The girls laughed and were full of compliments when they spoke to him following the ceremony. After he returned home, he sent Frances a note thanking her for inviting him to the school and added, "If I were not so inadequate in age & sex I would go there and take a term or two."[34]

Nobody at the school seemed to notice that he was feeling his age. In fact, he made a point of telling one of the Baltimore reporters, "I am just as young now as I was forty years ago. Why, I don't see any reason why I shouldn't live another hundred years."[35]

Thanks to Thomas Edison's film studio in New York, it is possible for later generations to see how easily Twain was able to give contemporaries the impression that he was still strong and healthy. Shortly after his return from Maryland, a film crew came to Redding to shoot a few scenes of the author at home. In May Edison's company had purchased the rights to make a short movie of *The Prince and the Pauper,* and the studio manager—Horace Plimpton—thought the feature should conclude with some footage of the author. He wanted the public to know that Twain had approved the film and was willing to promote it. As an advertising circular for the production boasted, "Mr. Clemens gave his full authority for the production of his celebrated story in motion pictures, and we believe it is the first time a writer of international fame has been so used."[36]

In an age of silent film Twain couldn't entertain viewers with humorous anecdotes and droll remarks, so he put on his usual white uniform and simply showed off for the camera. The brief footage is the only surviving example of Twain in motion. With his hair flying in all directions, he parades in front of his house and blows cigar smoke at the camera as he rounds the corner. Taking quick, vigorous strides, he doesn't look at all like a man with a bad case of angina.

The camera also captures him in a more relaxed pose, having tea outdoors with Clara and Jean. At one point the butler Claude (whom Clara had recently persuaded to return to Stormfield and serve the family again) appears in the scene and hands Clara a hat, which she puts on just before getting up to lead the others inside. The footage ends with a ghostly frame showing only Twain and Jean, who is wearing white like her father. Her thin summer dress is loosely gathered at the waist, and the sleeves are pushed up, as if she has come to the house straight from her work at the farm.

In the fall, when Twain was offered the chance to view the film at a theater, he seized the opportunity, saying that he had always been curious to see what he was "really like to others." Afterward, a magazine reported his verdict: "He said it was like looking in a mirror, but it was so lifelike it gave him a creepy feeling." What his voice sounded like, we may never know. Though he once made a recording on a wax cylinder, the original was apparently destroyed and no duplicates have yet to surface.[37]

· · ·

DR. QUINTARD WARNED TWAIN repeatedly that he needed to take better care of himself. In addition to his angina, he was also suffering from high blood pressure. But as long as he was able to keep the pain in his chest from hurting too much, Twain didn't want to talk about his health problems or make much of an effort to follow his doctor's orders, especially with regard to smoking. "It is the pains that persuade you to behave yourself," he said. "Nothing else could do it."

One problem, he joked, was that Quintard couldn't tell him whether his disease was "the kind that carries a man off in an instant or keeps him lingering along and suffering for twenty years or so." He wanted to figure out whether it was worth planning ahead or not. "I was in hopes that Quintard would tell me that I was likely to drop dead any minute; but he didn't. . . . He didn't give me any schedule."

And then one day that summer—while he was entertaining himself with books on astronomy, and his own amateur efforts to calculate the distances between stars—he announced to Paine that if he couldn't make long-term plans, he would prefer to stick to a schedule set ages ago that promised a reasonably quick, and suitably spectacular, exit. "I came in with Halley's comet in 1835. It is coming again next year, and I expect to go out with it. It will be the greatest disappointment of my life if I don't go out with Halley's comet. The Almighty has said, no doubt: 'Now here are these two unaccountable freaks; they came in together, they must go out together.' Oh! I am looking forward to that."[38]

All his life Twain had been fascinated by the fact that at his birth the skies had blazed with the light of a famous comet. Visiting Earth every seventy-five years, the comet takes it name from the British astronomer Edmond Halley, who first spotted it in 1682. In 1835, it reached perihelion—its closest approach to the sun—on November 16, and its light was still visible from Earth when Twain was born on the 30th.

"The most absorbing topic of interest," said the *New York Tribune* in a June 1909 article on astronomy, "has been the expected return of Halley's comet." But, as the paper went on to report, astronomers were worried. So far their telescopes had not picked up any sign of the comet's approach. "Probably it has been declining in size," the article speculated, "and may not be so imposing a sight as popular imagination has pictured it."[39]

Twain didn't seem to doubt that it would return right on time, and that it would look as splendid as ever. Only a few years before making his dramatic announcement to his biographer, he had described a feeling of mystical connection with comets in a manuscript note for his short work *No. 44, the Mysterious Stranger:* "How do you know, when a comet has swum into your system? Merely by your eye or your telescope—but I, I hear a brilliant far stream of sound come winding across the firmament of majestic sounds & I know the splendid stranger is there without looking." Such a feeling was probably picked up at his mother's knee. Jane Clemens was fond of stargazing and took the name for her oldest son, Orion, from the constellation.[40]

Twain enjoyed keeping track of the latest discoveries in astronomy, but had little use for scientific jargon. At the beginning of 1909, when the Harvard Observatory announced that "perturbations in the orbital movement of Neptune" might indicate the presence of a new planetary body, he offered his own interpretation of the discovery. Writing in the *Harper's Weekly* of January 30, he said that he was an old expert on perturbations, having learned all about them from youthful encounters with dogs guarding watermelon patches.

> These recent perturbations are considered remarkable because they perturbate through three seconds of arc, but really that is nothing. . . . There isn't any Neptune that can outperturbate a dog. . . . You let a dog jump out at you all of a sudden in the dark of the moon, and you will see what a small thing three seconds of arc is: the shudder that goes through you then would open the seams of Noah's ark itself, from figurehead to rudder-post, and you would

drop that melon the same as if you had never had any but just a casual interest in it.[41]

One day that summer he had a chance to take a close look at something that had come from outer space. While on a short visit to New York, Twain and his biographer stopped by the Museum of Natural History on the Upper West Side to admire the collection of meteorites on display in the lobby, including the three famous ones from Cape York, Greenland — the massive Ahnighito or "The Tent," and "The Dog" and "The Woman" — all of which had been transported to New York by the Arctic explorer Robert Peary in the 1890s.

Weighing more than thirty tons, the Ahnighito was then the heaviest and largest meteorite known to scientists. "Never," said Peary, "have I had the terrific majesty of the force of gravity and the meaning of the words 'momentum' and 'inertia' so powerfully brought home to me as in handling this mountain of iron." When it was shipped to New York, the massive load of iron caused the vessel's compass to freeze in its direction. Moving it from the docks to the museum required a specially built cart pulled by "a block-long line of twenty-eight horses."

It isn't surprising that Twain was in awe of this exhibit, and also of the one in the Hall of Dinosaurs. "To him," Paine recalled, "these were the most fascinating things in the world. He contemplated the meteorites and the brontosaur, and lost himself in strange and marvelous imaginings concerning the far reaches of time and space whence they had come down to us."[42]

· · ·

WHILE TWAIN WAS MUSING on the great questions of eternity and mortality, a friend of the family lay seriously ill at a hospital on the Upper East Side of New York. The patient was Ossip Gabrilowitsch, who had entered the Manhattan Eye, Ear, and Throat Hospital in the first week of July for an operation to treat a severe case of mastoiditis. In May he had given the last of his New York performances for the year and was preparing to return to Europe when he had suddenly fallen ill. His on-again, off-again relationship with Clara had entered another low period, and they had not seen much of each other in the last few weeks. She was aware that he was going to have an operation, but didn't know that complications had arisen, and that his doctors were worried he might not survive.

One day at Stormfield a visitor who didn't know of her relationship with the pianist mentioned the bad news in passing.

"What a shame he is dying!" the visitor said of Gabrilowitsch. "Such a fine fellow, they say!"

Clara dropped everything and raced to catch the next train to New York. When she arrived at the hospital, she found Ossip in the grip of a high fever and too weak to sit up. "He cannot possibly live," she was told.[43]

She stayed at his side day and night, and summoned Dr. Quintard to see if he could help. On July 9, one day after the *New York Times* reported that the pianist was "dangerously ill," the fever abated, and Clara was cautiously optimistic that he would pull through. "Gabrilowitsch seems a little better today," she wrote her father on the 9th, "& the doctors think that they are getting control of the fever at *last*."[44]

His recovery was slow but sure, and Clara believed that it was her prayers and constant presence that had helped to save him. When he expressed the fear that she might drift away from him again after he was well, she "hinted" that the ordeal of his illness had permanently affected their relationship, and that she was ready to think of marriage.

"Do you mean it?" he asked.

"Yes," she said, "I mean it."

Instead of staying in New York after his release from the hospital, Gabrilowitsch went to Stormfield with Clara to continue his recovery in one of the guest rooms. For more than a month he remained in a weakened state, and stayed in bed much of the time, attended by Clara and Katy Leary. As Paine would recall of that period, the pianist "rarely appeared, even at meal-times."[45]

With Ossip convalescing, and Twain suffering from angina, the last thing anyone at Stormfield wanted to hear was that Isabel Ashcroft was coming back home to contest the seizure of her cottage. But on Wednesday, July 14, when the liner *Carmania* docked in New York, Isabel was aboard. She was returning in style on one of the most elegant ships in the Cunard fleet, and her husband—who would follow her two weeks later—had alerted the newspapers to her arrival. Reporters and photographers were waiting as she came down the gangplank. One newspaperman described her as "a pretty, Quakerish-looking little woman, the kind you expect to wear a folded kerchief over her shoulders and dove-colored frocks."[46]

After a month abroad, the Ashcrofts seemed to have concluded that one of them should return and try to make peace with Twain. As her reason for leaving in the first place, Isabel told the press that she and her husband had gone on their honeymoon, and that the seizure of her cottage had forced her to come home early to defend herself against false charges. Though the honeymoon excuse was a new twist in the story, it made sense to the newspapers, one of which ran a headline the next day saying, "Mrs. Ashcroft Hurries Back from Her Honeymoon Abroad to Find Out About $4,000 Suit."[47]

With a convincing air of innocence, Isabel insisted that she couldn't understand why Twain would have taken action against her. "I loved him as a daughter loves a father," she said. "For seven years I relieved him of every care I could."

The problem, she suggested, could be traced either to a misunderstanding with Twain's older daughter or to mischief from some unnamed enemy. "She is of a highly artistic temperament," she said of Clara, "which is apt to lead her very far afield. And yet I don't think that she would do this of her own accord either. There must be somebody acting behind her—somebody who doesn't like me."[48]

One way or the other, she vowed to the press, she was going to make things right, and was leaving immediately for Redding to see Twain and resolve the matter face-to-face. "The whole case will be settled, but the shame of it is that I should have been placed in an improper and false light."[49]

She did indeed travel straightaway to Redding, but couldn't summon the courage to enter the grounds of Stormfield. Instead she let herself into her cottage and waited for Twain to come to her. He didn't take the bait, but sent Charles Lark to say that if she deeded the house back to him, the suit against her would be dropped and no further action would be taken. As a witness, Lark brought along Jean, who sat quietly during the visit, never once saying anything to rebuke the woman who had done so much to undermine her place in the family. For the most part, Isabel ignored Jean and tried not to look at her. Though she supposedly believed that Jean was unstable and prone to violent outbursts, she didn't seem in the least bit worried about her safety.

Lark was a persuasive advocate and didn't have much trouble talking Isabel into giving back the house. Ralph Ashcroft may have been hoping that his wife would prevail by using a softer approach, but in the end she simply gave up and signed over the deed. At Jean's suggestion, she was given six weeks to vacate the property. When Ashcroft learned of this development, he was livid. Returning to New York at the end of July, he immediately fired off a letter accusing Lark of using "threats and intimidations" to trick Isabel into surrendering the cottage.[50]

The feud took a turn for the worse on August 4 when the *New York Times* allowed Ashcroft to launch a major attack against Twain's family on the front page of the paper. After a few words of introduction by the editors, the article simply quoted Ashcroft's written account of his side of the dispute. Running to about 1,200 words, his statement filled one column of the first page and part of another on page two. Knowing that the public wouldn't be sympathetic to criticisms of Twain himself, Ashcroft directed most of his fire at Clara, but also took a few shots at Jean.

He tried to depict both women as troublemakers and hinted that each suffered from some vague malady affecting their mental stability. "For two years or more after their mother's death, both girls were in sanitaria most of the time, and the younger daughter has been under the care of nerve specialists ever since. Under these circumstances, Miss Lyon naturally became Mr. Clemens's hostess. . . . Both daughters, however, became jealous of her, were afraid that Mark Twain would marry her, and often endeavored to destroy his confidence in her."

Obviously, Ashcroft had no interest in establishing the truth. In his anger over the loss of the cottage, he simply wanted to stir up a scandal and force Twain to buy him off with a quick and generous settlement. He made it clear that he was willing to do anything to smear the daughters. In Jean's case, he played on a cruel stereotype of epileptics by hinting that she was an emotional wreck. In Clara's case, he used some hard truths to hit her where she was most vulnerable, lambasting her for neglecting her father while spending money on a career of dubious worth and a male friend of questionable character. She wasted her ample allowance, he wrote, on "the delightful experience of paying for the hire of concert halls

destined to be filled with 'snow' or 'paper,' for the maintenance of her accompanist, Charles E. Wark, and to defray other cash expenditures that an
embryonic Tetrazzini is naturally called upon to make."

To rub in the fact that Clara's talents couldn't match those of Luisa
Tetrazzini—then one of the biggest and best-paid opera stars—Ashcroft
observed sarcastically, "One's vocal ambitions . . . sometimes exceed one's
capabilities . . . and the bitter realization of this has, in this instance,
caused the baiting of a woman who has earned and kept the admiration
and respect of all of Mark Twain's friends."[51]

Disgusted by the sheer nastiness of Ashcroft's statement, Twain refused to speak to the *Times* when the paper called the house to ask for a
response. Though Ashcroft was now desperate enough to go after Clara
with some of his most damaging criticism, and to do it in such an influential paper, the attack failed to win him any sympathy from the public,
and it didn't intimidate anyone in the family. Instead it made him look
petty and vindictive. Nevertheless, for Twain and his family, it was the
kind of humiliating public exposure that Livy had always dreaded, and
that, ironically, Isabel had worked so hard to guard against during her
time as the family secretary.

During the rest of August, Ashcroft tried in vain to win concessions
from Twain's lawyers. He sent bills for various fees and charges that he
claimed were owed to him for previous services, and for expenses incurred by Isabel. He demanded that Twain return the cottage and promise not to file any more suits, and he wanted compensation for agreeing to
cancel his employment contract with the Mark Twain Company. His
lawyer and Twain's hotly debated whether the audit of the household expenses proved conclusively that money was missing. The question is one
that scholars still debate. But Twain was convinced that thefts had occurred, and his opinion was reinforced by the behavior of both Ashcrofts
in the aftermath of Isabel's dismissal. They had acted like scoundrels, he
believed, and therefore they must be scoundrels.

It soon became obvious that Ashcroft's threats and demands were not
going to work. On almost every issue Twain stood his ground and refused
to make concessions. As the deadline was approaching for Isabel to vacate the cottage, she realized that it was time to go. She knew Twain well
enough to understand that her husband couldn't make him budge once

he had made up his mind. And, no doubt, Ashcroft was disappointed by his failure to gain any advantage from his lengthy attack in the *New York Times*. If dragging the names of Twain's daughters through the mud couldn't bring the great man to his knees, nothing could. So, in the last week of August, Isabel moved out, joining her husband at his home in Brooklyn.

Twain relished the news. "That rotten-hearted pair of professional thieves, liars & forgers have cleared out . . . & are not likely to return," he told Elizabeth Wallace, who had been quick to take his side in the dispute and to end her friendship with Isabel. "I feel nearer to the Lord than I ever was before," he continued. "I feel as He feels of a Saturday night when the weekly report is in & He has had a satisfactory clean-up of the human race."[52]

About two weeks later, he noted proudly that Ashcroft had resigned from the Mark Twain Company "to keep from being thrown out." As a condition of his resignation, he had asked that Twain send him a concil-iatory note accepting his departure "with regret," but the request was re-fused. In the end Ashcroft's schemes came to nothing. And though the dispute cost Twain hundreds of dollars in legal fees, the author consoled himself for this loss by listing three ways in which the Ashcrofts were now much worse off as a result of their chicanery:

1. They are married;
2. They live in Brooklyn;
3. She adores Society—& she ain't in it any more.[53]

Twain may have thought he had heard the last of the troublesome pair, but Ashcroft wasn't quite finished tormenting the family. An oppor-tunity would soon arise for him to deliver one last nasty shock.

After a couple of broken engagements, Clara and Ossip finally married in October 1909. "What! Again?" was Twain's response when Clara brought him the news of her third—and last—engagement to the pianist.

TWENTY

Letters from the Earth

I am only human, although I regret it.
Mark Twain[1]

. . .

BY THE MIDDLE OF SEPTEMBER the mood at Stormfield had brightened considerably. The weather was good, Jean was busy with her new life, Gabrilowitsch was feeling better and was almost his old self again, Clara was glad to be rid of Isabel, and Twain was writing the final parts of his manuscript about the feud. He felt as though he had finally awakened from a bad dream, and though his heart trouble was showing no sign of going away, he was learning to live with it. "I guess it's all right," he wrote Dorothy Quick in response to a question about his health. "Infirmities & disabilities are quite proper to old age."[2]

He missed having his angelfish visit him, but he lacked the strength to keep up with them, and didn't want to be dull company. For the first time in almost three years, however, both his daughters were living under his roof, and he was happy to see so much of them. In fact, they all agreed that a celebration was in order, and it was decided that a concert would be given at Stormfield featuring Clara and Ossip. Invitations were quickly sent out to a large number of friends and neighbors, who were asked to pay a small admission price for the benefit of the Redding Library. A well-known opera singer in New York, the distinguished-looking baritone David Bispham, was invited to join Clara and Ossip on the program, and he gladly accepted. A crowd of two hundred or so was expected, but more than twice that number of tickets were sold.

All the excitement of the concert—which took place on Tuesday, September 21—made Twain forget his heart trouble, and he thoroughly enjoyed the event. "If we hadn't stopped the sale of tickets a day and a half before the performance," he later wrote, "we should have been swamped. We jammed 160 into the library (not quite all had seats), we filled the loggia, the dining-room, the hall, clear into the billiard-room, the stairs, and the brick-paved square outside the dining-room."[3]

A few hours before the concert began, David Bispham visited Twain in his room, where he found him propped up in bed smoking a pipe and looking as though he had no plans to go anywhere. But when the crowd began to fill up the house, the author appeared right on schedule in his white suit to host the event. "He was in great fettle," recalled Bispham, who shook with laughter when Twain introduced him to the audience. After making much of the fact that both Bispham and Gabrilowitsch were international stars, Twain said, "My daughter is not as famous as these gentlemen, but she is ever so much better-looking."

After the concert, there was a dance, and the festive atmosphere seemed to reflect a general sense of relief among the family and their close friends that the Ashcroft ordeal was over. As Paine recalled, Jean looked especially happy and healthy. She "danced down that great living-room as care-free as if there was no shadow upon her life."[4]

Meanwhile, out on the lawn in the warm night air, Ossip and Clara were admiring the stars and talking about their future. Now that he was almost well again, it was time for the pianist to resume performing in Europe, if his fragile health could bear it. But he wasn't going to leave Clara behind, and made it clear that he would need her help. While they stood together on the lawn, he asked if she would marry him, and the answer was yes.

"What! Again?" was Twain's response when Clara brought him the news of her engagement. Then he shrugged and said, "Well, anyway, any girl would be proud to marry him." After Clara's two previous engagements to Ossip had fallen through, Twain was understandably reluctant to believe this one would hold until the wedding day. But the couple decided not to make Twain or anyone else wait long to find out. Clara announced that the wedding would be a small one at home and would take place in two weeks.[5]

On Sunday the 26th she wrote Reverend Twichell asking him to come to Stormfield and marry her on October 6. To explain the haste, she said that Ossip needed to sail for Europe on October 12. "Because of concerts which he *can* not cancel," she wrote, "we have to be married at once." And then she added, "I couldn't get married without you." Of course, he replied at once that he would come. Thirty-nine years earlier he had presided over the marriage of her father and mother in Elmira.[6]

In large part, it was her experience of nursing Ossip through his long illness that had swayed Clara in the direction of marriage. But after enduring the attacks of the New York music critics in the spring, and the scandalmongering of the Ashcrofts in the summer, she seemed to welcome the chance to escape from her old life for a while and try living as a famous pianist's wife after thirty-five years of being a famous novelist's daughter. She had already scheduled another concert tour of her own in the autumn, but marrying Ossip at the last minute provided her with a ready excuse for canceling the tour and making a quick getaway from her past. With Jean at home, and the Ashcrofts banished, it must have seemed to her impulsive nature a good time to bolt.

All the same, she didn't want anyone to think that Ossip had won her hand by taming her independent spirit. She told Twichell, "There is one great favor I have to ask of you—just one—my very last. Please exclude the word 'Obey' from my marriage vows." He agreed, but after getting to know Ossip a little, he couldn't see why Clara was concerned that he might try to dominate her. As far as Twichell could tell, the pianist was a harmless fellow who wasn't in the least bit intimidating. After the wedding he described him as "a refined, gentle-mannered young man, quite modest and unaffected and not at all foreign in mien."[7]

In a great rush Clara went to Altman's department store and picked out a wedding dress, and also purchased a dress for her bridesmaid, Jean.

Her Elmira cousin and childhood playmate, Jervis Langdon, agreed to serve as Ossip's best man. The pianist Ethel Newcomb—who had studied with Clara and Ossip in Vienna under Leschetizky—was asked to play the wedding march. At Stormfield, Claude searched the surrounding fields for colorful wildflowers and autumn foliage to use as decorations in the living room, where the wedding was to take place. Besides the immediate family, about two dozen guests were invited.

At the wedding rehearsal on October 5, Twain seemed less than enthusiastic about the prospect of losing a daughter who had only recently moved back home. When his presence was requested at the rehearsal in the living room, he was playing billiards and didn't want to be interrupted for the purpose of merely going through the motions of a pretend ceremony. Clara's good friend the violinist Marie Nichols came to get him, but he refused to leave his game. It was no use arguing with him, though Nichols tried. As it happened, he had donned his Oxford garb earlier in the day, thinking he would try it out as part of his wedding outfit, and when Nichols wouldn't leave him alone, he turned to her in exasperation and did something unexpected. "He put the mortar board on my head and the robe over my arm," she recalled, "and told me to go in and take his place."[8]

The next day, however, during the real ceremony, he behaved himself. He gave the bride away without incident, and then posed for pictures wearing his cap and gown. In a photograph taken outside, Clara looks happy but uncomfortable in her heavy wedding dress, and Ossip's thin frame shows the effects of his recent illness. Pale, with short hair and pinched features, he bears little resemblance to his younger, more flamboyant self, when he had a full head of dark curls and a fresh, boyish expression.

Twain appears to be scowling at the camera, but he often looked that way whenever a photographer asked him to pose. No doubt he was unsettled by the speed with which Clara went from engagement to marriage, but he seemed content with his daughter's decision. When Elizabeth Wallace wrote to get his reaction to the marriage, he replied that he approved of it. "Happily it is congratulations, not condolences. We have known Gabrilowitsch intimately for 11 years. . . . They were engaged years ago—twice. Broken both times, to Mrs. Clemens's great regret. Gab is a very fine human being in every way." Because he liked and respected Wallace, and enjoyed giving her his unvarnished opinions of the Ashcrofts, it is unlikely that he would have shared with her his praise of Ossip if he didn't mean it.[9]

···

THE NEWLYWEDS HONEYMOONED in Atlantic City, but their plan to go abroad on October 16 ran into trouble when Gabrilowitsch faced another medical crisis. While they were staying in the seaside resort, he began having pains in his side and was advised by doctors that he needed an appendectomy. He felt well enough to return to New York, and an operation was scheduled for October 18 at a private hospital. Despite his weak condition, he went to the pier on the 16th to cancel his passage on the liner that he and Clara were supposed to have taken to Germany. To his surprise, he was approached by a couple of reporters who wanted an interview.

It wasn't his latest illness that interested them. What they wanted was his reaction to the recent rumor that a lawyer representing Mrs. Charles E. Wark was intending to bring a suit against Clara for alienation of affection. Some of the New York newspapers had received an anonymous letter "saying that every effort was being made to serve Mrs. Gabrilowitsch, the former Miss Clemens, with papers in an alienation suit." What did Mr. Gabrilowitsch know about this suit? asked the reporters.

Ossip did his best to give a dignified reply. "My wife and I are at a loss to know what it all means. There has been no suit for alienation against her, nor is she engaged in any other litigation. Mr. Wark is a personal friend of both of us, and I am sure he has nothing to do with it." Ossip was careful not even to acknowledge the existence of a Mrs. Wark, and dismissed the anonymous letter as a lie circulated out of "maliciousness."

Hoping that there was more to the story, a reporter telephoned Stormfield for a response and was fortunate to get Jean rather than Twain. She didn't mind saying exactly who was responsible for the rumor. The culprits, she declared, were the Ashcrofts. Isabel, she explained, "still felt revengeful as a result of the recent litigation between her and Mark Twain."

This comment brought a forceful denial from Ralph Ashcroft, who insisted "that neither he nor his wife had anything to do with the circulation of the rumors of Mrs. Wark's suit."[10]

There is no evidence that Wark's wife ever intended to file such a suit. As Jean indicated, it was one last effort by the Ashcrofts to embarrass Twain and his family. For Ossip and Clara, however, it was the worst possible time to have a fresh rumor hanging over their heads. He was ill and was going to have a serious operation in just two days. "Once more a hospital and days of misery," Clara was to recall of this period. They must have feared that their marriage might end in death and scandal before they were given a proper chance to make it work.

But once again Ossip survived a close call and was soon able to recover his health. In early November he felt well enough to return to Atlantic City with Clara and to resume their honeymoon. He even gave a few "informal recitals" at the hotel where they stayed, the Marlborough-Blenheim. Meanwhile, the European concerts that he had wanted so much to play were canceled or postponed. It wasn't until the end of November that the couple rebooked their passage to Europe and sailed away to start a new life.[11]

Before Ossip's appendectomy Twain had written to Clara's manager and made excuses for why she couldn't honor her engagements. The manager—R. E. Johnston—was understandably angry, but seemed to appreciate having a personal letter from Twain explaining the situation. "I am very, very sorry for these untoward things," he told Johnston, "but you see how they come about, and that neither you nor I could have helped it."[12]

Privately, Twain was relieved that Clara's marriage had given her a chance to give up performing. It wasn't that he begrudged her a career. He never failed to show her support. But he knew that her talent was limited, and that there were better ways to spend one's life than traveling from town to town trying to entertain audiences who might applaud or sit in silence. After her marriage he wrote, "She is done with the concert-stage—permanently, I pray. . . . I had a 'career' on the platform. I could not learn to like it."[13]

In some ways, Twain may have thought that touring made it easier for Clara to conduct her affair with her accompanist. Though her father could speak freely to her on many subjects, it is unlikely they ever had a frank discussion about Charles Wark. Yet it does seem that Ashcroft's campaign to undermine her reputation had the effect of increasing Twain's sympathy for women accused of adultery. As his biographer recalled, Twain spent much of the period immediately following Clara's marriage writing a new work titled "Letters from the Earth," and one of its most interesting sections includes a brutal analysis of male hypocrisy on the question of female adultery.

In sexual matters, Twain says in one of the "Letters," women are "*competent*. As competent as the candlestick is to receive the candle. Competent every day, competent every night. . . . But man is only briefly competent. . . . After 50 his performance is of poor quality, the intervals between are wide, and its satisfactions of no great value to either party; whereas his great-grandmother is as good as new."

By the laws of nature, Twain contends, a woman should be allowed not merely the occasional adulterous fling, but "the high privilege of unlimited adultery." The problem, as he sees it, is that society refuses to acknowledge the obvious and sanction this privilege. "Does she live in the free enjoyment of it? No. Nowhere in the whole world. She is robbed of it everywhere. Who does this? Man."

In a welcome moment of comic relief Twain illustrates the proper exercise of the woman's privilege by recalling the case of "a buxom royal princess" in the Sandwich Islands whose funeral was attended by her harem of "36 splendidly built young native men." As he explains, the princess had often boasted "that she kept the whole of them busy, and that several times it had happened that more than one of them had been able to charge overtime."[14]

Like many of the other manuscripts he was hoarding, Twain knew it would be a long time before any publisher might be willing to print his "Letters from the Earth." The only person he allowed to see the manuscript was Paine, but he did threaten to read selected parts of it to Elizabeth Wallace. "This book will never be published," he told her; "in fact, it couldn't be, because it would be a felony. . . . Paine enjoys it, but Paine is going to be damned one of these days, I suppose."[15]

Except for the comments on adultery, and a few similar remarks about masturbation and sexual appetites in general, "Letters from the Earth" doesn't contain much that might have provoked a prosecution for obscenity. Most of the time he is on the rampage against his favorite examples of divine injustice, biblical horrors, and religious hypocrisy. But it is worth noting that no one tried to publish the work until 1939, when Harper & Brothers decided it was safe to issue a collection of Twain's "uncensored writings"—including "Letters from the Earth."

At the last minute, however, the project was killed, and the person responsible wasn't a nervous executive or moral crusader. It was Clara, who "objected to the publication of certain parts of it on the ground that they presented a distorted view of her father's ideas and attitudes." There was nothing distorted in the work. It is more likely that she didn't want anyone raising questions about her father's controversial views of adultery. It must have been a sensitive subject for her because she continued for another twenty years to block publication. It was only shortly before her death that she changed her mind and allowed the work to appear. The whole collection came out in 1962 under the title *Letters from the Earth: Uncensored Writings,* by which time her relationship with Charles Wark was long forgotten.[16]

· · ·

A T SOME POINT in the autumn *Harper's Bazaar* asked Twain to write a short essay on "the turning point of my life." He didn't like the premise because he didn't believe that anyone's life had just one "turning point." As he saw it, there was "a very long chain of turning points" in each person's history, and no link in this intricate chain meant much without the others. Looking back over the events of his early life, he saw five or six crucial links—or turning points—starting with the day his mother "apprenticed me to a printer." His vagabond life as a young printer led to adventures along the great waterways of the American frontier, which aroused his interest in becoming a steamboat pilot. When "boats stopped running" during the early days of the Civil War, he went farther west and caught "the silver fever" in Nevada. When he didn't strike it rich, he traded a miner's shovel for a journalist's pen and made a name for himself in the West, which inspired him to try his luck as an author back East.

He believed that he had stumbled from one turning point to the other, allowing his temperament to react to circumstances as they arose rather than making a clear plan and sticking to it. Sometimes he had made a good choice, at other times a bad one. "Circumstance furnished the capital, and my temperament told me what to do with it. Sometimes my temperament is an ass."

The main trouble, he was convinced, is that "by temperament I was the kind of person that *does* things. Does them, and reflects afterwards. . . . I have been punished many and many a time, and bitterly, for doing things first and reflecting afterward. . . . When I am reflecting, on those occasions, even deaf persons can hear me think."[17]

Though he couldn't say it to the readers of *Harper's Bazaar*, the circumstance of finding Isabel Lyon at his elbow ready and willing to wait on him after Livy's death had started him doing things that he now had lots of time to think about. And, as Paine could have attested, Twain was doing some very loud reflecting that autumn.

"He still had violent rages now and then, remembering some of his most notable mistakes; and once, after denouncing himself, rather inclusively, as an idiot, he said: 'I wish to God the lightning would strike me; but I've wished that fifty thousand times and never got anything out of it yet.' "

All this violent reflecting only made his chest pains worse. After he had written the first part of his *Harper's Bazaar* essay, he started to read it one night to Jean and Paine, but was forced to stop. Clutching his chest, he said, "I must lie down," and Paine helped him upstairs. When he was in bed, his biographer gave him hot water, and Jean came in to make sure her father was all right. He seemed to be struggling and couldn't speak.

"We sat there several moments in silence," Paine remembered. "I think we both wondered if this might not be the end."

But the trouble passed, and soon he was feeling so much better that he insisted on getting up and playing a game of billiards.

On another occasion, when Jean came to him and said that a woman caller was waiting to see him, he waved her away with the words "Jean, I can't see her. Tell her I am likely to drop dead any minute and it would be most embarrassing."[18]

After years of being treated like an invalid, Jean now found herself in the strange position of having to look after her father. It wasn't easy. He was often grumpy, wouldn't follow his doctor's orders, and would make a fuss over little things. "Although he is very good and generous," Jean wrote her friend Marguerite Schmitt, "when he has an idea in his head, it's like melting marble with a piece of ice to make him change his mind!!"

If he opened a letter and didn't think it was worth answering, he would wad it up and throw it away. But Jean would rescue it from the wastebasket and write a reply for him. She thought that "all letters deserved the courtesy of an answer." Twain forgave her, remarking that "her mother brought her up in that kindly error."[19]

As the weather grew colder, he went outside less often, but would often stand at one of the windows and admire "the autumn splendors," with their "cozy, soft colors," and "the far hills sleeping in a dim blue trance." Though he was content to spend the winter at Stormfield, Dr. Quintard was worried that any bout with the flu or an attack of bronchitis might aggravate his heart. He advised a trip to a warmer climate, and once again Bermuda seemed the best place to go.[20]

This time, however, Twain wasn't sure he should attempt it. He thought he could make the voyage, but was worried about leaving Jean in charge of Stormfield with only the servants to keep an eye on her. He may also have felt that Bermuda now held too many painful memories as a place where he had spent a great deal of time in the company of Isabel Lyon, and where he had shared a long holiday with Rogers, whose death still weighed on his mind.

"I've got to make a trip, by the doctor's orders," he wrote Dorothy Quick. He told her that he preferred to stay home, "but I must obey, I suppose." He turned for help to Paine, who arranged the voyage and agreed to accompany him. Twain wasn't sure when they would return. "Perhaps we shall be back by the middle of December—we can't tell yet."[21]

He said goodbye to Jean, who seemed to think she could manage the big house well enough during his absence. On Saturday, November 20, he and his biographer sailed to Bermuda, arriving in Hamilton on Monday.

· · ·

THEY WERE MET at the dock by Marion Allen, the mother of his angelfish Helen, and she invited Twain to stay in the guest room at the family's bungalow, Bay House. He was happy to accept, and didn't regret passing up the chance to stay with Paine in one of the island's big hotels.

Pleased to have him back in Bermuda, Mr. and Mrs. Allen and their daughter did everything they could to make him feel comfortable in their home. Calling himself a "grateful & contented guest," he observed, "You *can't* make a home out of a hotel, & I can't be completely satisfied outside of a home."[22]

He joked that he had come to Bermuda to escape the Thanksgiving celebrations, but Marion soon realized that he had come to the island hoping that the climate would once again work its magic on his health. Over the next few weeks he did seem to improve. A change for the better was soon apparent to Paine, who visited him at Bay House nearly every day. Not long after their arrival on the island he noted that Twain "was looking wonderfully well after a night of sound sleep, his face full of color and freshness, his eyes bright and keen."[23]

Writing to Clara at the end of his first week, Twain said, "Everything—weather included—is in perfection here now. Paine & I drive in a light victoria about 3 hours every day, over the smooth hard roads, with the dainty blues & greens & purples of the sea always in sight." In a letter to Frances Nunnally, he claimed that the ocean breezes and the calm atmosphere had driven "the dyspeptic pain in my breast almost entirely away. Also the furious thoughts about Miss Lyon & Ashcroft, that pair of professional traitors & forgers."[24]

On November 30 he celebrated his seventy-fourth birthday with a quiet ceremony at Bay House. It was raining, so he sat by the fire and played cards and told stories. While he was spinning some yarn, he forgot a word and complained, "I'll forget the Lord's middle name some time, right in the midst of a storm, when I need all the help I can get." After dinner, the Allens gave him a birthday cake, and he returned the favor by treating them to a reading from *Tom Sawyer.*[25]

As another way of repaying the family for their hospitality, Twain ordered from Harper's a set of his works in the Author's National Edition, and inscribed all but four volumes for Helen. In her copy of *The Prince and the Pauper,* he wrote, "Up to 18 we don't know. Happiness consists in not knowing." When Marion noticed that he had not written anything in a few of the books, he explained that it was "so he would have to come back to finish them." In fact, he often did such things when he visited places he didn't want to leave. In the days when he used to spend the summers in Elmira, he "would never take away all his things." According to Paine, "He had an old superstition that to leave some article insured return."[26]

The Allens definitely wanted him to come back. "He was an ideal guest," Marion recalled, "enjoying everything, and most appreciative of any little thing done for his pleasure." It helped that she was an uncommonly easygoing hostess. She didn't mind that he liked to smoke in bed, and that he would usually stay there until noon, littering the sheets with pipe tobacco, matches, discarded pieces of writing paper, and some of his favorite books—Thomas Carlyle's *French Revolution,* Samuel Pepys's *Diary,* and various works by Kipling. In his gown and slippers, he would sometimes wander outside for a stroll on the lawn, oblivious to the way he looked. Marion wondered what the neighbors thought of the spectacle, but never said anything to him about it.

While he was living under her roof, she came to know him well, and he seemed to enjoy confiding in her. She liked his funny stories and appreciated his endless curiosity. In her view he was essentially a simple man with a good nature, and she believed that "all that was mean and small in others came as a surprise to him." One day he told her that he had always "craved affection, but found it very hard to express this feeling."

While Helen was away at school during the day, he and Marion would often have long conversations, and one of their favorite topics was the history of the island. He was especially intrigued by the possibility that Shakespeare's *The Tempest* might have been inspired by tales of sailors shipwrecked on Bermuda, which the play calls "the still-vex'd Bermoothes." His friend Kipling—who knew the island well and was convinced of the play's debt to reports from returning mariners—once remarked that anyone visiting "a certain beach some two miles from Hamilton will find the stage set for Act II. Scene 2 of *The Tempest*— a bare beach, with the wind singing through the scrub at the land's edge, a gap in the reefs wide enough for the passage of Stephano's butt of sack, and (these eyes have seen it) a cave in the coral within easy reach of the tide, whereto such a butt might be conveniently rolled ('My cellar is in a rock by the seaside where my wine is hid'). There is no other cave for some two miles . . . and here the currents strand wreckage."[27]

Twain would quiz Marion on the subject, checking her knowledge of local legends and culture for connections to the play. When she speculated on the various ways that Shakespeare might have picked up information on Bermuda in London, he was quick to correct her casual use of the name, saying that she must have meant to say "the man who wrote the Shakespeare plays." It was her opinion that "Caliban, with his gruntings and groanings, was probably suggested by the wild hogs which were the only sign of animal life on the island." As for Ariel, it made sense to her that a creature "who so lightly flitted about, was probably suggested by the almost always present refreshing breeze." At her suggestion, he found more information on the subject in J. H. Lefroy's two volume *Memorials of the Discovery and Early Settlement of the Bermudas or Somers Islands 1511–1687*, and this massive tome soon joined the select group of books kept on or near his bed.[28]

At peace in this home away from home, Twain paid little attention to news from the outside world. In early December he wrote Clara, "Never in my life before, perhaps, have I had such a strong sense of being *severed* from the world, & the bridges all swept away."[29]

· · ·

AT STORMFIELD, Jean was enjoying her independence and her new authority as head of her father's house in his absence. She was a good manager and reacted calmly and intelligently whenever problems arose. One night, when the new burglar alarm began ringing loudly after everyone had gone to sleep, Claude went downstairs to investigate with Jean's German shepherd at his side. Hoping the dog would chase away any burglars, Claude tried giving him commands in some of the German phrases he had heard Jean use. But he mixed them up and was frustrated when he mistakenly shouted "Leg dich!" (Lie down!), and the dog obediently stretched himself on the floor. As Twain later explained in his version of the story, which was based on an account his daughter sent him, "Jean came running, in her night clothes, & shouted 'Los!' (Go! fly! rush!) & the dog sped away like the wind, tearing the silences to tatters with his bark."[30]

Though her father wasn't eager to leave Bermuda, Jean asked him to come home for Christmas, and he agreed. He knew how much the holiday meant to her, and didn't want to disappoint her. She had big plans, making up a gift list with fifty names on it. She and Katy Leary—who had decided to remain at Stormfield after Clara's marriage—went on frequent shopping expeditions, coming home from New York with armloads of gifts, including a world globe for her father. The house was decorated with greenery, and in the loggia she and Katy put up a large Christmas tree with bits of silver foil on the branches.

On Monday, December 20, Jean was at the pier to welcome her father home. It was a gloomy, bitterly cold day, and after a month in Bermuda, the nasty weather was a shock to his system. The moment he arrived his angina began troubling him. "When I got down to Bermuda," he told the usual gang of waiting reporters, "that pain in the breast left me; now, on my return, I have got it again."[31]

The reporters tried to cheer him up, hoping he would deliver some fresh examples of his quotable humor, but they didn't have much luck. As the New York Tribune lamented the next morning, "He was not in the jovial mood so apparent on his return from the Bermudas last year with his close friend, the late H. H. Rogers. Whenever Mr. Clemens met the reporters he always had something humorous up his sleeve to drop casually when an interview was under way. It was different yesterday. The reporters clutched at straws to bring forth some droll remark."[32]

The newspaper accounts of his return were so uniformly glum that Jean worried about the effect of such stories on Clara, who would probably see them in the European press. Jean didn't want her thinking that their father's health was so bad he might die at any minute. After they got home, she urged him to send an upbeat holiday message to the Associated Press. To humor her, he dictated a brief message, and she gave it to the wire service over the telephone: "I hear the newspapers say I am dying. The charge is not true. I would not do such a thing at my time of life. I am behaving as good as I can. Merry Christmas to everybody! Mark Twain."[33]

Anxious to make their holiday celebrations a success, Jean hurried to get everything ready. She wrapped gifts, mailed cards and packages, checked menus, did her usual chores at the farm, and tried to keep her father from sneaking a peek at the Christmas display she was preparing in the loggia. On the night before Christmas Eve she was worn out and suffering from a cold. After dinner she was ready to go straight to bed, but spent an hour downstairs talking with her father, who wanted to discuss his plan for returning to Bermuda.

Would she be able to manage on her own again, he asked, if he went back in February and stayed a month or so? She agreed that he should go back, but suggested that if he waited until March, they could go together. Thrilled that she wanted to come along, he approved the idea and began talking excitedly of finding a house for their stay on the island.

With Jean's dog trailing behind, they went upstairs for bed and said good night at his door. Because of her cold, she didn't want to give him a kiss, so he bent and kissed her hand. As he later wrote, "She was moved I saw it in her eyes—& she impulsively kissed my hand in return. Then with the usual gay 'Sleep well, dear!' from both, we parted."[34]

· · ·

THE NEXT MORNING Jean was eager to ride to the post office and mail the last of her Christmas cards. As usual she was up early, and at seven she lowered herself into the tub for a quick bath. The water was cold, but that was the way she liked it. One of the maids was nearby, and became suspicious when she didn't hear anything from the bathroom for a while.

The maid called out to Katy, "Miss Jean is still in the tub. You'd better go in there, Katy."

Alarmed, Katy raced into the bathroom and saw Jean lying motionless in the tub. When she tried to lift her up, Jean's head fell against her shoulder, and she knew then that the worst had happened.

"Oh, come! Come! Miss Jean is dead," Katy cried.[35]

With the maid's help, she lifted Jean and placed her on a large towel spread across the floor. They tried to revive her, but there was no sign of life. Covering her with a sheet, Katy gave orders for the other servants to bring the nearest doctor, who lived a few miles away, and then she ran down the hall to Twain's room.

"Katy entered," he would soon write in his own anguished account of the tragedy, "stood quaking & gasping at my bedside a moment, then found her tongue: *'Miss Jean is dead!'* "

Twain wrote, "Possibly I know now what the soldier feels when a bullet crashes through his heart."

He rose from bed and made his way to her room. "In her bathroom there she lay, the fair young creature, stretched upon the floor & covered with a sheet. And looking so placid, so natural, & as if asleep."[36]

The local doctor thought at first that she had drowned as a result of losing consciousness during a seizure, but then it was decided that the seizure had caused her heart to fail, and drowning was ruled out. In any case she was always at risk of being seriously hurt or killed in the aftermath of a severe attack. Without someone close at hand and ever vigilant, she was never truly safe, and if she had escaped death in her bath one day, she might have died the next while she was working on her farm or riding. As Clara later said of her sister, "She chafed at the chains in her life which could not be entirely removed."[37]

If Dr. Peterson had not been misled by Isabel Lyon for so long, he might have had better success persuading Jean to accept her limitations and to live accordingly. But after having endured the many months of moving from place to place without a chance to see her own home, she relished her new freedom more than her safety. All her pent-up energy came out like a shot and led her in many directions at once. As a result, she pushed herself in ways that would have been discouraged at a sanitarium or even in her own home under the supervision of qualified attendants. No doubt this overexertion contributed to her death.

But no matter what Twain might have done to protect her or to improve the quality of her life, he couldn't have made her well. Knowing that, he found some comfort in the thought that she had finally been released from her long ordeal. "Now that dear sweet spirit is at rest," he wrote Twichell.[38]

As soon as he heard the news, Paine came to the house to comfort the grieving father and to stare in disbelief at Jean's lifeless body after Katy had dressed her. He had seen her at Stormfield the night before, and was now shocked to think that the vibrant young woman who had said goodbye to him on the stairs as he left was no longer alive. While he sat quietly with Twain, Katy telephoned Jervis Langdon in Elmira to discuss

The report of Jean's death in the
New York Tribune showed her in
one of her favorite photographs,
riding horseback.

funeral plans. Jervis agreed to come to Stormfield and arrange for the
body to be taken to Elmira for burial in the family plot.

Taking up his pen, Twain began writing about Jean in an effort to
fathom what had happened, and "to keep my heart from breaking." He
wrote about their last night together, her high spirits as they discussed
their plans for the coming year, and the flood of memories that now overwhelmed him, going back to her childhood when she was free of illness
and enjoying the magical life that he and Livy had created for their family in Hartford. Closing his eyes, he could see them all in their home
again, the children playing happily, and his wife at his side.

"How poor I am," he wrote in his grief, "who was once so rich!"[39]

If he went to Elmira, he knew it would kill him. He couldn't face another funeral. "He said he could never see another person belonging to
him laid in the grave," Katy recalled. The next day—Christmas—he went
downstairs to the living room, where Jean was lying in her coffin, and
said goodbye. She was wearing the white silk dress she had worn as

Clara's bridesmaid. Katy added a bright buckle that Twain had brought home from Bermuda. It was to have been one of Jean's Christmas presents.[40]

A cable was sent to Germany, giving the sad news to Clara and Ossip. Because it would take too long for them to return home, and because Ossip's health was still fragile, Twain advised the couple to stay where they were. "Clara must not grieve about Jean," he later wrote Ossip, "but rejoice that she has escaped and is free."[41]

On Christmas afternoon the skies turned dark and a steady snowfall began, blanketing the countryside. "There was not the least wind or noise," Paine recalled, "the whole world was muffled." Lanterns were placed at the door, and at six the hearse came up the drive. Standing at an upstairs window, Twain watched as the coffin was carried outside and placed in the black carriage. Downstairs, a Schubert impromptu was playing on the orchestrelle. Twain remained at the window, watching, until the hearse started on its journey and faded from view, "spectral in the falling snow."[42]

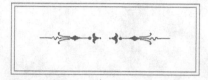

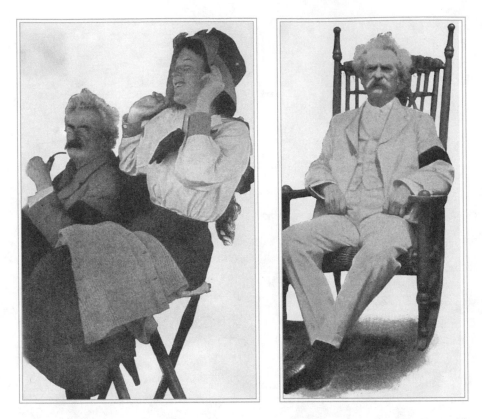

These are some of the last photographs taken of Mark Twain. The time is early April 1910, and the place is Bermuda. They are the work of Marion Schuyler Allen, whose daughter, Helen, is sitting beside Twain in the first picture. The black armband was for Jean, who had died four months earlier.

TWENTY-ONE

Revels Ended

*I am able to say that while I am not ruggedly well, I
am not ill enough to excite an undertaker.*

Mark Twain[1]

. . .

IT ALL FELL APART so quickly. In just a year and a half Twain's seemingly charmed life as a proud new homeowner in Redding had turned
tragic and left him alone and ill in a house far too large for his needs, and
already haunted by sad memories. What had he done to deserve such misfortune? He asked himself that question over and over. Bewildered by his
fate, he glanced through some of the condolence letters he was receiving
and noticed that many contained variations on the sentiment "God does
not willingly punish us."

Turning to Paine, he said, "Well, why does He do it then? We don't invite it. Why does He give Himself the trouble?"[2]

His losses weighed so heavily on him that he was beginning to wonder
why he had bothered in the last few years to build his house or compose
a single line. He vowed that his handwritten pages on Jean's death would

mark the end of his writing career, and would form the final chapter of his autobiography. There was no point in continuing it, he said. Much of his motivation for accumulating new material, and for zealously protecting his copyrights, had come from his desire to provide income for his daughters after he was gone.

But now what good could all that literary property do for a family that seemed to have disappeared before his eyes in a flash?

"Poor Jean, has no use for it now," he told himself; "Clara is happily and prosperously married & has no use for it."[3]

So much time and effort had been spent to further Clara's career ambitions, and now she was completely absorbed in her new life as Mrs. Gabrilowitsch, and was living thousands of miles away. So much time and effort had also been spent to treat Jean's illness, and to make sure that her expenses were met for as long as she lived. At her death she was still a young woman—only twenty-nine—and Twain had always assumed that she would survive him by many years. Until the very last day of her life, he was worried about what would happen to her when he was gone.

In the aftermath of her death, he told Twichell that his old habit of worrying about her future had, in her last days, become a "terror" that had cost him "much sleep." As he explained in a letter to Clara on December 29, "I was in such distress when I came to realize that you were gone far away & no one stood between her & danger but me—& I could die at any moment, & *then*—oh then what would become of her!"[4]

But now his future suddenly looked much different. For the first time in almost forty years, he was entirely on his own. And he didn't know what to do with himself. Lonely and restless, he felt that he couldn't stay at Stormfield. It was now a paradise lost. Writing to the actress Margaret Illington, he said the house "was desolation, its charm gone." Rather than linger there, enduring the cold weather and confronting sad reminders of better days, he decided to go back to Bermuda as soon as possible.[5]

Paine agreed to look after Stormfield while he was gone, and Claude was asked to accompany him on the trip, with the idea that once again Twain would stay at Bay House, and his assistant would stay at a hotel. On January 3 Paine sent an urgent letter telling the Allens that Twain would sail on the 5th, and that the author was looking forward to having his old room again if they approved. This time, however, Twain felt that it was only proper to pay for the privilege, and his biographer's letter made it clear that he wouldn't stay on any other terms.

"He feels that he could not take advantage of this generosity on your part for any length of time without some compensation. He would not feel comfortable, otherwise, and he would not be happy. He has suggested to me that you accept from him the sum of $25 per week during the period of his stay, and I sincerely hope you will not refuse to fall in with this arrangement."

Hoping to prevent any problems, Paine offered Mr. and Mrs. Allen some earnest tips on the proper care and maintenance of their famous guest. His advice was remarkably candid, and unintentionally funny. Be wary, he said, of creating too many social obligations for him. "Mr. Clemens is very impulsive, and likely to fall in with a suggestion, social or otherwise, and then be very sorry of it an hour or two later. We who have lived with and about him a long time have learned these things, and try to act accordingly."

Given the author's long history of mismanaging his business affairs, Paine was especially keen to warn the Allens not to let anyone talk their guest into making a financial investment. "He has never made an investment that brought him a return, however promising it may have seemed in the beginning. He does not wish ever to make an investment again. But, as I have said, he is impulsive, enthusiastic, and likely to fall in with the suggestion of a plan which would only mean discomfort, worry and nightmare for him later on, and he has had enough of such things. . . . If he should seek your advice in any matter, advise him only to wait a few days and think it over himself, and write to me about it."[6]

Just before he sailed Twain came down with a cold, and at the pier his biographer had to remind him to button his overcoat in the freezing weather. According to one report, his response was "that he never could remember buttons anyway, and that he had a habit of forgetting that there was weather." Before he sailed, someone asked why he wasn't taking a friend with him to Bermuda, as he had in the past. He shrugged and held up his cigar. "This is my only companion and solace. It is about all I care for now, and I have been warned about making it too constant a companion. I detest the idea of shaking him though, for he and myself have been companions such a long time."[7]

When the Allens met him on his arrival, Marion was shocked at the change in his appearance. It wasn't simply that he looked worn and a little older. It was worse than that. To her eye, Jean's death had left a terrible mark on him: "It was pathetic and unreal to see Mark Twain crushed!"

She was particularly attentive during his first day back, and commiserated with him over the loss of his daughter. The next day, when they were alone, he came to her clutching the manuscript of his comments on Jean's death, and handed it to her with tears in his eyes. "I want you to know how it all happened," he said. "I have not been able to speak of it; this will tell you."[8]

Hoping to take his mind off his sorrows, she tried to keep him active, gently easing him out of the house and accompanying him to lectures, tea parties, picnics, and concerts. One day when the weather was especially ideal, she and Helen went with him on a long tour of the island by motorboat, and Twain enjoyed himself, summing it up afterward as "several hours' swift skimming over ravishing blue seas, a brilliant sun."[9]

His spirits picked up, and he began to smile and joke in his usual manner. To Paine, he wrote, "Again I am living the ideal life.... There isn't a fault in it—good times, good home, tranquil contentment all day & every day without a break."[10]

On January 25 a front-page headline in the *New York Sun* declared, "Mark Twain's Health Good Again." That was supposedly the general impression on the island. "Passengers on the Quebec Line steamship Bermudian, which arrived here yesterday ... brought word that Mark Twain has recovered his health. They said that Mr. Clemens has donned a white suit again and is taking an active part in the social life of the resort." As the only indication of his recent loss, he wore a black armband with his suit.

Reports of dreadful weather back home made him all the more grateful to be in sunny Bermuda. "I am glad you are out of this awful winter," Howells wrote him in February from frigid New York, "where one spell of weather follows another like the rows of words in McGuffey's spelling-book. We are just starting in for our third blizzard tonight."[11]

One night he ran into his old friend Woodrow Wilson, who had recently escaped the bad weather in Princeton to enjoy a brief holiday on the island, but without the company of Mrs. Peck. Apparently, Wilson's romance with her was already in decline, but the island had drawn him back on the strength of its tranquil atmosphere, and perhaps its associations with better days. After a warm chat with the author, Wilson wrote home with the news that he was once again enjoying the company of "Mark Twain, who is staying here with such content that he says he does not see why he should ever leave Bermuda again. . . . He seems weaker than when I last saw him, but very well. He speaks of the tragical death of his daughter with touching simplicity. He is certainly one of the most human of men. I can easily understand how men like [President] Cleveland and [the actor] Joseph Jefferson learned to love him."[12]

Near the end of Wilson's stay, Twain was able to coax him into paying a visit to Bay House for a friendly game on Mr. Allen's nine-hole putting green. The score was close for eight holes, but on the last one the septuagenarian author beat the future president of the United States by sinking a long putt. It didn't seem to matter that he wasn't a golfer. Marion understood the secret of his success, pointing out that his many years at the billiards table had given him a keen eye for knocking round objects into small holes.

Before he had come to Bermuda, Twain asked himself, "Shall I ever be cheerful again, happy again?" And, even then, he had answered yes, telling himself, "My temperament has never allowed my spirits to remain depressed long at a time." Now, after a few weeks on the island, he was demonstrating the truth of that statement, reveling in the pleasures of the isolated colony and becoming immersed in the lives of his new "make-believe" family, who seemed happy to play the part. To make "the illusion more perfect," as Marion put it, he urged the family to call him by the affectionate nickname his daughters had often used for him, "Marcus."[13]

Marion thought he was at his best when the family gathered around him on rainy days, and—"storm-bound"—they gave him their complete attention. "We were in his room all day long, talking, or he would read to us. We discussed everything, including equal suffrage, in which he was a firm believer, and said that women were excusable for any lengths they went in gaining their point."[14]

He made a show of employing Helen as his secretary, dictating letters that seemed intended to entertain multiple readers—first, his young assistant and her family, and then the actual recipient. On February 15 he sent a letter to one of his bankers in New York, a former postmaster general named Thomas L. James. It begins like an ordinary business letter. The author writes to complain about a delayed parcel sent from New York to Bermuda by Wells Fargo Express. Then he shifts gears: "I mention it mainly to put you on your guard against sending anything to Bermuda or elsewhere by any express company, because the persons connected with those companies have been dead 30 years. This often causes delay."

A little while later, when a cable arrived asking Twain to make an appearance in New York on a date that had already passed, he replied, "I am very, very sorry, but all last week's dates are full. I will come week before last, if that will answer."

After Howells received one of the dictated letters, he jokingly complained in his response, "I have not got a Fairy Princess to take my profane and abusive dictation."[15]

All this dictating may have tempted Twain to write something for print, despite his vow not to do so again. He couldn't suppress his urge to tell a story or flesh out an idea, and he didn't want to be unprepared if a new work suddenly demanded to be written. In February he gave Paine a special request: "Please send me the *Standard Unabridged* that is on the table in my bedroom. I have no dictionary here."[16]

He was getting ready for a long stay, and even toyed with the notion of taking over Mr. Allen's largely honorary post as American vice consul. As always, his views were subject to change without notice. When he was feeling good, he would banish all thoughts of death and talk as if he had all the time in the world. To Elizabeth Wallace, he wrote, "I think I could live here always and be contented." And then he added, "You go to heaven if you want to—I'd druther stay here."[17]

Writing to Margaret Illington, he drew on his knowledge of Bermuda's history to portray himself as the latest in a long line of seafarers to wash up on its shores and to discover a perfect retreat. He also seemed to have in mind the example of Prospero in *The Tempest*, an exiled prince whose books are the source of his magical powers, and who was cast adrift on stormy seas until he reached his enchanted island. "My ship has gone down," he wrote Margaret, "but my raft has landed me in the Islands of the Blest, and I am as happy as any other shipwrecked sailor ever was."[18]

· · ·

THOUGH TWAIN SEEMED to be doing well, there were signs of trouble ahead. The chest pains had been mild of late, but they were always there. He tried to ignore them or to minimize their significance. If he happened to be around Helen when his angina or high blood pressure acted up, he would do his best to make a joke about it or to turn away and suffer in silence. But the problem wasn't going to disappear, especially because he refused to part company with his cigars and pipes.

"One morning," Marion was to recall, "he had a very serious bleeding of the nose in the garden, and the entire family were busy, maids, valet, and all bringing wet cloths for his relief. Amused at such a fuss being made over him, he said, with a quick chuckle, 'Helen, run quickly and get a pencil and paper, so that you can take down my last words. It is the only thing that has been forgotten.' "[19]

The family laughed off his request, even as they worried that his poor health was nothing to joke about. The nosebleed was a sign of his worsening hypertension, and it soon became obvious that he was suffering from a range of circulatory problems. His ankles began to swell, and the problem became so painful that he couldn't wear ordinary shoes. Instead he wore house slippers, shuffling around in them wherever he went, whether he was going for a walk on the lawn or to tea with some of the local dowagers.

His slippers caused Helen a great deal of embarrassment, but only because he insisted at first on wearing them with pairs of brightly colored socks. He was quite a spectacle when he left the house in his white suit with a mourning band and pink or yellow socks. Marion dropped polite hints to Claude, who usually spent part of each day at the house attending to his boss's needs. The next day Marion saw that Twain had added to Claude's list of errands the comment, "Miss Helen says I must have black socks!"[20]

To make his discomfort even worse, he came down with a cold that turned into a bad case of bronchitis. It was difficult to shake, and gave him terrible coughing fits. One visitor to Bay House recalled him complaining to her that all he did was "bark, bark all the time," and then she watched as "he started to cough, a miserable, nerve-wracking cough that shook the whole of his slight frame and left him nervous and trembling." The only thing that seemed to help was a vaporizer that Woodrow Wilson had thoughtfully recommended to him.[21]

His determination not to surrender to sickness amazed the Allens, but living in the same house with an old man in declining health wasn't easy for Helen, who was going to turn sixteen in September, and who was beginning to look and act more like a woman than a girl. She had her own friends and interests, and wasn't always willing to listen patiently while Twain talked about subjects that didn't particularly excite her. He was disappointed when she showed no interest in discussing Halley's comet or Kipling, but preferred instead to talk about "clothes & dancing & the theater."[22]

The merry figure in white who had charmed her when she was thirteen was a different man now, and she was different, too. The longer he stayed at Bay House, the harder it became for her to humor him. Her long silences annoyed him, and he took it hard. "It is as if someone to whom you were offering a politeness, has slapped you in the face; you feel that somebody's got to *speak*—or make a noise of some kind or other, the silence is so uncomfortable." Her mood wasn't helped when she caught his cold and had to spend three days in bed.

On at least a couple of occasions they quarreled, and the experience left Twain feeling miserable and bewildered. Writing in one of his notebooks, he observed that although Helen had "a most winningly sweet nature," it was "tempered by outbursts resembling the wrath of God. She will break out in an amazing fury over any little disappointment." After one unpleasant outburst, Twain blamed himself, telling Marion—who tried to soothe hurt feelings on both sides—"That is always my way, I hurt those whom I love; now I suppose I must lose all three of you just when I need you the most."[23]

Illness and his difficulties with Helen dampened whatever enthusiasm he still had left for his Angelfish Club. During the turmoil of his feud with the Ashcrofts, he had neglected his correspondence with the girls, and had come to realize that Stormfield was no longer a cheerful place for entertaining them. Now Helen was making him feel that he had suddenly worn out his welcome at Bay House, and that he was getting too old and weak to hold the interest of the young—the one group to which he had always felt the closest affinity.

Feeling unappreciated, he left the house one day without telling anyone and went off to watch a cricket match with some friends he found at the Princess Hotel. "He ran away—just as a bad boy would when he saw his chance," Marion later remarked. When he came home late, he looked sheepish and was accompanied by one of his new friends, who offered apologies for him. Afterward, Twain was appropriately contrite and was forgiven. He confided to Marion that though he didn't know much about cricket, he liked what he had seen of it and figured "it must be a good game if an entire nation thought it so."[24]

In March another angelfish—Dorothy Quick—briefly appeared in Bermuda, traveling with her mother. They stayed at the Hamilton Hotel, and Twain promptly came to see them. Unlike Helen, she was as full of admiration and affection for Twain as ever, and he was glad to see her. But she couldn't help noticing that age had suddenly caught up with him, and that his manner with her seemed strangely distant at times. He spoke with his eyes half closed and cut short the one evening they were able to be together at the Hamilton Hotel, saying that he had to retire early. "I'm not as young as you, dear," he told her as they were parting, "and I have to keep my hours."[25]

On March 22, while he and Marion were visiting the aquarium at Agar's Island, he suffered one of his most severe angina attacks. "He was so ill," she would recall, "that we feared we might not get him home." After the pain passed, he struggled to regain his composure and insisted that he could travel back to Bay House without assistance. When he made it back home, he tried to sleep but couldn't. "From this time on," wrote Marion, "he slept little, and the shortness of breath began."[26]

Fearing that he might not have much longer to live, Twain decided that he should go back to Stormfield in April and die in his own bed. On March 25 he wrote Paine that he had booked his return passage for April 23. "But don't tell anybody," he said. "I don't want it known. I may have to go sooner if the pain in my breast does not mend its ways pretty considerable. I don't want to die here, for this is an unkind place for a person in that condition. I should have to lie in the undertaker's cellar until the ship would remove me & it is dark down there & unpleasant."[27]

When he was feeling strong and jaunty, he could scoff at death and laugh at the notion of an afterlife that was anything like this life. But when he stared extinction in the eye, all he saw was his poor dead body lying by itself in a dank, cold cellar, and he didn't like it. It wasn't right.

And then, without missing a beat, he began telling Paine some of his plans for the summer, as if another change of scenery might be all that was needed to keep him going. To Clara in Europe, he also wrote of plans that went far beyond spring, discussing the idea of spending the fall with her in Berlin. One way or the other, he knew it was time to say goodbye to Bermuda. After three months of living in close quarters with his "make-believe" family, he could see that he had stayed too long, and that his illness didn't make him an easy guest—not so much for Marion, whose patience with him seemed endless, but for Helen, a restless teenager who was clearly tired of being a full-time "make-believe" granddaughter.

But Twain's talk of death was enough to make his biographer come running. After checking with the Allens and learning that their guest was indeed seriously ill, he sailed for Bermuda on April 2. Before leaving, he sent a cable advising Clara and Ossip to come home, and he also took the precaution of supplying himself with hypodermic needles and "opiates" from Dr. Quintard, just in case the patient required them to survive a return voyage. He left so quickly, however, that he didn't even bother to tell Twain he was coming.

When he entered Bay House unannounced on April 4, he found Twain sitting calmly in the bedroom looking pale and thin, but not as ill as he had been led to believe.

After welcoming him, and finding out why he had come, Twain dismissed any talk of death, saying that he had not meant for his words to be taken so seriously. "You shouldn't have come on *my* account," he said.

But when Paine spoke to the Allens he heard a different story. The local doctor believed that Twain's condition was very serious, and Mr. Allen had already arranged for the author to sail home on the 12th. To make it easier to take him directly to the ship, a tugboat had been hired to pick him up at Bay House's small landing.

For a week Paine waited and worried, fearing that Twain would die before their date of departure. Some days he seemed to be doing better, and then in the night the pains would return and leave him exhausted and fighting for breath in the morning. "That breast pain stands watch all night and the short breath all day," he said. "I am losing enough sleep to supply a worn-out army."[28]

On the morning of the 12th, Twain was so weak he couldn't be dressed, and had to be carried to the tug in a canvas chair by some of the strong sailors. He was wearing his nightclothes under a long overcoat and nursing a pipe.

A day or so before departing Bay House, he had made a point of leaving behind a rather large reminder of his visit. He opened the two-thousand-page dictionary that Paine had sent earlier in the year and wrote on the front flyleaf, "Given by Mark Twain to Marion Schuyler Allen, Bermuda, April 1910." Under normal circumstances, leaving his dictionary behind would have meant that he intended to return. But he knew that wasn't going to happen. So he parted company with it. The gesture left no doubt that his long career with words was finally at an end.[29]

It was a Prospero-like farewell, both to the island and to art. He was familiar with the relevant speech in *The Tempest*, not least because it alluded to the process from which he had taken the name Mark Twain—the use of a plummet to sound the depth of the water. As Prospero says near the end of the play, "But this rough magic / I here abjure. . . . And deeper than did ever plummet sound / I'll drown my book."[30]

· · ·

IT WAS HELL GOING HOME. For much of the voyage Twain was trying to fight off his angina, gasping for air. Paine tried to relieve his suffering with morphine injections—"hypnotic injunctions," as Twain called them—but they didn't do enough to help. At one point he was in so much agony that he begged Paine to kill him. "Can't you give me enough of the hypnotic injunction to put an end to me?" he asked.[31]

To keep him going, Paine reminded him that Ossip and Clara were also on the ocean and headed for New York, racing to be with him at Stormfield. He needed to hold on for their sake. But Twain wasn't sure he could do it. Every hour seemed to leave him weaker, and on at least one occasion he cried out that he thought he would die any minute. Yet when the ship approached New York, he was not only alive but sitting up and talking coherently.

While still at sea Paine wrote Mr. Allen, "It has been a ghastly trip for all of us, and I thank God we will soon be ashore."[32]

Around ten in the morning on Thursday, April 14, the ship docked. Robert Collier was among the friends who showed up to offer their help. He brought his best automobile and was willing to drive Twain to Stormfield or anywhere else. But the author was in such bad shape that Dr. Quintard didn't want to move him right away. It was not until the early afternoon that the doctor thought it was safe to take him to an ambulance. Claude and a porter carried his chair down the gangway as he sat slumped under heavy blankets and looked out at the skyline with a forlorn expression.

At the train station a special compartment was waiting for him on the express that would take him home. Quintard and another doctor rode beside him the whole way, and Twain felt well enough to look through the afternoon papers as the cars groaned and rattled in their usual way. On the drive from Redding station he was disappointed to see that spring was coming along slowly, and that there were only a few spots of green on the landscape.

Paine's wife, Dora, and Katy Leary were waiting for him at the door of Stormfield. He insisted on standing up and walking into his home under his own power, but he made it only a few feet and had to sit down and be carried upstairs. Against all odds, he had made it home, and that night he was able to get some sleep in his own bed, more than three months after leaving it.

Late Saturday night Ossip and Clara arrived in New York, and the next morning they came to Stormfield. There was a warm reunion, and for most of the day Twain sat up in bed talking. He apologized to Clara for not having his financial affairs in better order, and shared doubts with her about the future of his work. "He appeared skeptical," she later wrote, "as to whether the sale of his books would continue for more than a brief period after his death."[33]

He was so far removed now from contemporary literary life that he had begun to doubt his own popularity. He didn't seem to be aware that the news of his failing health was being followed anxiously by millions of people around the world. Slowly, he was withdrawing from life, looking down on it from a great height and wondering what would happen, after he was gone, to all the things he had made. It had always been difficult for him to think of the world without him in it, hovering somewhere. He knew he was dying, yet he spoke in his last days as though dying was just a phase. As soon as it was over, he would go back to doing something fun again.

His main complaint in the very last stage of his illness wasn't about the pain. That seemed to be fading. What bothered him was that his disease lacked diversions. It was almost as if he wanted to trade it for something else more interesting "This is a peculiar kind of disease," he told Paine. "It does not invite you to read; it does not invite you to be read to; it does not invite you to talk, nor to enjoy any of the usual sick-room methods of treatment. What kind of a disease is *that*?"[34]

After so many years of doing such a good job of entertaining himself and the world, he couldn't stop asking questions that were both funny and profound. And he tried to keep the old patter going right up to the end, even after his speech began to slur, and he thought no one could understand him but his foreign son-in-law, Gabrilowitsch, who may have captured his waning attention by telling him a secret. Clara was five months pregnant.

For some reason, Clara was reluctant to tell him the good news. But one of the last things he wrote may have been an attempt to question her on the subject. Written on Thursday, April 21, his one-sentence note to her is unfinished, but it seems plausible that he was trying to add to it some version of the phrase "are going to have a baby":

"Dear—You did not tell me, but I have found out that you—"[35]

He wrote the note in the morning. By the afternoon he had dozed off, and his breathing became weaker. At half past six, as the sun was going down, he slipped away. "The noble head turned a little to one side," Paine wrote, "there was a fluttering sigh, and the breath that had been unceasing through seventy-four tumultuous years had stopped forever."[36]

· · ·

Earlier that morning, before dawn, a scientific team at Harvard left their offices to go outside and look up at the sky. They were led by Professor O. C. Wendell, who had been in charge of the large telescope at the College Observatory for twenty years. For half an hour, they stared at the heavens, making notes as they watched in wonder at a spectacle no one had seen with the naked eye for almost seventy-five years.

"Harvard Observes Comet," said the headline the next day in the *New York Tribune*. The dateline was Cambridge, Massachusetts, April 21. "Visible to the naked eye for almost half an hour," the article began, "Halley's comet was watched with great interest by members of the Harvard College Observatory early to-day. The comet appeared in plain view at 3:48 A.M., and disappeared from sight at 4:12 A.M. From observations taken by Lee F. Campbell, of the observatory staff, the comet was 15 degrees east of Venus, had a tail one and one-half degrees long, and was in the fourth magnitude."[37]

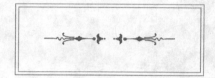

Dying man couldn't make up his mind which
place to go—both have their advantages,
"heaven for climate, hell for company!"

MARK TWAIN[1]

. . .

AFTER A FUNERAL SERVICE on Saturday, April 23, at the Brick Presbyterian Church on Fifth Avenue, during which a long stream of mourners filed past the open casket where Twain lay in his white suit, the body was taken to Elmira. On Sunday afternoon he was buried at Woodlawn Cemetery next to Livy, his son, Langdon, and his daughters Susy and Jean. During the graveside service, rain poured down and beat "fiercely against the canvas cover." Wearing a heavy black veil, Clara watched as her father was laid to rest.[2]

Life at Stormfield went on for a little while longer. Ossip and Clara lived there for most of the summer. And then in mid-August Nina Gabrilowitsch was born in Clara's room, with Katy Leary helping the doctor in the delivery. Only six weeks later the new parents and their baby girl moved to Europe. "I left behind me a home," Clara said, "which in two short years had seen a robbery, a wedding, two deaths, and a birth."[3]

In 1912, Paine's massive biography of Twain was published and earned him both high praise and considerable royalties. For the rest of his life—he died in 1937 at the age of seventy-five—he was protective of Twain's legacy, but often to the point of annoying other writers who wanted access to important papers that he controlled. As an editor of Twain's work, he took unscholarly liberties, making unwarranted changes to some of the texts. But despite his faults as a "keeper of the flame" in his later years, his biography still stands as an indispensable portrait of the man he knew so well.

For the most part, Stormfield remained vacant—standing "like a deserted castle," said a local paper—until Clara sold it in December 1922 to a couple from New York named James and Margaret Givens for $30,000. On July 25, 1923, while the house was undergoing some renovations, a fire broke out, apparently as the result of a cigarette left burning by a house painter. The destruction was devastating. The house burned to the ground, with only a brick fireplace and the archways of the loggia still standing among the smoking rubble.[4]

At the time of the fire, Clara and Ossip were living in Michigan. In 1918, Gabrilowitsch had become the conductor of the Detroit Symphony. He enjoyed a long and successful career with the orchestra and remained its leader until his death from cancer in September 1936. By that point, strangely enough, Clara had become a great believer in the religion founded by Mary Baker Eddy, and even called on a Christian Science healer to attend Gabrilowitsch in his final days.

Money left her by Ossip, and income from her father's estate, provided Clara with the means to move to California in 1939 and to buy a large Spanish-style mansion at the foot of the Hollywood Hills. Her only child, who was then an aspiring twenty-nine-year-old actor, joined her and tried getting into films. Mother and daughter got along well in California until Clara made the mistake in 1944 of marrying again.

Her new husband—a minor musician named Jacques Samossoud— was fifty and she was seventy (though she told the *Los Angeles Times* she was fifty-one). A gambler who loved horse racing, Samossoud didn't take long to do what Clara had once feared the Ashcrofts would do—he fleeced her, emptying her bank accounts to pay his gambling debts. In just the first six years of their marriage he ran through $350,000 of her money. In the process he also helped to turn mother and daughter against each other, and Nina drifted away, living on her own in Hollywood and drinking too much.

By 1951, Clara's annual trust income couldn't keep up with her husband's needs, and she was forced to do something desperate. She agreed to sell her home and many of her prized possessions. In April Jacques organized an auction that took place on the lawn, offering the public the chance to buy letters and manuscripts in Twain's hand, hundreds of books from the author's personal library, and various pieces of family furniture. At the edge of the property Jacques set up a hot dog stand to make a few extra dollars from the auction-goers, which prompted the *Los Angeles Times* to write, "At the five-acre estate, 2005 La Brea Terrace, there was the air of a circus, with none of a circus's gaiety."[5]

Clara pretended that she was tired of living in luxury and wanted to sell her things so that she and her husband wouldn't be tied down by possessions and could wander as they pleased. "Jacques and I are going to become gypsies," she declared.[6]

When Clara died eleven years later, she and Jacques were living at the Bahia Motor Hotel, where the neon sign advertised it as "San Diego's Finest Bay Resort." Her husband was continuing to spend the annual income from her father's estate as fast as it came in, and the amount was substantial. In April 1962—seven months before her death at the age of eighty-eight—the *New York Times* reported that Clara's trust fund earned $75,556 during the previous year.[7]

As Twain had fervently hoped would be the case, his work was still valuable property even fifty years after his death. Yet in spite of all his careful plans, there was one last swindler waiting to exploit his legacy. Instead of providing for the comfort of his daughter and grandchild, the estate was being used to bankroll a reckless gambler. In an odd reversal of the drama that had played out in 1909 between Twain and the Ashcrofts, Clara had become so dependent on her husband at the end of her life that she agreed to make him the principal beneficiary in her will, and to leave nothing to Nina. The will was contested, and under the pressure of expensive litigation, Jacques finally agreed to let Nina have a third of the trust income.[8]

But it was a hollow victory for Nina. After years of struggling to make a life of her own in California, and falling more and more under the influence of alcohol, she was living by herself in a small penthouse apartment overlooking Hollywood Boulevard, and was often depressed. "Nina was handicapped by being the descendant of brilliant people on both sides—her father and her grandfather," said one of her lawyers. "She was bright and had abilities, but she suffered because she felt she didn't measure up to her ancestors."[9]

One weekend in January 1966 she left her apartment at the Highland Towers and checked into a motel across the street. On Sunday night a friend went looking for her and found her lying facedown in the motel room, "which was strewn with bottles of pills and liquor." She was only fifty-five at the time of her death. As the obituaries noted, she was Mark Twain's last direct descendant.[10]

Jacques Samossoud, the inveterate gambler who spent twenty-two years wasting Mark Twain's money on bad bets, died only five months after Nina.

And what of the couple whom Twain banished for plotting to seize control of his estate in 1909? For years, Clara worried that they would resurface and try to lay claim to her inheritance or to sell some stolen manuscript, but she had little to fear from them. After only a few years of marriage the Ashcrofts went their separate ways and finally divorced in the early 1920s. To her deep dismay, Isabel discovered that Ralph was "fundamentally dishonest," as she put it, and "very unsatisfactory" as a husband.[11]

Moving to Canada, Ashcroft became an executive in advertising and broadcasting. He was the manager of the Trans-Canada Broadcasting Company and is frequently mentioned as a radio pioneer in a scholarly study of Canadian broadcasting by Mary Vipond, *Listening In*. He remarried and won respect in his new hometown of Toronto as a talented businessman. He died there in 1947.[12]

Isabel's life after her marriage was humdrum. She found a job as a purchasing agent at the Home Title Insurance Company in Brooklyn and worked there for a quarter of a century. But her heart was still drawn toward the area of Manhattan where she had enjoyed her best years as Twain's secretary. In the 1930s she found a small apartment at 7 Charles Street, only a few blocks away from 21 Fifth Avenue, and stayed there for the rest of her life. She was almost ninety-five when she died in 1958.

Shortly before her death, she was visited by a young actor who was working to refine his performance as Mark Twain in a one-man show, which he had been trying out at various small venues, including a Greenwich Village nightclub not far from her apartment. "She impressed me very strongly," Hal Holbrook would recall, "and the image of Mark Twain which she gave to me is the strongest one I have and, I believe, the truest one."[13]

In April 1959, five months after Isabel died, Holbrook made his debut at New York's Forty-first Street Theater in *Mark Twain Tonight!* It was an overnight sensation that brought the author to life in such a convincing fashion that critics lavished praise on Holbrook for bringing a new generation "close to Mark Twain and a roaring period in American life." The young actor was only thirty-four at the time, but with the proper makeup, a white wig and mustache, a convincing drawl, a well-paced delivery, a mischievous twinkle in the eye, a black cigar, and—of course—a white suit, he made it possible for New Yorkers to imagine for a moment that Mark Twain had never left.[14]

ACKNOWLEDGMENTS

Every student of Twain's life must be thankful for the Mark Twain Project at the University of California's Bancroft Library in Berkeley, which holds the original or a copy of all known Mark Twain letters—more than ten thousand. The library also has an enormous archive of the author's unpublished tales, travel pieces, essays, notebooks, and family papers, as well as interviews and uncollected articles from hundreds of periodicals. The Berkeley collection is so vast that no visitor could begin to make sense of it without considerable help from the resident team of scholars who use it every day.

I owe my largest debt of thanks to the editor and curator of Twain's papers at the Mark Twain Project, Robert H. Hirst, who gave me unfettered access to the files, and who generously shared his encyclopedic knowledge of the man and the works. During my several visits to Berkeley he was always a kind host and frequently put aside his own business to help me navigate the vast sea of papers under his charge. His colleagues were also unfailingly supportive. I received expert guidance and encouragement from Robert Pack Browning, Victor Fischer, Michael B. Frank, Lin Salamo, Kenneth M. Sanderson, and Harriet Elinor Smith. In their labors as custodians of the archives, and as scrupulous editors of Twain's work, this scholarly group has made an invaluable contribution to American literature and has eased the burdens of every researcher who follows in their footsteps.

My understanding and appreciation of my subject have also been enhanced by the efforts of many other scholars and critics, beginning with the pioneering work of Twain's official biographer, Albert Bigelow Paine, who preserved hundreds of vital documents and interviewed a number of crucial sources during the early 1900s. Above all, Paine had the advantage of intimate acquaintance with the author. Although his long, rambling biography may strike modern readers as old-fashioned and sentimental, it is indispensable for its vivid portrait of the literary lion in winter. The reader is given a strong sense of what it was like to be in Mark Twain's company—to observe his physical features and movements, to hear his jokes and opinions. Also of great usefulness are biographical and critical works by Howard Baetzhold, Louis J. Budd, Harold K. Bush, Jr., John Cooley, James M. Cox, Paul Fatout, Shelley Fisher Fishkin, Alan Gribben, Donald Hoffmann, Michael Kiskis, Edward Connery Lathem, Karen Lystra, Bruce Michelson, R. Kent Rasmussen, Gary Scharnhorst, Barbara Schmidt, Laura Skandera Trombley, and Dixon Wecter.

Several people helped me during my visits to locations associated with Mark Twain and his family, including a number of friendly guides and residents who offered useful information in Bermuda, Elmira, Hannibal, Hartford, Redding, and Virginia City. I especially want to acknowledge Amanda Outerbridge—former director of the Bermuda National Trust—for her gracious assistance during one of my visits to the island; and Dr. Paul Rutkowski for giving me a tour of his farm in Redding, Connecticut, which once belonged to Albert Bigelow Paine, and for showing me the original location of Mark Twain's Stormfield. In Hollywood Robert Tymchuk and Brenda Mattox showed me the penthouse apartment where Nina Gabrilowitsch lived until just before her suicide brought the Clemens line to an end.

I also want to thank several of my former colleagues at the London *Daily Telegraph* and the *Baltimore Sun* who gave me encouragement and support during my work on this book: John Coldstream, Paul Davies, Sir Max Hastings, Charles Moore, Mike Ollove, Michael Pakenham, Richard Preston, George Thwaites, Melissa Whitworth, and especially Corinna Honan, an ideal editor whose help was indispensable.

For assistance of various kinds I want to acknowledge Brenda J. Bailey, Ronald Baker, Keith Byerman, Thomas Derrick, Mary Ann

Duncan, Joe and Nancy Fisher, Kit Kincade, Julie Loehr, Dr. Lee McKinley, Maria McKinley, the late Charles M. Nelles, Robert Perrin, Mary Burch Ratliff, Dr. Wesley Ratliff, Nicole Remesnik, June Shelden, Dorothy Stowe, Judy Tribble, and Robert E. Van Est.

Special thanks are due to my agent and friend, Bill Hamilton, who has been a patient and steadfast supporter of this book from the very beginning.

Editorial suggestions from Kate Medina and Frankie Jones have done much to improve this book, and I am grateful to them for their expert help. I also want to thank Millicent Bennett for skillfully guiding me through the publication process. In the final production stage I am very fortunate to have benefited from the steady diligence of Steve Messina and his colleague Judy Eda.

For their love and unfailing encouragement, I am immeasurably indebted to Sue, Sarah, and Vanessa.

SOURCES AND BIBLIOGRAPHY

Unless otherwise indicated, CU-MARK is the source of all references in the notes to letters and other manuscript materials. The Mark Twain Collection at the University of California, Berkeley, has made available to me either the originals or their copies acquired from other collections.

ABBREVIATIONS

Names

CC	Clara Clemens
HHR	Henry H. Rogers
IVL	Isabel V. Lyon (When not coupled with the name of a correspondent, this abbreviation refers to entries in Isabel Lyon's journals, copies of which are in CU-MARK.)
JC	Jean Clemens (When not coupled with the name of a correspondent, this abbreviation refers to entries in Jean Clemens's journals, copies of which are in CU-MARK.)
MT	Mark Twain (Samuel L. Clemens)
WDH	William D. Howells

Manuscript Sources

AD	Autobiographical Dictations by Mark Twain (typescript in CU-MARK)
AFB	American Foundation for the Blind
BmuHA	Bermuda Archives, Hamilton, Bermuda
CLjC	James S. Copley Library, La Jolla, California
CtHSD	Stowe-Day Memorial Library and Historical Foundation, Hartford, Connecticut
CU-MARK	University of California Library, Berkeley, Mark Twain Collection
DSI-AAA	Smithsonian Institution, Archives of American Art, Washington, D.C.

LOC	Library of Congress, Washington, D.C.
MMP	Private Collection, courtesy of Mary M. Palmer, Canaan Town Clerk, Connecticut
NjWoE	Edison National Historic Site, West Orange, New Jersey
NYAML	New York Academy of Medicine Library, New York City
ViU	University of Virginia Library, Charlottesville

Books

Because the major books Twain published in his lifetime are available in so many different editions, I cite only chapter numbers for these works in my notes and don't abbreviate the titles.

Autob/AMT	*The Autobiography of Mark Twain.* Ed. Charles Neider. New York: Harper & Row, 1959.
Autob/MTA	*Mark Twain's Autobiography.* Ed. Albert Bigelow Paine. 2 vols. New York: Harper & Brothers, 1924.
Autob/MTIE	*Mark Twain in Eruption: Hitherto Unpublished Pages About Men and Events.* Ed. Bernard DeVoto. New York: Harper & Brothers, 1940.
Autob/NAR	*Mark Twain's Own Autobiography: The Chapters from the "North American Review."* Ed. Michael J. Kiskis. Madison: University of Wisconsin Press, 1990.
BAMT	*The Bible According to Mark Twain: Writings on Heaven, Eden, and the Flood.* Ed. Howard G. Baetzhold and Joseph B. McCullough. Athens: University of Georgia Press, 1995.
CT	*Collected Tales, Sketches, Speeches, and Essays.* Ed. Louis J. Budd. 2 vols. New York: Library of America, 1992.
Fab. of Man	*Mark Twain's Fables of Man.* Ed. John S. Tuckey. Berkeley: University of California Press, 1972.
HF & TS	*Huck Finn and Tom Sawyer Among the Indians and Other Unfinished Stories.* Ed. Dahlia Armon and Walter Blair. Berkeley: University of California Press, 1989.
Lets. Earth	*Letters from the Earth: Uncensored Writings.* Ed. Bernard DeVoto. New York: Harper & Row, 1962.
LFA	Howells, William Dean. *Literary Friends and Acquaintance: A Personal Retrospect of American Authorship.* Ed. David F. Hiatt and Edwin H. Cady. Bloomington: Indiana University Press, 1968.
Ltrs-1	*Mark Twain's Letters, Vol. 1, 1853–1866.* Ed. Edgar Marquess Branch, Michael B. Frank, and Kenneth M. Sanderson. Berkeley: University of California Press, 1988.
Ltrs-2	*Mark Twain's Letters, Vol. 2, 1867–1868.* Ed. Harriet Elinor Smith, Richard Bucci, and Lin Salamo. Berkeley: University of California Press, 1990.
Ltrs-4	*Mark Twain's Letters, Vol. 4, 1870–1871.* Ed. Victor Fischer, Michael B. Frank, and Lin Salamo. Berkeley: University of California Press, 1995.
Ltrs-5	*Mark Twain's Letters, Vol. 5, 1872–1873.* Ed. Harriet Elinor Smith and Lin Salamo. Berkeley: University of California Press, 1997.
Ltrs-6	*Mark Twain's Letters, Vol. 6, 1874–1875.* Ed. Michael B. Frank and Harriet Elinor Smith. Berkeley: University of California Press, 2002.
Ltrs-Angelfish	*Mark Twain's Aquarium: The Samuel Clemens Angelfish Correspondence, 1905–1910.* Ed. John Cooley. Athens: University of Georgia Press, 1991.

Ltrs-Fairbanks   *Mark Twain to Mrs. Fairbanks.* Ed. Dixon Wecter. San Marino, California: Huntington Library, 1949.

Ltrs-Howells   *Mark Twain–Howells Letters: The Correspondence of Samuel L. Clemens and William D. Howells.* Ed. Henry Nash Smith and William M. Gibson. 2 vols. Cambridge: Harvard University Press, 1960.

Ltrs-Mary   *Mark Twain's Letters to Mary.* Ed. Lewis Leary. New York: Columbia University Press, 1963.

Ltrs/Paine   *Mark Twain's Letters.* Ed. Albert Bigelow Paine. New York: Harper & Brothers, 1917.

Ltrs-Publs   *Mark Twain's Letters to His Publishers, 1867–1894.* Ed. Hamlin Hill. Berkeley: University of California Press, 1967.

Ltrs-Rogers   *Mark Twain's Correspondence with Henry Huttleston Rogers, 1893–1909.* Ed. Lewis Leary. Berkeley: University of California Press, 1969.

MSM   *Mark Twain's Mysterious Stranger Manuscripts.* Ed. William M. Gibson. Berkeley: University of California Press, 1969.

MTB   Paine, Albert Bigelow. *Mark Twain: A Biography; the personal and literary life of Samuel Langhorne Clemens, by Albert Bigelow Paine; with letters, comments and incidental writings hitherto unpublished; also new episodes, anecdotes, etc.* New York: Harper & Brothers, 1912.

MTFWE   *Mark Twain's Four Weeks in England, 1907.* Ed. Edward Connery Lathem. Hartford, Connecticut: Mark Twain House and Museum, 2006.

MT & JB   Baetzhold, Howard G. *Mark Twain and John Bull: The British Connection.* Bloomington: Indiana University Press, 1970.

MTMB   *Mark Twain's Travels with Mr. Brown. Being Heretofore Uncollected Sketches Written by Mark Twain for the San Francisco "Alta California" in 1866 & 1867.* Ed. Franklin Walker and G. Ezra Dane. New York: Alfred A. Knopf, 1940.

MTN   *Mark Twain's Notebook.* Ed. Albert Bigelow Paine. New York: Harper & Brothers, 1935.

MTS   *Mark Twain's Speeches.* New York: Harper & Brothers, 1910.

MT Speaking   *Mark Twain Speaking.* Ed. Paul Fatout. Iowa City: University of Iowa Press, 1976.

MTSFH   *Mark Twain Speaks for Himself.* Ed. Paul Fatout. West Lafayette, Indiana: Purdue University Press, 1997 [1978].

MTTCI   *Mark Twain: The Complete Interviews.* Ed. Gary Scharnhorst. Tuscaloosa: University of Alabama Press, 2006.

MTWS   *Mark Twain's Weapons of Satire: Anti-Imperialist Writings on the Philippine-American War.* Ed. Jim Zwick. Syracuse, New York: Syracuse University Press, 1992.

N&J-1   *Mark Twain's Notebooks and Journals. Vol. 1: 1855–1873.* Ed. Frederick Anderson, Michael B. Frank, and Kenneth M. Sanderson. Berkeley: University of California Press, 1975.

N&J-2   *Mark Twain's Notebooks and Journals. Vol. 2: 1877–1883.* Ed. Frederick Anderson, Lin Salamo, and Bernard L. Stein. Berkeley: University of California Press, 1975.

N&J-3   *Mark Twain's Notebooks and Journals. Vol. 3: 1883–1891.* Ed. Robert Pack Browning, Michael B. Frank, and Lin Salamo. Berkeley: University of California Press, 1979.

Newspapers

NYEW   *New York Evening World*
NYT   *New York Times*
NY Trib   *New York Tribune*
WP   *Washington Post*
WSJ   *Wall Street Journal*

BIBLIOGRAPHY

Aldrich, Lilian. *Crowding Memories.* Boston: Houghton Mifflin, 1920.

Andrews, Kenneth Richmond. *Nook Farm, Mark Twain's Hartford Circle.* Cambridge: Harvard University Press, 1950.

Arthur, Anthony. *Radical Innocent: Upton Sinclair.* New York: Random House, 2006.

Bair, Deirdre. *Jung: A Biography.* Boston: Little, Brown, 2003.

Barrymore, Ethel. *Memories: An Autobiography.* New York: Harper & Brothers, 1955.

Beard, Dan. *Hardly a Man Is Now Alive: The Autobiography of Dan Beard.* New York: Doubleday, Doran, 1939.

Belford, Barbara. *Bram Stoker: A Biography of the Author of "Dracula."* New York: Alfred A. Knopf, 1996.

Bennett, Arnold. *Your United States: Impressions of a First Visit.* New York: Harper & Brothers, 1912.

Bernays, Anne, and Justin Kaplan. *Back Then: Two Literary Lives in 1950s New York.* New York: Harper Perennial, 2003.

Berret, Anthony J. *Mark Twain and Shakespeare: A Cultural Legacy.* Lanham, Maryland: University Press of America, 1993.

Bierman, John. *Dark Safari: The Life Behind the Legend of Henry Morton Stanley.* London: Sceptre, 1990.

Biographical Directory of Fellows and Members of the American Psychiatric Association. New York: Bowker, 1963.

Bispham, David. *A Quaker Singer's Recollections.* New York: Macmillan, 1920.

Brooks, Van Wyck. *The Ordeal of Mark Twain.* New York: E. P. Dutton, 1920.

Budd, Louis J. *Mark Twain: Social Philosopher.* Bloomington: Indiana University Press, 1962.

——. *Our Mark Twain: The Making of His Public Personality.* Philadelphia: University of Pennsylvania Press, 1983.

Burke, Billie. *With a Feather on My Nose.* New York: Appleton-Century-Crofts, 1949.

Bush, Harold K. *Mark Twain and the Spiritual Crisis of His Age.* Tuscaloosa: University of Alabama Press, 2007.

Bynner, Witter. *Selected Letters.* Ed. James Kraft. New York: Farrar, Straus & Giroux, 1981.

Cameron, Mabel Ward. *The Biographical Cyclopaedia of American Women.* 2 vols. New York: Halvord, 1924–1925.

Camfield, Gregg. *The Oxford Companion to Mark Twain.* New York: Oxford University Press, 2003.

Carnegie, Andrew. *Autobiography of Andrew Carnegie.* Boston: Northeastern University Press, 1986 [1920].

Cather, Willa. *Collected Stories.* New York: Vintage, 1992.

Chernow, Ron. *The House of Morgan: An American Banking Dynasty and the Rise of Modern Finance.* New York: Grove, 1990.

——. *Titan: The Life of John D. Rockefeller, Sr.* New York: Random House, 1998.

Chotzinoff, Samuel. *A Lost Paradise: Early Reminiscences.* New York: Alfred A. Knopf, 1955.

Clemens, Clara. *My Father, Mark Twain.* New York: Harper & Brothers, 1931.

——. *My Husband, Gabrilowitsch.* New York: Harper, 1938.

Coburn, Alvin Langdon. *Alvin Langdon Coburn, Photographer: An Autobiography.* Ed. Helmut Gerusheim and Alison Gernsheim. New York: Dover, 1978 [1966].

A Companion to Mark Twain. Ed. Peter Messent and Louis J. Budd. Oxford: Blackwell, 2005.

Conway, Moncure Daniel. *Autobiography.* 2 vols. Boston: Houghton Mifflin, 1904.

Copyright Hearings, December 7 to 11, 1906, Arguments Before the Committees on Patents of the Senate and House of Representatives, Conjointly, on the Bills S.6330 and H.R. 19853. Washington, D.C.: Government Printing Office, 1906.

Cortissoz, Royal. *The Life of Whitelaw Reid.* 2 vols. New York: Scribner's, 1921.

Cotton, Michelle L. *Mark Twain's Elmira: 1870–1910.* Elmira, New York: Chemung County Historical Society, 1985.

Cox, James M. *Mark Twain: The Fate of Humor.* Princeton: Princeton University Press, 1966.

Crews, Frederick. *The Critics Bear It Away: American Fiction and the Academy.* New York: Random House, 1992.

Critical Essays on Mark Twain, 1867–1910. Ed. Louis J. Budd. Boston: G. K. Hall, 1982.

Davis, Malcolm W., and "Henry Williams." *In the Clutch of Circumstance: My Own Story by a Burglar.* New York: D. Appleton, 1922.

De Courcy, Anne. *The Viceroy's Daughters: The Lives of the Curzon Sisters.* New York: Harper Perennial, 2003.

Devinsky, Orrin. *Epilepsy: Patient and Family Guide.* Philadelphia: F. A. Davis, 2002.

Dias, Earl J. *Mark Twain and Henry Huttleston Rogers: An Odd Couple.* Fairhaven, Massachusetts: Millicent Library, 1984.

Dolmetsch, Carl. *"Our Famous Guest": Mark Twain in Vienna.* Athens: University of Georgia Press, 1992.

Duncombe, Frances. *Katonah: The History of a New York Village and Its People.* Katonah, New York: The Society, 1961.

Edel, Leon. *Henry James: A Life.* One-volume edition. New York: Harper & Row, 1985 [1953–1972].

Etherington-Smith, Meredith, and Jeremy Pilcher. *The "It" Girls: Lucy, Lady Duff Gordon, the Couturière "Lucile," and Elinor Glyn, Romantic Novelist.* San Diego: Harcourt Brace, 1986.

Fatout, Paul. *Mark Twain on the Lecture Circuit.* Bloomington: Indiana University Press, 1960.

Faude, Wilson. *The Renaissance of Mark Twain's House.* Larchmont, New York: Queens House, 1978.

Fishkin, Shelley Fisher. *Lighting Out for the Territory: Reflections on Mark Twain and American Culture.* New York: Oxford University Press, 1997.

——. *Was Huck Black? Mark Twain and African-American Voices.* New York: Oxford University Press, 1993.

Foster, R. F. *W. B. Yeats: A Life.* 2 vols. Oxford: Oxford University Press, 1997–2003.

Friedlander, Walter J. *The History of Modern Epilepsy: The Beginning, 1865–1914.* Westport, Connecticut: Greenwood, 2001.

Fulton, Joe B. *The Reverend Mark Twain: Theological Burlesque, Form, and Content.* Columbus: Ohio State University Press, 2006.

Garland, Hamlin. *Hamlin Garland's Diaries.* Ed. Donald Pizer. San Marino, California: Huntington Library, 1968.

——. *Roadside Meetings*. New York: Macmillan, 1930.

Gill, Gillian. *Mary Baker Eddy*. Reading, Massachusetts: Perseus, 1998.

Gillman, Susan. *Dark Twins: Imposture and Identity in Mark Twain's America*. Chicago: University of Chicago Press, 1989.

Gilmour, David. *Curzon: Imperial Statesman*. New York: Farrar, Straus & Giroux, 2003.

Giroud, Françoise. *Alma Mahler or the Art of Being Loved*. Oxford: Oxford University Press, 1991.

Glyn, Anthony. *Elinor Glyn: A Biography*. London: Hutchinson, 1968 [1955].

Glyn, Elinor. *Three Weeks*. New York: Duffield, 1909 [1907].

Goodman, Susan, and Carl Dawson. *William Dean Howells: A Writer's Life*. Berkeley: University of California Press, 2005.

Gottschalk, Stephen. *Rolling Away the Stone: Mary Baker Eddy's Challenge to Materialism*. Bloomington: Indiana University Press, 2006.

Grace King of New Orleans: A Selection of Her Writings. Ed. Robert Bush. Baton Rouge: Louisiana State University Press, 1973.

Gribben, Alan. *Mark Twain's Library: A Reconstruction*. 2 vols. Boston: G. K. Hall, 1980.

Harnsberger, Caroline Thomas. *Mark Twain, Family Man*. New York: Citadel, 1960.

——. *Mark Twain's Clara*. Evanston, Illinois: W. Schori, 1982.

Harper, J. Henry. *The House of Harper: A Century of Publishing in Franklin Square*. New York: Harper & Brothers, 1912.

Hawthorne, Hildegarde. *The Lure of the Garden*. New York: Century, 1911.

Hayward, Walter Brownell. *Bermuda Past and Present*. New York: Dodd, Mead, 1911.

Henderson, Archibald. *Mark Twain*. London: Duckworth, 1911.

Herts, Alice M. *The Children's Educational Theatre*. New York: Harper & Brothers, 1911.

Hill, Hamlin. *Mark Twain, God's Fool*. New York: Harper & Row, 1973.

A Historical Guide to Mark Twain. Ed. Shelley Fisher Fishkin. Oxford: Oxford University Press, 2002.

Hodgson, Godfrey. *Woodrow Wilson's Right Hand: The Life of Colonel Edward M. House*. New Haven: Yale University Press, 2006.

Hoffmann, Donald. *Mark Twain in Paradise: His Voyages to Bermuda*. Columbia: University of Missouri Press, 2006.

Holmes, Thom. *Electronic and Experimental Music*. New York: Routledge, 2002.

Hoopes, James. *Van Wyck Brooks: In Search of American Culture*. Amherst: University of Massachusetts Press, 1977.

Howe, Irving. *World of Our Fathers*. New York: Harcourt Brace, 1976.

Howells, William Dean. *Selected Letters*. 6 vols. Ed. William C. Fischer and Christoph K. Lohmann. Boston: Twayne, 1979–1983.

——. *Selected Literary Criticism*. Vol. 3: 1898–1920. Bloomington: Indiana University Press, 1993.

Hubbard, Elbert. *Little Journeys to the Homes of the Great*. Vol. 11. New York: William H. Wise, 1916.

Hulbert, Mary Allen. *The Story of Mrs. Peck: An Autobiography*. New York: Minton, Balch, 1933.

Hutton, Laurence. *Talks in a Library*. New York: G. P. Putnam's, 1905.

Ingersoll, Ernest. *Rand, McNally & Co.'s Handy Guide to Washington and the District of Columbia*. Chicago: Rand, McNally, 1897.

The Intimate Papers of Colonel House. Ed. Charles Seymour. 4 vols. Boston: Houghton Mifflin, 1926–1928.

Irwin, Wallace. *At the Sign of the Dollar*. New York: Fox Duffield, 1905.

James, Henry. *The American Scene*. Ed. Leon Edel. Bloomington: Indiana University Press, 1968 [1907].

Johnson, Merle. *A Bibliography of the Work of Mark Twain, Samuel Langhorne Clemens*. New York: Harper & Brothers, 1910.

Johnson, Robert Underwood. *Remembered Yesterdays*. Boston: Little, Brown, 1923.

Johnson, Willis Fletcher. *George Harvey: A Passionate Patriot*. Boston: Houghton Mifflin, 1929.

Josephson, Matthew. *The Robber Barons: The Great American Capitalists, 1861–1901*. San Diego: Harcourt Brace, 1962 [1934].

Kaplan, Fred. *The Singular Mark Twain: A Biography*. New York: Doubleday, 2003.

Kaplan, Justin. *Mr. Clemens and Mark Twain: A Biography*. New York: Simon & Schuster, 1966.

Keller, Helen. *Midstream: My Later Life*. Garden City, New York: Sun Dial Press, 1937 [1929].

———. *Selected Writings*. Ed. Kim E. Nielsen. New York: New York University Press, 2005.

———. *The Story of My Life: The Restored Edition*. Ed. James Berger. New York: Modern Library, 2003 [1903].

King, Grace. *Memories of a Southern Woman of Letters*. New York: Macmillan, 1932.

Kipling, Rudyard. *From Sea to Sea: Letters of Travel*. 2 vols. New York: Doubleday & McClure, 1899.

———. *The Letters of Rudyard Kipling*. Vol. 3: 1900–1910. Ed. Thomas Pinney. Iowa City: University of Iowa Press, 1996.

Klein, Maury. *The Life and Legend of E. H. Harriman*. Chapel Hill: University of North Carolina Press, 2000.

Kunhardt, Philip B., Jr., Philip B. Kunhardt III, and Peter W. Kunhardt. *P. T. Barnum: America's Greatest Showman*. New York: Alfred A. Knopf, 1995.

Lash, Joseph P. *Helen and Teacher: The Story of Helen Keller and Anne Sullivan Macy*. New York: AFB Press, 1997 [1980].

Lawson, Thomas W. *Frenzied Finance: The Crime of Amalgamated*. New York: Ridgway-Thayer, 1906.

Lawton, Mary. *A Lifetime with Mark Twain: The Memories of Katy Leary, for Thirty Years His Faithful and Devoted Servant*. New York: Harcourt, Brace, 1925.

Lefroy, J. H. *Memorials of the Discovery and Early Settlement of the Bermudas or Somers Islands, 1515–1685*. 2 vols. London: Longmans, Green, 1879.

Lessard, Suzannah. *The Architect of Desire: Beauty and Danger in the Stanford White Family*. New York: Dial, 1996.

Levin, Phyllis Lee. *Edith and Woodrow: The Wilson White House*. New York: Scribner, 2001.

Limerick, Patricia. *The Legacy of Conquest: The Unbroken Past of the American West*. New York: W. W. Norton, 1987.

Long, E. Hudson. *Mark Twain Handbook*. New York: Hendricks House, 1957.

Lorant, Stefan. *The Life and Times of Theodore Roosevelt*. Garden City, New York: Doubleday, 1959.

Lowell, James Russell. *Letters of James Russell Lowell*. Ed. Charles Eliot Norton. 2 vols. New York: Harper & Brothers, 1893.

Lucy, Henry W. *Sixty Years in the Wilderness*. London: Smith, Elder, 1909.

Lystra, Karen. *Dangerous Intimacy: The Untold Story of Mark Twain's Final Years*. Berkeley: University of California Press, 2004.

Macnaughton, William R. *Mark Twain's Last Years as a Writer*. Columbia: University of Missouri Press, 1979.

Mahler, Alma. *Gustav Mahler: Memories and Letters*. New York: Viking, 1969.

Manchester, William. *The Last Lion: Winston Spencer Churchill; Visions of Glory, 1874–1932*. New York: Dell, 1989 [1983].

Mark Twain: The Contemporary Reviews. Ed. Louis J. Budd. Cambridge: Cambridge University Press, 1999.

Mark Twain: The Critical Heritage. Ed. Frederick Anderson. London: Routledge & Kegan Paul, 1971.

The Mark Twain Encyclopedia. Ed. J. R. LeMaster and James D. Wilson. New York: Garland, 1993.

Mark Twain in Elmira. Ed. Robert D. Jerome and Herbert A. Wisbey, Jr. Elmira, New York: Mark Twain Society, 1977.

Mark Twain in Hartford. Hartford: Mark Twain Memorial, 1958.

Mark Twain's Helpful Hints for Good Living: A Handbook for the Damned Human Race. Ed. Lin Salamo, Victor Fischer, and Michael B. Frank. Berkeley: University of California Press, 2004.

Masters, Brian. *Now Barabbas Was a Rotter: The Extraordinary Life of Marie Corelli*. London: Hamish Hamilton, 1978.

Michelson, Bruce. *Mark Twain on the Loose: A Comic Writer and the American Self*. Amherst: University of Massachusetts Press, 1995.

Milford, Nancy. *Savage Beauty: The Life of Edna St. Vincent Millay*. New York: Random House, 2001.

Milmine, Georgine [Willa Cather]. *The Life of Mary Baker G. Eddy*. Grand Rapids, Michigan: Baker Book House, 1971 [1909].

Moore, Patrick, and John Mason. *The Return of Halley's Comet*. New York: W. W. Norton, 1984.

Morris, Edmund. *Theodore Rex*. New York: Random House, 2001.

Morrison, Michael A. *John Barrymore: Shakespearean Actor*. Cambridge: Cambridge University Press, 1997.

Mosley, Oswald. *My Life*. London: Thomas Nelson, 1968.

Nasaw, David. *Andrew Carnegie*. New York: Penguin, 2006.

The National Cyclopedia of American Biography. New York: James T. White, 1940.

Nesbit, Evelyn. *Prodigal Days: The Untold Story*. New York: Messner, 1934.

Nevins, Allan. *Study in Power: John D. Rockefeller, Industrialist and Philanthropist*. 2 vols. New York: Scribner's, 1953.

Newcomb, Ethel. *Leschetizky as I Knew Him*. New York: Da Capo, 1967.

Orwell, George. *Essays*. Everyman's Library edition. New York: Alfred A. Knopf, 2002.

Osborn, Henry Fairfield. *The American Museum of Natural History: Its Origin, Its History, the Growth of Its Departments, to December 31, 1909*. New York: Irving Press, 1911.

O'Toole, Patricia. *When Trumpets Call: Theodore Roosevelt After the White House*. New York: Simon & Schuster, 2005.

The Outrageous Mark Twain: Some Lesser-Known but Extraordinary Works. Ed. Charles Neider. New York: Doubleday, 1987.

Paine, Albert Bigelow. *Captain Bill McDonald, Texas Ranger: A Story of Frontier Reform*. Austin, Texas: State House Press, 1986 [1909].

——. *Dwellers in Arcady: The Story of an Abandoned Farm*. New York: Harper & Brothers, 1919.

——. *The Lure of the Mediterranean: The Ship Dwellers: A Story of a Happy Cruise*. New York: Harper & Brothers, 1910.

Peel, Robert. *Mary Baker Eddy: The Years of Authority*. Boston: Christian Science Publishing Society, 1982 [1977].

Phelps, William Lyon. *Autobiography with Letters*. New York: Oxford University Press, 1939.

Pond, James B. *Eccentricities of Genius: Memories of Famous Men and Women of the Platform and Stage*. New York: G. W. Dillingham, 1900.

Powers, Ron. *Mark Twain: A Life*. New York: Free Press, 2005.

Preston, Douglas. *Dinosaurs in the Attic: An Excursion into the American Museum of Natural History*. New York: St. Martin's, 1986.

Quick, Dorothy. *Mark Twain and Me: A Little Girl's Friendship with Mark Twain*. (Originally published as *Enchantment: A Little Girl's Friendship with Mark Twain*.) Norman: University of Oklahoma Press, 1961.

Rasmussen, R. Kent. *Mark Twain A to Z: The Essential Reference to His Life and Writings*. New York: Facts on File, 1995.

Reid, H. *The Virginian Railway*. Milwaukee: Kalmbach, 1961.

Ridley, Jo Ann. *Looking for Eulabee Dix: The Illustrated Biography of an American Miniaturist*. Washington, D.C.: National Museum of Women in the Arts, 1997.

Robertson-Lorant, Laurie. *Melville: A Biography*. New York: Clarkson Potter, 1996.

Roosevelt, Theodore. *Letters to Kermit from Theodore Roosevelt, 1902–1908*. Ed. Will Irwin. New York: Scribner's, 1946.

———. *The Wisdom of Theodore Roosevelt*. Ed. Donald J. Davidson. New York: Citadel, 2003.

Sachs, Harvey. *Rubinstein: A Life*. New York: Grove, 1995.

Sackville-West, Vita. *The Edwardians*. Garden City, New York: Doubleday Doran, 1930.

The Sagebrush Anthology: Literature from the Silver Age of the Old West. Ed. Lawrence I. Berkove. Columbia: University of Missouri Press, 2006.

Sangster, Margaret. *From My Youth Up: Personal Reminiscences*. New York: Fleming H. Revell, 1909.

Seelye, John D. *Mark Twain in the Movies: A Meditation with Pictures*. New York: Viking, 1977.

Shaw, Bernard. *Collected Letters: 1898–1910*. Ed. Dan H. Laurence. New York: Dodd, Mead, 1972.

Sinclair, Upton. *The Brass Check: A Study of American Journalism*. Urbana: University of Illinois Press, 2003 [1919].

———. *Mammonart: An Essay in Economic Interpretation*. Pasadena, California: Published by the Author, 1925.

———. *The Moneychangers*. New York: B. W. Dodge, 1908.

Small, Herbert. *Handbook of the New Library of Congress*. Boston: Curtis & Cameron, 1906.

Spratling, William P. *Epilepsy and Its Treatment*. Philadelphia: W. B. Saunders, 1904.

Stoneley, Peter. *Mark Twain and the Feminine Aesthetic*. Cambridge: Cambridge University Press, 1992.

Strong, Leah A. *Joseph Hopkins Twichell, Mark Twain's Friend and Pastor*. Athens: University of Georgia Press, 1966.

Strouse, Jean. *Morgan: American Financier*. New York: Random House, 1999.

Study and Stimulants; or, the Use of Intoxicants and Narcotics in Relation to Intellectual Life. Ed. A. Arthur Reade. Philadelphia: Lippincott, 1883.

Swafford, Jan. *Charles Ives: A Life with Music*. New York: W. W. Norton, 1996.

Tarbell, Ida. *All in the Day's Work: An Autobiography*. New York: Macmillan, 1939.

Taylor, Coley B. *Mark Twain's Margins on Thackeray's "Swift."* New York: Gotham House, 1935.

Teachout, Terry. *The Skeptic: A Life of H. L. Mencken*. New York: HarperCollins, 2002.

Temkin, Owsei. *The Falling Sickness: A History of Epilepsy from the Greeks to the Beginnings of Modern Neurology*. Baltimore: Johns Hopkins University Press, 1971.

Tenney, Thomas Asa. *Mark Twain: A Reference Guide*. Boston: G. K. Hall, 1977.

Thomas, Robert David. *"With Bleeding Footsteps": Mary Baker Eddy's Path to Religious Leadership*. New York: Alfred A. Knopf, 1994.

Trombley, Laura Skandera. *Mark Twain in the Company of Women*. Philadelphia: University of Pennsylvania Press, 1994.

Uruburu, Paula. *American Eve: Evelyn Nesbit, Stanford White, the Birth of the "It" Girl, and the Crime of the Century*. New York: Riverhead, 2008.

Utley, Robert M. *Lone Star Justice: The First Century of the Texas Rangers*. New York: Oxford University Press, 2002.

Vaidhyanathan, Siva. *Copyrights and Copywrongs: The Rise of Intellectual Property and How It Threatens Creativity*. New York: New York University Press, 2001.

Vipond, Mary. *Listening In: The First Decade of Canadian Broadcasting, 1922–1932*. Montreal: McGill-Queen's University Press, 1992.

Wall, Joseph Frazier. *Andrew Carnegie*. Pittsburgh: University of Pittsburgh Press, 1989 [1970].

Wallace, Elizabeth. *Mark Twain and the Happy Island*. Chicago: A. C. McClurg, 1913.

Ward, Geoffrey C. *A First-Class Temperament: The Emergence of Franklin Roosevelt*. New York: Harper & Row, 1989.

Washington, Booker T. *The Booker T. Washington Papers*. Ed. Louis R. Harlan and Raymond W. Smock. 14 vols. Urbana: University of Illinois Press, 1981.

Wecter, Dixon. *Sam Clemens of Hannibal*. Boston: Houghton Mifflin, 1952.

Wilson, Francis. *Francis Wilson's Life of Himself*. Boston: Houghton Mifflin, 1924.

Wilson, Woodrow. *The Papers of Woodrow Wilson*. Ed. Arthur S. Link. 69 vols. Princeton: Princeton University Press, 1966–1994.

Wolfe, Theodore F. *Literary Haunts and Homes: American Authors*. Philadelphia: Lippincott, 1899.

Woodress, James. *Willa Cather: A Literary Life*. Lincoln: University of Nebraska Press, 1987.

Woolf, S. J. *Here Am I*. New York: Random House, 1941.

Wright, Orville, and Wilbur Wright. *Miracle at Kitty Hawk: The Letters of Wilbur and Orville Wright*. Ed. Fred C. Kelly. New York: Da Capo, 1996.

Yarsinske, Amy Waters. *Jamestown Exposition: American Imperialism on Parade*. 2 vols. Charleston, South Carolina: Arcadia, 1999.

Yount, Sylvia. *Cecilia Beaux: American Figure Painter*. Berkeley: University of California Press, 2007.

PROLOGUE: HOW THE MAN IN BLACK
BECAME THE MAN IN WHITE

1. MT, "More Maxims of Mark," *CT*, 2:942.

2. Twain appeared at the hearing in the Senate Reading Room on December 7, 1906, accompanied by his friend and biographer Albert Bigelow Paine. He gave interviews at the Capitol earlier in the day and allowed reporters a preview of his white suit. My account of his afternoon appearance is based on the following sources: "Twain's Fancy Suit," *WP*, December 8, 1906; "Mark Twain in White Amuses Congressmen," *NYT*, December 8, 1906; "Twain Awes Capitol," *Washington Herald*, December 8, 1906 (MTTCI, 556–61); *Copyright Hearings, December 7 to 11, 1906*, 114; Ingersoll, *Rand, McNally & Co.'s Handy Guide to Washington and the District of Columbia* (1897); Charles Goodrum, "The Congressional Reading Room," *Library of Congress Information Bulletin*, May 5–19, 1997; *MTB*, 1346–47.

3. "Mark Twain Bids Winter Defiance," *New York Herald*, December 8, 1906. The *Washington Times* worried that Twain might catch cold wearing "summer apparel" on "the coldest day of the season thus far" ("Mark Twain Demands Thanks of Congress," December 8, 1906); *MTTCI*, 556; quotations from the *New York World* are taken from Budd, *Our Mark Twain*, 210–11; the quotation from the *Boston Herald* is taken from "The Milky Way," *WSJ*, December 20, 1906.

4. *MTB*, 1346. The *New York Tribune* expressed surprise that Twain would "show such disdain for the December air" by wearing "a summer suit" ("Mark Twain's Views," December 8, 1906).

5. AD, October 8, 1906 (*Autob/NAR*, 136–37).

6. Small, *Handbook of the New Library of Congress*, 8.

7. MT, "More Maxims of Mark," *CT*, 2:944; *Autob/MTIE*, 375. In *Copyrights and Copywrongs*, Siva Vaidhyanathan uses the standard sources to set the scene of Twain's appearance before Kittredge's committee, but it is difficult to agree with his assertion that Thomas Nelson Page and Edward Everett Hale "warmed up the crowd for Twain" with their remarks at the hearing (35). The statements of those two authors seem uninspired, and Page spoke long before Twain showed up. It was announced at the hearing that Twain would appear at four in the afternoon, and the speakers who immediately preceded him were Frank Millet of the National Academy of Design,

W. A. Livingstone of the Print Publishers' Association, H. N. Low of the music roll industry, and Hale, whose comments were short.

8. *MT Speaking,* 534.

9. *MTB,* 1347; "Mark Twain in White Amuses Congressmen," *NYT,* December 8, 1906.

10. "A Humorist at His Best," *NYT,* December 10, 1906; *MTB,* 1347. At eighty-four, Edward Everett Hale was probably the oldest man in the room.

11. *WP,* December 17, 1906; *Suburbanite Economist* (Chicago), December 14, 1906; *LFA,* 319; WDH, *Selected Letters: 1902–1911,* 5:234. Even the *Washington Post* had a swift change of heart, acknowledging the appeal of "Twain's famous white suit" only a few months after dismissing it ("A Woman's Story of 'Dr.' Mark Twain's Latest Trip Across the Atlantic," *WP,* August 4, 1907).

12. *Mark Twain's Speeches* (1910), 137. In *Dark Twins,* Susan Gillman doesn't agree that the white suit enhanced Twain's efforts on behalf of copyright reform, but argues that it was a distraction, and that Twain was "competing with himself" (182).

13. *MT Speaking,* 463.

14. Ibid., 575.

15. Ibid., 530; MT, *Adventures of Huckleberry Finn,* chapter 18.

16. *LFA,* 257–58; CC, *My Father, Mark Twain,* 153; "Mark Twain's Views," *NY Trib,* December 8, 1906.

17. *MTB,* 1341–42.

18. MT to JC, December 7, 1906; *MTTCI,* 557; MT to Frances Nunnally, March 28, 1909 (*Ltrs-Angelfish,* 256).

19. MT to Thomas Bailey Aldrich, June 6, 1904; *MTN,* 388.

20. Of course, in earlier years, Twain had often worn a white suit in summer, but he didn't adopt it as a year-round uniform until after December 1906. Some critics seem to think that Twain put on the suit as a stunt and rarely wore it in public after his appearance in Washington. A distinguished contributor to *The Mark Twain Encyclopedia* asserts that Twain didn't wear his white suit "regularly . . . during the last three years of his life, and did not (except at one banquet) wear it while speech making" (390). In *Mark Twain: A to Z,* R. Kent Rasmussen echoes this erroneous statement (512–13). In fact, Twain wore the suit so regularly that the *Washington Post* referred to it in the spring of 1907 as his "copyrighted white flannel suit" ("Mark Twain in Gloom," *WP,* May 1, 1907), and he gave several speeches in the outfit in just the first half of 1907, including a talk at the statehouse in Annapolis, Maryland, before which he was specifically asked if he planned to wear it and replied, "Why, of course, I'm going to wear it. Why not? You just ought to see me in it. I look at least 10 years younger" ("Mark Twain in Clover," *Baltimore Sun,* May 10, 1907; *MTTCI,* 595). He had worn it only a few days earlier when he spoke at the Actors' Fund Fair in New York, and he wore it in mid-April when he spoke on the stage of the Educational Alliance theater, also in New York ("Actors' Fund Fair Opens with Vim," *NYT,* May 7, 1907; "Mark Twain Tells of Being an Actor," *NYT,* April 15, 1907). Over the next two years he made countless public appearances in the suit, and wore it when he gave his last important speech in New York, as a reporter noted in the *New York Sun:* "Mark Twain [was] very noticeable indeed in his white flannels among the black swallowtails and boiled shirts" ("A Great Night for Jerome," *New York Sun,* May 8, 1909).

21. MT, "Old Age," *CT,* 2:719; AD, October 8, 1906 (*Autob/NAR,* 137).

22. "Mark Twain Amused," *New York Journal,* June 2, 1897 (*MTTCI,* 317); Frank Marshall White, "Mark Twain as a Newspaper Reporter," *The Outlook,* December 24, 1910; *Autob/MTIE,* 253. (The version that Clara Clemens used in *My Father, Mark Twain* is, "The report of my death has been grossly exaggerated," 184.)

23. Kunhardt et al., *P. T. Barnum*, 343; "Amended Obituaries," *Harper's Weekly*, November 15, 1902; Budd, *Our Mark Twain*, 228.

24. *Hartford Courant*, July 24, 1901 (Harnsberger, *Mark Twain, Family Man*, 190).

25. Theodore Dreiser, "Mark the Double Twain," *English Journal*, October 1935.

26. MT to WDH, June 17, 1906 (*Ltrs-Howells*, 2:811); "Our Original Superstar," *Time*, July 14, 2008.

27. "Mark Twain in Cream-Colored Summer Flannel," *New York World*, December 8, 1906; "Mark Twain in White Amuses Congressmen," *NYT*, December 8, 1906 (*MTTCI*, 562.)

28. WDH, *Selected Literary Criticism*, 3:197.

29. MT, "Notebook 42" (quoted in Dolmetsch, *"Our Famous Guest,"* 107).

30. MT to WDH, August 31, 1884 (*Ltrs-Howells*, 2:501).

31. MT to Joseph Twichell, June 24, 1905.

32. CC, *My Husband, Gabrilowitsch*, 178; MT to Emilie Rogers, October 24, 1906 (*Ltrs-Rogers*, 618).

33. *MTB*, 1292.

34. It is a strange truth that modern accounts of Twain's last years tend to portray them as a largely dull and bleak conclusion to an otherwise colorful and exciting life. A recent biography of several hundred pages devotes only two dozen to his last decade, and summarizes it with the hollow remark "He aged, and he died" (Powers, *Mark Twain*, 618). Another biography describes him as an emotional wreck who was "crippled" by "despair, pessimism, frustration, and insensitivity." This same writer also argues that Twain's decision to wear white in Washington is evidence of "erratically disquieting behavior" (Hill, *Mark Twain, God's Fool*, 272 and 157). In his highly praised biography Justin Kaplan attributes Twain's fondness for white to hidden psychological problems, speculating that the author struggled with "the fetish of what had become an obsession with guilt, with forbidden and therefore unclean thoughts" (Kaplan, *Mr. Clemens and Mark Twain*, 380). Interpreting a preference as a fetish is one of the dangers of putting Mark's old ghost on the modern Freudian couch. But the image of Twain as a dark, guilt-ridden creature lies at the heart of Justin Kaplan's biography. From the beginning, Kaplan's purpose in writing about Twain was to explore the author's "dark side" and subject it to a Freudian interpretation. Freud was the great-uncle of Kaplan's wife, Anne Bernays, and in their joint memoir, *Back Then*, Kaplan recalls that he was inspired to write his biography as a Freudian case study of "a nocturnal creature . . . guilt-ridden and dream haunted, his middle life a daydream of glory, his later life a nightmare" (305). In *Dangerous Intimacy* Lystra offers a lively argument against "the myth of Twain's sustained geriatric despair" (62). In "Mark Twain and Whiteness," Richard S. Lowry suggests that in wearing white Twain may have been making a point about racism, that the suit was a "parodic exposure of racial whiteness," but he cites no evidence to support this theory (*A Companion to Mark Twain*, 59).

35. MT to Mary Fairbanks, June 3, 1876 (*Ltrs-Fairbanks*, 199–200).

36. Brooks, *The Ordeal of Mark Twain*, 13–14; Woodress, *Willa Cather*, 210. Twain liked young Cather's verse, calling her poem "The Palatine""a fine poem, a great poem" (*MTB*, 1501). Brooks adapted his comment about the derelict from Twain's remark concerning Lord Clive and Warren Hastings: "There is no figure for the human being like the ship; no such figure for the storm-beaten human drift as the derelict— such men as Clive and Hastings could only be imagined as derelicts adrift, helpless, tossed by every wind and tide" (*MTB*, 1500). But, like others, Brooks wanted to use Twain's works and life as a way of addressing his own obsessions. In his books on Twain and Henry James, he "focused many of the feelings of guilt and inadequacy that troubled him all his life," writes his biographer James Hoopes, *Van Wyck Brooks*, 1.

37. MT, *Life on the Mississippi*, chapter 14.

38. *LFA*, 322.

39. "Too Bleak for Mark," *Washington Herald*, December 9, 1906; "Mark Twain Demands Thanks of Congress, and Right Away, Too," *Washington Times*, December 8, 1906 (*MTTCI*, 568).

40. *MT Speaking*, 557.

41. *MTB*, 1267; "Twain's Daughter Talks About Him," *NYT*, June 14, 1908; Budd, *Our Mark Twain*, 212.

42. In the issue of January 31, 1907, *Life* joked that Twain was "paid a dollar a word by philanthropic publishers" (*Critical Essays on Mark Twain*, 189); but Colonel George Harvey corrects this figure in "Mark Twain's Exclusive Publisher Tells What the Humorist Is Paid," *WP*, March 3, 1907. As Twain's secretary recalled many years later: "He was always interested in selling his full value in the word-count of any article he wrote & sold to Harpers, for his contract gave him 30 cents a word, and I counted every word of every article published" (IVL to William Howe, October 25, 1936).

43. *MT Speaking*, 605; *MTB*, 1072.

44. MT, "Notebook 44" [1901]; Lawton, *A Lifetime with Mark Twain*, 256; CC, *My Father, Mark Twain*, 258; AD, October 30, 1906.

45. MT to Alfred Arthur Reade, March 14, 1882 (*Study and Stimulants*, 120–22).

46. *MT Speaking*, 529.

47. *St. Louis Post Dispatch*, December 10, 1899; Jane Lampton Clemens to Olivia Clemens, January 7, 1885 (Wecter, *Sam Clemens of Hannibal*, 44 and 81) .

48. Jane Lampton Clemens to Orion Clemens, April 25, [1880?] (*HF & TS*, 313–14).

49. *HF & TS*, 91; *Autob/MTA*, 1:108.

50. *HF & TS*, 83.

51. "Mark Twain's Experiences in the Hands of British Interviewers," *NYT*, June 30, 1907.

52. MT to Margery H. Clinton, August 27, 1909. For examples of the phrase "tobacco heart," see MT to Frances Nunnally, July 15, 1909 (*Ltrs-Angelfish*, 262), and MT to Charlotte Teller, [July 1909]; and MT to Joe Goodman, May 16, 1902.

53. *MTB*, 1340 and 1318.

54. MT to CC, July 27, 1907.

PART ONE: BLITHE SPIRIT
CHAPTER ONE: RAGTIME ON TAP

1. MT, *A Connecticut Yankee in King Arthur's Court*, chapter 22.

2. "Magic Music from the Telharmonium," *NYT*, December 16, 1906; "Mark Twain and Twin Cheer New Year's Party," *NYT*, January 1, 1907; "1907 Comes in Noisily; Moon Scatters Fog," *NYT*, January 1, 1907; "Mark Twain in White Greets 1907," *New York Herald*, January 1, 1907 (*MTTCI*, 575); *MTB*, 1364; MT to JC, January 1, 1907.

3. "Twain and the Telephone," *NYT*, December 23, 1906 (*MTTCI*, 573).

4. "Mark Twain in White Greets 1907," *NY Trib*, January 1, 1907; "Twain Gives 1906 a Merry Funeral," *New York World*, January 1, 1907 (*MTTCI*, 574–76).

5. "Mark Twain and Twin Cheer New Year's Party," *NYT*, January 1, 1907.

6. In her diary for December 28, 1906, Jean refers to plans for "a sort of reception and partially impromptu performance at home on Monday night"; MT, "Personal Habits of the Siamese Twins," *CT*, 1:296–98. As Twain no doubt knew, the real story of the Barnum twins was almost as bizarre as his joke suggests. Married to a pair of American sisters after leaving their native Siam, the twins purchased a plantation in

North Carolina with some of the money they earned exhibiting themselves for Barnum and other showmen. Their wives gave birth to a total of twenty-two children, who were cared for in part by some of the thirty-three slaves acquired by the twins to work the plantation. The Civil War caused them financial ruin after their slaves were freed, and the pair had to go back to work on the theatrical circuit in the North, where one reporter remarked wittily, "As long as they go in for Union, they will do. . . . United they stand; divided the show is ended" (Kunhardt et al., *P. T. Barnum*, 144–47).

7. Bynner, *Selected Letters,* 37. Bynner is identified as Twain's "twin" for the night in MT to JC, January 1, 1907 (CC, *My Father, Mark Twain,* 263), and JC, December 28, 1906.

8. See *MTTCI,* 575, for quotations from articles in the *New York Herald* and *New York American,* January 1, 1907.

9. "Tributes to Poet by Men of Letters," *NYT,* February 24, 1907 (*MTTCI,* 578).

10. Burke, *With a Feather on My Nose,* 70. Twain's praise of Burke is quoted in Long, *Mark Twain Handbook,* 250.

11. Barrymore, *Memories,* 155; "Benefit of College Women's Club," *NY Trib,* March 13, 1907.

12. IVL, January 5, 1908.

13. MT to JC, March 5, 1907. An excellent account of Mary Ann Cord's importance in Twain's life can be found in Fishkin, *Was Huck Black?,* 31–33 and 99.

14. IVL, January 1, 1907.

15. "Won at Billiards by a Single Point," *NYT,* March 6, 1907; "Battle of the Cues," *NY Trib,* March 6, 1907. The tournament was held at the Liederkranz Hall on East Fifty-eighth Street. Demarest's violent streak is reported in "Billiardist Assails Wife," *NYT,* June 17, 1915.

16. "Social Gossip," *WP,* February 16, 1907. The paper reported that Twain's public reading at the event was done "rather glibly and fast—for him."

17. "Keats-Shelley Meeting Pleases," *NYT,* February 15, 1907.

18. MT, *Adventures of Huckleberry Finn,* chapter 19.

19. *MTB,* 846; Gribben, *Mark Twain's Library,* 1:106

20. Gribben, *Mark Twain's Library,* 2:640; "For the Keats-Shelley Fund," *The Publishers' Weekly,* February 16, 1907.

21. "Mark Twain Sails South," *New York Herald,* March 17, 1907 (*MTTCI,* 579).

22. Advertisement, "Summer Vacations," *WP,* June 22, 1907. In early 1907 Twain made two trips to Bermuda, one in January and one in March.

23. MT, "Some Rambling Notes of an Idle Excursion."

24. MT to Dorothy Quick, March 12, 1908 (*Ltrs-Angelfish,* 121).

25. MT, *Life on the Mississippi,* chapter 4. Hoffmann takes a similar view in *Mark Twain in Paradise,* 26.

26. AD, January 28, 1907 (*Autob/MTIE,* 71–72). It appears likely that Twain was invited to the Clark dinner by his friend from the Lotus Club, Frank Lawrence ("Dinner to Senator Clark," *NYT,* January 27, 1907).

27. Limerick, *The Legacy of Conquest,* 114; "Senator Clark Fights Auto Suit: Montana Man Wants Boy Whom His Car Injured to Deposit Cost Money," *NY Trib,* November 19, 1907.

28. "As a Goddess She Won Him," *Oakland Tribune* (California), July 29, 1905. Clark's marriage to his ward, Anna La Chappelle, took place secretly in 1901 and wasn't announced until 1904 ("Marriage of Senator Clark," *NYT,* July 13, 1904).

29. AD, January 28, 1907 (*Autob/MTIE,* 74–76).

30. AD, November 8, 1906 (*Autob/NAR,* 190); MT to WDH, January 16 and March 14, 1904 (*Ltrs-Howells,* 2:778, 782).

31. MT to Henry Rogers, June [17?], 1906 (*Ltrs-Rogers,* 611).

CHAPTER TWO: DOMESTIC CIRCLE

1. *MTB*, 1265.
2. MT to Muriel Pears, October 23, 1904.
3. AD, April 6, 1906.
4. The old Grosvenor Hotel was located at 37 Fifth Avenue. A sample advertisement can be found in *NYT*, October 10, 1909. Livy and Twain stayed there in 1903 before sailing to Italy, and Twain returned to live there in 1904 while 21 Fifth Avenue was being renovated (MT to Muriel Pears, October 23, 1904). His praise for it can be found in MT to Frances Nunnally, March 31, 1908 (*Ltrs-Angelfish*, 125). As for the Brevoort, Raymond Orteig bought it in 1902, when he was only thirty-two, and ran it for thirty years ("When Hotels Mirrored New York's Life," *NYT*, March 6, 1932; "Raymond Orteig, Hotel Man, Dies," *NYT*, June 8,1939). In the 1920s Orteig offered a prize for the first person to fly between New York and Paris. It was won by Charles Lindbergh.
5. Cather, "Coming, Aphrodite!," *Collected Stories*, 65; both the Brevoort and 21 Fifth Avenue were demolished in the 1950s to make way for a high-rise apartment building. Fortunately, a few photographs of the buildings survive, including one by Berenice Abbott, who photographed the two structures in the 1930s for her WPA project, *Changing New York*. A plaque on the side of the modern building marks the spot where Twain once lived.
6. *Autob/MTA*, 1:226. The Renwick family owned 21 Fifth Avenue. James Renwick, Jr. (1818–1895) also designed the Smithsonian Building. His mother was Margaret Brevoort, whose family owned the land on which both the Brevoort Hotel and 21 Fifth Avenue stood. Isabel Lyon recalls the reference to "The House of Mirth" in the margin of her annotated copy of *MTB*, xii, and also in her journal, June 8, 1906. (Edith Wharton's *The House of Mirth* was a best-seller in 1905.)
7. Quoted in Tenney, *Mark Twain*, 119.
8. Faude, *The Renaissance of Mark Twain's House*, 26.
9. MT to Joseph Twichell, January 19, 1897.
10. *LFA*, 260.
11. MT to Mary Rogers, November 7, 1906 (*Ltrs-Mary*, 85); for evidence of Clara's explosive temper, see "Putting a Happy Face on an Often Unhappy Twain," *NYT*, April 22, 2000.
12. *Mark Twain in Elmira*, 149. On the day of Livy's funeral in Elmira, her nephew Jervis made this cryptic note in his diary, "Clara's illness at the grave." More than half a century later Caroline Thomas Harnsberger—who was a friend of Clara— wrote in *Mark Twain, Family Man* (211) that Clara tried to jump into Livy's grave. Presumably, this detail came from Clara herself, who was still alive when Harnsberger's book was published in 1960, but it seems an exaggeration. As Livy's headstone notes, the grave holds not her body but her "ashes." Twain's comment on the "crushing" effect of Livy's death was made in a letter to Muriel Pears, October 23, 1904.
13. CC to MT, November 7, 1904.
14. "In the World of Music," *Atlanta Constitution*, October 21, 1906.
15. Harnsberger, *Mark Twain, Family Man*, 183.
16. "Miss Clemens in Concert. Mark Twain Makes a Speech at His Daughter's Debut," *NYT*, September 23, 1906; *MT Speaking*, 528–29.
17. AD, October 4, 1906.
18. MT to Mary Rogers, [September 22, 1906] (*Ltrs-Mary*, 65); AD, October 4, 1906; CC, *My Father, Mark Twain*, 272.
19. MT to JC, February 21, 1907; "Concert at Cumings Theater," *Fitchburg Daily*

Sentinel (Massachusetts), March 7, 1907. Built in 1899, the theater was demolished in the 1950s. Its name is usually spelled in later documents as "Cummings."

20. MT to Samuel E. Moffett, April 23 [1900].

21. MT, "Jean's Illness," unpublished ms [1899].

22. "Hillbourne Club: A Private Health Resort" (NYAML; 1913); Spratling, *Epilepsy and Its Treatment,* 341. For information about Dr. Edward A. Sharp and the sanitarium in Katonah, I am indebted to Virginia Fetscher of the Katonah Village Library, and to Bedford Town Historian Katharine Kelly. Called by various names, including Hillbourne Farms, the "health resort" was incorporated in 1904 (Incorporation Records, Westchester County) and was located half a mile from the village along what is now Route 22. In the late twentieth century part of the old property became the home of the Katonah Museum of Art. The only surviving copy of the twenty-page brochure titled "Hillbourne Club: A Private Health Resort" is signed by Dr. Edward A. Sharp and by his successor, Dr. S. T. Armstrong. As Dr. Sharp told a medical association in 1904, he established his sanitarium in that year on a forty-two-acre farm in Katonah with the primary purpose of helping epileptics (*Transactions of the National Association for the Study of Epilepsy and the Care and Treatment of Epileptics,* 1904). A respected expert on the disease, Sharp had worked closely with William P. Spratling, author of the then standard textbook on the subject, *Epilepsy and Its Treatment,* and at Katonah had followed Spratling's guidelines for the ideal sanitarium treating epileptics. For information on contemporary public attitudes to epilepsy, see Amy L. Fairchild, "Policies of Inclusion: Immigrants, Disease, Dependency, and American Immigration Policy at the Dawn and Dusk of the 20th Century," *American Journal of Public Health,* April 2004, and Sydney Brooks, "A New York 'Colony of Mercy,' " *American Monthly Review of Reviews,* vol. 21 (January–June 1900).

23. JC, September 26, 1906. By October 5, Jean had grown more positive in her attitude, confiding in her diary that "she very much want[ed] to" go to the sanitarium for the winter.

24. MT to Mary Fairbanks, January 18, 1893 (*Ltrs-Fairbanks,* 269); MT to CC, October 20, 1905.

25. King, *Memories of a Southern Woman of Letters,* 84; WDH, *Selected Literary Criticism,* 3:197.

26. JC, "A Programme and Program," *NYT,* November 24, 1906: Doris Webster's interview with IVL, 1953.

27. Interview with Nancy Brush Bowditch, January 30, 1974, conducted by Robert Brown for the Archives of American Art, Smithsonian Institution; MT to Mary Fairbanks, January 18, 1893 (*Ltrs-Fairbanks,* 269); MT to Laurence Hutton, February 20, 1898.

28. Paine says of Jean, "she dressed always in white" (*MTB,* 1308); in Vienna, Leschetizky liked to call Clara and her friend Ethel Newcomb "Day and Night" because of the contrast between Ethel's fair hair and her taste for bright clothing and Clara's dark hair and taste for dark clothing (see Lawton, *A Lifetime with Mark Twain,* 163, and Newcomb, *Leschetizky as I Knew Him*); JC, May 29, 1905.

29. As Dr. Orrin Devinsky—the head of New York University's Epilepsy Center—has pointed out, "The false association between epilepsy and aggressive behavior is one of the most damaging stigmas cast on people with epilepsy" (Devinsky, *Epilepsy,* 329). Lyon was quick to see the worst in Jean's own guilty confession that she had hit the family housekeeper—Katy Leary—during an epileptic seizure. The blow was no doubt accidental and minor—Katy makes no mention of it in her 350-page memoir of her service to the family—but Jean apparently felt that she had done something wrong, and Lyon concluded that the young woman had actually meant to kill the

housekeeper. Lyon, however, didn't witness the seizure itself, and there is no evidence that Jean's illness ever posed a serious danger to anyone but herself. In any case Katy survived many more months in close company with Jean and lived until the ripe age of seventy-eight, dying almost a quarter of a century after her service to the Clemens family ended.

30. MT to CC, October 20, 1905; MT to JC, October 29, 1906.

31. Information about Paine's life and career is taken from *The National Cyclopedia of American Biography,* 28:113–14, which notes that he worked at *St. Nicholas* magazine from 1899 to 1909; Paine's biography of Thomas Nast is 583 pages; for the origin of "Great White Way," see *Brewer's Dictionary of Modern Phrase and Fable,* 16th edition; Milford, *Savage Beauty,* 7.

32. *MTB,* 1260–67 and 1325–27.

CHAPTER THREE: PIRATES OF BROADWAY

1. AD, June 2, 1906.

2. "Wants a Business Man in the Hall of Fame," *NYT,* February 3, 1907.

3. T. Quiller Wright, "Mark Twain as a Motorist," *Motor Talk: A Magazine of Outdoor Sports,* May 1906; *Springfield Republic* (Massachusetts) quoted in "Henry H. Rogers as Viewed by the Newspaper Press," *WSJ,* May 22, 1909.

4. AD, April 1904 (*Autob/MTA,* 1:251).

5. MT, "A Tribute to Henry H. Rogers" (*Ltrs-Rogers,* 710); MT to Olivia Clemens, February 15, 1894; MT to HHR, December 21, 1897 (*Ltrs-Rogers,* 310).

6. Klein, *The Life and Legend of E. H. Harriman,* 214.

7. The article "Standard Oil Tells Who Has Its Stock," *NYT,* September 21, 1907, lists Rogers as the fourth-largest individual stockholder with sixteen thousand shares valued at over $7 million. A listing of all his stocks at the time of his death two years later includes shares in more than eighty companies ("Three Noted Men Left $79,196, 371," *NYT,* July 23, 1914). Among them is the Richmond Railroad and Lighting Co., which operated the streetcars on Staten Island. For information on Rogers's control of this company, see "Staten Island to Ask Help from the Courts," *NYT,* August 12, 1906.

8. Limerick, *The Legacy of Conquest,* 115. It was rumored that Senator Clark later made secret deals to sell his mining interests to Rogers and his associates.

9. MT to Olivia Clemens, February 15, 1894; MT, "A Tribute to Henry H. Rogers" (*Ltrs-Rogers,* 711); "Real Popularity," *Mansfield News* (Ohio), July 25, 1907 (quoting the *Birmingham Age-Herald* of Alabama).

10. HHR to MT, June 2, 1894 (*Ltrs-Rogers,* 64).

11. Chernow, *Titan,* 222–23.

12. "You Must Pass by a Woman," *Kansas City Star,* February 18, 1904.

13. Tarbell, *All in the Day's Work,* 216.

14. Hubbard, *Little Journeys to the Homes of the Great,* 11:392.

15. Chernow, *Titan,* 223; "Mainly About People," *Kansas City Star,* November 1, 1907. The Standard Oil lawyer was Fred Hagerman, who had known Twain many years earlier in Keokuk, Iowa, when he was a boy and Twain was a young man.

16. Chernow, *Titan,* 393; MT to HHR, October 4, 1899 (*Ltrs-Rogers,* 412).

17. "Mr. Dooley's Friends," *Atlantic Monthly,* September 1963 (*Ltrs-Rogers,* 7).

18. See note in *Ltrs-Rogers,* 486.

19. MT to HHR, October 4, 1907 (*Ltrs-Rogers,* 640–41); MT to WDH, October 4, 1907 (*Ltrs-Howells,* 2:827).

20. Garland, *Hamlin Garland's Diaries,* 193.

21. Josephson, *The Robber Barons,* 325; Chernow, *Titan,* 378. As Chernow points

out in *Titan,* a government report in 1907 found that Standard Oil "was more than twenty times the size of its most serious competitor, Pure Oil" (537).

22. Tarbell, *All in the Day's Work,* 217; Josephson, *The Robber Barons,* 280.

23. MT to HHR, July 13, 1905 (*Ltrs-Rogers,* 591).

24. MT, "A Tribute to Henry H. Rogers" (*Ltrs-Rogers,* 710).

25. *MTB,* 984.

26. MT to HHR, February 19, 1899 (*Ltrs-Rogers,* 389).

27. Beard, *Hardly a Man Is Now Alive,* 348.

28. Keller, *Selected Writings,* 62; Washington, *The Booker T. Washington Papers,* 10:126.

29. *Autob/MTIE,* 258; "Mark Twain Talks on Graft (from the *Boston Transcript*)," *WSJ,* November 11, 1905; Pond, *Eccentricities of Genius,* 197.

30. *Autob/NAR,* 4.

31. MT, *The Adventures of Tom Sawyer,* chapter 8; MT, *Life on the Mississippi,* chapter 4.

32. AD, June 2, 1906; "I go out very frequently & exhibit my clothes. Howells has dubbed me the Whited Sepulchre" (MT to CC, February 24, 1907).

33. MT to HHR, March 21–22, 1904 (*Ltrs-Rogers,* 560); Tarbell, *All in the Day's Work,* 10.

34. Built in 1899, the *Kanawha* was acquired by Rogers in 1901. It displaced 575 tons. "Yacht Kanawha Won the Lysistrata Cup," *NYT,* July 25, 1903.

35. MT, *The Gilded Age,* chapter 27.

36. MT to HHR, December 19, 1908 (*Ltrs-Rogers,* 658)

37. MT, "Notebook 48."

38. HHR to MT, June 12, 1907 (*Ltrs-Rogers,* 627).

39. Dias, *Mark Twain and Henry Huttleston Rogers,* 100–101.

40. IVL, August 24, 1906 (*Ltrs-Rogers,* 616).

41. "Rogers's Deepwater Railroad," *WSJ,* January 28, 1907. There had been rumors in late December that the two rail lines were going to operate as one, but the report in the *Wall Street Journal* was the first to offer convincing details.

42. "Two Million for Tidewater Pier," *Richmond Times Dispatch,* March 4, 1907; "Mark Twain Is Going to Be a Buccaneer," *New York American,* April 23, 1907 (*MTTCI,* 583).

43. "Roosevelt Won't Drop Trust War," *NYT,* August 21, 1907; the cartoon of Teddy and the serpent appeared in *Puck,* May 23, 1906 (Lorant, *The Life and Times of Theodore Roosevelt,* 479).

44. *Autob/MTIE,* 49.

45. Roosevelt, *The Wisdom of Theodore Roosevelt,* 36; IVL, November 28, 1905; MT to JWT, February 16, 1905 (*Ltrs*/Paine, 2:766–67).

46. The various attractions of the fair are illustrated in a collection of photographs at the Sargeant Memorial Room of the Public Library in Norfolk, Virginia.

47. "Mark Twain Is Going to Be a Buccaneer," *New York American,* April 23, 1907 (*MTTCI,* 583–84); "Mark Twain on the Scope of the Children's Theater," *Brooklyn Eagle,* November 24, 1907 (*MTTCI,* 657); *Autob/MTIE,* 48; *MTTCI,* 657.

48. *MTWS,* 156–60.

49. Yarsinske, *Jamestown Exposition,* 2:8; Theodore Roosevelt to Kermit Roosevelt, April 29, 1907 (Roosevelt, *Letters to Kermit from Theodore Roosevelt,* 191.) The event might have been more inspiring—or maybe just frightening—if Wilbur and Orville Wright had pulled off their planned stunt to fly to Hampton Roads, where they would take, in Orville's words, "an unexpected part in the parade," buzzing the fleet. As it happened, however, they were forced to abandon the idea when negotiations with a syndicate in Europe required them to go overseas. But it was the kind of

daring feat that might have won Roosevelt's admiration—and perhaps even Twain's. The great Barnum himself couldn't have dreamed up a three-ring circus as spectacular as one involving the president and his fleet, Mark Twain and his sidekick's yacht, and the Wright brothers' flying machine (Wright and Wright, *Miracle at Kitty Hawk,* 411–12).

50. Reid, *The Virginian Railway,* 30–32; "Mark Twain's Joke in Face of Death," *Daily News* (Frederick, Maryland) May 1, 1907.

51. "President in Danger," *WP,* May 1, 1907.

52. "Roosevelt Opens Exposition," *WSJ,* April 27, 1907; "The Artful Dodger," *WSJ,* January 9, 1906.

53. MT to CC, May 2, 1907.

54. "Roosevelt Day at Jamestown," *WP,* April 27, 1907.

55. MT to CC, May 2, 1907; "Mark Twain Investigating," *NYT,* May 5, 1907.

56. "Mark Twain Gloomy," *Washington Herald,* May 1, 1907.

57. "Mark Twain in Gloom," *WP,* May 1, 1907.

58. "Joke on Mark Twain," *WP,* May 5, 1907. This article makes the convincing case that Rogers deliberately spread the false story of Twain's disappearance at sea, saying, "There is also an inkling somewhere that Mr. Rogers' act is retaliatory."

59. "Twain and Yacht Disappear at Sea," *NYT,* May 4, 1907; "Mark Twain and Yacht Missing," *NY Trib,* May 4, 1907.

60. "Mark Twain Investigating," *NYT,* May 5, 1907; " 'I'm Not Lost at Sea,' Says Twain," *New York World,* May 5, 1907; "Not Lost, Says Twain," *NY Trib,* May 5, 1907; "Twain Hesitates to Admit He's Dead," *New York American,* May 5, 1907 (*MTTCI,* 586–87).

CHAPTER FOUR: BODY AND SOUL

1. MT, "Notebook 42" (Fulton, *The Reverend Mark Twain,* 16).

2. MT to Lyman Powell, May 27, 1907.

3. MT, "The Secret History of Eddypus, the World-Empire," *Fab. of Man,* 321; MT, *Christian Science,* chapters 7, 12, and 15.

4. Milmine [Cather], *The Life of Mary Baker G. Eddy,* 480. In "Willa Cather and The Life of Mary Baker G. Eddy," *American Literature,* May 1982, L. Brent Bohlke revealed that the *McClure's* series on Eddy and the subsequent publication of the articles in hardcover were in fact the work of Cather, with the exception of some introductory material. She admitted her authorship in a letter Bohlke found at the New York Public Library. See also David Stouck's Introduction and Afterword to the University of Nebraska Press edition of *The Life of Mary Baker G. Eddy* (1993), and Woodress, *Willa Cather,* 193.

5. Milmine [Cather], *The Life of Mary Baker G. Eddy,* 482. In "Mark Twain and Mary Baker Eddy: Gendering the Transpersonal Subject," *American Literature,* March 1998, Cynthia Schrager argues that Twain's critique of Eddy is "marred by a tendency to denigrate the feminine." In his biography of Eddy, Robert David Thomas says that Twain's attack on the church's female leader indicates that the author "could not conceive of a woman as an independent person" ("With Bleeding Footsteps," 302). For an excellent rejoinder to these arguments, see Fulton, *The Reverend Mark Twain,* 20–21.

6. Camfield, *The Oxford Companion to Mark Twain,* 87; "Topics of the Times," *NYT,* October 2, 1900, November 8, 1900, and July 12, 1904.

7. MT, *Christian Science,* chapter 15; MT to J. Wylie Smith, August 7, 1909; MT, "The Secret History of Eddypus, the World-Empire," *Fab. of Man,* 315–85. At her

death in 1910, Eddy left her estate of $3 million to her church (Gill, *Mary Baker Eddy,* 553).

8. MT to Frederick Peabody, December 5, [1902] (private collection).

9. *LFA,* 309–10; MT, *Christian Science,* chapter 2.

10. Ibid. In defense of Eddy's prose style, Peter Stoneley writes this sixty-three-word sentence that unintenionally proves Twain's point about the unreadability of her writing: "But her reiterative technique, which uses unconventional word-orders and demanding clausal structures, does not so much build up to a 'grand total' as create a quality of concentration: if we suffer our minds to become familiar with Mrs. Eddy's syntax, this process institutes a provisional malleability of mind, even if we, through some stronger prerogative, reject the message it is intended to convey" (*Mark Twain and the Feminine Aesthetic,* 126).

11. Gottschalk, *Rolling Away the Stone,* 57.

12. Peel, *Mary Baker Eddy,* 204.

13. "Actors' Fair Promoters Row over Twain," *NYEW,* May 1, 1907.

14. "Century Club in Quandary," *NY Trib,* May 4, 1907; "Warm Apologies to Mark Twain," *NYT,* May 2, 1907.

15. "Flower Booth the Favorite," *NY Trib,* May 9, 1907.

16. "Actors' Fund Fair Opens with Vim," *NYT,* May 7, 1907.

17. *NY Trib,* May 9, 1907; Barrymore, *Memories,* 155.

18. "Actors' Fund Fair Opens with Vim," *NYT,* May 7, 1907. The Rosenfeld controversy was covered in great detail in a series of *NYT* articles published in 1907 between May 1 and May 11.

19. *BAMT,* 318–31.

20. "To the Person Sitting in Darkness," *CT,* 2:461; "The United States of Lyncherdom," *CT,* 2:486 (this essay wasn't published until after Twain's death).

21. WDH to MT, October 9, 1899 (*Ltrs-Howells,* 2:707); and MT, "The New Wildcat Religion," *The Golden Era* (San Francisco), March 4, 1866 (*MTMB,* 134). Twain makes fun of the Model Boy in *The Adventures of Tom Sawyer,* chapter 5. A helpful overview of Twain's attitudes toward religion can be found in Harold K. Bush, " 'A Moralist in Disguise': Mark Twain and American Religion," *A Historical Guide to Mark Twain,* 55–94; see also Bush, *Mark Twain and the Spiritual Crisis of His Age,* and Fulton, *The Reverend Mark Twain.*

22. IVL, March 9, 1907.

23. "Oxford Degree for Twain," *NYT,* May 11, 1907; "As Mark Twain Watched Drill," *Baltimore American,* May 11, 1907 (*MTTCI,* 595–600).

24. Bentztown Bard [Folger McKinzie], "Mark Twain at Annapolis" (quoted in Charles J. Nolan, Jr., and David O. Tomlinson, "Mark Twain's Visit to Annapolis," *Mark Twain Journal,* Fall 1987).

25. William Oliver Stevens, *Annapolis: Anne Arundel's Town* (quoted in Charles J. Nolan, Jr., and David O. Tomlinson, "Mark Twain's Visit to Annapolis," *Mark Twain Journal,* Fall 1987).

26. "Mighty Mark Twain Overawes Marines," *NYT,* May 12, 1907 (*MTTCI,* 600–601).

27. "As Mark Twain Watched Drill," *Baltimore American,* May 11, 1907 (*MTTCI,* 598).

28. "Mark Twain Departs," *Baltimore Sun,* May 12, 1907 (*MTTCI,* 605).

29. *MTB,* 1379; CC, *My Father, Mark Twain,* 270.

30. "Mark Twain an Honored Guest," *Baltimore American,* May 10, 1907 (*MTTCI,* 594).

31. AD, May 23, 1907 (*Autob/AMT,* 348).

32. Gribben, *Mark Twain's Library,* 2:797.

33. AD, May 23, 1907 (*Autob/AMT*, 348–49).

34. *MT Speaking*, 237.

CHAPTER FIVE: AUTOBIOGRAPHY HOUSE

1. *Autob/MTA*, 1:226.

2. Frank Kintrea, "Tuxedo Park," *American Heritage*, August–September 1978; MT to HHR, May 29, 1907 (*Ltrs-Rogers*, 625–26).

3. "Some New Twain Stories," *Kansas City Star*, October 6, 1907.

4. *MTB*, 676.

5. Isabel Lyon's account of how Paine lost Orion's manuscript is given in her annotated copy of *MTB*, 676.

6. Woolf, *Here Am I*, 78; MT to HHR, May 29, 1907 (*Ltrs-Rogers*, 625–26).

7. IVL, January 13, 1907; Doris Webster's interview with IVL, October 25, 1953, and May 17, 1953.

8. IVL, March 28, 1907.

9. Paine, *Dwellers in Arcady*, 114. Paine lived in Redding from 1905 to 1917 and gave a slightly fictionalized account of his life there in a book published in 1919, *Dwellers in Arcady: The Story of an Abandoned Farm*. For information about Redding, and for a tour of Paine's farm, I am indebted to the current occupants, Dr. Paul Rutkowski and Szilvi Meinert.

10. MT to CC, August 3, 1906.

11. *MTB*, 1446–47.

12. "Mark Twain's Wanderings at an End," *NYT*, March 31, 1907.

13. MT to Emilie Rogers, November [5?], 1906 (*Ltrs-Rogers*, 620).

14. JC, December 28, 1906.

15. IVL, March 25, 1907; IVL to Raffaello Stiattesi, January 25, 1907.

16. MT to CC, May 2, 1907.

17. MT to CC, February 24, 1907. Not much is known about the background of Charles Wark, though an article of 1908 in a Washington paper does identify him as "Charles Wark, of this city" ("Mark Twain Quits Gay Old New York," *Washington Times*, September 7, 1908).

18. JC, July 4, 1906.

19. JC, October 4 and 5, 1906.

20. Swafford, *Charles Ives*, 471 (Ives knew Gabrilowitsch in America, where the Russian pianist became a conductor of the Detroit Symphony in 1918); Sachs, *Rubinstein*, 35.

21. Ossip Gabrilowitsch, "Memoir of Leschetizky," *NYT*, December 7, 1930.

22. For the background of Clara's relationship with Ossip, see her *My Husband, Gabrilowitsch*, 16 and 43. For information about Ossip's brief affair with Alma Mahler, see Giroud, *Alma Mahler*, 68–69 and 72.

PART TWO: AMERICAN IDOL
CHAPTER SIX: COLLEGE OF ONE

1. *Autob/MTA*, 1:264.

2. Cortissoz, *The Life of Whitelaw Reid*, 2:380–81.

3. *MTB*, 461.

4. MT to Olivia Clemens, September 11, 1872 (*Ltrs-5*, 155).

5. MT to WDH, March 14, 1904 (*Ltrs-Howells*, 2:782); MT to Mary Mason Fairbanks, November 2, 1872 (*Ltrs-5*, 206).

6. *MTB,* 1379.

7. JC, May 21, 1907; JC, July 22, 1906.

8. JC, June 8, 1907.

9. *MTB,*1381.

10. IVL, June 21, 1907.

11. MT to HHR, April 8–9 and June 13, 1900 (*Ltrs-Rogers,* 440 and 446); *LFA,* 308–9.

12. IVL, June 21, 1907; "Mark Twain at Windsor," *The Observer* (London), June 23, 1907 (*MTFWE,* 29).

13. MT to John McComb, June 8, 1867 (*Ltrs-2,* 61).

14. *MT Speaking,* 364.

15. "Mark Twain Sails for Oxford Honors," and "Weather," *NYT,* June 9, 1907 (*MT Speaking,* 554–55), with additional quotations from "Mark Twain Sails, Will Get Degree," *Washington Times,* June 9, 1907.

16. "Mark Twain Tells Literary Secret and Many Other Things," *Baltimore News,* May 10, 1907 (*MTTCI,* 589).

17. *MTFWE,* 142–43; " 'G.B.S.' and Mark Twain," *Pall Mall Gazette* (London), June 18, 1907 (*MTFWE,* 18).

18. "Matters of Moment," *Daily Express* (London), June 19, 1907 (*MTFWE,* 144); "Mark Twain London's Lion," *NYT,* June 20, 1907; "Mark Twain on Secrets of Youth," *Morning Leader* (London), June 19, 1907 (*MTFWE,* 15).

19. Ward, *A First-Class Temperament,* 15.

20. Kaplan, *Mr. Clemens and Mark Twain,* 372; *MTB,* 1382.

21. Churchill is singled out as one of the politicians welcoming Twain in "Twain in the Commons," *NYT,* June 25, 1907; Manchester, *The Last Lion,* 388.

22. MT, "Introducing Winston S. Churchill," *CT,* 2:455; *Autob/MTIE,* 330.

23. *Mark Twain: The Critical Heritage,* 290.

24. The figure of eight thousand guests was reported in the *Illustrated London News* (June 29, 1907); "Twain Amuses the King and Queen," *NYT,* June 23, 1907; *MT Speaking,* 557.

25. *LFA,* 306.

26. AD, August 28, 1907 (*MTFWE,* 95).

27. HHR to MT, June 27, 1907 (*Ltrs-Rogers,* 630).

28. "Mark Twain in England," *Harper's Weekly,* July 20, 1907.

29. The description of the bathrobe is Twain's (*MTTCI,* 629).

30. "Twain Startles London," *NYT,* June 21, 1907.

31. "Mark Twain and the Bathrobe," *NYT,* June 24, 1907.

32. IVL, June 21, 1907; CC, *My Father, Mark Twain,* 270.

CHAPTER SEVEN: A YANK AT OXFORD

1. *MT Speaking,* 574.

2. Curzon's words are quoted in Simon Schama, "Superior Person," *The New Yorker,* June 9, 2003. The best photographs of the Oxford procession can be found in *Harper's Weekly,* July 27, 1907.

3. Phelps, *Autobiography with Letters,* 63; MT to JC, June 30, 1907.

4. Rudyard Kipling to John Kipling, June 27, 1907 (*The Letters of Rudyard Kipling,* 3:242).

5. Rudyard Kipling to Anna Smith Balestier, [June 30, 1907] (*The Letters of Rudyard Kipling,* 3:248–49).

6. Kipling, *From Sea to Sea,* 2:170.

7. Rudyard Kipling to Anna Smith Balestier, [June 30, 1907] (*The Letters of Rudyard Kipling,* 3:248).

8. "Mark Twain for Penny Post," *New York Sun*, July 2, 1907 (*MTTCI*, 635).

9. "Mark Twain, D. Litt., Oxon.," *NYT*, June 27, 1907; *MTB*, 1393; *MT & JB*, 246; *Harper's Weekly*, July 20, 1907.

10. A translation of Curzon's Latin sentence appears in a caption for one of the photos in *Harper's Weekly*, July 27, 1907. A shorter, slightly different translation appears in *MTB*, 1394.

11. *MT & JB*, 246.

12. "Dr. Mark Twain," *Daily Graphic* (London), June 27, 1907 (*MTFWE*, 53).

13. AD, July 30, 1907 (*MTFWE*, 64).

14. MT to JC, June 30, 1907. For background information on the pageant, see "The Oxford Pageant," *The Bookman*, June 1907; and "Pageant Took Pride of Place," *Oxford Mail*, June 25, 2007.

15. "A Woman's Story of 'Dr.' Mark Twain's Latest Trip Across the Atlantic," *Washington Post*, August 4, 1907. (A similar description of the birds and swans can be found in MT to CC, June 30, 1907.)

16. Masters, *Now Barabbas Was a Rotter*, 12.

17. Ibid., 231.

18. MT to J.Y.W. MacAlister, April 6, 1897.

19. *Autob/AMT*, 350.

20. Ibid., 350–51.

21. *MT Speaking*, 677, quoting from *The Times* (London), July 1, 1907. For Twain's memory of "persistent retreating" in the Civil War, see *Autob/AMT*, 102.

22. *Autob/AMT*, 350–53

23. *MT Speaking*, 574–75.

24. "Mark Twain's Experiences in the Hands of British Interviewers," *NYT*, June 30, 1907.

25. "Twain's Daughter Talks About Him," *NYT*, June 14, 1908.

26. The Fleet Street pub was Ye Olde Cheshire Cheese. See Belford, *Bram Stoker*, 313; and Gribben, *Mark Twain's Library*, 2:668.

27. *MT & JB*, 250; Shaw, *Collected Letters: 1898–1910*, 697.

28. Fatout, *Mark Twain on the Lecture Circuit*, 288; *Autob/MTIE*, 331.

29. "Samuel L. Clemens Interviews the Famous Humorist, Mark Twain," *Seattle Star*, November 30, 1905 (*MTTCI*, 528).

30. *MT Speaking*, 582–83; Charles Vale, "Mark Twain as Orator," *Forum*, July 1910. Twain said his source for the seafaring anecdote was Richard Henry Dana's *Two Years Before the Mast*. The relevant passage, which he adapted for his own purposes, can be found in chapter 35 of Dana's book (Gribben, *Mark Twain's Library*, 1:171). Kittery Point is probably a sly reference to William Dean Howells, whose beloved summer home was located in that part of Maine. Kittery isn't mentioned in Dana's book.

31. "Twain Postpones Funeral," *NYT*, July 13, 1907.

CHAPTER EIGHT: YOUNG AND OLD

1. "Mark Twain Comes in White," *New York Sun*, July 23, 1907 (*MTFWE*, 123).

2. IVL, June 23 and 24, 1907.

3. Ibid.

4. Ibid., March 26, 1907, and March 30, 1905.

5. Harnsberger, *Mark Twain, Family Man*, 236–37. Though this book gives a fairly accurate report of the Halifax incident, it mistakenly says the collision took place in the fall.

6. "Crash in Halifax Harbor: The Rosalind Cuts Down the Senlac—Mark Twain's Daughter on the Former," *New York Sun*, July 2, 1907. A typical press story of the

incident is "Mark's Daughter Cool as Cucumber," *Fort Wayne Daily News* (Indiana), July 2, 1907. Also see "Steamers in Collision: Daughter of Mark Twain a Passenger—All Are Rescued," *Washington Herald,* July 2, 1907; "Steamer Run Down by Liner Rosalind," *NYT,* July 2, 1907; and "Steamers Crash, Thrilling Rescues," *Trenton Evening News* (New Jersey), July 2, 1907.

7. "Social and Personal," *WP,* July 4, 1907.

8. "Mark Twain Will Not Marry Again," *WP,* July 6, 1907. The source of the article is cited as the *New York Herald.*

9. "Marry Mr. Twain? Well I Guess Not," *Fort Wayne Daily News* (Indiana), July 3, 1907.

10. MT to CC, July 12, 1907 (*MTFWE,* 218).

11. "A Woman's Story of 'Dr.' Mark Twain's Latest Trip Across the Atlantic," *WP,* August 4, 1907. This article also appeared in the *New York Sun* on the same day under the headline "Traveling with Mark Twain."

12. MT, "From Twain by Wireless," *NYT,* July 18, 1907; "Dr. Mark Twain Slaps King's Back," *Trenton Evening News* (New Jersey), July 24, 1907.

13. "Twain Home with English Jokes at 30 Cents a Word," *New York American,* July 23, 1907 (*MTTCI,* 639); "Mark Twain Comes in White," *New York Sun,* July 23, 1907 (*MTFWE,* 123).

14. *MT Speaking,* 585–86; "Mark Twain Comes in White," *New York Sun,* July 23, 1907 (*MTFWE,* 123); "Dr. Mark Twain Home with His Honors," *New York Herald,* July 23, 1907 (*MTTCI,* 645); "Twain Home with English Jokes at 30 Cents a Word," *New York American,* July 23, 1907 (*MTTCI,* 639).

15. "Mark Twain Comes in White," *New York Sun,* July 23, 1907 (*MTFWE,* 123).

16. "Mark Twain's Daughter Demurs," *Fitchburg Daily Sentinel* (Massachusetts), October 4, 1907.

17. *MTB,* 1404.

18. MT to HHR, July 29, 1907 (*Ltrs-Rogers,* 631). Despite the best efforts of the Rogers family, press speculation about Rogers's illness was rampant. See "Wall Street Gossip," *WP,* July 30, 1907; and "Henry H. Rogers Ill," the Associated Press and the *New York American,* July 26, 1907. Urban Broughton recalled moving his father-in-law to Long Island in "H. H. Rogers Had Stroke Last July," *NYT,* September 17, 1907.

19. Emilie Rogers to MT, August 12, 1907 (*Ltrs-Rogers,* 632).

20. "Oil Fine," *NY Trib,* August 4, 1907; "Fined 29 Millions," *WP,* August 4, 1907.

21. MT, "Notebook 48" [1907].

22. HHR to MT, August 30, 1907 (*Ltrs-Rogers,* 636).

23. "Oil King Rogers Is Well, Though Reporting Sick," *NYEW,* September 18, 1907; "H. H. Rogers Drives Auto," *NYT,* September 18, 1907.

PART THREE: THE WORLD ACCORDING TO MARK
CHAPTER NINE: PRINCES AND PAUPERS

1. *MTB,* 964.

2. William Justus Boies, "Trust Companies and the Panic," *The American Review of Reviews,* December 1907. In a letter of January 16, 1906, Katharine Harrison first suggested to Twain that he put his money in the Knickerbocker Trust Company (*Ltrs-Rogers,* 606). Stillman's National City Bank was closely associated with Standard Oil. The Aeolian Company and Aeolian Hall were located at 362 Fifth Avenue in 1907.

3. MT to Dorothy Quick, [October 19, 1907] (*Ltrs-Angelfish,* 76).

4. IVL, October 22, 1907; "Pays Out $8,000,000 and Then Suspends," *NYT,* October 23, 1907.

5. JC to Nancy Brush, October 31, 1907; IVL, October 23, 1907. The suicide of

Knickerbocker depositor Valentine Hayerdahl is described in "Trust Depositor a Suicide," *NYT,* November 27, 1907.

6. "Preachers Exhort Depositors to Calm," *NYT,* October 28, 1907.

7. "C. T. Barney, Deposed President of Knickerbocker Trust Co., a Suicide," *NYEW,* November 14, 1907.

8. IVL, October 23, 1907; *MTB,* 1445.

9. "Mr. Rockefeller Talks," *NY Trib,* January 25, 1908.

10. Strouse, *Morgan,* 589 and 593; Chernow, *Titan,* 543.

11. Sinclair, *The Moneychangers,* chapter one.

12. MT to the *New York World,* [typed letter circa October 27, 1907] (carbon in Special Collections, ViU; published in Macnaughton, *Mark Twain's Last Years as a Writer,* 235). In 1906 Upton Sinclair had given a copy of *The Jungle* to Twain (Gribben, *Mark Twain's Library,* 2:644), who later replied that he had been forced to put the book down halfway through it because, according to Sinclair, Twain "could not endure the anguish it caused him." For his recollections of Twain in 1906–1908, see Sinclair's *Mammonart,* 327–28, and Arthur, *Radical Innocent,* 110–11.

13. Ralph Ashcroft to Julien T. Davies, November 26, 1907 (Special Collections, ViU); Davies was a lawyer for the Knickerbocker's directors.

14. *WP,* January 27, 1908. "Twain Out $32,000 in Plasmon Failure," *New York American,* December 21, 1907 (*MTTCI,* 660.) To add to his troubles in 1907, the Plasmon Company of America went broke at the end of the year, but Twain had already given up hope of seeing his investment returned, and was grateful that some of the money he had poured into the food supplement over the years was still returning 6 percent from the solvent British branch of the business.

15. "To Make Good Citizens—The Theatre for Children," *NYT,* November 12, 1911. Bennett describes his visit to the Lower East Side in *Your United States,* 186–87.

16. MT, *The Outrageous Mark Twain,* 38.

17. Quoted in Howe, *World of Our Fathers,* 234.

18. "Mark Twain Tells of Being an Actor," *NYT,* April 15, 1907. On March 14, 1885, Twain had written to J. B. Pond, "You ought to have been here to-night to see Susie & Clara & a dozen of the neighbors' children play half a dozen stirring scenes from the Prince & the Pauper." As the basis of her production, Herts used the dramatization prepared by Abby Sage Richardson in 1889 for a Broadway performance.

19. Chotzinoff, *A Lost Paradise,* 362.

20. Herts, *The Children's Educational Theatre,* 60.

21. MT to Frances Nunnally, October 28, 1907 (*Ltrs-Angelfish,* 80).

22. Nasaw, *Andrew Carnegie,* 693–96.

23. MT to Andrew Carnegie, February 6, 1901 (quoted in Carnegie, *Autobiography of Andrew Carnegie,* 282).

24. *MTB,* 964.

25. "Greet Mark Twain," *NY Trib,* November 20, 1907.

26. *MTB,* 1412; "Uptown Audience at Children's Play," *NYT,* November 20, 1907. The *New York Times* reported that Carnegie was among the guests attending the performance.

27. "Uptown Audience at Children's Play," *NYT,* November 20, 1907; "Mark Twain on the Scope of the Children's Theater," *Brooklyn Eagle,* November 24, 1907 (*MTTCI,* 656).

28. Herts, *The Children's Educational Theatre,* 80. Collier was not the only important donor, and it was expected that others would come forward in the months ahead to help build the new theater. But Collier's position as the chief benefactor to the children's theater is confirmed in "Children's Theater Split by a Quarrel," *NYT,* February 11, 1909 ("Mr. Collier guaranteeing the payment of immediate expenses"), and "End of Children's Theater," *NYT,* August 10, 1909 ("It is said that of late Mr.

Collier has contributed most of the funds toward maintaining the theater"). Twain's announcement of the plan for the new building is reported in "Child Actors Warm to Their Mark Twain," *NYT,* April 24, 1908. Though Carnegie may have donated some money to the project, whatever he may have given doesn't seem to have satisfied Twain's expectations or Alice Herts's. In 1905–1907 Twain had helped Collier in another charitable cause—the purchase of the Kentucky farm where Abraham Lincoln was born, and the subsequent establishment of a Lincoln birthplace memorial. Collier's most famous, and most enduring benefaction, is the prestigious aviation prize awarded annually in his name by the U.S. National Aeronautic Association, the winners of which have included Neil Armstrong, Howard Hughes, and Orville Wright. The publisher loved flying and bought his first plane from the Wright brothers.

29. Twain's criticisms of Carnegie can be found in AD, December 2, 1907 (Autob/*MTIE*, 36–51).

30. Herts, *The Children's Educational Theatre,* x. According to press reports at the time ("Children's Theater Split by a Quarrel," *NYT,* February 11, 1909; and "Twain's Theater to Close," *Chicago Tribune,* June 30, 1909), Alice Herts and her assistant Emma Sheridan Fry clashed over questions of interference from the stage manager Jacob Heniger. Fry objected that she couldn't work with Heniger, but Herts took his side in the argument and dismissed Fry. Some of the older children in the acting company petitioned Twain for help, asking him "to use your great influence in having Mrs. Fry restored to her former position" ("Children's Theater Split by a Quarrel," *NYT,* February 11, 1909). But there was little Twain could do to resolve such a dispute. After Herts recovered from her breakdown, she married Jacob Heniger in 1913. She taught at Columbia University and wrote two books on the subject of teaching children to act. She died in the 1930s. For Paine's comment on the failure of the acting company, see *MTB,* 1412.

CHAPTER TEN: TO HEAVEN AND BACK

1. MT, "Extract from Captain Stormfield's Visit to Heaven," *CT,* 2:838.

2. Andrew Carnegie to MT, [May 22,] 1909 (Nasaw, *Andrew Carnegie,* 722).

3. "Happy Pessimist Is Mark Twain," *Boston Herald,* November 6, 1905 (*Critical Essays on Mark Twain,* 180), "Twain's Plan to Beat the Copyright Law," *NYT,* December 12, 1906.

4. Kipling, *From Sea to Sea,* 2:174.

5. AD, August 29, 1906 (Autob/*MTIE*, 247).

6. AD, August 30, 1906 (*BAMT,* 137).

7. MT, "Extract from Captain Stormfield's Visit to Heaven," *CT,* 2:829 and 846.

8. *BAMT,* 137 (for the reader's convenience, grammatical errors in Lyon's comment have been silently corrected).

9. *N&J-1,* 253; *BAMT,* 139.

10. MT, *Roughing It,* chapter 50.

11. MT, "Extract from Captain Stormfield's Visit to Heaven," *CT,* 2:850, 838, and 832.

12. IVL, Notes for William Howe on *A Connecticut Yankee in King Arthur's Court,* 1933. William T. H. Howe (1874–1939) was president of the American Book Company and a Mark Twain collector for whom Isabel Lyon prepared several sets of notes as guides to Twain's life and works. In the 1930s she often visited Howe at Freelands, his estate in northern Kentucky. After his death Howe's large library became part of the Berg Collection of the New York Public Library.

13. *MTB,* 1430–31.

14. MT to Carl Thalbitzer, November 26, 1902. When he corresponded with Twain, Thalbitzer was a twenty-six-year-old writer in Copenhagen.

15. IVL, Notes for William Howe, April 1933.

16. Ibid., June 1935.

17. MT, *Is Shakespeare Dead?,* chapter 6.

18. "Miss Clara Clemens Sings," *NY Trib,* November 10, 1907.

19. JC, October 7, 1907; MT to JC, October 8, 1907.

20. JC to Nancy Brush, November 7, 1907.

21. "Table Gossip," *Boston Globe,* December 1, 1907. Quotations from the *Boston Transcript* are taken from Harnsberger, *Mark Twain, Family Man,* 237, and appear to have come from an article in Clara's own scrapbook. Clara's scheduled appearance at the YWCA, November 9, is noted in "Renewed Activity in the World of Music," *NYT,* November 3, 1907. Chickering Hall was a short distance from Boston's Symphony Hall, and next door to Horticultural Hall. It operated as a movie theater in later years and was demolished in 1968.

22. MT to CC, September 5, 1907. The idea that Clara's success in Boston was "decisive" is mentioned in "Miss Clemens on Tour," *Syracuse Herald* (New York), March 17, 1908.

23. IVL, October 5, 1907. In a letter to Nancy Brush of December 5, 1907, Jean writes with great joy about the carving of herself. In his professional writings Dr. Peterson did argue on occasion that, in extreme cases, some epileptics could do violence to others, but he thought such cases were rare and involved patients suffering not only from epilepsy but also from insanity.

24. JC to Nancy Brush, December 26, 1907.

CHAPTER ELEVEN: MANHATTAN MELODRAMA

1. *Autob/MTIE,* 317.

2. J. H. Twichell to A. B. Paine, February 26, 1908 (*The Twainian,* September–October 1970).

3. "Bill McDonald, Evangelist," *NYT,* November 1, 1908. See also Utley, *Lone Star Justice,* 257.

4. *The Intimate Papers of Colonel House,* 1:20–21.

5. Ibid., 1:21.

6. Paine, *Captain Bill McDonald, Texas Ranger,* 394–95 and 14. McDonald's guide at Coney Island was Paine, who was something of an expert on the place, having written a long article about it for the *Century Magazine* in August 1904 ("The New Coney Island").

7. *The Intimate Papers of Colonel House,* 1:21.

8. IVL, January 3, 1908.

9. Ibid., January 5, 7, and 8, 1908; Barrymore, *Memories,* 155.

10. Ibid., January 16 and 17, 1908.

11. "Mark Twain Sick," *Boston Globe,* January 19, 1908; "Mark Twain No Worse," *NYT,* January 20, 1908.

12. IVL, January 19 and 23, 1908. The neighbor who sent the oysters was Maud Littleton, wife of attorney Martin Littleton.

13. Ibid., January 19, 1906.

14. At twenty-four, Paine married his first wife, Wilhelmina Schultz, of Fort Scott, Kansas (*National Cyclopedia of American Biography,* 28:113–14). IVL, June 6 and September 30, 1906.

15. Lyon's comments on Paine's emotions are taken from the private annotations she later made in his biography of Twain.

16. IVL, January 22, 1908; IVL, Notes for William Howe, 1936.

17. MT to WDH, January 22, 1908, and WDH to MT, February 4, 1908 (*Ltrs-Howells*, 2:828–29).

18. Albert Bigelow Paine to IVL, January 28, 1908.

19. "Elinor Glyn Talks About Her American Critics," *NYT*, October 6, 1907; "Mrs. Glyn on Her Own Book," *NYT*, December 18, 1907; De Courcy, *The Viceroy's Daughters*, 21; Glyn, *Three Weeks*, 15.

20. IVL, Notes for William Howe, [1937]; Margaret Illington's "statuesque" figure is praised in Burke, *With a Feather on My Nose*, 51. Without citing any evidence, Anthony Glyn writes that Twain and Elinor Glyn had met before the "dinner given by Daniel Frohmann [sic]" (Glyn, *Elinor Glyn*, 144). But Lyon's recollection of the event is more detailed and seems the best available source in this case.

21. AD, January 13, 1908 (*Autob/MTIE*, 313); "Critics Idiots—Mrs. Glyn," *NYT*, November 17, 1907; "Pilgrim Mothers Amused Mrs. Glyn," *NYT*, December 23, 1907; "Mrs. Glyn's Fire Uncovers Opponent," *NYT*, December 24, 1907; "Mrs. Glyn Sails Away," *NYT*, February 9, 1908.

22. IVL, Notes for William Howe, [1937].

23. Glyn, *Elinor Glyn*, 143; AD, January 13, 1908 (*Autob/MTIE*, 314–16); Etherington-Smith and Pilcher, *The "It" Girls*, 107.

24. AD, January 13, 1908 (*Autob/MTIE*, 315); AD, June 25, 1906 (*BAMT*, 330).

25. MT to Elinor Glyn, January 24, 1908 (Glyn, *Elinor Glyn*, 144).

26. *MTB*, 1407.

27. "Littleton Pleads Insanity for Thaw," *NYT*, January 30, 1908; and *MT Speaking*, 592. For information on Twain's interest in Thaw's first trial, see Susan Gillman, " 'Dementia Americana': Mark Twain, 'Wapping Alice,' and the Harry K. Thaw Trial," *Critical Inquiry*, Winter 1988 (later published in Gillman, *Dark Twins*).

28. Nesbit, *Prodigal Days*, 56.

29. Sinclair, *The Brass Check*, 24. Sinclair wrote "Is Chicago Meat Clean?" for the April 22, 1905, issue of *Collier's*, but felt that the magazine didn't give enough space to his article and didn't do enough to promote the campaign against the unsanitary practices of the meatpacking industry. For details of Collier's "dog ballet" party, see MT to JC, February 14, 1908; "Collie Ballet for Collier," *NYT*, February 14, 1908; and "Social Gossip," *WP*, February 15, 1908.

30. Gibson's *The Eternal Question* was so popular that *Collier's* published a mounted print suitable for framing in a 1905 booklet, *Charles Dana Gibson: A Study of the Man and Some Recent Examples of His Work*. Looking back on her life in old age, Nesbit concluded that Robert Collier was one of the few men who had treated her well in her youth. When Twentieth Century-Fox produced a film in 1955 about her relationship with Thaw and White—*The Girl in the Red Velvet Swing*—Nesbit was hired to work on it as a script consultant, and she made sure that Robert Collier's character was given an influential and respectable part in her story. For details about Collier's life, see his obituary in *NYT*, November 9, 1918.

31. Uruburu, *American Eve*, 327.

32. Morrison, *John Barrymore*, 43; Uruburu, *American Eve*, 328; "Fled from White, Thaw's Wife Says," *NYT*, February 9, 1907.

33. *A Connecticut Yankee in King Arthur's Court*, chapters 22 and 41; Isabel Lyon's annotated copy of *MTB*, 764.

34. *NYEW*, February 8, 1908.

CHAPTER TWELVE: TOURIST TRADE

1. This quotation has appeared in many versions over the years. My source is the typescript "Our Friend Mark Twain," by Twain's friend in Bermuda Marion Schuyler Allen (BmuHA). For slightly different versions, see Wilson, *Francis Wilson's Life of Himself,* 299; Budd, *Mark Twain,* 196; and Dias, *Mark Twain and Henry Huttleston Rogers,* 160. In 1905 the phrase "tainted money" was widely used in the press after some Congregational ministers objected to a Rockefeller donation of $100,000 to the Congregational Board of Foreign Missions because Standard Oil money was considered "tainted" by greed and corruption (Nevins, *Study in Power,* 2:345–46).

2. MT to Frances Nunnally, January 21, 1908; MT to Dorothy Quick, [January 21, 1908] (*Ltrs-Angelfish,* 99–100).

3. "Better Copper Feeling," January 23, 1908, and "Prosperity of the Prosecuted," February 18, 1908, *WSJ.*

4. Quotations from Twain and Rogers have been drawn from the following reports: "Rogers Pits His Humor Against Mark Twain's," *NYEW,* February 22, 1908; "Rival Jokesmiths Off for Bermuda," *New York World,* February 23, 1908; "Mark Twain and Rogers at Sea," *Oakland Tribune* (California), February 23, 1908; " 'Rogers Is Busted' — Twain," *New York American,* February 23, 1908 (*MTTCI,* 662–63). The headline "Two Jokers; One Deck" appeared in the *New York Tribune.*

5. IVL, February 28, 1908; "Rogers Pits His Humor Against Mark Twain's," *NYEW,* February 22, 1908.

6. "Two Jokers; One Deck," *NY Trib,* February 23, 1908.

7. IVL, February 24, 1908; Wallace, *Mark Twain and the Happy Island,* 57.

8. The baseball game at Richmond Ground in Hamilton was reported a few days later in the *St. Louis Post-Dispatch* on March 8, 1908 ("Mark and Baseball," *Mark Twain Quarterly,* Winter–Spring 1945); Rogers's shaky condition after the game was noted in "H. H. Rogers Feeble," *WP,* March 6, 1908; IVL, February 28, 1908.

9. Quoted in *Ltrs-Angelfish,* 106; Wallace, *Mark Twain and the Happy Island,* 55. For information on Elizabeth Wallace, see the entry for her in Cameron, *The Biographical Cyclopaedia of American Women.*

10. Wallace, *Mark Twain and the Happy Island,* 56–57; HHR to MT, December 18, 1908 (*Ltrs-Rogers,* 657).

11. MT to Dorothy Quick, March 10, 1908 (*Ltrs-Angelfish,* 118).

12. Hulbert, *The Story of Mrs. Peck,* 176 (Mrs. Peck's full name was Mary Allen Hulbert Peck); Wallace, *Mark Twain and the Happy Island,* 68–69.

13. John S. Monagan, "The President and Mrs. Peck," *The Bermudian,* February 1984 (Levin, *Edith and Woodrow,* 127).

14. Levin, *Edith and Woodrow,* 126; Mary Peck published the photo of her with Twain in her autobiography, *The Story of Mrs. Peck,* where she also refers to Twain and Rogers as "those two old dears" (175).

15. Woodrow Wilson to Mary Peck, February 6, 1907 (*The Papers of Woodrow Wilson,* 17:29).

16. Woodrow Wilson to Ellen Wilson, January 26 [and 27], 1908 (*The Papers of Woodrow Wilson,* 17:607). In letters of this period to his wife, Ellen, Wilson pretended that his interest in Mary Peck was purely social. The letter dated January 26 is a long one and seems to have been written over the course of two days, since Twain's first winter visit to Bermuda began Monday, January 27, 1908.

17. Mary Peck to Woodrow Wilson, October 11, 1915 (Levin, *Edith and Woodrow,* 137); O'Toole, *When Trumpets Call,* 216; Levin, *Edith and Woodrow,* 131.

18. Woodrow Wilson to Mary Peck, January 10, 1922 (Levin, *Edith and Woodrow,* 126).

19. Woodrow Wilson to Ellen Wilson, February 4, 1908 (*The Papers of Woodrow Wilson,* 17:612).

20. Woodrow Wilson to John Grier Hibben, January 26, 1907 (*The Papers of Woodrow Wilson,* 17:17); "A Petition," 1908 (*The Papers of Woodrow Wilson,* 17: 609–10).

21. Gene Weingarten, "An Honorable Affair," *WP,* January 10, 1999.

22. "An Outline and Two Drafts of Statements," [circa September 20, 1915] (*The Papers of Woodrow Wilson,* 34:496).

23. Hulbert, *The Story of Mrs. Peck,* 177. In her journal entry for February 24, 1908, Isabel Lyon notes that rain upset the plan for Twain and Rogers to visit Peck and Wilson at Shoreby on Wilson's last day in Bermuda. Another celebrated person in Bermuda whom Rogers failed to meet was Upton Sinclair, who was staying on the island for the winter. Twain had visited Sinclair on the previous trip, but must have decided that too many sparks would fly if his friend from the Standard Oil Trust met the writer whom a Bermuda newspaper called the "assailant of the beef trust" (*Royal Gazette,* February 8, 1908).

24. MT to Emilie Rogers, March 2, 1908 (*Ltrs-Rogers,* 644).

25. AD, April 17, 1908, and February 12, 1908 (*Ltrs-Angelfish,* xx and xvii).

26. "News from Mark Twain," *NYT,* March 27, 1908. The saying originally appeared in MT, *Pudd'nhead Wilson,* chapter 8.

27. Wallace, *Mark Twain and the Happy Island,* 44.

28. AD, February 13, 1908 (*Ltrs-Angelfish,* 105–6).

29. Fishkin, *Was Huck Black?,* 49. Twain's sketch "Sociable Jimmy" appeared in the *New York Times* on November 29, 1874. I am grateful to my former student Nicole Remesnik for locating information about William Evans in her hometown of Paris, Illinois. For more details about Remesnik's discovery, see *Ltrs-5,* 20–21.

30. Marion Schuyler Allen, "Our Friend Mark Twain" (BmuHA). One of the main streets in Belmont, New York, is named after Marion's family, but it was also the hometown of the Allens. For information about his family, I am grateful to Helen Allen's son, Charles M. Nelles, who lived in Victoria, British Columbia, until his death in 2006 at the age of eighty-nine.

31. MT to Helen Allen, April 25, 1908 (*Ltrs-Angelfish,* 144).

32. "Mark Twain at Bermuda," *Human Life,* May 1910 (*MTTCI,* 694–95).

33. Marion Schuyler Allen, "Our Friend Mark Twain" (BmuHA).

34. AD, February 12, 1908 (*Ltrs-Angelfish,* xvii). Twain met Margaret Blackmer during the first of his two winter visits to Bermuda and sent out the first angelfish pin in early February. In AD, April 17, 1908, he sets out his ideas for the Aquarium and the club's badge and says that he bought the angelfish pins in Bermuda, but that they were made in Norway.

35. "Mark Twain Faced 2 Perils," *New York American,* April 14, 1908; "Twain Was 'Soused,' " *NY Trib,* April 14, 1908; and "Mark Twain a Hero? He Won't Admit It," *New York World,* April 14, 1908 (*MTTCI,* 664–65).

CHAPTER THIRTEEN: FAREWELL, FIFTH AVENUE

1. "Twain Was 'Soused,' " *NY Trib,* April 14, 1908 (*MTTCI,* 666).

2. MT to Dorothy Sturgis, April 13, 1908 (*Ltrs-Angelfish,* 133).

3. *MTB,* 1415–17.

4. "Children Celebrate Mass in New York," *Washington Times,* April 29, 1908; "Twain, Child at Seventy, at Children's Mass," *Fort Wayne Journal-Gazette* (Indiana), April 30, 1908. For background on the centennial celebrations of the archdiocese, see

"Laity Pays Tribute to Cardinal Logue," *NYT,* April 30, 1908; and "Thousands Fight for Prelate's Blessing," *NYT,* May 3, 1908.

5. MT, *The Innocents Abroad,* chapter 55; MT, *A Connecticut Yankee in King Arthur's Court,* chapter 8.

6. "Whole City Arrested," *NY Trib,* May 10, 1908.

7. *MT Speaking,* 623–24; "Jubilee Dedication for City College," *NYT,* May 15, 1908; "Twain for Citizenship," *NY Trib,* May 15, 1908.

8. AD, December 2, 1907 (*Autob/MTIE,* 50–51).

9. Willard B. Gatewood, "Theodore Roosevelt and the Coinage Controversy," *American Quarterly,* Spring 1966; *Autob/MTIE,* 50.

10. *MT Speaking,* 624; "Jubilee Dedication for City College," *NYT,* May 15, 1908.

11. "Fight for Coin Motto," *NY Trib,* November 12, 1907; William B. Gatewood, "Theodore Roosevelt and the Coinage Controversy," *American Quarterly,* Spring 1966.

12. *MTB,* 1444–45.

13. JC to Nancy Brush, January 16 [1908].

14. MT to JC, June 19, 1908; MT to Dorothy Sturgis, May 24, [1908] (*Ltrs-Angelfish,* 160); MT to JC, Thursday night [May 21, 1908].

15. JC to MT, May 26, 1908; Hawthorne, *The Lure of the Garden,* 130–33.

16. JC to MT, May 26, 1908.

17. An advertisement for Clara's concert appears in the *Atlanta Constitution* of April 2, 1908; Clara's tour of the South and Midwest is reported in "Miss Clemens on Tour," *Syracuse Herald* (New York), March 17, 1908. (The Grand Opera House in Atlanta later became the Loew's Grand and was the site of the premiere of *Gone with the Wind* in 1939.) MT to CC, March 23 and April 5, 1908.

18. IVL, May 8, 1908.

19. Ibid., May 2, 1908.

20. "The Sunderlands of Stormfield," *Redding Times,* June 19, 1958. This special issue of the paper (a copy of which is available in CU-MARK) celebrates the fiftieth anniversary of Twain's move to Redding.

21. MT to CC, May 19, 1908.

22. "Daughter of Mark Twain to Make Stage Debut Sunday," *Washington Times,* May 29, 1908.

23. MT to CC, June 3, 1908.

24. MT to JC, June 5, 1908.

25. MT to CC, May 19, 1908.

26. Burke, *With a Feather on My Nose,* 70. Twain's praise of Burke is quoted in Long, *Mark Twain Handbook,* 250.

27. MT to Dorothy Quick, [May 12, 1908] (*Ltrs-Angelfish,* 154 and 195). Producer Dan Frohman discovered the actress Maude Light, of Bloomington, Illinois, and made her a Broadway star after changing her name to Margaret Illington, creating the stage name by a combination of Illinois and Bloomington. In 1903 they married, but divorced seven years later. Her career peaked not long after her divorce, and in 1934 she died at fifty-two. Her second husband was Major Edward Bowes, whose *Amateur Hour* radio show helped to launch the career of Frank Sinatra.

28. MT to Carlotta Welles, [late May 1908] (*Ltrs-Angelfish,* 164).

CHAPTER FOURTEEN: CONNECTICUT YANKEE

1. *Autob/NAR,* 152.

2. MT to Mary Rogers, June 15, 1908 (*Ltrs-Mary,* 117).

3. *MTB,* 1448.

4. Coley B. Taylor, quoted in Harnsberger, *Mark Twain, Family Man,* 243.

5. *MTB,* 1450. I have closely followed Paine's eyewitness account for my description of Twain's arrival at his new house.

6. Detailed descriptions of Twain's Redding estate can be found in several sources, including an issue of the *Twainian* for November–December 1948, and Dan Beard's "Mark Twain as a Neighbor," *American Review of Reviews,* May 1910. Twain's comment about the house being "perfect" comes from *MTB,* 1450; he sent his praise to John Howells in a letter of July 3, 1908 (*Ltrs-Howells,* 2:830). The Spring–Fall 2006 issue of the *Mark Twain Journal* includes many photos of both the exterior and interior of the house and copies of the original architectural plans (Kevin Mac Donnell, "Stormfield: A Virtual Tour").

7. MT to Dan Beard, August 28, 1889; *MT Speaking,* 473.

8. Beard, "Mark Twain as a Neighbor," *American Review of Reviews,* May 1910. From 1910 until his death in 1941, "Uncle Dan" Beard held the largely ceremonial title of national scout commissioner in the Boy Scouts of America, but throughout that period he remained an influential voice in the organization as a result of his frequent contributions to its national magazine, *Boys' Life.* In later years he managed so successfully to shed his old persona as an urbane illustrator that many scouts assumed he was an actual pioneer of the Old West when they saw him at camp meetings dressed in buckskin and wearing a white goatee like Buffalo Bill's.

9. MT to JC, June 19, 1908.

10. MT to CC, [June 20, 1908].

11. "Twain's Daughter Talks About Him," *NYT,* June 14, 1908.

12. MT to Mary Rogers, Monday [summer 1908] (*Ltrs-Mary,* 121).

13. Lawton, *A Lifetime with Mark Twain,* 305; "The Lounger," *Putnam's Monthly,* September 1908.

14. IVL, August 8, 1908.

15. Ibid., August 2, 1908.

16. Ibid., August 6, 1908.

17. MT to Mary Rogers, August 17, 1908; MT to Mary Rogers, Monday [summer 1908] (*Ltrs-Mary,* 123 and 121).

18. MT to Emilie Rogers, August 6, 1908, and August 12, 1908 (*Ltrs-Rogers,* 650–52.)

19. Louise Paine Moore, "Mark Twain as I Knew Him," *Redding Times,* June 19, 1958.

20. "Mark Twain Cannot 'Bubble Humor,' He Says, as Demanded," *New York American,* September 8, 1908 (*MTTCI,* 667).

21. Quoted in *Ltrs-Angelfish,* 191–95.

22. Quick, *Mark Twain and Me,* 189.

23. MT to JC, Tuesday [July 28, 1908] (CLjC).

24. MT to Helen Allen [summer 1908] (*Ltrs-Angelfish,* 195).

25. MT to Mary Rogers, Monday [summer 1908] (*Ltrs-Mary,* 120–21).

26. IVL, September 3, 1908.

27. MT to Helen Allen, August 13, 1908 (BmuHA).

28. AD, July 3, 1908 (*Autob/MTIE,* 293–94).

29. AD, July 3, 1908 (*Autob/MTIE,* 295).

30. *MTB,* 1455; AD, July 8, 1908 (*Autob/MTIE,* 299).

31. *MT Speaking,* 679.

32. "In the Interpreter's House," *The American Magazine,* July 1910; AD, July 9, 1908 (*Autob/MTIE,* 303); *MTB,* 1456.

33. MT, "Ashcroft-Lyon Manuscript" (1909).

34. Ibid.

35. MT to JC, Thursday night [July 2, 1908] (CLjC).

36. AD, July 3, 1908 (*Autob/MTIE*, 295). The Thomas Bailey Aldrich Memorial Association, founded by Lilian, continued to oversee the boyhood home until 1979, when it became part of a large museum district in old Portsmouth called Strawbery Banke.

37. MT to JC, Tuesday [July 28, 1908] (CLjC).

38. MT to Mary Rogers, August 17, 1908 (*Ltrs-Mary*, 123).

39. JC to Isabel Lyon, August 5, 1908; JC to Nancy Brush, August 1, 1908.

40. IVL, September 26, 1908.

41. "Editor Moffett Dies, Struggling in Surf," *NYT*, August 2, 1908.

42. MT to Emilie Rogers, August 6, 1908 (*Ltrs-Rogers*, 651); IVL, August 4, 1908; "Samuel E. Moffett's Funeral," *New York Sun*, August 5, 1908.

43. IVL, August 6, 1908.

44. MT to Susan Crane, August 12, 1908 (*MTB*, 1459).

45. In the spring of 1908 Twain saw Kennedy's *The Servant in the House* in New York and called it "a noble play" (*Ltrs-Angelfish*, 169). One of his angelfish, Dorothy Sturgis, recalled in 1967, "Also there was Mr. Ashcroft, known as 'Benares,' because of *The Servant in the House*, a very popular current play" (Gribben, *Mark Twain's Library*, 1:368). In a letter to Margaret Blackmer of January 3, 1909, Twain refers to Ashcroft as "Lord Bishop of Benares" (*Ltrs-Angelfish*, 245).

46. IVL, October 26, 1908.

47. "Weddings of a Day: Wark-Cullis," *NYT*, October 11, 1903. For other information about Wark and Clara, see Laura Skandera Trombley, "Mark Twain's *Annus Horribilis* of 1908–1909," *American Literary Realism*, Winter 2008. Trombley gives an earlier date for the Wark marriage than that recorded in the *New York Times*, but she includes the intriguing information from a Wark relative that Charles and Edith were the parents of twins. She points out that when the marriage ended in 1912, Charles wed New York socialite Ruth Sands. When asked about Wark in 1909, Clara's manager, R. E. Johnston, told the *New York Herald*, "I did not know he was married" ("Mystery in Quest of Pianist's Wife," October 14, 1909).

48. CC to IVL, June 24, 1908.

49. "Mark Twain No More a Gay New Yorker," *New York World*, September 7, 1908; this article was reprinted in the evening *Washington Times* as "Mark Twain Quits Gay Old New York," but with the added fact that Wark had been a resident of Washington, D.C. He kept an apartment in New York, but his wife may have lived at his old address in Washington, which would help to explain why the New York press seemed unaware of her.

50. MT, "Ashcroft-Lyon Manuscript" (1909).

51. "Mark Twain Cannot 'Bubble Humor,' He Says, as Demanded," *New York American*, September 8, 1908 (*MTTCI*, 668).

52. "New York Loses Mark Twain," *NYT*, September 8, 1908; "Weddings of a Day: Wark-Cullis," *NYT*, October 11, 1903.

53. "Miss Clara Clemens Returns Home," *NY Trib*, September 10, 1908.

54. IVL, September 9, 1908.

55. MT, "Ashcroft-Lyon Manuscript" (1909).

CHAPTER FIFTEEN: BREAKING AND ENTERING

1. *N&J-2*, 469.

2. Davis and "Williams," *In the Clutch of Circumstance*, 168–69. In the 1920s the burglar calling himself Henry Williams wrote a memoir with the help of a professional ghostwriter and discussed his career in detail, including the night he

broke into Twain's villa. Much of his story rings true, but a lot of the book is obviously exaggerated or false, and must be carefully weighed against more reliable sources.

3. MT to Frances Nunnally, [October 24–31, 1908] (*Ltrs-Angelfish,* 224).

4. "Mark Twain Robbed," *NYEW,* September 18, 1908. This was the first report of the burglary and, in many respects, it seems the most convincing. But I have used several sources to describe the crime, reconciling as best I can different accounts of the same events. Quotations from my other sources are cited in subsequent notes. A description of Williams's physical features can be found in the *New York Evening World.*

5. "Burglar Chase at Mark Twain's Ends in Shooting," *New York World,* September 19, 1908 (*MTTCI,* 670).

6. MT to Theodore Bingham, 2:30 A.M. [September 18, 1908] (Wallace Shugg, "The Humorist and the Burglar: The Untold Story of the Mark Twain Burglary," *Mark Twain Journal,* Spring 1987). In her memoir *My Father, Mark Twain,* Clara mistakenly says that after Twain came downstairs at two o'clock in the morning "he returned to bed, unmindful of the stolen silver" (275).

7. "Burglar Chase at Mark Twain's Ends in Shooting," *New York World,* September 19, 1908 (*MTTCI,* 671).

8. "Mark Twain Robbed," *NYEW,* September 18, 1908.

9. "Mark Twain's Burglar: Now a Devoted Reader of Man He Robbed," *NYT,* December 28, 1924.

10. "Burglar Chase at Mark Twain's Ends in Shooting," *New York World,* September 19, 1908 (*MTTCI,* 671).

11. "Mark Twain Robbed," *NYEW,* September 18, 1908.

12. Davis and "Williams," *In the Clutch of Circumstance,* 174–75.

13. "Mark Twain Robbed," *NYEW,* September 18, 1908.

14. Dan Beard, "Mark Twain as a Neighbor," *American Review of Reviews,* May 1910. The carnage of the chase was described succinctly in the *Tribune:* "Deputy Sheriff George F. Banks was shot in the thigh, and one of the cracksmen was wounded in the leg, while the other was beaten insensible" ("Mark Twain's Robbers," *NY Trib,* September 19, 1908).

15. Dan Beard, "Mark Twain as a Neighbor," *American Review of Reviews,* May 1910.

16. Davis and "Williams," *In the Clutch of Circumstance,* 177–78.

17. "Sheriff Banks Apprehends a Burglar," *Danbury Evening News,* September 18, 1908 (reprinted in the *Redding Times,* June 19, 1958).

18. Dan Beard, "Mark Twain as a Neighbor," *American Review of Reviews,* May 1910.

19. *Danbury Evening News,* September 18, 1908; Wallace Shugg, "The Humorist and the Burglar: The Untold Story of the Mark Twain Burglary," *Mark Twain Journal,* Spring 1987; "Mark Twain's Robbers," *NY Trib,* September 19, 1908; Davis and "Williams," *In the Clutch of Circumstance,* 180.

20. MT to WDH, September 24, 1908 (*Ltrs-Howells,* 2:835).

21. "Burglars Invade Mark Twain Villa," *NYT,* September 19, 1908; "Mark Twain's Robbers," *NY Trib,* September 19, 1908; "Burglar Chase at Mark Twain's Ends in Shooting," *New York World,* September 19, 1908 (*MTTCI,* 669–70); "Burglarized at Last!," *Baltimore Sun,* September 19, 1908 (Wallace Shugg, "The Humorist and the Burglar: The Untold Story of the Mark Twain Burglary," *Mark Twain Journal,* Spring 1987). "Notice. To the Next Burglar" is reprinted in full in *MTB,* 1463, and with minor corrections in *Mark Twain's Helpful Hints for Good Living,* 57.

22. Margaret Blackmer to MT, September 20, 1908 (*Ltrs-Angelfish,* 209); *Mark Twain's Helpful Hints for Good Living,* 56–57.

23. MT to Marjorie Breckenridge, October 7, 1908; MT to Dorothy Quick, October 7, 1908; MT to Margaret Blackmer, October 6–9, 1908 (*Ltrs-Angelfish,* 214 and 217–18). Clara's apartment was at 17 Livingston Place. The street was later renamed Nathan D. Perlman Place.

24. MT to Emilie Rogers, October 7 and October 12, 1908 (*Ltrs-Rogers,* 652–54); MT to Dorothy Quick, October 7, 1908 (*Ltrs-Angelfish,* 218).

25. Charles Henry Meltzer, "Twain Says He Told Her 'Book a Mistake,' " *New York American,* September 27, 1908 (*MTTCI,* 674); IVL, Notes for William Howe, 1937.

26. The fact that Wark was a witness to the burglary was reported in "Burglars Invade Mark Twain Villa," *NYT,* September 19, 1908; and "Mark Twain's Robbers," *NY Trib,* September 19, 1908. Describing Wark's activities on the night of the burglary, Paine's biography discreetly leaves out his name and refers to him only as a "guest" (*MTB,* 1462). In her account of the burglary, Harnsberger refers to Wark by name (*Mark Twain, Family Man,* 246).

27. MT to Frances Nunnally, October 10–12, [1908] (*Ltrs-Angelfish,* 219). A veteran Cunard captain, Daniel Dow was in charge of the *Caronia,* on which Clara and Wark sailed to and from Europe in 1908. He was later captain of the *Lusitania,* but took sick leave in early 1915, and thus was not aboard when the ship was sunk by a German U-boat in May. He retired in 1919.

28. Davis and "Williams," *In the Clutch of Circumstance,* 180.

29. "Twain's Burglars on Trial," *NYT,* November 11, 1908; AD, November 12, 1908. Isabel Lyon also attended the trial and gave testimony.

30. Davis and "Williams," *In the Clutch of Circumstance,* 185 and 247–48. After his release from prison, Williams wrote contrite letters to Clara and asked permission to make a film about the burglary. Nothing came of the idea (CC, *My Father, Mark Twain,* 275). Williams married, became a foreman in an automobile factory, wrote his autobiography, and lectured on prison reform. Clara met him a couple of times and even loaned him money, which he repaid (Harnsberger, *Mark Twain, Family Man,* 248–49).

31. "Twain Is Bitter Against Burglars," *Trenton Evening News* (New Jersey), October 31, 1908, and *MTS,* 214. There is a slightly different version of Twain's speech in *MT Speaking,* 630–31.

32. MT to JC, October 2, 1908; MT to Marjorie Breckenridge, December 1, 1908 (*Ltrs-Angelfish,* 238).

33. "Mark Twain's First Sweetheart, Becky Thatcher, Tells of Their Childhood Courtship," *Kansas City Star,* November 25, 1917.

34. Elizabeth Davis Fielder, "Familiar Haunts of Mark Twain," *Harper's Weekly,* December 16, 1899 (*HF & TS,* 323).

35. "Mark Twain's First Sweetheart, Becky Thatcher, Tells of Their Childhood Courtship," *Kansas City Star,* November 25, 1917.

36. MT, *The Adventures of Tom Sawyer,* chapter 3; Keene Abbott, "Tom Sawyer's Town," *Harper's Weekly,* August 9, 1913 (*HF & TS,* 323).

37. Twain misspelled Frazer, Laura's married name. She kept the photo until her death in 1928, after which it was acquired by the Mark Twain Birthplace State Historic Site in Florida, Missouri. See *HF & TS,* 323.

CHAPTER SIXTEEN: THE MARK TWAIN COMPANY

1. *MT Speaking,* 496.
2. Ibid., 630.
3. See Gribben, *Mark Twain's Library,* 1:xxvii–xxviii, 198, 217, and 436. In the accession records compiled by the Redding librarian, Twain's first contribution is

listed as *The Holy Bible,* Illus., Springfield, Mass.: W. J. Holland, n.d. (Gribben, 1:64). From 1908 to 1911, an unused chapel housed the Redding library (*MTB,* 1471–72).

4. Wallace, *Mark Twain and the Happy Island,* 116–17; MT to WDH, November 23, 1908 (*Ltrs-Howells,* 2:838).

5. *MTB,* 1447; MT to Marjorie Breckenridge, December 1, 1908 (*Ltrs-Angelfish,* 238).

6. *MTB,* 1465.

7. Wallace, *Mark Twain and the Happy Island,* 111.

8. MT to Frances Nunnally, November 1, 1908 (*Ltrs-Angelfish,* 229–30).

9. IVL to Mary Moffett, October 20, 1908 (ViU).

10. Doris Webster's interview with IVL, 1953.

11. IVL, October 26 and October 6, 1908.

12. MT to Dorothy Quick, August 10, 1908 (*Ltrs-Angelfish,* 198); Doris Webster's interview with IVL, n.d.

13. *MTN,* 393.

14. Revocation of Power of Attorney (November 14, 1908), signed and witnessed on June 1, 1909, by Albert Bigelow Paine and Charles Lark (Hill, *Mark Twain, God's Fool,* 212–13).

15. MT, "Ashcroft-Lyon Manuscript" (1909).

16. "Mark Twain Turns into a Corporation," *NYT,* December 24, 1908.

17. MT to CC, March 11, 1909; "Mark Twain Turns into a Corporation," *NYT,* December 24, 1908; "Copyright by Incorporation," *New York Sun,* December 25, 1908.

18. "The Test of the Primary Laws," *Washington Times,* December 25, 1908; quoted in "Meeting of Twain Trust," *WP,* December 26, 1908.

19. MT, "Ashcroft-Lyon Manuscript" (1909). The Mark Twain Company was incorporated on December 22, 1908.

20. In March 1909 Frederick Duneka at Harper's alerted Twain to the danger of having his signature on the stock certificates, and the problem was corrected. But Twain didn't realize just how great the danger had been until later in the year, when Ashcroft's dishonesty became clear to him. At which point he exclaimed in amazement, "If I had died while my transfer signature was still attached to the stocks, bonds, & Mark Twain Company stock in the Safe Deposit vault! . . . The children would have been paupers. However, I didn't die" ("Ashcroft-Lyon Manuscript").

21. Doris Webster's interview with IVL, n.d; IVL to Hattie Whitmore Enders, February 16, 1909.

22. Coburn, *Alvin Langdon Coburn, Photographer,* 36.

23. IVL, December 21, 1908. (See Robert H. Hirst and Lin Salamo, "Mark Twain Photo Op—December 21, 1908: Alvin Langdon Coburn, Mark Twain, and Isabel V. Lyon," *Bancroftiana,* Spring 2002.)

24. Henderson, *Mark Twain,* 183.

25. Quoted from a BBC program broadcast in 1954 (Robert H. Hirst and Lin Salamo, "Mark Twain Photo Op—December 21, 1908: Alvin Langdon Coburn, Mark Twain, and Isabel V. Lyon," *Bancroftiana,* Spring 2002).

26. Quotations taken from Joseph J. Firebaugh, "Coburn: Henry James's Photographer," *American Quarterly,* Autumn 1955, and Robert M. Poole, "In Living Color," *Smithsonian Magazine,* September 2007.

27. Quick, *Mark Twain and Me,* 89. Exposure times for indoor autochrome portraits ranged from ten to thirty seconds, according to the manufacturer (C. H. Claudy, "The Autochrome Plate—Some First Experiences," *The Camera,* December 1907). A short time before Coburn photographed Twain, William Ireland Starr attempted to make an autochrome picture of Twain, but failed.

28. Coburn, *Alvin Langdon Coburn, Photographer,* 66 and 68.

29. "The Boston Orchestra," *New York Sun,* December 4, 1908; "The Boston Orchestra," *NYT,* December 4, 1908. Though the critics liked Gabrilowitsch's performance, they were less impressed by Rachmaninoff's composition.

30. IVL, December 30, 1908.

31. Ossip Gabrilowitsch, "Memoir of Leschetizky," *NYT,* December 7, 1930.

32. See the following accounts published on December 21, 1908: "Miss Clemens in Accident," *NY Trib;* "Saves Miss Clara Clemens," *NYT;* "Miss Clemens Hurt," *Boston Globe;* "Says Her Escape Was Marvelous," *Washington Times.* There is also an unidentified newspaper source quoted in Harnsberger, *Mark Twain, Family Man,* 251.

33. "Concerts and Recitals," *NY Trib,* January 10, 1909. For further reasons why the accident in the snow may have been invented, see Laura Skandera Trombley's informative article "Mark Twain's *Annus Horribilis* of 1908–1909," *American Literary Realism,* Winter 2008. Trombley believes that Twain had a plan "to force Clara to give up Wark and choose a life of respectability with Gabrilowitsch." She makes an interesting case for this view, but it is based partly on a statement made by Isabel Lyon in 1940 that is contradicted by more reliable evidence from 1908 to 1909.

34. Sylvester Rawling, "Gabrilowitsch Charms at His Recital in Carnegie Hall," *NYEW,* January 11, 1909; "Ovation for Gabrilowitsch," *NYT,* January 11, 1909.

35. Quoted in Kevin Mac Donnell, "Stormfield: A Virtual Tour," *Mark Twain Journal,* Spring–Fall 2006. The original passage can be found in Act I, Scene i of *Titus Andronicus.*

36. MT, "Ashcroft-Lyon Manuscript" (1909).

37. Mary Louise Howden, "Mark Twain as His Secretary at Stormfield Remembers Him; Anecdotes of the Author Untold Until Now," *New York Herald,* December 13, 1925. (This article was located and transcribed by Barbara Schmidt of Tarleton State University.) For more of Howden's recollections of life at Stormfield, see "She Knew Mark Twain," *Hartford Courant* (Connecticut), July 26, 1925.

38. *MTB,* 1476.

39. MT to Clara Spaulding Stanchfield, xmas/08 [December 25, 1908] (MMP).

40. Howden, "Mark Twain as His Secretary at Stormfield Remebers Him," *New York Herald,* December 13, 1925; *MTB,* 1476–77. A slightly different version of Collier's prank was reported in "Joke on Mark Twain," *New York Sun,* December 29, 1908. The newspaper says the trainer identified himself as Professor May. A photograph of the toy elephant in the loggia has survived and is reprinted in Kevin Mac Donnell, "Stormfield: A Virtual Tour," *Mark Twain Journal,* Spring–Fall 2006.

PART FOUR: TEMPEST
CHAPTER SEVENTEEN: HANNIBAL-ON-AVON

1. MT, *Is Shakespeare Dead?,* chapter 12.

2. Keller, *Midstream,* 52–53; Keller, *The Story of My Life: The Restored Edition,* 289.

3. *MT Speaking,* 642; MT to Helen Keller, St. Patrick's Day, '03 [March 17, 1903] (*Ltrs/Paine,* 730).

4. Sangster, *From My Youth Up,* 285; Hutton, *Talks in a Library,* 391. The luncheon took place on March 24, 1895, at 229 West Thirty-fourth Street, where Hutton lived in a "substantial three-storied red brick house" until he moved to Princeton, New Jersey, a few years later (see Wolfe, *Literary Haunts and Homes,* 82–83).

5. *MTB,* 1274–75.

6. Keller, *Midstream,* 66–67.

7. Keller, *The Story of My Life: The Restored Edition,* 204.

8. Keller, *Midstream,* 54 and 58.

9. Gribben, *Mark Twain's Library,* 1:366; Keller, *Midstream,* 52.

10. IVL, January 10, 1909 (reproduced in IVL's Notes for William Howe, February 6, 1936).

11. Keller, *The Story of My Life: The Restored Edition,* 21; Keller's entry in the Stormfield guestbook, and Twain's comment on it, are quoted in Lash, *Helen and Teacher,* 360.

12. Twain's comment about "unreality" is quoted in Lash, *Helen and Teacher,* 306. The raft scene takes place in chapter 19 of *Adventures of Huckleberry Finn.*

13. MT to Anne Sullivan Macy, [January 11, 1909] (AFB); William Gibson, "Looking Back at *The Miracle Worker* on TV," *NYT,* October 14, 1979. Annie Sullivan died in 1936, Helen Keller in 1968.

14. IVL, January 10, 1909 (reproduced in IVL's Notes for William Howe, February 6, 1936); "Books Received," *New Shakespeareana,* September 1909; *MTB,* 1485 (Paine gives Booth's book the incorrect title *Some Characteristic Signatures of Francis Bacon,* and this error has often been repeated by others writing about Twain). *Some Acrostic Signatures of Francis Bacon* was published on April 24, 1909 ("Boston Gossip of Latest Books," *NYT,* March 6, 1909).

15. Gribben, *Mark Twain's Library,* 1:180 and 2:636 (AD, January 11, 1909).

16. MT, *Is Shakespeare Dead?,* chapters 4–5. Many modern Shakespearean scholars would dispute the claim that no manuscript in Shakespeare's hand has survived, citing the case of the so-called Hand D in the manuscript of the play *Sir Thomas More* as a likely—though not certain—example.

17. IVL, January 10 and 11, 1909, and February 5 and 17, 1909 (reproduced in IVL's Notes for William Howe, February 6, 1936); *MTB,* 1479.

18. MT, *The Innocents Abroad,* chapter 27. Greenwood's *The Shakespeare Problem Restated* arrived at Stormfield on February 4, 1909, according to IVL's Notes for William Howe, February 6, 1936.

19. MT, *Is Shakespeare Dead?,* chapter 11.

20. Ibid., chapter 12.

21. Ibid., chapter 11. Twain knew how reverent an "awed pilgrim" could be standing before Shakespeare's bust. In 1873 he played a trick on Livy, "an ardent Shakespearian," by taking her to visit Holy Trinity Church in Stratford without alerting her beforehand that it was the place where Shakespeare was buried. When she saw the famous words on the grave, "Good friend, for Jesus' sake forbear . . ." she was shocked and exclaimed, "Heavens, where am I?" Twain's friend Moncure Conway was in on the joke and recalled, "Mark received her reproaches with an affluence of guilt, but never did lady enjoy a visit more than that to Avonbank" (Conway, *Autobiography,* 2:145).

22. MT, *Is Shakespeare Dead?,* chapter 11.

23. Ibid., chapter 6.

24. Twain's comment written in the margins of Greenwood's book is quoted in Berret, *Mark Twain and Shakespeare,* 26.

25. MT to JC, February 26, 1909; IVL's Notes for William Howe, February 6, 1936.

26. IVL's Notes for William Howe, February 6, 1936.

27. George Greenwood's copy of *Is Shakespeare Dead?* is now owned by the Folger Shakespeare Library in Washington, D.C. See Michael D. Bristol's "Sir George Greenwood's Marginalia in the Folger Copy of Mark Twain's *Is Shakespeare Dead?,*" *Shakespeare Quarterly,* Winter 1998.

28. "Can Mark Twain Be a Literary Pirate?," *NYT,* June 9, 1909.

29. In 1905 Rutger Bleecker Jewett was appointed managing director of John Lane's New York office. He was later Edith Wharton's editor at Appleton. His letter giving Twain permission to use excerpts from Greenwood's book is quoted in "Can

Mark Twain Be a Literary Pirate?," *NYT,* June 9, 1909. Twain liked the arguments in Greenwood's book so much that he was tempted to use a great deal more of it than he did. In the early stages of his work he was as irreverent about "stealing" from Greenwood as he was about Shakespeare's authorship of the plays, telling John Macy that he wanted to "stuff yards & yards" of it "in my vast Autobiography and make it look like my own" (MT to John Macy, February 25, 1909). But his attitude was more restrained when it came time to submit the final manuscript of *Is Shakespeare Dead?* The excerpt was far short of being "yards & yards," though the letter of permission from Jewett would have permitted such wholesale borrowing.

30. Johnson, *A Bibliography of the Work of Mark Twain, Samuel Langhorne Clemens,* 103. See *The Bookman* of August 1909 for an example of the blurb that Lane created from Twain's remarks in "Twain's Footnote Lost," *NYT,* June 11, 1909.

31. "Twain's Footnote Lost," *NYT,* June 11, 1909.

32. MT to the Editor of the London *Spectator,* September 20, 1872 (*Ltrs-5,* 164).

33. MT to James Beauchamp (Champ) Clark, September 16, 1909; MT to Champ Clark, June 5, 1909.

34. *Ltrs/Paine,* 831; *MTB,* 1494.

35. Frank Evina, "Mark Twain Lobbied for International Copyright Protection," *Copyright Lore,* May 2004 (U.S. Copyright Office).

36. MT to Frances Nunnally, February 9, 1909 (*Ltrs-Angelfish,* 249).

37. JC to IVL, December 11, 1908.

38. JC to MT, March 5, 1909.

39. MT to Dorothy Quick, March 3, 1909 (*Ltrs-Angelfish,* 251).

40. MT to JC, February 26, 1909; JC to MT, March 5, 1909.

41. On February 24, 1909, Lyon wrote to Twain from the Heublein, which was built in 1891 on a downtown corner facing Bushnell Park and the state capitol. Advertising slogans for the old Heublein Hotel are displayed at the Heublein Tower at Talcott Mountain State Park, Connecticut. In the "Ashcroft-Lyon Manuscript" (1909) Twain speculates on the cost of Lyon's stay at the hotel.

42. MT to CC, March 11–14, 1909.

43. Dora Paine to Albert Bigelow Paine, March 8, 1909 (Hill, *Mark Twain, God's Fool,* 218–19).

CHAPTER EIGHTEEN: END OF THE LINE

1. *Autob/MTIE,* 324.

2. "Twain's Secretary to Wed," *NYEW,* March 17, 1909; James, *The American Scene,* 93. Also see "Mark Twain Directors to Marry," *New York Sun,* March 18, 1909, which notes that the couple "obtained a license yesterday at the City Hall."

3. "Mark Twain's Secretary to Wed," *NY Trib,* March 18, 1909.

4. IVL to MT, February 24, 1909.

5. The first part of this quotation is taken from MT to Elizabeth Wallace, August 27, 1909, and the second part (after the ellipsis) comes from MT, "Ashcroft-Lyon Manuscript" (1909).

6. MT to Elizabeth Wallace, August 27, 1909; Doris Webster to Dixon Wecter, December 10, 1947.

7. MT, "Ashcroft-Lyon Manuscript" (1909).

8. The agreements are dated March 13, 1909, and are notarized by John N. Nickerson (ViU).

9. MT to CC, March 11–14, 1909.

10. WDH to Elinor Howells, March 24, 1909 (*Selected Letters,* 5:272).

11. *LFA,* 320–21.

12. WDH to Elinor Howells, March 24, 1909 (*Selected Letters,* 5:272); MT to Frances Nunnally, March 28, 1909 (*Ltrs-Angelfish,* 256).

13. "Great Coal Road Formally Opened," *Richmond Times-Dispatch* (Virginia), April 3, 1909.

14. Reid, *The Virginian Railway,* 42; "Praise for Rogers," *WP,* April 4, 1909.

15. *MT Speaking,* 640–43.

16. "Mark Twain Delighted the Little Ones," *Norfolk Ledger-Dispatch* (Virginia), April 5, 1909 (*MTTCI,* 677).

17. JC to Joseph Twichell, June 14, 1909 (CtHSD); Doris Webster, Notes on the Diaries of IVL, n.d.

18. Jean Clemens's letter was written on March 29 in response to the article "Indians in Revolt; Six Whites Killed," *NYT,* March 29, 1909.

19. MT, "Ashcroft-Lyon Manuscript" (1909).

20. Harnsberger, *Mark Twain, Family Man,* 249; "Mark Twain Carries Roses to Daughter," *New York Herald,* April 14, 1909.

21. "Miss Clara Clemens Sings," *NYT,* April 14, 1909; "Miss Clemens's Concert," *New York Sun,* April 14, 1909; Harnsberger, *Mark Twain, Family Man,* 250.

22. In his "Ashcroft-Lyon Manuscript" Twain gives a slightly different sequence of events, saying that Clara's big argument with Peterson took place two days before her concert. In JC to Joseph Twichell, June 14, 1909 (CTHSD), Jean provides a sequence that seems more logical, and I have chosen to follow it here. Overall, I find her journals and letters to be remarkably reliable with regard to the basic facts of her family's story. Though Clara may have seen Peterson on April 11, Jean is clear in her account that the most important meeting between the two took place on April 15. Writing from Stormfield only two months after the events, Jean provides this summary: "The Ashcrofts got my physician up here the day of Clara's concert [April 13], when neither she nor Father was here and dinned lies into his ears, until, when Clara saw him two days later, he refused to believe that Father wished me back. Clara talked, argued for 45 minutes & only succeeded in wringing his consent to a one week's trial visit."

23. Samuel and Doris Webster's interview with IVL, January 5, 1950.

24. Isabel Ashcroft to MT, April 15, 1909. Information also taken from Samuel and Doris Webster's interview with IVL, January 5, 1950.

25. MT, "Ashcroft-Lyon Manuscript" (1909).

26. Lowell, *Letters,* 1:375.

27. Gribben, *Mark Twain's Library,* 1:426; MT to Orion and Mollie Clemens, October 19 and 20, 1865 (*Ltrs-1,* 324). In referring to 1866 as the time when he was tempted to commit suicide, Twain may have been influenced by the 1866 date of Lowell's letter. His own letter to Orion and Mollie about suicide makes 1865 a more likely time for this early crisis in his life.

28. MT to JC, April 19, 1909.

CHAPTER NINETEEN: CRIME AND PUNISHMENT

1. *LFA,* 300.

2. MT, "Ashcroft-Lyon Manuscript" (1909).

3. JC to Joseph Twichell, June 14, 1909 (CtHSD).

4. MT, "Ashcroft-Lyon Manuscript" (1909).

5. JC to Joseph Twichell, June 14, 1909 (CtHSD).

6. *MTB,* 1492.

7. Ibid., 1484, 1522, and 1505.

8. HHR to MT, April 23, 1909.

9. Ralph Ashcroft to MT, April 29, 1909.

10. Ralph Ashcroft to Archibald Henderson, May 27, 1909 (Hill, *Mark Twain, God's Fool,* 227).

11. MT to HHR, May 4, 1909 (*Ltrs-Rogers,* 662).

12. CC, *My Father, Mark Twain,* 278.

13. *MTTCI,* 678. Two reliable accounts of the events surrounding Rogers's death are "H. H. Rogers Dead from Apoplexy," *NY Trib,* May 20, 1909; and "Mark Twain Grief-Stricken," *NYT,* May 20, 1909.

14. *MTB,* 1491. Paine mistakenly gives the date of Rogers's death as May 20.

15. "Rockefeller's Plea Vain," *NYT,* May 20, 1909.

16. Andrew Carnegie to MT, May 22, 1909 (Nasaw, *Andrew Carnegie,* 722).

17. "Pastor Praises Rogers," *NY Trib,* May 22, 1909.

18. *MTB,* 1491–92.

19. *Autob/AMT,* 259 and 263.

20. Ibid., 259.

21. MT, "Ashcroft-Lyon Manuscript" (1909).

22. JC to Joseph Twichell, June 14, 1909 (CtHSD).

23. Ralph Ashcroft to MT, June 3, 1909.

24. Lark didn't find out until June 17 that the Ashcrofts had left New York on June 9 as passengers on a steamship of the Northwestern Transportation Line bound for Holland (Charles T. Lark to Albert Bigelow Paine, June 17, 1909).

25. MT, "Ashcroft-Lyon Manuscript" (1909).

26. "Mark Twain Sues," *NY Trib,* June 20, 1909.

27. *The Mark Twain Encyclopedia,* 44; Stoneley, *Mark Twain and the Feminine Aesthetic,* 149.

28. IVL, Notes for William Howe, June 1935.

29. Hill, *Mark Twain,* 230.

30. Susan Crane to Albert Bigelow Paine, October 27, 1912 (*The Twainian,* July–August 1967).

31. *MTB,* 1497–98; MT to Frances Nunnally, [July 15, 1909] (*Ltrs-Angelfish,* 262).

32. MT to Elizabeth Wallace, August 27, 1909; *MTB,* 1504–5.

33. Quotations come from the following articles: "Twain Puts Blame on the Typesetter," *Baltimore News,* June 10, 1909; "Mark Twain Their Guest," *Baltimore Sun,* June 11, 1909; and "Two Dozen White Suits Are Twain's," *Baltimore News,* June 11, 1909 (*MTTCI,* 679–87).

34. MT to Frances Nunnally, June 18, 1909 (*Ltrs-Angelfish,* 260).

35. "Twain Puts Blame on the Typesetter," *Baltimore News,* June 10, 1909 (*MTTCI,* 680).

36. Horace Plimpton to Frank Dyer, June 8, 1909; "Sales Department Bulletin No. 39," July 23, 1909, Edison Manufacturing Company (NjWoE). The Edison studio paid only $150 for the film rights to *The Prince and the Pauper,* which was made quickly with a main cast of twenty-two and more than sixty extras for crowd scenes. It was released in August 1909 and featured a woman—the popular stage actress Cecil Spooner—playing both the prince and the pauper.

37. Marion Schuyler Allen, "Our Friend Mark Twain" (BmuHA); Marion Schuyler Allen, "Some New Anecdotes of Mark Twain," *The Strand Magazine,* September 1913.

38. MT to Frances Nunnally, [July 15, 1909] (*Ltrs-Angelfish,* 262); *MTB,* 1511.

39. Mary Proctor, "Gossip of Starland," *NY Trib,* June 6, 1909.

40. MT, *MSM,* 439. The Clemens family used an unusual pronunciation for Orion's name, placing the accent on the first syllable.

41. MT, "The New Planet," *CT,* 2:875. See also "New Planet Is Indicated," *NYT,* January 3, 1909.

42. Preston, *Dinosaurs in the Attic*, 40–41; *MTB*, 1519. See also Osborn, *The American Museum of Natural History*, 44 and 144.

43. CC, *My Husband, Gabrilowitsch*, 47–48.

44. "Pianist Dangerously Ill," *NYT*, July 8, 1909; CC to MT, July 9, 1909.

45. CC, *My Husband, Gabrilowitsch*, 49; *MTB*, 1505.

46. "She Will Make Twain Explain His $4,000 Suit," *NYEW*, July 14, 1909.

47. "Wants Mark Twain to Explain to Her," *NYT*, July 15, 1909.

48. "Mark Twain's Ex-Secretary," *New York Sun*, July 15, 1909.

49. "Wants Mark Twain to Explain to Her," *NYT*, July 15, 1909.

50. Ralph Ashcroft to John Stanchfield, July 30, 1909. (Charles Lark and Stanchfield were legal associates, and both worked for Twain.)

51. "Ashcroft Accuses Miss Clara Clemens," *NYT*, August 4, 1909.

52. MT to Elizabeth Wallace, August 27, 1909.

53. MT, Notes for September 10 [1909], "Everything cleaned up & arranged with the Ashcrofts." To make his defeat look better, Ashcroft gave a false story to the *Times* that Twain had "signed a document acquitting Mrs. Ashcroft of all blame for her conduct of his affairs," and that Ashcroft himself had "offered to resign" from the Mark Twain Company, but that the author had "requested him to continue" ("Mark Twain Suits All Off," *NYT*, September 13, 1909).

CHAPTER TWENTY: LETTERS FROM THE EARTH

1. AD, February 10, 1907 (*Autob/NAR*, 129–30).

2. MT to Dorothy Quick, September 10, 1909 (*Ltrs-Angelfish*, 264).

3. *MTB*, 1521.

4. Bispham, *A Quaker Singer's Recollections*, 341; *MTB*, 1522.

5. CC, *My Husband, Gabrilowitsch*, 50.

6. CC to Joseph Twichell, September 26, 1909 (CtHSD).

7. CC, *My Husband, Gabrilowitsch*, 51; Harnsberger, *Mark Twain, Family Man*, 259.

8. Quoted in Laura Skandera Trombley, "Mark Twain's *Annus Horribilis* of 1908–1909," *American Literary Realism*, Winter 2008.

9. MT to Elizabeth Wallace, November 10, 1909.

10. "Twain's Daughter Made Defendant?," *Richmond Times-Dispatch* (Virginia), October 18, 1909; see also quotations from the *New York Herald* and the *New York American* in Laura Skandera Trombley, "Mark Twain's *Annus Horribilis* of 1908–1909," *American Literary Realism*, Winter 2008.

11. "Gabrilowitsch in Atlantic City," *Musical America* [November 29, 1909]. On November 27 Jean wrote Joseph Twichell, "Clara is still at Atlantic City" (CtHSD).

12. MT to R. E. Johnston, October 12, 1909, quoted in "Marriage Good Excuse for Canceling Tour," *Musical America*, October 23, 1909.

13. MT to Augusta Ogden, October 13, 1909.

14. MT, *CT*, 2:914–15.

15. *MTB*, 1531.

16. MT, *Lets. Earth*, vii–viii.

17. MT, "The Turning Point of My Life," *CT*, 2:932–35.

18. *MTB*, 1528–29.

19. JC to Marguerite Schmitt, December 21, 1909; MT, "Closing Words of My Autobiography" (Lystra, *Dangerous Intimacy*, 254).

20. *MTB*, 1531.

21. MT to Dorothy Quick, November 18, 1909 (*Ltrs-Angelfish*, 266).

22. MT to Frances Nunnally, December 14, 1909 (*Ltrs-Angelfish*, 267); MT to CC, December 6, 1909.

23. *MTB*, 1544.

24. MT to CC, November 26, 1909; MT to Frances Nunnally, December 14, 1909 (*Ltrs-Angelfish*, 267).

25. *MTB*, 1545.

26. Helen's inscribed copies of the Author's National Edition, all of which are dated December 18, 1909, can be found in the Allen Collection, BmuHA. For an account of Twain's habit of visiting places and leaving things behind on purpose, see *MTB*, 825.

27. Quoted in Hayward, *Bermuda Past and Present*, 119–20.

28. Marion Schuyler Allen, "Our Friend Mark Twain" (BmuHA).

29. MT to CC, December 6, 1909.

30. MT, "Closing Words of My Autobiography" (Lystra, *Dangerous Intimacy*, 254).

31. "Mark Twain Feeling Blue," *New York Sun*, December 21, 1909 (*MTTCI*, 692).

32. "Mark Twain Home," *NY Trib*, December 21, 1909.

33. *MTB*, 1549.

34. MT, "Closing Words of My Autobiography" (Lystra, *Dangerous Intimacy*, 248).

35. Lawton, *A Lifetime with Mark Twain*, 321.

36. MT, "Closing Words of My Autobiography" (Lystra, *Dangerous Intimacy*, 248).

37. CC to Mrs. [?]Wilson [1910] (CLjC).

38. MT to Joseph Twichell, December 27, 1909.

39. MT, "Closing Words of My Autobiography" (Lystra, *Dangerous Intimacy*, 249).

40. Lawton, *A Lifetime with Mark Twain*, 323.

41. Quoted in Harnsberger, *Mark Twain, Family Man*, 262.

42. MT, "Closing Words of My Autobiography" (Lystra, *Dangerous Intimacy*, 257).

CHAPTER TWENTY-ONE: REVELS ENDED

1. Quoted in Harnsberger, *Mark Twain, Family Man*, 265.

2. *MTB*, 1553.

3. MT, "Closing Words of My Autobiography" (Lystra, *Dangerous Intimacy*, 247).

4. MT to Joseph and Harmony Twichell, December 27, 1909; MT to CC, December 29, 1909 (*MTB*, 1554).

5. MT to Margaret Illington, January 26, 1910 (*Ltrs-Angelfish*, 271).

6. Albert Bigelow Paine to W. H. Allen, January 3, 1910 (*The Twainian*, January–February 1948).

7. "Mark Twain Off to Bermuda," *New York Sun*, January 6, 1910; "Mark Twain Hastily Returns to Bermuda," *New York World*, January 6, 1910 (*MTTCI*, 694).

8. Marion Schuyler Allen, "Our Friend Mark Twain" (BmuHA).

9. MT to Albert Bigelow Paine, February 5, 1910 (*MTB*, 1560).

10. MT to Albert Bigelow Paine, January 11 and January 24, 1910 (*MTB*, 1558 and 1560).

11. WDH to MT, February 11, 1910 (*Ltrs-Howells*, 852).

12. *The Papers of Woodrow Wilson*, 20:133.

13. *MTB*, 1552; Marion Schuyler Allen, "Our Friend Mark Twain" (BmuHA).

14. Marion Schuyler Allen, "Some New Anecdotes of Mark Twain," *The Strand Magazine*, September 1913.

15. MT to Thomas L. James, February 15, 1910 (CLjC); Marion Schuyler Allen, "Some New Anecdotes of Mark Twain," *The Strand Magazine*, September 1913; WDH to MT, February 11, 1910 (*Ltrs-Howells*, 852).

16. MT to Albert Bigelow Paine, February 5, 1910 (*MTB*, 1560).

17. MT to Elizabeth Wallace, March 12, 1910 (Wallace, *Mark Twain and the Happy Island,* 139).

18. MT to Margaret Illington, January 26, 1910 (*Ltrs-Angelfish,* 271).

19. Marion Schuyler Allen, "Some New Anecdotes of Mark Twain," *The Strand Magazine,* September 1913.

20. Marion Schuyler Allen, "Our Friend Mark Twain" (BmuHA).

21. "Mark Twain at Bermuda," *Human Life,* May 1910 (*MTTCI,* 697).

22. "Helen Allen Manuscript," *Ltrs-Angelfish,* 276.

23. Ibid., 272; Marion Schuyler Allen, "Our Friend Mark Twain" (BmuHA).

24. Marion Schuyler Allen, "Our Friend Mark Twain" (BmuHA); Marion Schuyler Allen, "Some New Anecdotes of Mark Twain," *The Strand Magazine,* September 1913. In *Mark Twain, God's Fool,* Hamlin Hill speculates that Twain may have antagonized the Allens and their daughter by some unspecified "inappropriate" behavior of a sexual nature (260–61). There is no evidence to support this. Marion Allen doesn't even hint at such a thing in the forty-nine-page typescript of her memoir, "Our Friend Mark Twain," written after the author's death. Hill's suggestion that Twain was jealous of another man named Arthur, supposedly Helen's sweetheart, is unfounded. As both Paine and Marion Allen wrote, Arthur was only a boy in the neighborhood who was one of Helen's friends. Twain's dismissive comments about him were jokes. Moreover, in a letter to me on September 20, 1995, the late Charles M. Nelles, Helen's son, wrote that his mother had never mentioned to him any trouble with Twain. In fact, in her later years, she didn't seem to think his visit was all that noteworthy: "Mother seldom mentioned her early days, and nothing about Mark Twain until one day I got her to say he had been at the house, Bay House, a great deal. And that was all."

25. Quick, *Mark Twain and Me,* 215.

26. Marion Schuyler Allen, "Some New Anecdotes of Mark Twain," *The Strand Magazine,* September 1913.

27. *MTB,* 1562–63.

28. Ibid., 1564 and 1568–69.

29. Robert T. Slotta, "Mark Twain, Halley's Comet, and Some Trails Left Behind," *The Twainian,* November 30, 1993. Slotta bought Twain's dictionary in 1991 after the last of the Allen heirs donated or sold off the contents of Bay House.

30. Shakespeare, *The Tempest,* Act V, Scene i.

31. *MTB,* 1571.

32. Quoted in Robert T. Slotta, "Mark Twain, Halley's Comet, and Some Trails Left Behind," *The Twainian,* November 30, 1993.

33. CC, *My Father, Mark Twain,* 290.

34. *MTB,* 1575–76.

35. MT to [CC] [April 21, 1910] (ViU).

36. *MTB,* 1578.

37. "Harvard Observes Comet," *NY Trib,* April 22, 1910.

EPILOGUE

1. *N&J-3,* 538.

2. *Mark Twain in Elmira,* 155.

3. CC, *My Husband, Gabrilowitsch,* 54.

4. "Stormfield, Mark Twain's Last Home, Razed by Fire," *Bridgeport Telegram* (Connecticut), July 26, 1923; Kevin Mac Donnell, "Stormfield: A Virtual Tour," *Mark Twain Journal,* Spring–Fall 2006.

5. "Bids Pour in for Mark Twain Books," *Los Angeles Times,* April 11, 1951.

6. "Twain's Possessions to Be Sold at Auction," *Los Angeles Times,* April 3, 1951.

7. "Twain Heirs Gain by $95,467," *NYT,* April 28, 1962.

8. See Isabelle Budd, "Clara Samossoud's Will," *Mark Twain Journal,* Spring 1987.

9. Diane Swanbrow, "The Lost Legacy of Mark Twain," *Los Angeles Times Magazine,* May 10, 1987.

10. "Rites for Mark Twain's Last Descendant Set," *Los Angeles Times,* January 19, 1966.

11. Samuel and Doris Webster's interview with IVL, January 5, 1950.

12. "Business Leader, Friend and Aide of Mark Twain," *The Globe and Mail* (Toronto), January 9, 1947.

13. Quoted in Jennifer L. Rafferty, " 'The Lyon of St. Mark': A Reconsideration of Isabel Lyon's Relationship to Mark Twain," *Mark Twain Journal,* Fall 1996.

14. Brooks Atkinson, "Good as New," *NYT,* April 19, 1959.

INDEX

Numbers in **boldface** refer to illustrations.

Title pages: Library of Congress, Prints and Photographs Division

Page xvi: The Mark Twain House & Museum, Hartford, Connecticut

Page xxv: Mark Twain Project, the Bancroft Library, University of California, Berkeley

Page xxvi: Mark Twain Project, the Bancroft Library, University of California, Berkeley

Page xl: *Harper's Weekly*, 1907

Page 2: Library of Congress, Prints and Photographs Division

Page 10: Left, *Burr McIntosh Monthly*, 1901; right: Library of Congress, Prints and Photographs Division

Page 20: Mark Twain Project, the Bancroft Library, University of California, Berkeley

Page 31: Reprinted from Albert Bigelow Paine, *Mark Twain: A Biography*, 1912

Page 40: Library of Congress, Prints and Photographs Division

Page 56: U.S. Naval Historical Center

Page 66: Mark Twain Project, the Bancroft Library, University of California, Berkeley

Page 72: Library of Congress, Prints and Photographs Division

Page 84: Reprinted from Albert Bigelow Paine, *Dwellers in Arcady*, 1919

Page 94: Library of Congress, Prints and Photographs Division

Page 96: Library of Congress, Prints and Photographs Division

Page 98: *Philadelphia Inquirer* cartoon reprinted in the *Washington Times*, June 28, 1907

Page 112: Reprinted from *Harper's Weekly*, July 27, 1907

Page 128: Library of Congress, Prints and Photographs Division

Page 142: Library of Congress, Prints and Photographs Division

Page 144: Library of Congress, Prints and Photographs Division

Page 159: Library of Congress, Prints and Photographs Division

Page 164: Cover of Mark Twain's book *Extract from Captain Stormfield's Visit to Heaven*, 1909

Page 178: Left: Library of Congress, Prints and Photographs Division; right: reprinted from a 1907 issue of *Putnam's Monthly*

Page 195: Library of Congress, Prints and Photographs Division

Page 200: Reprinted from Mary Hulbert's *The Story of Mrs. Peck*, 1933

Page 206: Mark Twain Project, the Bancroft Library, University of California, Berkeley

ABOUT THE AUTHOR

MICHAEL SHELDEN is the author of three previous biographies, including *Orwell*, which was a Pulitzer Prize finalist. He was a correspondent for the *Daily Telegraph* (London) and a fiction critic for the *Baltimore Sun*. He is currently a professor of English at Indiana State University.

ABOUT THE TYPE

This book is set in Excelsior, a typeface designed in 1931 by Chauncey H. Griffith, an American printer, compositor, and typeface designer. Griffith worked for the Linotype Corporation and helped to establish it as the industry standard in newspaper and book composition in the early twentieth century. One of five typefaces in the so-called Griffith's Legibility Group, Excelsior is a clear typeface of even color that reads easily in small sizes, producing a calm effect on the page. As such, it was widely adopted as a text and display face for newspapers across the United States, and it is also popular internationally.